Carlo Rosselli: Socialist Heretic and Antifascist Exile

Desperate Inscriptions: Graffiti from the Nazi Prison in Rome, 1943–1944

BITTER
SPRING

Farrar, Straus and Giroux
New York

BITTER SPRING

A Life of IGNAZIO SILONE

Stanislao G. Pugliese

FARRAR, STRAUS AND GIROUX
18 West 18th Street, New York 10011

Library of Congress Cataloging-in-Publication Data
Pugliese, Stanislao G., 1965–
    Bitter spring : a life of Ignazio Silone / Stanislao G. Pugliese.— 1st ed.
      p. cm.
    Includes bibliographical references and index.
    ISBN-13: 978-0-374-11348-3 (alk. paper)
    ISBN-10: 0-374-11348-3 (alk. paper)
    1. Silone, Ignazio, 1900–1978.   2. Authors, Italian—20th century—
Biography.   3. Socialists—Italy—Biography.   4. Anti-fascist movements—
Italy—Biography.   I. Title.

PQ4841.I4 Z78 2009
853'.912—dc22
[B]

                          2008050410

Designed by Cassandra J. Pappas

www.fsgbooks.com

10 9 8 7 6 5 4 3 2 1

For Giulia, Alessandro, and Jennifer:

fontana della vita

Perhaps those who . . . search through these miserable papers will understand enough to seize a spark of the great struggle of our time.

—*IGNAZIO SILONE*, *Memoir from a Swiss Prison*, December 1942

At the Grave of Silone

HARRY CLIFTON

Lost in a fog at four thousand feet
When the lights come on, I can see them all,
The mountain villages, so small
A blind man feels his way about
Without a stick, and everyone overhears
Everyone else, as they quarrel and shout,
And still they are all alone—
And the places, the years,
Who redeems them? I think again
Of you, Ignazio Silone,
Ten years dead . . .
On this freezing Apennine chain,
A body interred, forever looking out
On an endlessly fertile plain—

And how we had visited you, one day
When August blew the crops awake
And harvesters toiled, in the drained lake
Of human promise . . . Skies were passing away
But nothing had changed on the ground.
Heat and apathy, absence of sound
In your natal village. Unsuccess
With its local dreamers, revving their motorbikes,
Punishing the slot machines.
Fontamara . . .
Without knowing it, we had come to pray
At the shrine of ordinariness . . .

We, who were running away.
. . . .
Unconsciousness everywhere . . . Fifty years ago,
In exile, writing Bread and Wine—
The War was coming. Now, below your shrine
Memory tries to wake
Blind monuments, to the Fascist dead,
Disheartened villages, men who cannot shake
The ant of toil from their Sunday clothes,
Slatternly women, old for their years,
The Christian cross, the Communist rose,
With the human word you said.

Contents

Illustrations

IN TEXT

The illustrations accompanying each chapter are reproduced from *Clément Moreau/Carl Meffert: Linolschnitte zu Ignazio Silone* (Berlin: Lit Pol, 1980). They were originally used to illustrate a German edition of Silone's *Fontamara* and *Die Reise nach Paris* as well as the English edition, *Mr. Aristotle*.

FOLLOWING PAGE 170

A Note to the Reader with Some Thoughts on Biography

The destiny of names, like that of men, is strange.

Although he was born Secondino Tranquilli and known by more than a dozen aliases during his period of clandestine political work for the Italian Communist Party (PCI) and with the American Office of Strategic Services (OSS), the subject of this book is referred to throughout as Ignazio Silone. Silone was fully cognizant of the ramifications of changing names so often: He once described a man "compelled to use so many names" that he was in danger "of forgetting his own." When it came time to join the Communist underground, choosing a new name was a decision fraught with political, cultural, and psychological ramifications. After adopting and sloughing off names in an effort to remain unknown to the police, Silone confessed, "We have acquired too many names . . . and one of them, probably not the most pleasant, has stuck." The effect on personal identity was sweeping. Silone compared it to the case of a monk entering the monastery, requiring "a break with his family and every private relationship, and his installation in a separate world."

Silone's works are referred to by their English titles. I have used Eric Mosbacher's translations (revised by Darina Silone) in *The*

Abruzzo Trilogy for Silone's first three novels (*Fontamara, Bread and Wine*, and *The Seed Beneath the Snow*) and Harvey Fergusson's 1968 translation of *Emergency Exit*, checking the English renditions against the Italian originals. Unless otherwise noted, all other translations are my own. When necessary—because of the inexact art of translating—I have included the original word or phrase. I have retained Silone's use of "man" and "mankind" rather than use gender-neutral terms, as they would be anachronistic.

Throughout the text I have also retained Silone's use of a contentious word—*cafone*—to describe the southern Italian peasant. Silone was painfully aware that the term was one of derision and contempt in most of Italy (including the south), but he insisted on using it with the hope that "when suffering ceases to be shameful, it will become a term of respect, and perhaps even of honor." That hope, sad to say, has not yet been fulfilled in Italy, or any other country. Today, the *cafoni* are known by other names: *marocchini, zingari, clandestini, extracomunitari*, but their suffering is unchanged.

I have sought in this work to counter two current trends in the writing of biography: the massive eight-hundred-page doorstop and the use of the omniscient biographer's voice. James Atlas has warned us against pedantry, "the insistence—prevalent especially among academics—upon entering every fact, however insignificant, into the biographical ledger merely because it has been found." More dangerous, I think, is the belief that after having spent nearly a decade living with a subject, the biographer has attained some mystical union with him and privileged insight or wisdom. To give one banal example: Someone casually remarked to me that the title of this book had been rendered in cyberspace as *Bitter Spring: The Life of Ignazio Silone*. I immediately tried to set the record straight in that the definite article was incorrect. The subtitle of the book has been since its inception *A Life of Ignazio Silone*. I hope to have avoided Jay Parini's criticism that, in most contemporary biographies, "the biographer remains invisible, a kind of God who toys with the strings of his puppets, who dance across the page, or—in most cases—fail to dance." While never known to have danced in real life, if Silone fails to do so in these pages, the fault is entirely my own.

The reconstruction of Silone's life is made more difficult by his desire, voiced to his wife Darina Laracy and included in his last testament, that his personal letters (both those he wrote and those he received) be destroyed after his death, a wish only partially carried out by his widow. Nonetheless, vast quantities of correspondence and documentation remain in Rome, Florence, and Pescina, as well as Zurich, Bern, Amsterdam, Washington, D.C., and elsewhere.

The idea for this book was born while I was seated on the mountainside next to Silone's tomb. I was in Pescina, Silone's hometown, in March 2000 to accept the International Ignazio Silone Prize for my first book, *Carlo Rosselli: Socialist Heretic and Antifascist Exile*. Because of its genesis, I cannot claim scientific objectivity for this book; I can only profess that I have tried to be faithful to Gaetano Salvemini's belief that "impartiality is a dream, honesty a duty." In one of the last essays before his death, Arthur M. Schlesinger Jr., who won Pulitzer Prizes for his works of history and biography, wrote that "all historians are prisoners of their own experience. We bring to history the preconceptions of our personalities and our age. We cannot seize on ultimate and absolute truths. So the historian is committed to a doomed enterprise—the quest for an unattainable objectivity."

A premise of this book is that much of Silone's writing is autobiographical; it follows that the writing of biography is also, in some sense, autobiographical. Ideally, the biography of an individual can be a prism through which we may gain insight not only into the life and times of the subject but into our own as well. Consequently, it is best that the biographer confront the enigmatic and ambiguous relationship between subject and author in a straightforward manner. Therefore, it is necessary to clarify some points here before the reader begins what may be—in the end—an arduous journey. Perhaps my stance can best be described by Silone himself who, on commenting about his autobiographical writing, once confessed, "I can guarantee its sincerity, not its objectivity."

No birth is without its complications. Two essays by prominent scholars have dogged me during this project. Just as the proofs of the Rosselli biography were arriving on my desk in 1999, an op-ed piece by Stanley Fish raised all manner of doubt in my mind. Fish noted that although biographies are popular with both the reading public and reviewers, as a reader, beginning a biography always made him feel "queasy," and that queasiness turned into something close to "a feeling of illness" by the third sentence. There was "nothing to stop the spiral sprawl of unconvincing speculation" except bald statements of fact, mostly uninteresting. Since the master narratives of biography have been dismissed along with most other master narratives in the West, biographers are reduced to piling on details divorced from a story line (hence the eight-hundred-page behemoths). Bad enough; but Fish charged biographers with a far graver offense, one that has haunted me for the past decade. "Biographers," he argued, "can only be inauthentic, can only get it wrong, can only lie, can only substitute their own story for the story of their announced subject. (Biographers are all autobiographers, although the pretensions of their enterprise won't allow them to admit it or even see it.)"

I have tried not to substitute my own story for that of Silone; hence the refusal to adopt the voice of an omniscient scholar. And although I have crafted a story that accepts contingency and embraces ambiguity, the reader will still, I trust, discern some "general truths."

Equally important in crafting this biography was an address by the historian Joseph Ellis at the 2004 meeting of the American Historical Association. An eminent biographer, Ellis noted that the genre was something of a "bastard" in the historical profession. While most members of the public get their history from biographies, the genre is seen as "an orphan periodically adopted by history or English departments." It has now been two generations that the historical profession has been dominated by social history and a professional disdain for the "dead white male" and "great man" narratives. But this, according to

Ellis, is a mistaken conception of biography as a form of writing that "invariably imposes a simplistic set of assumptions about human agency, namely that men make history rather than the other way around." This, insists Ellis, is a "patent falsehood." A falsehood that I hope will be borne out by this telling of Silone's life.

Ellis questions Jill Lepore's assertion that historians who write biography tend to succumb to hagiography. "Every great man," quipped Oscar Wilde, "has his disciples and it is always Judas who writes his biography." This is only partially true in Silone's case, where, until recently, hagiographies and character assassinations have more or less canceled each other out. If Lepore thinks historians are falling in love with their subjects, Janet Malcolm argues that they are driven by an Oedipus complex. "The intellectual health of biography," Ellis mischievously asserts, "is largely a function of its outlaw character."

The irony should not be overlooked: Ellis, a noted historian who had won the National Book Award for his biography of Thomas Jefferson and a Pulitzer Prize for his book *Founding Brothers: The Revolutionary Generation*, and who had been caught fabricating details of his own biography (that he had served in the Vietnam War and was active in the antiwar and civil rights movements), influencing a biography of Silone, a man who was himself accused of fabricating and hiding aspects of his own life.

Speaking to a group of nuns late in life, Silone confessed to "a tremendous fear of the terrible ambiguity of words." The reader of Silone's work (and the biographer) should be cautioned not to see the author in his idealized protagonists. Certainly, this biography will please neither Silone's many admirers nor his myriad critics. I must confess that after nearly a decade of being haunted by my subject, I am not at all sure whether I have exorcised his ghost or avoided Fish's criticism, only that Silone remains—surely now more than ever—an enigmatic yet representative figure of the twentieth-century intellectual swimming in the rough seas of history and ideology.

Pescina / New York
March 2009

BITTER SPRING

The LANDSCAPE of MY SOUL

*What the "true" image of each of us may
be in the end is a meaningless question.*
—*PRIMO LEVI*, "Lorenzo's Return"

I n 1923, "Ignazio Silone" was born in a Spanish prison. Perhaps it was no coincidence—and surely appropriate—that at the time he was reading Dostoevsky. Secondino Tranquilli, the person whose identity he erased with his new name, had been born twenty-three years earlier in the rural Abruzzo region of Italy and burdened with the given name "Secondino," which, in the local dialect, meant "prison guard." In Spain, he had been writing for Andrés Nin's journal *La Batalla* and imprisoned as a Communist. Significantly, he derived "Silone" from the ancient warrior Poppedius Silo, a native of Silone's beloved Abruzzo. Silo had led a successful revolt against the tyranny of Rome in 90 B.C. and thereby gained official recognition of the local population's autonomy. "Ignazio" he borrowed from the Spanish Counter-Reformation saint Loyola in order to "baptize the pagan surname." In this defiant act of self-appellation and identity creation, he synthesized a classical, pagan past with the Christian tradition.

Silone has most often been associated with the protagonist of his novels *Bread and Wine* and *The Seed Beneath the Snow*, Pietro Spina. ("Read my books," he once said, "only in them do I fully recognize myself.") A Communist intellectual and activist, Spina is returning from exile to his native Abruzzo, hunted by the Fascist police. In order to elude arrest and move about the countryside, he dons the robes of a priest and becomes Don [Father] Paolo Spada. The metamorphosis from Pietro Spina (literally Peter [the] Thorn) to Paolo Spada (Paul [the] Sword) is revealing: The Communist "thorn" is transformed into the religious "sword." The American literary critic Edmund Wilson, after reading Silone's novels while sitting on the benches of the Villa Borghese Gardens in Rome, Italian dictionary at his side, perceptively sensed that Silone was "a queer mixture of priest and communist." Nicola Chiaromonte, Silone's fellow founder and editor of the literary-cultural journal *Tempo Presente*, and one of the few people who could claim to be close to the writer, intuited that Silone was in some ways a "*prete contadino*," a peasant priest.

Yet Silone's life and experience are reflected in many of his characters, not just Pietro Spina/Paolo Spada. There is the peasant Berardo Viola in *Fontamara*, Thomas the Cynic in *The School for Dictators*, the disillusioned party intellectual Rocco De Donatis in *A Handful of Blackberries*, the doggedly persistent Andrea Cipriani in *The Secret of Luca*, the compassionate Daniele of *The Fox and the Camelias*, self-effacing Pope Celestine V in *The Story of a Humble Christian*. But there is always a clear, explicit, and sincere identification with the poor Christ, the suffering Christ, the peasant Christ who figures in the mythology of the rural poor. And in his last, unfinished work, *Severina*, Silone for the first and only time identifies himself with a female protagonist. Severina, a young convent initiate who refuses to give false testimony in court even though ordered to do so by her mother superior, grew out of Silone's fascination at the end of his life with Simone Weil. A member of the French underground, a writer, and a Jew who died by self-starvation in 1943, Weil inspired Silone to create Severina as bystander to a crime, thus embodying what writing meant for him: "the absolute necessity of bearing witness."

Representativeness was imposed on Silone, wrote R.W.B. Lewis in a profile that, now almost a half century old, is still the best critical analysis of the writer. "He scarcely had a chance to be Italian." Further complicating his portrait is the essential paradox that defined him: his entrance into politics because of an essentially religious conception of the world. "He became a socialist," Lewis writes, "because he wanted to become a saint." As a priest says of one of Silone's characters, "socialism was his way of serving God."

Silone is a particularly difficult subject for the biographer because of the labyrinthine meanderings of his own identity and his enigmatic autobiographical comments. He believed that the true nature of any person could not be known because—following the Neapolitan philosopher Giambattista Vico—he insisted that man is not nature. "Every man," he wrote, "is much more complicated than what he appears and that which he believes himself to be . . . to hell with psychology and facile suppositions."

Did Silone knowingly encourage a misreading and a conflation of his heroic and morally pure main characters with his own biography? Is it true, as others now insist, that Silone offered a confession for his transgressions as a police spy in a minor protagonist? The transfiguration from Secondino Tranquilli to Ignazio Silone was neither the first nor the last of his many self-transformations.

When I asked Silone's widow about his fate in Italian literary circles and why no biography on him had been written in English, Darina Silone replied, "That situation was Silone's own fault; his—to say the least—extremely difficult character." When I noted the challenge of tracking down documents in various archives and trying to fashion an identity from them, she was quick to respond. "There are things that are not found in any archive," she insisted. "Silone's character was difficult; his personality very complex. Of the few people alive who knew him personally, I am perhaps the one who knew him best, even if certainly not completely (no one ever knew him completely)."

Where, exactly, does identity lie? C. H. Cooley's "looking-glass" theory of self ("I am not who I think I am; I am not who you think I am; I am who I think you think I am") doesn't help us in Silone's case, for he simply did not care what others in the Italian political and literary establishments thought of him. But the biographer has a fertile mine in Silone's own writings. Rarely has an oeuvre been so autobiographical. All of Silone's novels except one take place in the Abruzzo region of Italy, as do his two plays. Rarely has so cosmopolitan a writer been so closely identified with the place of his birth. "Look at Silone," said Albert Camus, noting the paradox in an interview after winning the Nobel Prize in Literature, "he is radically tied to his land but is the most European of writers . . . Silone speaks to all of Europe. If I feel myself tied to him it is because he is incredibly rooted in his national and even local tradition." Not that Silone engaged in any sentimental or nostalgic mythmaking of his origins. Indeed, one is struck by his complicated and ambivalent relationship with his hometown of Pescina. Notwithstanding all the autobiographical detail in his work, the problem of uncovering his identity still remains almost insurmountable for the biographer. "There is no single truth about Silone," Darina Silone once said, "only many truths."

The writing is deceptively simple and presents the biographer with multiple challenges. Silone recognized himself in Hugo von Hofmannsthal's dictum that writers are a human category for whom writing is more difficult than it is for anyone else. "I live in a close communion with the characters in my stories that cannot be broken from one day to the next," Silone wrote. So close was that identification that the necessity of actually finishing a book was "an arbitrary and painful act, an act against nature, at any rate, my nature."

The flawed, tragic hero is only one possible trope in crafting a biography of Silone. Like an ancient Hebrew prophet or one of the early persecuted Christians, Silone insisted on a moral vision of the world.

His writing—"bearing witness"—was to become the testimony of an age. This is related to what might be called "the Christian quandary" or Silone's "wrestling with the Lord." He refused to take the more facile path of an easy atheism or agnosticism. Christianity for Silone was both a historical movement, tied to a certain place and time, and a transcendent, timeless moral force. This conflicting tension between an adamant historicism and a desire for transcendence are ever-present in his thought and writing. Silone and his main protagonists are not so much searching for a hidden God as being hounded by the Lord. A doggedly persistent deity haunts Silone and his characters, seeking them out in desolate landscapes and humble farmhouses, donkey stalls, and empty churches. The moral and ethical impetus is more St. Augustine's *Confessions* than Beckett's *Waiting for Godot*. There is, as Irving Howe noted, an irreducible tension in all of Silone's writings between the secular promise of Socialist liberation and the Christian promise of spiritual transcendence. Despite his identification with both Christianity and socialism, Silone indelibly defined himself as "a Socialist without a Party, a Christian without a Church."

Silone was honest enough to recognize the potential and contemporary failure of the Catholic church just as he fearlessly recognized the potential and failure of orthodox Marxism. There was no Dantean "comedic" vision of Christianity in Silone; he confessed to being an "absurd Christian." Theologically, orthodox Christianity cannot accept absurdity or nihilism, yet for Silone, these must be confronted before they can be transcended. For Silone, the promise of Christianity as embodied in the Easter Resurrection has not come to pass. Instead, for the peasants of southern Italy—indeed, for peasants and workers around the world—it is, he insisted, still—and always—Good Friday. While the writer felt himself hounded by the Lord, Silone's peasants ask, like Christ on the cross, "My God, my God, why hast thou forsaken me?" Surely the most anguished and—for the Christian—the most disturbing line in the Bible.

Nor could Marxism offer salvation or redemption. In an early work he concluded: "The future belongs to Socialism." Years later, Silone repudiated that sentiment and the entire work in which it was written and strictly forbade its reprinting. Just as he could not bring himself simply to accept a comedic teleology of Christianity, he eventually came to question and then reject Marxist eschatology and teleology.

William Faulkner thought him Italy's greatest living writer, and intellectuals as diverse as Thomas Mann, Albert Camus, Graham Greene, and Edmund Wilson agreed. Yet even his most astute readers, focused on his moral and political seriousness, often fail to note Silone's irony and humor. He once wrote that since pathos cannot be eliminated from human life, "a touch of irony is required to make it acceptable." Silone's irony could indeed be bitter, but it was always moderated by a critical spirit and an independence of judgment. Although tragedy and sorrow were inherent in the human condition—he often wrote of "our inhuman fate upon the earth"—there remained the possibility of hope. His politics could be described as a humanistic socialism combined with a compassionate libertarianism. He was an admirer of the anarchists Pierre-Joseph Proudhon, Peter Kropotkin, and Camillo Berneri (the last assassinated by Stalin's agents during the Spanish Civil War). When Berneri's widow, Giovanna, in her journal *Volontà*, implied that Silone was an anarchist, the writer responded, saying he would be honored to be counted as an anarchist, if only to distinguish himself from the various forms of socialism then current in Italy. "But a great respect toward those who have studied, struggled and suffered to give the anarchist ideal a precise shape" prevented him from identifying himself as such. Nine years later, in a sympathetic response to the student uprisings of 1968, Silone commented that "democracy has a duty to respect utopia."

By nature silent, meditative, and melancholy, Silone belied the stereotype of the gregarious, outgoing, extroverted southern Italian. In *The Seed Beneath the Snow*, a sympathetic character remarks to Pietro Spina's grandmother (modeled on Silone's own maternal grandmother): "There's a kind of sadness, a subtle kind of sadness that must not be confused with the more ordinary kind that's the result of remorse, disappointment, or suffering; there's a kind of intimate sadness and hopelessness that attaches itself for preference to chosen souls . . . That kind of sadness has always been very prevalent among sensitive individuals in this part of the world. Once upon a time, to avoid suicide or madness, they entered monasteries."

Unable or unwilling to enter a monastery, Silone gravitated to politics at an early age. But painfully shy, uncomfortable in the public light, and perpetually doubtful of himself, Silone never had any of the qualities necessary for a successful political career. He was a difficult husband, an exasperating friend, a mediocre politician, an aloof acquaintance, a morose presence in public, a distant and cool relative, often manic-depressive, sometimes suicidal, and he carried out an epistolary exchange with a police official that has shadowed his reputation for the last decade. Yet, starting in the 1930s, he crafted a body of work that testifies to a searing political and spiritual crisis and still bears fruitful reading. Silone offers us today a critical commentary on everything that we as human beings experienced in the twentieth century: from the failed promise of political utopia to the disillusionment with art; from the nihilism of totalitarianism to the moral temptations and seductive corruption of an affluent but savage, consumerist culture.

Curiously, Silone has never been the subject of a biography in English. Even in Italy, when not neglected by the literary and cultural establishment, he was often the object of scorn and derision, accused of writing "bad Italian." Awash in a sea of hagiographical works, there is some discerning, insightful scholarship on Silone in Italian for the serious reader. But considering the ethical dimensions of his writing and the wide range of his literary production, it is surprising that his work has not attracted greater attention in America. While known mainly for his novels, Silone mastered the art of the essay (*Emergency Exit*), the theoretical treatise (*Fascism: Its Origins and Development*), political satire (*The School for Dictators*), as well as drama (*And He Hid Himself*; *The Story of a Humble Christian*). When *The School for Dictators* first appeared in 1938 (with dictators ascendant), Silone was acclaimed "a second Machiavelli" by some overly enthusiastic critics, as, conversely, his *Manifesto for Civil Disobedience* of December 1942, in which he urges the peoples of Europe to rise up against the Fascist and Nazi dictatorships with nonviolent public resistance, makes one think of Mahatma Gandhi and Martin Luther King Jr.

Critics and readers of twentieth-century Italian literature are now familiar with the so-called *caso Silone* (Silone case), first broached in the postwar years: Why was Silone so beloved and read abroad and so neglected at home in Italy? It was only late in his life that the Italian literary establishment issued a collective mea culpa and showered Silone with literary prizes. Robert Gordon has concisely delineated Silone's postwar critical reputation:

> Ironically, the foreign writers and critics who had championed Silone in the 1930s and 1940s as a great writer gradually lost interest in his later work, unable or unwilling to stomach his increasingly intense libertarian Christianity. For them Silone would always be a standard-bearer of the cause of anti-Fascism and of the necessity for moral enquiry in literature. As such, he was to be set alongside Camus, Koestler, Malraux, Orwell, and others, and to be remembered principally for his earlier works, including *Fontamara*. Other critics more open to his later work did emerge, but in turn they tended to neglect *Fontamara*, where the themes of introspective morality and crisis are muted and poverty and politics are to the fore. They tried to fit Silone into another company of writers, of Christian moralists such as Bernanos, Péguy, and Greene. Despite their best efforts, however, it is undeniable that Silone's international reputation faded somewhat, along with that of the anti-Fascist or existentialist generation.

By 1967, Iris Origo could write that admiration for Silone "has now become not only the fashion, but almost a certificate of integrity." Almost as soon as Origo had penned these words, another "Silone affair" exploded: It was discovered that the Congress for Cultural Freedom, of which Silone was a leading member, and his beloved journal, *Tempo Presente*, were being indirectly financed by the Central Intelligence Agency with funds laundered through the Ford Foundation. Silone immediately resigned from the CCF and in 1968 closed down the journal, but the allegations that he was a spy for the CIA persisted. Documents from the National Archives in Washington, D.C., however, demonstrate that during World War II Silone was working with the OSS in trying to overthrow fascism and establish democracy in Italy. His fervent letters and telegrams depict a man who was desperate that the Italian people, victims of fascism for more than twenty years, should not have to pay the price for the sins of Mussolini's regime. A careful reading of these documents reveals that Silone was no spy. It hardly seems likely that Silone was a spy for the CIA when, despite the intervention of both Adlai Stevenson and Clare Boothe Luce, he was denied a visa to visit the United States until the mid-1960s. (He had, during World War II, been offered asylum by no less a person than Eleanor Roosevelt.) In light of his beleaguered circumstances—denied by both the right and the left—Silone was adopted by the democratic socialists of the United States and lauded by the intellectual and literary circles of *Partisan Review, Dissent,* and *The Nation.* Critics and writers such as Clement Greenberg, Alfred Kazin, Mary McCarthy, and Irving Howe worked to bring his work to the attention of an American audience.

Slowly but surely Silone's reputation survived all these charges. After his death in 1978, it seemed that his place in the literary establishment was secured, especially after the distinguished publishing house Mondadori published much of Silone's oeuvre in its prestigious Meridiani series in two deluxe volumes. But over the last decade another *caso* Silone has darkened his reputation. In 1996, an Italian historian uncovered documents supposedly proving that Silone had been spying for the Fascist police. Over the next few years, new revelations appeared in the press and academic journals. Apparently, Silone had spent a decade in an epistolary exchange with a high-ranking police official in Rome. Once again, Silone was at the center of political, literary, and cultural scandal.

This latest *caso* Silone did not arise in a vacuum. Silone had not been a stranger to controversy in life. Perhaps the ur-scandal was his class betrayal: For although he and his family were petite bourgeoisie, owning some properties in the Fucino plain of the Marsica region in the Abruzzo, he cast his lot with the *cafoni* all over the world in their myriad guises. As his alter ego Pietro Spina muses in a letter, "Perhaps the real cause of my distress is my defiance of the ancient law, my way of living in cafés, libraries, and hotels, my having broken the chain that for centuries linked my forefathers to the soil." Later, there followed another scandal in his expulsion from the Italian Communist Party (PCI) in 1931 and his subsequent exile in Switzerland. Although his 1933 novel, *Fontamara*, was a critical and commercial success, there was the scandal of his writing's critical reception in Italy, where, upon returning from exile in 1944, he faced a domestic literary ostracization that was no less devastating than his physical exile. For decades, the classically trained literary establishment refused to countenance Silone's work. It was said that he didn't write "proper Italian." He was often passed over for major literary awards. His subject matter—the rural Abruzzo and the cafoni—was considered beneath "proper" litera-ture by the conservative establishment while the cultural elites of the left, dominated by the PCI, could not forget his expulsion from the party in 1931 or forgive his criticism of communism during the cold war. When his account of disillusionment with communism, "Emer-gency Exit," appeared in Richard Crossman's anthology *The God That Failed* in 1950, Silone was mercilessly criticized by his former com-rades, and when that essay became the central piece in the auto-biographical volume *Uscita di sicurezza* (*Emergency Exit*, 1965), the Communist-dominated committee of the prestigious Viareggio Prize refused to accept it for consideration, thus generating further contro-versy (the book was awarded the Marzotto Prize instead). Italian critics began asking themselves why it was that Silone was so esteemed abroad and so derided at home. As the American scholar Michael P. McDonald has written, it was a classic case of *Nemo propheta acceptus est patria sua* (No prophet is accepted in his own country). Contempo-rary neo-Fascists (or post-Fascists, as they like to fashion themselves) as well as paleo-Communists are loath to forget Silone's "betrayal": his effective demolition of their precious myths.

The most recent scandal, that Silone was engaged in a decadelong spying operation against his comrades in the Italian Communist Party, has come to overshadow everything else, calling into question as it does Silone's status as a reluctant secular saint of the independent left in Europe, a persona that Silone worked hard to root in the public imagination. In Silone's second novel, *Bread and Wine*, Don Benedetto reads from an old essay of Pietro Spina's: "But for the fact that it would be very boring to be exhibited on altars after one's death, to be prayed to and worshiped by a lot of unknown people, mostly ugly old women, I should like to be a saint." But surely he would have echoed Dorothy Day's retort: "Don't call me a saint; I don't want to be dismissed so easily." And it was George Orwell, to whom Silone has often been compared, who wrote "saints should always be judged guilty until they are proved innocent," a sentiment that certainly would have provoked a wry smile and a knowing nod from the Italian writer. "Silone was the man of capital letters," his wife recalled. "He used to write the word 'verità' with a capital 'V'; 'libertà' with a capital 'L.' But his lowercase character was mysterious and unknowable."

How then, in this tangled thicket of representation, self-representation, and misrepresentation, is a historian and biographer to approach Silone? And how should these most recent revelations affect our perception of the writer? Perhaps a comparison with an earlier work—also a biography—might prove useful. Then, the subject (Carlo Rosselli), while a complex and charismatic figure, was a relatively "open" text, his thinking accessible through his essays, letters, anti-Fascist activism, and most important theoretical work. Silone, by contrast, has been "known" only through an association with the protagonists of his novels and his autobiographical essays. But this presents the reader and the biographer with a challenge. As Elizabeth Leake demonstrates in her recent analysis, Silone reinvented himself as a novelist who had passed through the inferno of the militant's life in the Communist underground, thereby giving his writings an aura of authenticity. Because of Silone's role as Fascist informer, Leake argues that his identity was based on "incoherent decisions" and that when the discrepancies between his life and his fiction are taken into account, the reader is unable to fix Silone's position on the moral spectrum. "The paradoxical nature of his identity," she concludes, "is thus insurmountable." But was Silone's transformation insincere and therefore, in some way, deceitful? There is no reason to doubt that Silone's transition from underground political activist to exiled solitary writer was as sincere and painful as he claimed.

Silone's notoriously difficult personality has sometimes been blamed on a certain strain of misanthropy. Yet, in May of 1936, he wrote to the German writer Bernard von Brentano:

> The difficulty Spina encounters (in *Bread and Wine*) in communicating with other men reflects in good measure my state of mind [*stato di anima*]. Relations with other people do not have a simple, natural, and direct character which I would love. This dissatisfaction sometimes pushes me toward solitude and willful silence. It is not misanthropy, but just the opposite: a love of man that remains unsatisfied, a need for friendship that fails to find its subject. This ends by irritating me and wearing me out. I begin again to love solitude as I loved it when I was 17: it is a very particular kind of solitude in which one chooses and invents one's friends, and one reads much.

This biography employs neither the psychoanalytical approach (for which I am not trained) nor the literary-critical method, for I am convinced that the "truth" of Silone's life lies neither hidden in the archives nor wholly revealed in his writings but in some contested and ambiguously mapped terrain between memoir, literature, and history.

That terrain was shaped by the forces of heresy in daring to challenge certain Marxist and Stalinist "truths," exile in Switzerland, and the twin tragedies of a failed politics and a disillusionment with the Catholic church. In the 1920s, as a major figure of the international Communist movement, Silone refused to accept the orthodoxy of

Stalin's cult and suffered the fate of the heretic, excommunicated from the Marxist church. Broken, disillusioned, told by his doctors that he was near death, and contemplating suicide, Silone retreated to Davos, where he began composing his most famous work, *Fontamara*, literally "Bitter Spring." The book's "unforeseen and unforeseeable" success "made me a writer," he recalled forty years later. Like a long line of Italian intellectuals before him, from Dante to Machiavelli, from Mazzini to Garibaldi, exile transformed Silone into an entirely new person. He was ostracized by the Communists and hunted by the Fascists. Rather than the relatively congenial exile of bohemian Paris, Silone chose austere, Protestant Zurich. He was accused of failing to change with literary taste, of refusing to accommodate the whims of the reading public, of writing the same book over and over again. But as his close friend and colleague the Polish writer Gustaw Herling wrote about him, "Anyone who is deeply convinced that he is saying something important is not ashamed to say things more than once. The secret is the gravity of the words, and what gives words their gravity is their unceasing vigilance."

It was this existential status as an outsider and exile—even after returning to Italy—that marked his life and work. An interviewer once noted a certain "Erasmian component" to his personality. But an Erasmus plucked from the aristocratic Renaissance and dropped into the Industrial Age, "not afraid to get his hands dirty in peasant revolts." This was an Erasmus who rendered Silone "a citizen of an invisible world community of free men, not very numerous, but united by cultural ties." This Italian had no homeland. Indeed, Silone claimed no other citizenship except that of this "imagined communion" with peasants and workers around the world, so different from the "imagined communities" of nationalism.

Silone's personal traumas (the loss of his father, the death of his mother in an earthquake, his precarious physical and mental health, his brother's imprisonment and death, his "spying") inevitably left their marks but were only obliquely played out in his work. It was only the public trauma of expulsion from the PCI that was explicit in his writing. His struggle with demons private and public may not have been as obvious as that of other intellectuals with whom he has often been compared, such as Jean-Paul Sartre, Albert Camus, or George Orwell, yet it was no less dramatic. His story is, in short, a modernist tragedy.

Silone represents a special genre of intellectual: passionately committed to a political ideology that eventually proves illusory; in the light of that failure desperately attempting not to succumb to nihilism; perhaps morally compromised by a relationship to the very powers of oppression; caught in a Sisyphean task of political liberation in a century that placed all the powers of modern mass communication, technology, and awesome violence in the hands of totalitarian states.

In 1962, Silone and Darina made a pilgrimage of sorts to the Holy Land. They had taken the road from Jerusalem to Bethlehem and found themselves in a barren valley bereft of trees, shrubs, plants, or flowers. There was no sign of water or human life. But near Bethlehem they came upon a woman dressed all in black, carrying a child and riding a dusty, gray donkey. The three silent figures passed Silone and his wife without so much as a glance in their direction. The vision created in Silone a particular state of mind and he was silent for a long time. Although he had never been in this part of the world, he had the distinct impression that he had already seen and lived this panorama. It was Darina who after a long while broke the silence by pointing out to her husband that this was the landscape of his novels. It was a revelation. "I saw once again," he later wrote, "outside of myself, something that I had carried within me for years, perhaps since birth: the landscape of my soul." In this landscape, bread, wine, wolves, donkeys, and water all had potent hold on his imagination, both in their literal and symbolic manifestations. Water in all its forms—from fountains and springs to snow and tears—is always critical in his work. (One is reminded of Picasso's famous remark: "I went to communism as one goes to a spring of fresh water.") In Silone's work, towns and people have names such as Acquasanta (holy water), Acquaviva (living water), and Pietrasecca (dry stone), indicating their interior life. The cover of his last work was graced with Giotto's fresco "Miracle of the Spring," depicting St. Francis of Assisi in prayer while a fellow pilgrim quenches his thirst nearby. But "if the spring is not clear," declares one of Silone's protagonists, "I refuse to drink."

ONE

SAINTS and STONECUTTERS

When September comes to Fontamara,
the old cornmeal is almost finished,
and the new is not yet ground.
When September comes to Fontamara,
the old meal is wormeaten,
and the polenta is bitter indeed.
—*SILONE*, "Viaggio a Parigi"

Homo Homini Lupus

Ignazio Silone came from a land where wolves still roamed the earth. They were sovereigns of the mountain passes that linked one small town to another in the rugged Abruzzo region of Italy. After years of merciless hunting, today the only wolves in the still-rugged Abruzzo are safely ensconced in a national park. But as unwary visitors may unexpectedly discover, their cousins—menacing wild dogs—still wander the hills above Silone's hometown of Pescina dei Marsi. Jealous of their inheritance, the dogs defend their domain while birds of prey lazily circle high above. Wolves in all their myriad forms haunted Silone's imagination and writing his entire life.

Their physical presence in Abruzzo was a defining feature of life in the region, especially in winter:

> The wolves would come down from the mountains in the afternoon and lie in wait near the watering troughs. There they lay buried in the snow until dusk. To their famished bellies the wind bore the plump, warm smell of the sheep. The moment it grew dark, they threw prudence to the winds. The smell of sheep made them desperate, mad, and capable of anything. They moved in groups of three, one behind the other, according to their ancient rule of war. Not even the sight of men waiting in ambush for them—not even certain death—would make them turn back.

Few readers of his masterful second novel, *Bread and Wine*, can forget its tormenting last lines, as the innocent Cristina desperately seeks to follow the fleeing Pietro Spina into the mountains during a snowstorm:

> Eventually a voice in the distance answered her, but it was not a human voice. It was like the howling of a dog, but it was sharper and more prolonged. Cristina probably recognized it. It was the howl of a wolf. The howl of prey. The summons to other wolves scattered about the mountain. The invitation to the feast. Through the driving snow and the darkness of the approaching night Cristina saw a wild beast coming toward her, quickly appearing and disappearing in the dips and rises in the snow. She saw others appear in the distance. Then she knelt, closed her eyes, and made the sign of the cross.

The wolves that permeate Silone's oeuvre are accompanied by another force of nature: the ever-present earthquake of 1915 that destroyed a good part of Silone's hometown. Wolves and the earthquake are mentioned in every one of Silone's novels, often seemingly in passing but freighted with power and symbolism. The earthquake affected Silone in much the same way that Dostoevsky's mock execution marked the Russian writer; neither man was the same afterward and their writing bears the often subtle and sometimes obvious imprint of the event. Pescina had a population of five thousand on the morning of January 13, 1915; within thirty seconds, thirty-five hundred people were dead, including Silone's mother. The son dug his mother out of the ruins with his own hands. After five days, Silone's last surviving sibling, a younger brother, Romolo, was pulled from the rubble. In a passage many years later, Silone conflated the wolves and the earthquake in a scene of deep despair that apparently was never far from his mind or his writing.

> It was a few days after the earthquake. Most of the dead were still lying under the ruins. Help was slow in coming. The terrified survivors lived among the ruined houses in temporary shelters. It was the dead of winter, and that year had been especially cold. New tremors and snowstorms were threatened. The donkeys, mules, cows, and sheep had been gathered in makeshift pens, since their barns and stalls had been destroyed. And at night the wolves came, attracted by the strong warm odor of the animals no longer protected by their stables. Night comes quickly in our part of the world, and in that season it's already dark at four o'clock. So it was dangerous to go too far from the shelters. On the mountain, unusually deep in snow, it was impossible for the wolves to get their customary food. Irresistible hunger drove them down into the valley. The smell of the herds in the open air made them bolder than usual, almost mad. To keep them away we had to keep big fires burning all the time. Some nights the cries of these beasts did not let us sleep.

In the bitter, piercingly cold nights after the earthquake, one could hear the wolves howling, each time a little closer to the ruins of the town. "You know," Silone sadly recounted to his wife a few days before his death in 1978, "even outside the ruins many people died in the snow . . . By day I tried digging with my hands in the rubble, but all I could see were the large fallen beams . . . One night I couldn't face the cold outside and pretended to sleep. I heard one of my uncles saying I must be wakened, then someone else replying, 'Let him sleep, he's better off dead, since he's got no one left.' "

The despair brought about by nature was compounded by horrors committed by friends and family: A wife fails to notify others that her husband is still alive beneath the ruins, ensuring that he perishes. And during the first evening after the earthquake, Silone witnessed a relative stealing his dead mother's purse. "I believe it was that night," he caustically recalled, "which colored my opinion of money in a veil of deep horror."

Until he was fifteen, Silone's entire world was circumscribed by the view from the hills above Pescina with the mountains encircling the Fucino plain below. Compared to other regions in Italy, Silone wrote, the Marsica had been very poor in terms of any civil history. "Its glories," he wrote dryly, "have been primarily religious." The area, Silone insisted, was not backward but rather "overburdened and exhausted by its load of medieval history." Yet in spite, or perhaps precisely because, of this, he felt that it was the only setting in which he could situate his "living" characters. The one novel not set in Abruzzo, *The Fox and the Camelias* (1960), takes place in the Ticino canton of Switzerland, and its main character, Daniele, is the son of an exiled Abruzzese peasant. Yet Silone once admitted: "In the judgment of the Abruzzesi, the countryside comes off poorly [*maltrattato*] in my books. I must say that they are absolutely right." He went on to insist that in a novel, the landscape is an integral part of the characters, the situations, and the problems represented. It was not until many years later, in a journey to the Holy Land, that he became fully cognizant of this.

He was acutely aware that the Mezzogiorno (the Italian south) was a society lacerated by profound contradictions. It had given Italy some of her most original philosophers (Benedetto Croce) and artists (Ovid), yet it was the part of the country in which ignorance was most widespread. It was a region of mystics such as Joachim of Fiore and sensualists such as Gabriele D'Annunzio; it was permeated by anarchists and overrun with police; it was populated by landless peasants and large landowners and *latifundisti.* "It is one of the most inhuman parts of the world (comparable in certain aspects with Spain) and its contradictions are so ancient," he wrote in 1938, "that they seem natural. The refusal to accept poverty, ignorance, and injustice as natural facts was the impetus for my non-conformity."

For Carlo Levi, a northern Italian Jewish intellectual, banished to the remote town of Aliano in the province of Matera for his political activities, contact with the Mezzogiorno was a revelation. Levi came to see it as "that other part of the world, hedged in by custom and sorrow, cut off from History and the State, eternally patient," a land and a people "without comfort or solace, where the peasant lives out his motionless civilization on the barren ground in remote poverty, and in the presence of death." What kinship did Silone have, an interviewer once asked rhetorically, to Italy? Pescina was not in Italy; it was "outside time and space, forgotten by God and men." And paraphrasing the title of Carlo Levi's most famous book, he concluded, "Christ did not arrive at Pescina."

A decade before his death, Silone looked back at the Abruzzo and its people as "quite ordinary, simple, taciturn, even crude and mean." But when the occasion demanded it, they could also be "capable of exceptional acts of generosity and courage." A South African prisoner of war, escaping from the Fascists and Nazis, had been hidden and succored by the peasants of Abruzzo. On meeting Silone, he recounted his promise to return to Italy and tell of how he had then, for the first time, "glimpsed the possibility of absolutely pure, selfless human relationships."

Pescina

In his famous autobiographical essay "Emergency Exit" (1949), Silone acknowledged that "everything that I may have written up to now, and probably everything I will write in the future, even though I have traveled and lived abroad for many years, refers only to that part of the country which can be seen from the house where I was born—no more than twenty or thirty miles in any direction."

The people of Pescina are justly proud of their history and jealous of their cultural inheritance. For centuries the seat of the local bishop, it was the central city of the Marsica region. When the bishop fled after the earthquake of 1915, the bishopric was transferred to nearby Avezzano. Protesting this decision landed the young Silone in court facing a stiff fine. Twenty years later, when that very same bishop was scheduled to officiate over the annual first Holy Communion Mass, he found himself facing an empty cathedral. The flock had neither forgotten nor forgiven their shepherd for abandoning them.

One arrives in Pescina dei Marsi from the drained lake bed of the Fucino plain. Today, most outsiders come via the railroad from Rome, cutting through the Apennine mountain range. "When I came from Rome by the night train," Pietro Spina recalls, "I realized I was approaching this part of the world by the slightly bitter flavor in the air." Centuries ago, the people of the area fled the malaria and warring factions of the plain for the relative safety of the mountains. There, small towns cling precipitously to the mountains, remote and aloof, the fear of malaria and war replaced by the peril of earthquakes and wolves.

Although Silone's childhood home was destroyed by the earthquake, the house he was born in still stands on the old via Botteghe, dark and abandoned in the ancient part of Pescina the writer called "Purgatory." This was at the top of the hill and "made up of a hundred or more hovels and stables where only the peasants dwelt." A half century after the earthquake, he could still paint a vivid picture of Purgatory over which reigned "the ruins of an ancient castle." Today, one wanders amid the ruins with Silone's words echoing off the walls: "a great rabbit warren of black peasant huts, stables for the animals carved out of the rock, a couple of churches and some uninhabited mansions." Yet in his time, the town was alive with a persistent vitality: "At the first light of dawn, there began on our street the daily procession of goats, sheep, donkeys, mules, cows, wagons of every description and use, and peasants, making their way down to the plain for the day's work. And every evening until late the same procession of men and animals passed in the opposite direction, showing clear signs of fatigue."

The peasant women of Pescina used to gather water from a small spring on a street recently renamed via Poppedio Silo but that all the inhabitants of the town continued to call by its ancient name, Fontamara. Silone recalled,

> I drank that water until I was fifteen. When I was small (from five to nine years old) I spent entire days by the spring with the goat or the pig. The spring was not bitter, but the life of the peasants of that neighborhood was very bitter. Fontamara was the road that led to the cemetery and the road that led to the Fucino plain.

Pescina is light-years distant from tourist Italy. Not far from L'Aquila, the town is circumscribed by the Maiella mountains and Monte Velino and situated on the left bank of the Giovenco River. In 1888, the German scholar of classical antiquity Ferdinand Gregorovius wrote that "Abruzzo" was a word that might sound harsh and strange to the ear but that the region itself was "of a singular beauty, proud and majestic . . . One could admire magnificent plateaus and rich plains of pastures and grain, and hills crowned with rocks and ancient cities, many of whose origins are hidden in the darkness of myth, all are the refuge of a hardy and industrious people."

Silone wryly pointed out that few Abruzzesi would have recognized this portrait of themselves. Worse, the political authorities in Rome had even less of an understanding of the region, as revealed in a curious expedition of politicians and journalists from Rome in July 1909 that set out to "discover the Abruzzo." Needless to say, Silone sardonically notes, the expedition, with its comic and grotesque overtones, failed; the accounts published in all the major newspapers of the time revealed far more about the politicians and the journalists than the people of the region. Only one writer was honest enough to admit that the explorers had discovered only their own ignorance. But the writer could not resist adding that this failure was reciprocated by the "natives" who failed to demonstrate any desire to make themselves known or to know their guests. Suspicion of the national government coupled with the mass wave of emigration meant that the peasants of the Abruzzo in 1909 knew New York and Philadelphia better than Rome or Milan.

The draining of the Fucino lake in the middle of the nineteenth century, while creating fertile farmland in the valley below (to the enormous benefit of the local lord, Prince Torlonia), was an environmental and ecological disaster for the mountain town. The lake had been responsible for retaining the little warmth necessary during the winter months to ensure the survival of a way of life; now the old olive groves were destroyed and the vineyards often afflicted with infectious diseases, with the result that the grapes oftentimes did not fully ripen. The peasants were forced to gather the grapes before the earlier frosts and snowfalls, with the result that the wine produced was "as sour as lemon juice." Sadly, "those who produce it are condemned to drink it." Silone always felt an insurmountable estrangement from Pescina: His depictions of the petite bourgeoisie of the small towns are so pitch-perfect because his family lived that life and shared those values. "Just because you are from somewhere," he remarked with bitterness to Gustaw Herling, himself an exile in Naples after the war, "does not mean that you can't be an exile from there, too."

At the age of sixty-five, Silone could still recall with crystal-clear clarity the first time he went beyond the confines of the village. His father consented to take the young boy, perhaps not yet ten, down to work in the fields five miles from town. The experience caused him to feel that he had passed the threshold of childhood into adulthood. Leaving home before the sun was up, father and son set out silently to work. On looking back over his shoulder, Silone was granted an unexpected panorama of the town: "I had never seen it as a whole before, outside myself, with its own valley. I hardly recognized it: a pile of houses jumbled together in a crack in the barren mountain."

Although Silone left Pescina for Rome as a seventeen-year-old youth and returned only sporadically, the town left an indelible impression on his psyche and his writing. He once returned and found a ten-year-old boy wandering the ruins of "Purgatory." Silone had known the boy's grandfather, the local postman. In trying to explain why he left, Silone tells the boy that life is made of choices—"some good and some less good"—and that one of his choices was to live far from Pescina. The boy, justifiably suspicious, asks, "But do you like Pescina?" As a light flickered in his eyes moist with emotion, Silone replies, "Pescina for me is everything: it is my life, it is my homeland, it is my family, it is in my dreams, it is a part of me." Only many years later did the boy discover the identity of the old man.

Exiled in Switzerland in 1930, hounded by an increasingly bitter struggle with the Italian Communist Party and the Communist International, tormented by an exchange of letters with a Fascist police official, told by his doctors that he was fatally ill, and plagued by mental illness to the point of suicide, Silone wrote *Fontamara*, a poignant and powerful novel set in his hometown, "so that at least I might die among my own people." It was a village like many others, "but to those born and bred there, it is the universe, for it is the scene of universal history—births, deaths, loves, hates, envies, struggles, and despair."

In a 1937 letter to the German writer and translator Rainer Biemel, Silone contrasted his own mental topography of the Abruzzo with that of another native son, Gabriele D'Annunzio. Drawing from Greek mythology, Renaissance imagery, and the primitive painters, D'Annunzio has given us beautiful, marvelous, and sensuous—but superficial—descriptions of the Abruzzo. Comparing D'Annunzio's Abruzzo to his own portrait in *Bread and Wine*, Silone wrote to Biemel, was like comparing the visible and the secret face of southern Italy.

Pescina, which had a population of no more than five thousand at the time of Silone's birth, is like innumerable other towns in the region, each one unique yet all sharing a common history of deprivation and hardship. L'Aquila, the provincial capital, was the town of the hermit Pietro da Morrone, called to the papacy by warring factions of aristocratic Roman families, taking the name Celestine V in 1294, who would inspire Silone's *The Story of a Humble Christian* (1968). Nearby Sulmona is renowned for its sweets. Cocullo celebrates the feast of St. Dominic on the first Thursday of May with a procession carrying the saint's statue draped by a mass of live, writhing snakes. Pescina's one claim to fame would be as the birthplace of Cardinal Jules Mazarin (born Giulio Raimondo Mazzarino), chief minister of state of King Louis XIV of France. In fact, the Mazarin house sits a mere stone's throw from what is left of the Silone home. Two more different men can hardly be imagined. Mazarin, first apprentice then successor to Cardinal Richelieu, represented everything that Silone fought against his whole life: the arrogance of those in power, the contamination of the church with secular power and its subsequent corruption, the contempt of the ruler for the ruled.

The houses of Pescina seem to huddle together for protection and warmth. For much of the twentieth century, most were one-storied with a single opening that served as door, window, and chimney for the hearth. Some houses had unpaved floors and had to shelter not only husband and wife and several children on a massive matrimonial bed, but sometimes livestock as well. A few families of the petite bourgeoisie, like the Tranquillis, had homes of two or even three stories. In these lived the local gentry: mayor, pharmacist, doctor, schoolteacher. The more modest homes were refuge for the *contadini* (peasants who owned scattered pieces of land) and *braccianti* (day laborers without any land at all who gathered in the piazza every day seeking work).

The one main road through the town witnessed an exodus every morning as men and animals made their way to the Fucino plain below, often leaving while it was still dark. After their departure, their place would be taken by carts from the local bauxite mine, rumbling through the streets.

Ruins dominate the town. Peering down from the mountain like two haughty old aunts are the remains of the Church of San Berardo and the ravaged castle of the baronial del Balzo family. For Silone, it was a town and region poor in civic history, dominated by a Christian and medieval past. Its only monuments of note were churches and monasteries and "its only illustrious sons were saints and stonecutters." The human condition there has always been particularly difficult, with suffering given primacy of place as "the first of natural calamities." For those who were determined not to be trampled by fate or overwhelmed by suffering, two ideals beckoned: the humble meekness of St. Francis of Assisi or the quixotic rebelliousness of the anarchists. The mysticism of a Joachim of Fiore, in which Christian charity would replace the laws of men, found more adherents in the Abruzzo than the theoretical Marxism of Antonio Gramsci. Far from being perceived by Silone as insignificant or as a burden in a secular age, this mystic Christian tradition was of fundamental importance, which had not been sufficiently understood. It was, he insisted, "a real resource, a miraculous reserve." The politicians were ignorant of it, while the priests feared its power. Only the "saints and stonecutters" knew it intimately.

Pescina, like all these mountain towns, has its own internal complexity, paradoxes, and irony. After having seen the mountain that hovers over the town in the distance for several hours from the town's piazza and narrow lanes, I decided to make the ascent. Upon touching the rose-colored stone, it unexpectedly broke off in my hand. At the age of seven, Silone and his family moved to another house, near the town's central piazza. That house was destroyed in the 1915 earthquake. Today, a local office of the CGIL, the Communist-dominated labor union, is next door. Across the piazza is a fountain built in the Fascist era. The Silone archive, donated to the town by his widow in 2000, is housed in what was once a former Franciscan convent, marking the spot where St. Francis visited the town in the thirteenth century. The convent was converted into a Fascist jail in the 1920s.

"I was born in 1900," Silone wrote in 1940 while in Swiss exile with his typical ironic humor, "in the month consecrated to the Virgin Mother of God, roses, and donkeys. This last circumstance has, unfortunately, had a great influence on my destiny." Silone often wrote—and biographers have often repeated—that he was born on May 1, the day consecrated by the Catholic church as a holy day to St. Joseph, patron saint of carpenters and workers, and by the Socialist parties of Europe to more contemporary workers. Surely he reveled in the fact that his birth date attempted to reconcile the two great ideologies of his life. (Yet as the town historian Diocleziano Giardini pointed out to me, Silone was actually born on April 30 and registered at the local church on May 2.) Silone's father, presenting himself at the town hall a day after his son's birth, wished to enter the patriotic names of Mameli or Cairoli as Silone's given name but the mayor objected: They were not recognized Christian names. Exasperated, Paolo Tranquilli replied that they should give the infant the acceptable name of the mayor, Severino, but the town secretary, present in his official capacity, offered his own, Secondino, and so Silone was burdened with a name that roughly translates in the local dialect as "jailer."

In an essay published in 1938 in *Partisan Review*, Silone insisted that his first memory of childhood went back as early as his weaning. Local custom dictated that mothers wishing to wean their children from the breast smear their nipples with coal. The unsuspecting child, when confronted with the life-nurturing breast suddenly disfigured, would recoil in horror. "I remember the combination of terror and disgust with which I discovered those mysterious marks on her maternal breasts. It was the first tragic moment of my life." Three years later when the youngest son, Romolo, was to be weaned, Silone was a spectator at the cruel rite of passage. While Romolo wept and howled, his mother remained silent and impassive. When Silone revealed to his mother that he remembered his own weaning and how he was shocked at how she could so deceive him, she sought to defend herself by explaining that it was time for him to be weaned. The older son was neither convinced nor consoled.

In an interview with the writer Iris Origo, Silone described his mother and maternal grandmother as "two grave, remarkable women, serious and extraordinary," the dominant influences of his childhood. That maternal grandmother would become the model for the indomitable Donna Maria Vincenza Spina in two of his novels. When Origo asked if there were any photographs of the women, Silone—

perhaps sardonically—told her that photographs were a frivolity, taken only for passports and tombstones.

One summer evening in Rome, struggling to sustain a conversation, Silone asked Irving Howe when he had become a Socialist. At age fourteen in the Bronx, Howe replied. Silone burst out laughing, "You too!" Although separated by thousands of miles of ocean, the melancholy boy from the Abruzzo and the Jewish kid from the Bronx recognized that "some thread of shared desire had linked our youth."

Silone often switched between the two registers of tragedy and comedy when writing about his own life. In 1940, he joked that "there were three great events of my adolescence: the appearance of Halley's Comet with the expectation of the end of the world; the epic war against the Turks for the conquest of Tripoli; and the cholera epidemic of 1911. When I have learned to write a little better than I do now and above all when the fear of those events has passed, perhaps I will recount them."

Secondino was the third of seven children. His father, Paolo Tranquilli, was a small landowner and the youngest of seven brothers; his mother, Marianna Delli Quadri, was a weaver. From his father, Silone inherited a stubborn nonconformism and a burning rage against all forms of injustice. Once, seated at the front steps of the family home, Silone witnessed a forlorn man being dragged away by the police. The young boy was amused by the spectacle and turning to his father said, "Look how funny he is!" Paolo Tranquilli was furious. Pulling his son to his feet by his ear, the father admonished him to have pity on the miserable wretch. "What have I done wrong?" asked the child. "Never make fun of a man who's been arrested!" the father insisted, "Never!" "Why not?" "Because he can't defend himself," replied the father. "And because he may be innocent. In any case, because he's miserable."

Paolo Tranquilli came from a family that was not desperately poor, possessing land in the Fucino plain. Silone once described his father as "the most restless" of the seven brothers, "the only one with any proclivity to insubordination." These men were "tall, strong and solemn, the oldest wearing long beards, and they all had huge feet and powerful knees, shoulders and hands. In spite of age and comfortable family circumstances, they continued to do the hard labor themselves; they drove the wagons, they guided the plows and supervised the threshing. The need to work seemed a physical necessity for them." The family enjoyed a standard of living considerably more fortunate than the overwhelming mass of peasants in the town. As Silone himself admitted, his orientation toward progressive ideas and toward the poor developed in direct contradiction to the dominant psychology of his origins. The phylloxera epidemic of 1908, which wiped out the family vineyard, along with the mysterious deaths of a few head of cattle, spelled economic ruin. Economic considerations, along with his innate nonconformism and status as the youngest of seven brothers, goaded Paolo Tranquilli to emigrate. Unlike most of the Abruzzesi, he decided to try his fortune in Brazil. But when Paolo Tranquilli stepped off the boat in Rio de Janeiro, he was confronted with the spectacle of striking workers being beaten by police. The police, in addition to assaulting the workers, appealed to the newly arrived Italians to accept jobs at lower wages. Disgusted, Paolo Tranquilli took the next boat back to Italy. He died in 1911, three years after his return. Silone was eleven.

As his mother was a weaver, Silone spent much of his youth assisting her at the loom. For him, these were rare idyllic moments of reprieve in his childhood, even as his mother counseled him in the traditional fatalism and resignation of the peasants. He listened with fascination to the stories the women told to pass the time: of bandits and hermits, villains and martyrs, episodes from the Bible and lives of the saints. He later likened the art of storytelling to weaving: placing one tangible, substantive word after another with patience and humility until the image appears woven together.

It was from his father that the boy discerned the possibility of another way. When, in 1907, the local aristocrat, Prince Torlonia, stood for election to parliament, Paolo Tranquilli and his older brothers met to discuss their options. A timid local unknown, an eye doctor named Mariano Scellingo, had announced his candidacy on the list of the

Catholic Partito Popolare Italiano. Since about eight thousand families of the region (the majority of the local population) were engaged in cultivating the prince's thirty-five-thousand-acre estate, it was simply assumed that everyone would vote for the prince, even though none of "his" eight thousand families had ever laid eyes on the man. Paolo Tranquilli was the only one who suggested that since the ballot was secret, they should all vote their conscience. His older brothers were aghast at this breach of protocol and tradition. Silone, seated by the fire, silently followed the proceedings, debate, and arguments with fascination. When Scellingo was scandalously elected, Prince Torlonia was compensated by King Vittorio Emanuele III by being named a senator, offering the boy another valuable lesson in politics. The glaring discrepancy between private and public life tormented him. "In school all my prayers ended with one request: 'Oh, God, help me to live without betraying myself.'"

As with many families of the Mezzogiorno, the Tranquillis had their share of misfortune and tragedy. Most typical were the early deaths of children. An older sister, Elvira, died in childhood. On May 6, 1903, Maria Tranquilli, a mere twelve days old, died. A year later, on May 23, 1904, a younger brother, Romolo, destined to play a critical role in two of the tragedies of Silone's life, was born. Three years after Romolo's birth, Marianna Tranquilli gave birth to another son. This time Paolo was able to assert his will and have the child named after a hero of the Risorgimento, Cairoli. But ten days after he saw the light of the world, little Cairoli too died. The scourge of infant mortality continued when another daughter named Maria died in 1910 shortly after her first birthday. "Many babies died in the first few months," Silone wrote later, "It was a periodic massacre of the innocents." Domenico, Silone's older brother, was forced to take the father's place in the fields, abandoning a promising academic career. But two months after their father's death, Domenico too died after fracturing his spine in a fall steps away from the family home. Marianna was forced to redouble her work at the loom. Malnutrition, malaria, tuberculosis, and accidents combined to ensure that the women of the Mezzogiorno wore the vestments of mourning for most of their adult lives. "My memories of childhood and adolescence are almost all sad," Silone wrote. "After the earthquake of 1915 which destroyed a good deal of the Marsica, I was an orphan and homeless . . . The events following led me to undergo three essential experiences: poverty, religion, and communism."

The novelist Ferdinando Camon has richly described the vanishing world of the Italian peasantry. Perhaps no country in the twentieth century besides Russia went through such a radical transformation from a rural peasant society to an urban and industrial one. In 1900, illiteracy was the norm in many areas of the Mezzogiorno. The standard of living had decreased since the unification of Italy in 1861. Economic prospects were dim. A Piedmontese army of occupation attempted to control brigandage and "primitive rebels" in the south. Thousands were imprisoned, exiled, or killed. There is no more eloquent testimony to the failure of Italian unification than the mass wave of emigration that sent millions of cafoni, braccianti, *mezzadri* (sharecroppers), and others sailing to the Americas, Australia, and other strange shores.

The mountain towns of the Apennines were particularly isolated well into the 1950s. Then, through the so-called "economic miracle," Italy transformed itself into a relatively affluent society. Although radios were available under the Fascist regime, they had been strictly controlled and a license was required to own one. Now, in addition to the radio, television made fateful inroads into Italian society. Fiat introduced the 500, the Italian version of the Model T Ford, a car affordable to the masses. By the early 1960s, Silone could write that Italian youth of the postwar generation simply could not imagine the monotony of life in the mountain towns of his childhood. While parents, relatives, and other adults discussed inscrutable matters, the children watched the fire. With his usual deadpan style and studied understatement, Silone remarked that "it was not a very stimulating life." Those evenings before the hearth could dull the mind or might fire the imagination of a future poet; one could also acquire a taste for reflection and meditation.

Enrolled in the local seminary school, Silone soon earned a reputation in Pescina as a studious if enigmatic child. "But the most interesting things I learned on the street going back and forth to school. Even later, I must confess, what I learned I learned from the street." The rural counterparts to the infamously cunning Neapolitan *scugnizzi*, the young village ruffians, constituted a separate community, with "its own laws, its own rites, and its own dialect . . . Mothers shouted at their sons from morning till night, and the air often resounded with the most terrible curses, but these were so frequent that no one took any notice."

Beginning in 1908, Silone surreptitiously began writing letters on behalf of an illiterate woman to her son in prison. Francesco Zauri had been convicted in 1897 of the premeditated homicide of Giuseppe Zauri and sentenced to life in prison. Francesco Zauri refused to defend himself against the charges and would not tell the court what he had been doing at the time of the murder. Nor did he have any explanation for the rather large sum of money on his person at the time of his arrest. In writing the letters, the eight-year-old Silone was soon convinced of the man's innocence. That lost soul would haunt Silone for forty years.

In spite of, or perhaps because of, the Tranquilli family's social standing as small landowners, the young Silone more often found himself drawn to the lowest rung of the social ladder in Pescina, the peasants. In the local dialect and throughout Italy, they were referred to as cafoni, then as now a truly derogatory term. Yet Silone sought to rescue the term: With his sardonic irony, he pointed out that it was poor peasants all over the world—whether they were fellahin, coolies, peons, muzhiks, or cafoni—who, by "sweating blood," made the soil fertile and grew the food yet were always hungry. "They form a nation, a race, a church of their own." The cafoni themselves have no illusions about their place in the world. A peasant in *Fontamara* simply and eloquently maps out their mental topography of the cosmos:

"At the head of everything is God, the Lord of Heaven. Everyone knows that. Then comes Prince Torlonia, lord of all the earth.

"Then come Prince Torlonia's guards.

"Then come Prince Torlonia's guards' dogs.

"Then, nothing at all.

"Then nothing at all.

"Then nothing at all.

"Then come the cafoni. And that's all."

On another occasion, a clerical worker in town sneeringly reminds the peasants that they are cafoni, "flesh used to suffering."

Silone cannot be charged with romanticizing the cafoni: He is quite conscious of the ridiculous tourist-industry image of southern Italy as a place of beautiful landscapes where "peasants go caroling joyfully to work, echoed prettily by a chorus of country girls dressed in traditional costume, while nightingales trill in the neighboring wood." The song-birds, Silone brutally reminds us, have been pitilessly exterminated for food; and besides, there "is not even a word for nightingale in the local dialect." The peasants, for their part, don't sing on their way to work; if anything, they curse, swear, and blaspheme—and not very creatively, at that. A reader can understand why the good people of the Abruzzo might be offended by Silone's portrait of the peasants; in his pages they are ignorant, scheming, torn by petty jealousies and an insatiable envy; and often the victims of townsfolk and the local bourgeoisie. At one point, Berardo Viola, the hero of *Fontamara*, even equates his status as a *cafone* with a donkey, but the careful reader of Silone will come to recognize the high regard the writer had for donkeys, the author's favorite animal. The donkey for Silone is the antithesis of the wolf; it is eternally patient and bears its suffering with dignity.

The cafone, Silone insisted, was in no way a "primitive"; on the contrary, in a certain sense he is "too civilized." The experience of generations has induced him to believe that the state is a criminal enterprise, just better organized than "organized" crime. Through their "intimate contact with animals and nature, through their direct experience of life's great events such as birth, love, and death, many peasants acquire an immense wisdom." He compared the cafoni to Europe's

Jews, "so crushed by their sorrowful experiences with the state that they can no longer imagine a government composed of human beings." A society could be said to be "developed" or "civilized" only when the classes that were most oppressed by their privations were recognized and judged by their effective worth. "I am proud," he wrote, "to have given a new name, that of cafoni, to those sufferings." Even after he had grown disillusioned with formal politics, he always insisted that in the workers and peasants of Europe he found "those traits of generosity, frankness, solidarity and lack of prejudice which were the genuine and traditional resource of Socialism in its struggle against bourgeois decadence and corruption." In the peasants, Silone found the possibility of a pure, "primitive" Christianity, a possibility of sharing bread and companionship, and it was this—paradoxically— that led him to left-wing politics.

Our Christian Heritage

Just as the mountains and Fucino plain exerted an enormous influence over the young Silone, so too did a native tradition of "primitive" Christianity. Benedictine and Franciscan monks, hermits, apocalyptic orators, visionaries, and alms seekers wandered the countryside. Local fables stressed the deep mysticism and frail humanity of believers. Well into the twentieth century, it was still common to greet visitors in the Mezzogiorno with a biblical "Peace be with you." Silone felt a lifelong attraction to a Christianity deeply rooted in the folk culture of the Abruzzo. In place of an elaborate theological definition, a Christmas custom of the region might serve as an example.

Although the Nordic Christmas tree is today ubiquitous in Italy, it was not always so. In the Abruzzo, it was customary to burn a log (*il ceppo*) in the fireplace on Christmas Eve; in fact, "il ceppo" is a colloquialism for Christmas in this part of the world. The log had to be oak or beech (a luxury) so as to burn all night. The Christmas meal was to be left on the table and the door to the house unlocked because that night the Holy Family was abroad in the land, refugees seeking shelter, persecuted by the authorities. With hearth ablaze and food prepared, the Holy Family could find refuge in any humble home of the Mezzogiorno that night. For a young boy like Silone, the tale exerted considerable influence. On Christmas Eve it was impossible to sleep, not in expectation of extravagant gifts (an orange was considered a rare present) but because the Holy Family might at any time suddenly appear on one's threshold. Besides that thrill of anticipation, the tale inculcated a respect and solidarity for the persecuted and oppressed. The moral complexity of such a worldview was not lost on Silone. It left an indelible impression on a susceptible soul and was an integral part of what he called "our Christian heritage."

He often admitted little formal training in literature and the arts, saying that the first time he attended the theater he was seventeen years old and living in Rome. Instead, his early cultural formation consisted almost entirely of the culture of the church. Before the earthquake, Pescina was a town of approximately five thousand people, mostly peasants. Yet there was a bishop's seat with curia, a seminary, seven churches, and a cathedral. "An imbalance," Silone once dryly remarked, "to be found only in the Mezzogiorno." In such an environment, it was only natural that the liturgical feasts and the solemn rites of the church would exert a singular and otherwise "unimaginable poetic fascination" on the young boy. Vespers, funeral rites, and popular festivals honoring local saints offered the only expression of "true art" that was accessible. The choreography of the priests, the haunting melodies of the Gregorian chant, the eloquence of the Latin, all in service of the "sacred mystery" left a profound mark on Silone. More than four decades after having left the church, "the work that today still touches me most profoundly is Bach's 'Saint Matthew Passion.'"

Ironically, it was a secular Jew from northern Italy who penetrated and best understood the primitive Christianity described by Silone. Carlo Levi was active in Giustizia e Libertà (Justice and Liberty), a movement founded in Paris in 1929 by Carlo Rosselli, Emilio Lussu, Alberto Tarchiani, and others. Justice and Liberty was critical of the dogmatism and orthodox Marxism of the Italian Communist Party and the passivity of the Italian Socialist Party. It soon acquired a reputation as the "party of intellectuals" as well as the party of "Jewish intellectuals." Carlo Levi had been sentenced to *confino* (domestic exile) in the Basilicata region in 1935. From that experience came his most famous book, *Christ Stopped at Eboli*. As Levi slowly came to realize, *cristiano* in the Mezzogiorno had no theological connotations; rather, it was synonymous with civilization and "being civilized." Hence, if, in the local parlance, Christ stopped at Eboli, a town near the coast, he never ventured far enough into the mountains to bring History and Civilization to the poor people of the Mezzogiorno. Small wonder, then, that an ancient pagan past is never far from the surface of a thin veneer of Christianity in southern Italy.

Michael P. McDonald has noted how Silone's "creative vision sprang from and remained rooted in Scripture" and compares Silone to André Gide, who also employs biblical stories to serve his fiction. But McDonald makes an astute distinction: "Whereas the Bible was a psychological sounding board to Gide, a means to plumb the paradoxes and perversities of human nature, to Silone it was less a means to promote greater individual self-awareness than a hallowed reminder of the perennial want of human solidarity."

An incident from childhood reveals Silone's tortured relationship with the institutional Catholic church. An animated discussion unfolded in catechism class between the children and the priest. The day before, the children had seen a puppet show in which a young boy, pursued by the devil, hid under a bed on stage. The devil, unable to locate the boy, turned toward the audience for assistance and politely asked where he might find the young scoundrel. Immediately and in unison, all the children responded that they had not seen the boy or that he had fled. As Silone points out, since none of the children had foreseen that they were to be questioned by the devil himself, their answers were entirely spontaneous and sincere; all children around the world would probably respond the same way. Yet to the astonishment of the children the next day, the priest charged with the catechism was not pleased. In fact, he told the children that he was disappointed in their behavior, for they had told a lie; a lie for a good end, perhaps, but a lie nonetheless, and they should never lie.

"Not even to the Devil?" we asked in astonishment.

"A lie is always a sin," answered the priest.

"Even before a judge?" asked one of the boys.

"I'm here to teach you Christian doctrine, not to talk nonsense," he said. "What goes on outside the Church does not concern me."

As the priest launched into a fine theoretical and theological exegesis, the children grew impatient: Should they or should they not have told the devil where the boy was hiding? With the devil on one side and the boy on the other, and the children eager to help the boy, they wanted to know what to do. Silone raised his hand and asked a question "of unheard of perfidy": "What should we have told the Devil if it had been a priest instead of a boy?" For his impertinence, Silone was required to kneel by the priest's feet for the remainder of the lesson. At the end of the session, the priest, sure that he had tempered the boy's impudence, asked if he had repented. "Of course," Silone answered. "If the Devil asks me for your address, I'll certainly give it to him."

Earthquake

At 6:52 on the morning of January 13, 1915, Pescina and the surrounding mountainous region of the Marsica were devastated by a massive earthquake. Tremors were felt as far away as Rome. Within thirty seconds, thirty-five thousand people were killed and more than five thousand dwellings destroyed. In Pescina, a huge crevice, nearly a thousand feet long, opened up from the mountain to the Giovenco River. Houses along the fissure simply tumbled into the gaping chasm, including parts of the ancestral home of Cardinal Mazarin. The only house left undamaged was, ironically, uninhabited at the time. "When the earthquake demolished the roofs," a character notes in *The Seed Beneath the Snow*, "it exposed things that generally remain hidden."

Forty years later, the effects of the earthquake were still vivid in Silone's mind.

All of a sudden there was a thick fog. Ceilings opened and the plaster fell to the ground. In the middle of the fog one could see children who, without saying a word, moved toward the windows. All this happened in twenty seconds, at most thirty seconds. When the haze of dust dissipated, there was a new world before us. Buildings that didn't exist anymore, streets that had disappeared, the town leveled . . . There were ghostlike figures among the ruins . . . An old miser, the village moneylender, was seated on a rock, wrapped in a sheet as though in a sauna. The earthquake had surprised him in bed, as so many others. His teeth were chattering from the cold. He asked for food. No one helped him. They said to him: "Eat your IOUs." He died like that . . . We witnessed scenes that overthrew every element of the human condition. Large families of which only an idiot child survived . . . the rich man who had not even a wool undershirt to defend him from the cold . . . After five days I found my mother. She was stretched out near the fireplace, without any evident injuries. She was dead. I am very sensitive, yet I didn't shed any tears. Some felt I didn't have a heart. But when suffering overwhelms everything, tears are stupid . . . My brother was found during another search. Because he had been shouting, his mouth was full of dust.

Trapped for days beneath the rubble, Romolo had suffered a broken shoulder; Silone saved himself by standing in the architrave of the seminary in Pescina where he was studying.

With his father dead four years, five of his six siblings dead in childhood, and now the death of his mother, Silone found himself alone in the village with eleven-year-old Romolo. Their maternal grandmother, Vincenza Delli Quadri, took them in and somehow managed to secure the patronage of Queen Elena of Italy for the boys. In the aftermath of the earthquake, Silone came to a bitter realization: Although the Italians had had more than their share of foreign invasions, wars, and natural calamities in more than two millennia of existence, the country would be destroyed not in war or earthquake but in the aftermath of catastrophe. That's when envy, jealousy, deceit, and greed—often just barely kept in check by society's forces of order in the form of the law and the church—came boiling to the surface. Surely the Italians would destroy themselves when foreigners failed. A pathetic letter to Romolo several months later, just days after Italy entered World War I, reveals the depths of Silone's despair.

Pescina 25 May 1915

Dearest brother,

Every misfortune is followed by misfortunes! After the earthquake came the war and after the war will come . . . who knows what will come after the war? Because of the war I had to return to Pescina since the seminary of Chieti was requisitioned by the government as a military hospital. Alas! I have returned to Pescina. I have seen again with tears in my eyes the horrible ruins. I have returned to the wretched hovels, some covered by a few rags as in the first days, where the people live with a horrible disregard of gender, age, or condition. I have seen again our house where I witnessed, with eyes exhausted from tears, our pale, ravaged mother pulled from the ruins. Now her body is buried and yet it seemed to me that her voice calls out. Perhaps the ghost of our mother now inhabits those ruins unconscious of our fate; it seems as though it calls us to be embraced in her bosom.

I saw the place where you fortunately were unearthed. I have seen everything again . . . And now? . . . Now what will I do? I cannot take the exams because I would have to go to some city and that would cost money that can't be found.

But then, then where will I go? How uncertain and perhaps terrible is my future. I see myself with studies interrupted, without any material or moral aid, yes even moral! But a glimmer of hope has appeared to me: While I was at Chieti a lady from the Royal

Court of Her Majesty Queen Elena came to see me and promised
to look after me. The lady was part of the charitable foundation of
Queen Elena for orphans and she told me that she had already been
to visit you at Sacro Cuore. I don't know the name of the lady, or
else I would write it to you; if you find out, write to me immediately.
I don't know what to do, I try to hope still, then . . . whatever
happens happens, I will accept it. If you only knew how one suffers
here! . . . If you can do something for me, please do it. Recommend
me to some lady who comes to visit you; consult with the superior,
to whom I send my most humble greetings.

Affectionate kisses,

Secondo

Romolo was treated for his broken shoulder in a hospital and,
under the patronage of Queen Elena, sent to a school in Rome. With
the collapse of the family home, Silone lived in the poorest and "least
respectable" part of town, which consisted of one-story huts lacking
running water or electricity. To reach this part of town, one had to cross
a ditch that the local authorities had dubbed the Tagliamento after the
river that acted as the front line between the warring Italian and Austrian armies in the north. In short, it was "enemy territory." In some
strange way, the inhabitants liked this nickname and they soon took
measures appropriate to a war zone. Street lamps were smashed,
plunging the neighborhood into perpetual darkness and making it
dangerous for the police—or anyone else—to enter at night. "Any
unlucky person," Silone recalled mischievously, "was welcomed by a
volley of stones from unknown provenance."

What surprised the young boy most was the matter-of-factness with
which the townspeople seemed to accept the catastrophe. It was this
eternal resignation that he could not countenance. In a world where
injustice was so infrequently punished, earthquakes were simply
accepted as plausible devices in a dramaturgical setting. If anything,
the peasants were surprised that earthquakes did not occur more frequently. "In an earthquake," Silone wrote a half century later, "every-

one dies: rich and poor, learned and illiterate, authorities and the people. An earthquake accomplishes what words and laws promise and never achieve: the equality of all. An ephemeral equality, for when fear had died down, collective misfortune became the opportunity for even greater injustices."

The injustices included massive corruption in the distribution of funds to alleviate the suffering of the earthquake's victims and to begin the process of reconstruction. Silone's first published essays were a young man's j'accuse against the local authorities for this breach of the public's trust. Two were published in the Socialist daily newspaper *Avanti!* The third essay was killed when a prominent Socialist lawyer intervened with the paper's editorial board. Silone soon discerned that the system of deception and fraud oppressing the people was vaster than he had imagined and had invisible ramifications.

In the aftermath of the earthquake, relief workers from the north appeared in Pescina. The people of Pescina were shocked: a millennial insularity had decreed that one simply buried the dead and attempted to take up the thread of life after a natural calamity; there had never been a tradition of mutual assistance. Now, the peasants of the Marsica region were inundated with well-intentioned volunteers and paid workers from the state and they were simply amazed. An anecdote reveals the wide gulf separating the victims from their benefactors.

A week or two after the earthquake, supplies began to arrive from Milan. Besides clothing and food, there were prefabricated houses. But the architects of the north had built these houses with a mistaken premise: The kitchen in modern times was to be used only for the preparation of food, while the actual consumption of food was to take place in a "dining" room. Supplies were to be stored in the cellar. The family was to spend most of its time in the "living" room. When the people of Pescina took possession of these houses, the first thing they did was take an ax and hammer and destroy the internal layout. Not the exterior, for they did not want to hurt the feelings of the kind people from Milan, but the interiors were totally reconfigured. The typical peasant family in Pescina, in Abruzzo, and in the Mezzogiorno spent most of the day in the kitchen (often the only room with heat). The pre-fabricated houses, built to be used for a period of six months, were still in use a half century later.

Now officially orphans, Silone and Romolo were charges of the state. In the autumn of 1915, Silone was sent to a school in Rome, but the experience proved disastrous. The school, named after the se-vere pope and saint Pius X, was run by a recently organized order of religious zealots and was built near the Campo Verano cemetery. The dismal architecture was compounded by the character of the neighbor-hood. The local shops were tied to the funeral business and sold tomb-stones. "In those days," Silone recalled, "the vehicles most frequently seen on the street were hearses." The gloom of the surroundings was matched by that of the headmaster and preceptor of the school. The other children were from Rome and sons of the petite bourgeoisie. Silone immediately felt the onus of being the outcast. To the other boys, he was a cafone, a rube, a hick, a simpleton from the countryside. Compounding the frustration was the fact that Silone was immediately recognized by his teachers as the brightest student of the lot and often held up as an example to the others. This, of course, did nothing to endear him to his classmates.

So it seemed almost preordained that one day, just before Christ-mas, Silone would flee school. It was simple enough: a coal truck mak-ing a delivery, the gate to the courtyard wide open, a few steps, and he was on the "outside." Wandering through the dismal streets, he didn't realize the impact of his gesture until he passed a police station. Then the magnitude of his "crime" became apparent. But the most disturb-ing aspect was that there was no explanation that he could offer his superiors upon his return three days later. The headmaster was under-standably furious but also baffled. When interrogated, the young boy could offer no reason for his insubordination. The headmaster "must have been surprised at my apathy, in strange contrast with my recent rebellion. Maybe he sensed the presence in me of something he could not understand." Silone was expelled.

Between Hope and Despair: Don Luigi Orione

At a certain point in his young adulthood, Silone abandoned the church. His departure was anything but unusual. In 1917, at the age of seventeen, when the country was in the midst of a world war and experiencing a profound political and moral crisis, Silone was astonished and dismayed that the Roman Curia could bring itself out of its lethargy only to condemn "women's immodest dress, promiscuous bathing on the beaches, new dances of exotic origin, and traditional bad language." He could no longer accept the "backwardness, the passivity, the conformist behavior of the clergy" in the face of such monumental questions as the war, the Russian Revolution, or the rise of fascism. More than half a century after the events, Silone still recalled the formation of the first peasant agrarian leagues and the response of the local curia: Private property was a divinely sanctioned institution and the very idea of organizing the peasants and workers anathema to God's law. The church was even against the much more modest and conservative demands of the new secular state. In the seminary schools, Silone was encouraged to read the works of Antonio Bresciani (1798–1862), a Jesuit priest. One passage in particular struck the young boy: In a fictional scene, the idealist hero of the Italian Risorgimento, Giuseppe Mazzini, exiled in London, is giving advice to a young Italian patriot: "Try to encourage vice," Bresciani depicts Mazzini as saying, "because only from vice can the sentiment for freedom be born." Silone would later plaintively ask: "How could one remain in such a Church?"

Yet there are indications from his autobiographical writings and the alter ego protagonists of his novels that he felt a great attraction to the vocation of religious life. In the first novel he wrote after his return to Italy after exile, a priest states that Rocco De Donatis "was the object of the clearest call from God that I have ever witnessed. That he did not follow it is one of those mysteries that only God can explain and judge. But although he did not obey his vocation he has constantly demanded from secular life the absolute quality that he could have found only in a monastery. For this reason he is in a tragic, absurd situation."

Yet an episode a day or two after the earthquake had planted a seed of hope in Silone's mind, a seed of hope that until his death never died yet never burst forth in full plenitude. While the survivors were digging through the rubble, still searching for the living and the dead, a slightly built priest arrived from Rome. In a torn, dirty cassock and a beard of several days' growth, Don Luigi Orione had collected a flock of forlorn children orphaned by the quake. Silone was among them. In the confusion, a spectacle never before seen in those parts unfolded before their eyes. King Vittorio Emanuele III and his entourage, in a public display of noblesse oblige and empathy, had arrived from Rome to inspect the damage. Don Luigi, sensing divine intervention, immediately attempted to commandeer one of the entourage's vehicles to take the orphans to Rome. (The rail lines had been broken by the earthquake.) The carabinieri (military police) guarding the car naturally protested. Don Luigi insisted to the point of almost coming to blows with them. The king, noticing the commotion, demanded to know what was happening. Without the slightest sense of intimidation, and fully aware of Vittorio Emanuele's rabid anticlericalism, Don Luigi calmly explained why he needed the vehicle in question. Under the circumstances, the monarch could hardly refuse. Silone witnessed this episode with amazement and admiration. Little did he know at the time that the "strange priest," Don Luigi Orione, would prove to be a decisive figure in his life. Of the three great traumas in Silone's life (the other being his expulsion from the Communist Party in 1931), Don Orione was a critical protagonist in two: the earthquake that killed Silone's mother and the arrest, imprisonment, torture, and death of his brother Romolo.

Don Luigi Orione (1872–1940) was born in Pontecurone in the Piedmont region and studied with Giovanni Luigi Bosco, who inspired in the young boy a life dedicated to the service of others. Orione founded the Piccola Opera della Divina Provvidenza, which included priests, monks, nuns, hermits, and lay associations dedicated to both the active and the contemplative life. Their mission was devoted to education and pastoral care. Don Orione, through his indefatigable efforts and inspired resourcefulness, established dozens of schools along the Italian peninsula. In 1980, Pope John Paul II proclaimed him "blessed," the penultimate stage before sainthood, and in May 2004, the same pope raised Orione to sainthood. The fact that Don Orione kept Silone's letters, before the latter had become famous as a writer, is indicative of the weight he gave their relationship.

The 1915 event was not Don Orione's first brush with earthquakes—or with wolves: In 1908, he had rushed to the Mezzogiorno in the aftermath of an earthquake that killed nearly one hundred thousand people. In 1915, before departing for Pescina, Orione had outfitted three houses in Rome to receive children orphaned by the quake. On arriving in the ravaged mountain region, his car was attacked by wolves. With five terrified children in the car, Don Orione calmly remarked, "how fond these big dogs are of us."

In the immediate aftermath of the earthquake, Silone remained for some time in Pescina with his maternal grandmother while Romolo was sent to the Istituto San Filippo in Rome. Silone eventually joined him in Rome but at the Istituto Pio X. After Silone's impetuous abandonment of the institute, Don Orione accompanied him to a new seminary, the San Romolo in San Remo (where Orione would die in March 1940). The train ride, taking an entire night, was recounted by Silone more than once. Accompanying them was another orphan from Pescina, Gaetano Piccinini, who had lost mother, father, and most of his extended family in the quake. (Piccinini would eventually join Orione's order and corroborate the most important episodes concerning the strange priest and the strange Socialist.)

After the debacle at the school in Rome, Silone had been sent back to Pescina. Propitiously, it was Silone's grandmother who made arrangements for the young man to be placed under the care and tutelage of Don Orione. Silone would travel to Rome, where Don Orione would accompany him to a new school in San Remo on the Ligurian coast. The San Romolo school had in fact been established by Don Orione after the disastrous earthquake of 1908. Romolo, meanwhile, had been taken by Don Orione to a seminary school in Tortona. On arriving at the train station and not recognizing the priest, Silone was disappointed in thinking that the authorities had sent not Don Orione but a lowly subordinate. To make clear his hostility, Silone demanded that the priest carry his luggage and, when asked if he would like something to read from the newsstand, impertinently asked for *Avanti!* the Socialist (and rabidly anticlerical) Party newspaper. When, on the train, the misidentification was cleared up, Silone was acutely embarrassed and apologized for making the priest carry his bags. Don Orione engaged the boy with a particularly brilliant response: "My real vocation, a secret which I want to tell you, would be to live like a real donkey of God, a real donkey of Divine Providence." This led to a spirited disquisition on the nature of donkeys. In the seminary, Orione had willingly shouldered the burdensome tasks avoided by the other boys, such as carrying heavy pails of water from the local well. Orione reveled in being the seminary's "donkey." Silone often returned to the icon of the donkey in his writings and his personal life. When Giuseppe Delogue, seeking to make fun of Silone's appearance, called Silone a "*cavallo di cartone*" (a papier-mâché horse), Silone shot back with his customary ironic humor: "better an *asino di cartone*, but perhaps you Tuscans don't have the same idea of the donkey as I do."

In Don Orione, Silone sensed "the goodness and clear-sightedness which are sometimes found in certain old peasant women, in certain grandmothers, who have patiently endured all kinds of trouble and who therefore know and can guess at the most secret sufferings." At times, Silone "had the impression that he saw me more clearly than I saw myself, but this was not an unpleasant impression." That evening as the train made its way up the coast with the sound of the Tyrrhenian Sea outside the compartment's windows, deeply engaged in conversation with Don Orione, the young boy sensed the beginning of a new life. "I seemed to be on my way to discovering the world." When the two travelers arrived in San Remo at noon, Don Orione told Silone that he would have to depart that day. Silone, perhaps thinking of losing his father and mother so recently, was heartbroken. "I began to feel an entirely new pain taking shape in the depths of my being."

Nearly a quarter century after Don Orione's death, Silone confessed that "certain things that he told me . . . I only understood much later." Among them: "In whatever difficult situation you find yourself in the future, do not be discouraged. God is everywhere and not just in church. He is the father of everyone, even those who do not go to church, even the atheists." For Silone, it had been impossible to fall asleep during that long train ride. "Side by side with many weaknesses, fears, cowardice, which were and are the raw material of my regrets, I carried within myself a dimension, excavated from my deepest self, almost unknown to me, in the first years of my life, in which every word from Don Orione had a very living resonance. That was the source of my nostalgia for the Word, in its original purity and audacity, and the intolerance for institutional compromises."

At the San Remo school, Silone failed to excel academically or even to integrate socially. In one of his letters to Don Orione, the question of a transfer was raised: "I would prefer to remain in one of your schools. This year, you are disappointed in me. It's only right: Even I am very disappointed in myself and so I have decided to straighten out. I beg you not to laugh at my proposals, which would be terrible for me." And he concluded, revealingly: "It's not always true that the wolf changes his skin but not his vice. And then, I don't really believe myself to be, all in all, a wolf."

He chafed under the harsh discipline. His difficult character, combined with a concern for his fragile health, prompted a transfer a year later to the San Prospero school in Reggio Calabria on the toe of the Italian peninsula. There, in the "deep south" of the Mezzogiorno, Silone felt more at ease among the students and faculty.

Silone felt he had found in Don Orione not just a father figure but something more. When Don Orione wrote and agreed to a change in schools, Silone was overjoyed. "It's been so long since I have heard such sincere, good, and affectionate words! In truth, only a father's heart can say certain things . . . I have heard the voice of my father, the breath of my mother, the wish of a saint."

Silone's portrait of the "strange priest" was no less powerful nearly a decade after Orione's death:

Don Orione, with his average height, his dark coloring, and other somatic traits, while Piedmontese, could be mistaken for a Sardinian peasant. But his gaze was extraordinary. He was benevolent and profound . . . he appeared as a man of rare simplicity and naturalness, so to induce even a young boy resisting it, to also be, *with him, simple and natural* . . . Don Orione clearly believed in the continuing presence and assistance of God, to the point of having the impression, in certain occasions, that for him any border between the natural and the transcendent disappeared.

From the San Prospero school, Silone wrote to Don Orione on October 29, 1916: "I have a great fear of myself and want to be in an isolated environment, but I have within myself an irresistible fire that pushes me to do good and to be in the middle of the world."

The children in Don Orione's schools were, whether they were willing or not, forced to take up the burden of poverty. In a note found among Don Orione's papers, Silone lists the entirety of his pathetic worldly possessions: a pair of bedsheets, two torn shirts, a single pair of socks, the uniform from San Remo and a pair of blue trousers, two pairs of broken shoes, an old beret, no quilt, no handkerchief, no pillowcase. But it was not the material deprivations that caused Silone anguish; he was convinced of his moral and spiritual corruption. In a letter of early 1917 to Don Orione, Silone confessed to a state of moral despair. A "corrupt environment," among other things, contributed to a cooling of his fervent promises to do well. "I thought I was finished once and for all with vacillating between good and evil, but I am disillusioned . . . and I was succumbing to evil." Although he finished the academic year in good standing, Silone returned to Pescina in the summer of 1917.

At eighteen, Silone definitely abandoned his studies. Two or three doctors ("fountains of science," he sardonically recalled) assured him that "you won't live more than a year." In his mordantly comic voice, he recalled years later: "Fate had decreed that my doctors would die one after the other, while at this moment, I am writing and drinking coffee. But at the time, I could not foresee this and so I abandoned my studies, faithful to the Italian proverb: 'Better a living donkey than a dead genius.'"

Finding it impossible to live with his relatives, Silone rented a house in town with friends. He described them as "students, vagabonds, workers, and happy people." To the principal of the Reggio Calabria school, Silone wrote an impertinent letter, telling Don Silvio Ferretti that the house is known as "the house of devils" and that he and his friends pass their time singing, drinking, and dancing. His only lament? That with the departure of the class of 1900 for military duty, he will be all alone and thus, perhaps, he'd seek a wife. He also toyed with the idea of entering the civil engineering office in Pescina. (Silone himself was exempt from the call-up to military service due to his ill health and, perhaps, some timely intervention by Don Orione.) But a few months later he is humble and dejected in a pathetic attempt to mend fences with Ferretti and asking for help. "Summing up: 1) studies = disastrous; 2) health = dangerous; 3) soul = (I no longer have one; I no longer believe!)." A letter the same day to Don Orione is more considered and reflective but no less desperate. He berates himself, a Socialist, for speaking of the soul and sin to Don Orione, but in going over the tenets of Marxism, he was overcome by a desolation, a sense of terror in realizing that his new faith (socialism and materialism) would surely lead him to suicide. "Father, my health is ruined, my studies are ruined, but I still want to rebuild, rebuild, rebuild! Help me!" Don Orione refused to offer easy counsel. "Read me with your heart and not your eyes. For me you are an enigma who becomes, day by day, bigger and more awesome . . . You have before you a great crossroad—a tremendous fork in the road."

An Italian biographer has called Orione "God's Fool," while Pope John Paul I thought of him as "the strategist of charity." Orione often referred to himself as "the porter of God." When Douglas Hyde—like Silone a former Communist but unlike Silone a convert to Catholicism—was in the process of writing a biography of Don Orione, he asked Silone for an interview. It was the Italian writer who suggested the title for Hyde's book: *God's Bandit*. When Hyde asked Silone if he had ever met anyone with such a temperament and personality as the humble priest, Silone answered without hesitation: "Lenin. I have met no one else of the intellectual stature of those two men, combined with the same magnetic and rebellious personality and the same immense drive. Don Orione might easily have been a Lenin." Silone sent his explication to the editor of the Italian translation of Hyde's biography: "The motive for the paradoxical paragon between Don Orione and Lenin is the following: two exceptional personalities, with a strong spirit, extremely simple, concentrated on a single point. For Don Orione, this was Christian charity; for Lenin, the social revolution. If Lenin had been a monk, he would have been a saint; if Don Orione had become a politician, he would have accomplished a revolution." Hyde seemed to agree with Silone's assessment of the priest. Although his biography of Orione often approaches hagiography, Hyde writes that he could well imagine Don Orione as a Lenin, for he "was a natural demagogue" and might have gone "far in fascist politics," even challenging Mussolini himself.

The "strange priest" saved Silone in more than one way. In an episode recounted to Domenico Sparpaglione (another biographer of the priest and formerly a fellow student with Romolo Tranquilli), Orione told how, meeting at the train station in Milan, and sensing that Silone, now a high-ranking figure in the PCI, was being followed, he walked arm in arm with him, making sure that the police agents couldn't get a good look at the fugitive. Orione was under the (correct) impression that the agents were "authorized to shoot [Silone] on sight should he attempt to escape." Orione was shrewd enough to understand the mentality of the police: Surely a man walking with a well-known priest could hardly be a dangerous Communist. So Orione was able to escort Silone to a waiting train destined for Switzerland.

Orione had a special desire to help those priests who were in danger of being defrocked or excommunicated. Perhaps he saw in Silone a heretical figure similar to the men he ministered to in the church. Silone, for his part, must have recognized a kindred spirit in the priest.

Young men who knew Orione in the seminary recalled that he often said that "if Christ had not kept his hand on my head I would have been a revolutionary." In March 1940, suffering from pulmonary infections and cardiac problems, Orione was sent back to the seminary at San Remo, protesting, "It is not among the palm trees that I would like to die but among the poor who are Jesus Christ." When his body was first exhumed in 1965, it was said to still be intact; the body now rests in the Sanctuary of the Madonna della Guardia, the church he founded in Tortona.

Romolo

With an athletic build and a love of sports, Romolo Tranquilli was very different from his older brother. Perhaps just as intelligent as Silone, but chafing under the necessary discipline to succeed academically, Romolo was Silone's last link with family and Pescina.

Pulled from the rubble of the earthquake after five days, his mouth full of dust and dirt after desperately calling for help, Romolo emerged with no more than a broken shoulder. Unlike his older brother, Romolo did not seem to suffer trauma from this event; at least he rarely mentioned it in his letters. He was brought to Palazza Madama, the official residence of Queen Elena, under her direct patronage. From there, he was sent to the Policlinico in Rome, where his shoulder was attended to. Unlike Silone, Romolo remained for some time in Rome, with the Salesians at the Institute of the Sacred Heart. Don Orione brought Romolo to the Istituto San Filippo in Rome and finally to the Paterno boarding school in Tortona, where he remained until 1920. From Rome, Silone wrote (February 21, 1919) to remind his brother that "our fate depends on us."

Don Orione was just as preoccupied with Romolo as he was with Silone. Romolo could never adapt himself to the communal life and self-discipline demanded in the boarding schools run by the church; even Don Orione's intervention failed to convince the boy. An episode in 1920 was cause for concern. Romolo decided to take part in a Socialist May Day demonstration in Tortona. Wearing a red neckerchief, he climbed on a chair in a crowd and began denouncing priests in general and Don Orione in particular, the latter for "starving" the boys in the boarding school. The president of the Socialist cooperative grabbed him by his collar and pulled him from his perch, angrily saying, "It's not true! I bring the bread to Don Orione's school and I know how much I bring every day. Don Orione doesn't let his boys go hungry." First wanting to expel him, Don Orione thought better of it and permitted Romolo to finish school, even sending the boy on a summer trip to Venice. Orione's portrait of Romolo was revealing:

> Romolo was not a wicked boy but very vivacious and inclined to follow the subversive ideas of his brother. Even in Tortona there were subversives . . . and they organized meetings against the state and against the church. Romolo often attended; indeed, he was one of the most ardent supporters of those movements . . . . How many times did I have to present myself at police headquarters to hear the complaints of the authorities and to suffer their reprimands, saying that in the boarding school I was creating youth unworthy of the *patria* [homeland] and of religion. But if we don't restrain these boys, where will they end up? Those at the police station were right, but they didn't know or had forgotten how Don Orione had to suffer to pull them from the ruins, or how poor Romolo had suffered because of the loss of his mother and almost all his relatives. Only his old grandmother remained, who placed her two grandsons in my care so that they wouldn't starve, that they would study and, above all, that I would act as their father!

But Tortona could no longer condone Romolo's outrageous behavior, so Don Orione arranged for his transfer to another boarding school. There, he started an apprenticeship as a typographer and joined the school band as a trumpet player. But once again, he managed to land in hot water, attended political rallies, and was expelled, returning to the patronage of the queen and a school in Velletri. On the

sixth anniversary of the earthquake, Don Orione wrote to Romolo, begging the young boy to mend his ways. Saying that he was soon departing for South America, Orione asked how he could watch over the boy
from such a distance. Be honest and brave, "we will always be spiritually close . . . Courage my son! Don Orione will be close to your heart,
like your mother and father." Romolo immediately replied in desperation that it was true: He was a poor student and a worse Christian.
"Leave me to my crazy fate! Clear your fields of the seeds of dissension." Orione, deeply perturbed, responded, "What are you saying, my
son, abandon you to your fate? . . . Fate doesn't exist and it is the child
of ignorance; but even if it did exist, your mother would never abandon
you to your crazy fate, and neither will Don Orione, as long as he can."

Notwithstanding his proper Christian denial of the concept of fate
or destiny, Don Orione tellingly wrote to the director of Romolo's
boarding school, "I'm sorry because he [Romolo] was a genius, who
could have been a good Christian; this way, perhaps, he'll end up like
his brother." Indeed, by the early 1920s, Romolo had already been
under surveillance, arrested, and *schedato* (that is, a file had been
opened on him) by the Fascist police: COMMUNIST, it declared in block
letters; "dangerous" and "denounced to the Special Tribunal," the
Fascist court established to suppress dissent and destroy all political
opposition.

At a state boarding school in Velletri, Romolo was expelled by the
local Fascist officials and sent home to Pescina. Silone introduced
his brother to an acquaintance in Rome who owned a typesetting stu-
dio/printing press, but the business soon failed and Romolo was again
without means of support. In August 1924, Romolo was called up to
serve his military duty and was honorably discharged in 1926. He continued to travel between Rome and Pescina, returning to the hometown when there was no work in Rome. In Pescina, where there was
even less work available, he often passed the day in the carpentry work-
shop of his cousin Pomponio Tranquilli, living off the generosity of
their maternal grandmother. The local *podestà* (an appointed Fascist
official who took on the duties of elected mayor) demanded that

Romolo's identity card be stamped *"sospetto in linea politica,"* effectively destroying any chance that the young man would be hired for work. Pomponio Tranquilli recalled that after Romolo's discharge from the military, Silone (at the time wanted by the Fascist police) made a dangerous trip back to Pescina, intent on convincing his younger brother to leave the country; Romolo refused. Don Orione tried to get Romolo a position in the Tipografia Vaticana, to no avail. Failing that, the priest found a spot for Romolo at the Tipografia Emiliana in Venice. In testimony after Romolo's arrest in 1928, Don Orione claimed that Romolo had asked him for a job so as to be able to marry, thus "removing him from the malevolent influence of his brother Secondino." Another priest, Antonio Ruggeri, claimed that Romolo once confided in him about having joined the Communist Party, declaring ambiguously, "I'm in trouble if I fall into my brother's hands!" Was it because he feared being dominated by his older brother or rather that he knew that Silone would not have approved of his brother's joining the party?

Romolo was Silone's last surviving link to Pescina. The writer often returned to the town in his thoughts and in his writings, seeking to understand the ancient way of life he had forsaken. When asked by his comrades in the revolutionary struggle about the apathy of the peasants of the Mezzogiorno, Silone would write, "It would be incorrect to conclude that what held them back was fear. The people were neither cowardly nor lazy." Instead, it was better to look at "centuries of resignation, the consequence of violence and deception" that weighed them down. "Experience seemed to justify the blackest pessimism." For Silone, the peasants were "wounded and humiliated souls" capable of experiencing the "worst torments without complaining, until they broke out in unexpected revolts."

TWO

The CHOICE of COMPANIONS

*I explained to him by gestures that two
persons who ate the same bread became*
cumpane, *companions, and that . . .
company came from* cumpaani.
—SILONE, *The Seed Beneath the Snow*

In the worldview of the southern Italian peasant, the state has always been
identified as "the Devil's own creation." Why, then, would any sane per-
son concern himself with politics? "A good Christian, if he would save
his soul, should avoid contact with it as much as possible," Silone
wrote, reflecting the worldview of the Mezzogiorno. "The State always
stands for theft, corruption and special privilege. It can be nothing
else. Neither law nor force can change that." If some calamity should
strike it, "it is the judgment of God alone." Yet as he ruefully acknowledged later in life, he simply could not follow the ancient admonition
about "minding one's own business" and threw himself into public
life. "In my rebellion," he reflected, "there was a point at which love
coincided with refusal to cooperate." The step from submission to sub-

version was very short. All he had to do was simply "apply to society the principles that were considered valid for private life."

One of Silone's earliest memories of politics focused on the peasant agrarian leagues established around Pescina in 1911–12. The major opposition to the peasant leagues came not from the great landowners but from the local parish priests. Almost all of the peasants joined the leagues but since they were all Christians, a conflict was inevitable. The priests rarely bothered to criticize the political and agrarian positions of the leagues; rather, they were against the very principle of organizing the peasants in any association outside the Catholic church. As soon as the peasants met in the piazza to discuss their affairs, the priests would give an order to ring the bells of the church, drowning out the voices of the speakers.

At the local school, administered by the church and staffed by priests, the children were instructed that private property was a divinely sanctioned institution. Yet even the youngest children were keenly aware of the history of the distribution of the land around the Fucino plain: how the land had been expropriated by the new nation-state in 1871, distributed among the few politically connected families in the region while the valley of the drained Fucino was granted— seemingly in perpetuity—to the aristocratic Torlonia family by royal decree. In fact, during the years before the Great War, the delicate economic balance between agriculture and artisan sectors was thrown into crisis, not by Socialist revolution but by the development of industrial capitalism with its cheaper products. It was neither paradoxical nor surprising that private property was being destroyed not by socialism but by capitalism itself.

In September 1911, the government of Prime Minister Giovanni Giolitti cynically manufactured a "crisis" with the Ottoman Empire as a pretext for war and the annexation of Libya, events that would eventually have a direct impact on Silone's life. The Italian Socialist Party (PSI) was riven by internal debates: Should the party support or denounce the imperialist war? When the reformist and moderate Socialists voted to support the war effort, revolutionary Socialists, led by Benito Mussolini, formally expelled them and seized control of the party. The PSI, born in 1892, would one day regret the opportunity it had created for a brash and impatient Mussolini.

Four years later, war came to Italy in May 1915, almost a full year after it had broken out in much of Europe. Italy, formally linked with Germany and Austria-Hungary in the Triple Alliance, argued for a creative reading of the treaty binding the three countries together: Italy was to come to the defense of its allies only if they were attacked. Since Germany and the Austrian-Hungarian Empire were actually the aggressors, Italy proclaimed neutrality. In fact, neutrality was an overwhelmingly popular stance in Italy. Few could imagine Italy joining military ranks with Germany and even less with the traditional enemy, Austria. Although the neutrality position resonated with the population, Italian politicians immediately entered into secret talks with Britain and France, seeking the best possible terms for Italy's participation in the war. At the same time, a small but vocal and persistent minority in Italy was calling for an immediate entry into the war. Mussolini, from his post as editor of the Socialist Party newspaper, *Avanti!* first argued for neutrality, then intervention. The PSI, the only European Socialist Party maintaining international solidarity by voting against the war, expelled him. Thus began Mussolini's political pilgrimage from left to right that eventually culminated in his assumption of the prime minister's office in October 1922. Nationalists and Futurists both perceived the war as a necessary endeavor, but for different reasons. Nationalists felt Italy had been unjustly deprived of its place in the sun and longed for colonial possessions. An 1896 expedition in Africa had ended in ignominy while the brief war with the Ottoman Empire had brought only Libya as an Italian colony. Nationalists were hungry for more. Some of the more idealistic felt that participation of the masses in the war would function as the final act in the drama of national unification begun in the nineteenth century. The Futurists welcomed war as "the world's best hygiene" and an occasion to revel in the glories of speed, technology, flight, and violence. In Pescina, though, the war was received as one of the natural calamities that periodically befall the poor. Most realized that Italy's entry into the war was not for idealistic or noble purposes but rather for the immediate and short-term gains afforded a small and corrupt band of inept and shortsighted politicians and their avaricious supporters. In Pescina, the war was viewed through the prism of an eternal fatalism. "The women went to church to pray for peace," remarked Silone a half century later, "but the men knew that impatience with fate never did any good."

At age sixteen, Silone was still too young for the call to arms, yet he was elected to be secretary of the Abruzzese Peasants' Youth Federation. He accepted the post in part because the federation adhered to a current of socialism proclaimed at Zimmerwald in Switzerland in September 1915, where Italian Socialists had reiterated their stand against the war. The year 1917 was one of revolts and revolution for Europe and Silone. He formally joined the Unione Socialista Romana, but his first brush with the law occurred during a public demonstration protesting the transfer of the bishop's office from Pescina—where it had been for centuries and lent the town its only measure of importance—to the nearby town of Avezzano. The transfer signaled the bishop's and the church's desire to be nearer an administrative center than to the poor peasants, a point not lost on the citizens of Pescina. A second revolt broke out in protest over the blatantly corrupt distribution of the wartime bread ration in Pescina. But it was the third revolt that carried the most serious consequences for Silone.

Three soldiers on leave had confronted the local carabinieri who, in the eyes of the soldiers, were paying too much attention to the wives and girlfriends of the local soldiers away at the front. (In their resplendent uniforms, the carabinieri may indeed have caught the eye of the lonely local women.) The accused carabinieri turned to their commanding officer, who had the soldiers arrested and decreed that they should be sent back to the front immediately. The mother of one of the three soldiers made a desperate appeal to Silone in his capacity as a member of the Unione Socialista Romana, and he, in turn, presented the appeal to the parish priest, the local judge, and the mayor, all to no avail. The arrogant sentence of the commanding officer, coupled with the impotence or indifference of the local authorities, sparked outrage among the townspeople. And so, with their innate sense of justice offended, the peasants were transformed into what Eric Hobsbawn has defined as "primitive rebels" initiating periodic, millennial, and rarely successful revolts against the autocratic powers that controlled their lives.

The three soldiers were detained in the local barracks, awaiting the next train back to the front. In the late afternoon, a crowd collected before the police and soon transformed itself into a mob, moving from simple shouts to throwing stones while the police responded by firing shots into the air. After several hours, the police fled to the nearby fields, the mob broke open the windows and doors of the barracks, and the three soldiers—"whom everyone had by now forgotten"— went home unobserved. Silone and the "revolutionaries" were left in control.

"What do we do now?" the other boys wanted to know from me. (My authority derived, more than anything else, from the fact that I knew Latin.)

"Tomorrow morning," I said, "the town will certainly be occupied by hundreds and hundreds of soldiers, carabinieri, and police who will arrive from Avezzano, from Sulmona, from L'Aquila, maybe even from Rome."

"But before they get here, what will we do tonight?" the other boys wanted to know.

"A single night evidently is not enough," I said, having guessed what they wanted, "to create a true new order."

"Couldn't we take advantage of the fact that the whole town is sleeping to make socialism?" some of the others proposed. They had heard the word only recently, without grasping its meaning; and perhaps they thought that now everything was possible.

"I don't think," I had to answer, "I really don't think that a single night is enough to establish socialism, even if the whole town is asleep."

"One single night could be enough to sleep in our own bed before going to jail," one of those present finally suggested.

And since we were tired, that advice was both timely and wise.

The spectacle cost Silone a trial and a fine of one thousand lire (several thousand dollars in contemporary numbers). One friend, less fortunate, was sent back to the front and later killed in action. Many years later, he looked back at the unfolding of events that led to the catastrophe and saw a world already in crisis. "The Great War," he wrote in 1954, "simply revealed the fragility of the myths about progress on which capitalistic society was based."

Silone and his cohort were born in times of momentous change. At the turn of the last century, "Italy" itself was a mere four decades old, having been unified in 1861, with Rome added to the new country only in 1871. Civil unrest coupled with (or caused by) desperate poverty, especially in the south, created a constant state of tension. Economic historians agree that conditions in the Mezzogiorno deteriorated after unification in the nineteenth century. In the year of Silone's birth, King Umberto I was assassinated by the anarchist Gaetano Pesci. (Pesci had traveled from Paterson, New Jersey, a hotbed of Italian anarchism, to kill the king in retaliation for the massacre of striking workers by the armed forces.)

Reconstructing Silone's early intellectual formation is no easy task. Educated in religious schools, it was the liturgy and theatricality of the church that left their mark on the young boy. "During my youth, the only music I knew was religious music; the only singing, Gregorian chant; the only spectacle was the liturgy." But at a certain point, Silone simply stopped attending Mass. It wasn't that church doctrines suddenly lost relevance but rather that the young boys of the town grew tired of those who were always in church. He recognized that his rebellion was similar to that of all youth against tradition and that it was rarely devoid of ambiguity (*spoglia di ambiguità*). Instead of priests and churchgoers, the young Silone was drawn more to the wretchedly poor peasants who often didn't even enter the church but remained outside in the piazza. "The companions I preferred," he wrote many years later, "were the sons of the poor peasants. My tendency not to mind my own business and my spontaneous friendships with the poorest of my contemporaries were to have disastrous consequences for me." "That which defined our revolt," he confessed, "was our choice of companions . . . It was not their psychology that attracted us, but their condition." And even that choice was sometimes foreordained, because "before we choose, we are chosen, without our knowing it."

The crisis of the war and the postwar period, combined with disgust at the events unfolding in his own town, were responsible for "a profound change" in his soul: "the conviction that in an old, exhausted and bored society," the poor peasants "represented life's last hope."

In his formation as a writer, even technically, Silone insisted that most influential were his contacts and association with the peasants and workers, especially those in difficult circumstances. He confessed (or boasted) that books did not play an important role in his intellectual formation. No teacher left a lasting impression. When an adolescent, he often took a book with him while wandering the mountainside, but he rarely opened it; books were most often used to sit on the wet grass. "Even in the best books I found some things unacceptable on a first reading." Years later, he returned to the Greek and Latin classics that he had failed to appreciate in school, while certain romantic novels that he had read surreptitiously, because they had been banned, later seemed unreadable. He developed an intellectual interest in the liberal and idealist philosopher Benedetto Croce (born in Abruzzo) as well as Sigmund Freud, and wrote, "Whatever I know of the functioning of capitalist society I learned from Karl Marx and the Italian [Marxist] Antonio Labriola." In midlife, after the success of his first two novels, he openly confessed that he had no personal theory about art. With characteristic irony and a slight maliciousness he added, "But I admire all those who do and I find that they are all correct, even when they contradict each other." Silone defended this apparent lack of theory by saying that if he had known he was to become a writer, surely he would have "fortified" himself with a personal theory of art. But he became a writer "by accident." He once asserted that from the age of seventeen, immersed in political struggle, he read only works of science, economics, and history. It wasn't until after the immense success of *Fontamara* in 1933 that he seriously began a study of literature. If he is to be believed, he had not even read the Sicilian realist writer Giovanni Verga.

If Silone's political education began with his involvement in the Peasant League, it continued with his joining the Socialist Youth Movement. In Pescina, the Peasant League had met in an impressive palazzo that had been an old Franciscan convent close to the Tranquilli home until both were destroyed by the earthquake. Later, the league was reconstituted in a dilapidated hut in the poorest section of town, surrounded by pigsties and donkey stables. Rescued from the ruins of the former headquarters was a picture of Christ the Redeemer appropriately dressed in red overalls. A banner over the painting proclaimed, "Blessed are those who hunger and thirst for righteousness." Under the painting hung the trumpet used to summon the peasants to meetings. The league attracted a few old peasants on Sunday nights. Other children were being called home by their mothers, but there was no one left to call Silone home so he often attended the meetings. "I felt strangely attracted to those poor people who, worn out by their day's labors, came at the summons of the trumpet." Although these were the same men one saw at church, in the fields, in the piazza, they were different here, "in the courtyard of an old Franciscan convent which in its day had been founded by another poor man, St. Francis of Assisi." The meetings made a profound impression on the young man. There he encountered "paradoxical opinions" that became a "bitter pain and torment" for him. He joined the Unione Socialista Romana and made preparations to move to Rome. "I left at night like a thief," he recalled many years later, "and I never dreamed that I would be away for so many years." On his leaving Pescina, his grandmother was distraught. At whose hearth would he warm himself, she asked him plaintively. "Who will bake your bread?"

Silone described his move to Rome in late 1917 as "a sort of flight, an emergency exit from an insupportable solitude." He likened it to a sailor who cries, "Land! Land!" upon sighting a new continent. For a lonely and melancholy youth, Rome must have seemed a frightening and overwhelming city. Silone did eventually find people with whom he could "bake bread" and share a hearth. His immersion into party politics and then the underground life would first sustain—then nearly destroy—the sorrowful young man.

In January 1921, he would be a catalyst at the birth of the Italian Communist Party. Membership in the PCI was unlike membership in any other political party. As he and others have pointed out, it was a "conversion," a manner of living completely differently from the vast majority. "Those were times when to call oneself a Socialist or Communist meant risking everything, breaking with one's relatives and friends and not being able to find work. The material consequences were therefore serious, and the difficulties in readjusting one's thinking were no less painful." The world embodied by Pescina, from which Silone had derived his first primitive instinct of rebellion, was "shaken to its foundations, as if by an earthquake." All established truths and eternal verities came into question. "Life, death, love, goodness, evil, truth all changed their meaning or lost meaning completely." How could he describe the private despair of a provincial youth in a squalid bedroom in the city who has lost his belief in the immortality of the soul? Unable to speak to anyone outside the party, Silone kept his despair to himself. "And so, unknown to anyone, the world changed its whole appearance for me." Rome beckoned with its siren song of liberation. There, in the Eternal City of the popes, was a possible politics of redemption.

Silone was not a stranger to Rome, having traveled to the city with Don Orione after the earthquake of January 1915. Then, he was under the tutelage of the kind and generous priest; now, he was a young man with no visible means of support, seeking relief from the cold in St. Peter's Basilica, and often reduced to sleeping under the baroque bridges that crossed the Tiber or in a niche of the Coliseum.

Despite his personal despair, his ascent through the political ranks of the left was astonishing: In August 1919, at age nineteen, he was elected secretary of the Unione Giovanile Socialista in Rome (USR); two months later, he was elected to the Central Committee of the Gioventù Socialista Italiana; a few weeks after that, Silone was named to the Communist Youth International; in January 1920, he assumed direction of the Socialist weekly newspaper *L'Avanguardia*; at the Socialist Party congress a year later, he represented the Socialist youth wing and brought it to the newly formed Communist Party of Italy and was named to the central committee; in June, he participated in the Third International. Almost as soon as he set foot in Rome, a police file had been opened in his name. In September 1919, he was already marked as "subversive" and "dangerous."

But the young man from the provinces was haunted by nostalgia and homesickness in Rome. An episode on Christmas Day 1920 is emblematic: Near St. Peter's Basilica, in Piazza Rusticucci, Silone comes across a modest inn, the Taverna del Trentuno. In spite of—or perhaps because of—the proximity to the basilica, he is in *mangia-prete* (priest-eater) territory. A popular refrain in the neighborhood was *"Abbasso preti e frati / Viva Giordano Bruno"* (Down with priests and monks / Long live Giordano Bruno). Standing outside the door hungrily looking over the menu and calculating his expenses, the young man figures that if he restrains himself, he can just afford a modest meal. Entering, he finds a *zampognaro*, one of the itinerant wandering bagpipe players from his native Abruzzo, and is overcome with nostalgia. In the bittersweet moment, Silone is carried away and soon he is adding his contributions to those of the other—less destitute—patrons for the wandering musician. When it comes time to pay the bill, Silone is short sixty *centesimi*. The owner (surely in a foul mood, having to work Christmas Day) threatens to call the police. Silone humbly proposes a deal: his hat and cape in exchange for the sixty cents until the debt can be paid. Walking out into the cold streets with neither hat nor cape, Silone is desperate. Then a moment of perhaps divine illumination: Not far off is the Church of Sant'Anna, which hosts priests from Don Orione's Order of Divine Providence. The surly porter who answers Silone's knock says brusquely that Don Orione is indeed present but cannot be disturbed. Defeated and discouraged, Silone turns to leave, only to be brought back by the voice of Don Orione himself. They embrace and the priest thanks Silone for so unexpected a Christmas visit, but Don Orione is shrewd and can read a human soul. Embracing the young man upon his departure, the old priest coolly slips a handful of lire into Silone's jacket pocket.

In Rome, Silone found some refuge with political friends. In August 1919, he was elected to the youth organization of the USR and quickly assumed the role of secretary-general, joining his colleagues in a critique of both reformist and democratic socialism. He was intransigent in his "maximalist" position within the PSI. The Russian Revolution had electrified Italy as it had the rest of Europe, and Silone too felt the immense hope that had been ignited with the events in St. Petersburg. Silone gravitated to the wing dominated by Amadeo Bordiga, editor of the official newspaper *L'Avanguardia*. Bordiga advocated expelling the more moderate members of the party, as demanded by Lenin. In this he was opposed by Antonio Gramsci and his Ordine Nuovo group from Turin. Gramsci, from a poor Sardinian family, had earned a scholarship to study at the University of Turin, where he met Palmiro Togliatti, who, unlike the other two, had been born into a middle-class family in Genoa. Gramsci and Togliatti, along with Silone, would be among the founders of the Italian Communist Party in January 1921. Silone, although the junior colleague, was not intimidated by his more learned comrades. While his later polemic with Togliatti became well known, his relationship with Gramsci was more complicated.

On January 10, 1920, Silone was named editor of *L'Avanguardia* and promulgated the more radical, "maximalist" position of the youth federation while establishing close contacts with the international cell in Zurich directed by Willi Münzenberg, considered Lenin's spokesperson. Silone would remain in contact with Münzenberg even after the Italian writer's divorce from politics, until Münzenberg's 1940 death by hanging in Marseilles. Silone was not alone in thinking that Stalin had a hand in Münzenberg's demise.

Silone continued his editorial work for the party with the weekly *L'Avanguardia* and as editor of *Avanti!* International developments were to have an inordinate impact on the evolution of socialism in Italy. The second congress of the Communist (Third) International met in Moscow in July and August 1920, closing with a list of twenty-one points that were required for admission to the Third International. Three points in particular had dire implications for Italian socialism. Point 7 declared that "notorious opportunists" such as Filippo Turati (the grand old man of Italian socialism who rejected the violent overthrow of society and advocated a peaceful and legal transition to socialism) and Giuseppe Emanuele Modigliani (brother of the painter Amedeo) could "not be tolerated." Point 17 insisted that any party that wished to belong to the Third International had to be named Communist Party of . . . (that is, "Communist Party of Italy," rather than "Italian Communist Party"; hence the official abbreviation of PCd'I rather than the more common PCI adopted later). The twenty-one points ended with an admonition: Those members who disagreed with the conditions and theses formulated by the Communist International were to be expelled from the party. The PSI in theory agreed to these conditions but in typically Italian fashion "reserved the right to apply the conditions in its own way." What the PSI revealed instead was a failure to understand how and why the Moscow International was created in the first place. The solution was put off to the next annual meeting of the PSI, scheduled for January 1921 in the resort city of Livorno.

With its severe neoclassical façade of stone and honey-colored stucco, the Teatro Goldoni was chosen as the site of the XVII Congress of the PSI attended by three thousand delegates on January 15, 1921. Beneath architect Giuseppe Cappellini's crystal dome, the delegates had arranged themselves from the left (Antonio Gramsci, Amadeo Bordiga, Umberto Terracini) to a center occupied by Giacinto Menotti Serrati; to the right were Turati and the reformists. Garlands (left over from the Christmas holidays) festively decorated the boxes while a large photograph of an imposing Marx hung over the stage. In the halls, Vincenzo Vacirca accused Nicola Bombacci of being an impotent revolutionary. Bombacci responded by drawing his pistol. Only the timely interventions of Bordiga and Terracini avoided the shedding of blood. (Revealingly, Bombacci went on to become a notorious Fascist, the so-called "Communist in a blackshirt"; fittingly, he ended his days alongside the executed Mussolini, hanged upside down in Milan's Piazzale Loreto.) Even an innocuous motion to send a message of protest to the current prime minister, Giovanni Giolitti, deploring Fascist street violence, was drowned out.

In this atmosphere, Silone took the podium. He was confident, almost to the point of arrogance. Not yet twenty-one but speaking on behalf of the Socialist Youth Federation and recalling the German Communist Karl Liebknecht (assassinated along with Rosa Luxemburg in 1919), Silone resolutely declared their adherence to the Third International, the expulsion of the reformists and moderates, and the creation of a new Communist Party of Italy. Bordiga and Terracini rose to second Silone. The latter appeared on stage in his hat and with briefcase in hand, melodramatically emphasizing that for the left wing of the PSI, "it was time to go." Antonio Gramsci did not have a speaking role as there was a worry that his support of Mussolini's 1914 thesis (from absolute neutrality in the Great War to "relative" neutrality and eventually intervention) would harm the cause. But Gramsci's newspaper in Turin, *L'Ordine Nuovo*, sported the headline "May Turati Take the Cadaver of the Late Socialist Party and Make It the Footstool for His Senile Ambition. Communists, Forward!" By the last day of the conference, January 20, a split was inevitable. The Bulgarian Hristos Kabakchiev and the Hungarian Matyas Rakosi, representing Lenin in place of Zinoviev and Bukharin (who were not permitted entry into Italy), were adamant: There could be no compromise. The twenty-one points were to be accepted in their entirety and without any reservation. Serrati realized the center could not hold. Bordiga then convened the Communists at the Teatro San Marco in Livorno to declare the birth of the Partito Comunista d'Italia (PCd'I, Communist Party of Italy, until May 24, 1943, and the end of the Comintern, when it became the PCI or the Italian Communist Party). In the waning days of January 1921,

Silone's group, now the *Communist* Youth Federation, met in Florence. For Silone, the stress of the past few weeks was overwhelming and he collapsed, coughing up blood. A period of rest was ordered.

So began his clandestine career in the PCI, with the resulting toll on his psyche and body. For years, he adapted himself to "living like a foreigner in my own country," relinquishing his name, his family, his hometown. "The party became family, school, church and barracks," he wrote in 1949. "Outside of it the rest of the world was to be entirely destroyed." A half century after the event, Silone recalled that the atmosphere in Livorno was "certainly not euphoric." There was a seriousness and consciousness of the gravity of the occasion, and even a painful awareness perhaps that—with Fascists controlling the streets of Italy—the revolutionary moment had already passed.

Notwithstanding his precarious health, Silone was named to the central committee of the youth federation. In addition, he was named to a delegation that would meet with Lenin at the International scheduled for June 1921. Years later in a radio interview, Silone recalled that "there were no hotels in Moscow and the food was scarce. But what did it matter? Every day I left the house and found the streets filled with people cleaning up, repairing a roof, deciding things. The Futurists were painting on walls, the poets recited verse to passersby, everyone was contributing to remaking society."

That first encounter with Lenin was still a vivid memory almost fifty years later: "The first time I saw him, in Moscow in 1921, the apotheosis had already begun. Lenin now lived between myth and reality." When Lenin entered a room, the result was a physical, palpable charge of electricity, a contagious enthusiasm, not unlike the presence of the pope in St. Peter's Basilica. The Russian exerted a religious fascination among the revolutionaries, based on what Silone called "the charisma of the victor." Surely Silone was conscious of the Greek and religious etymology of "charisma" as a gift, favor, or grace from the gods. And yet, even this very first meeting was tainted with the seed of doubt. Silone's comparison of Lenin to the pope was tinged with irony. Upon speaking with Lenin, Silone noted that the mystical façade soon faded and one was struck by the Russian's capacities (a skill for rapid synthesis) and defects (contemptuous judgments, peremptory decisions). Noting that Lenin read the Italian daily *Il Corriere della Sera* with the help of his knowledge of French, Silone remarked that he read with blinders on, refusing to recognize that the Italian situation was far different from the Russian. Lenin considered Bordiga closest to the Bolshevik position but criticized him for "anarchist" tendencies. The Russian also failed to discern the revolutionary potential of Gramsci's factory councils in Turin, likening them to traditional trade unions. Even Lenin's criticism of the PSI was unfair in that its leaders (Turati, Claudio Treves, and Modigliani) had always espoused positions different from traditional European democratic socialism first broached by Eduard Bernstein in 1899. And although Lenin had the good fortune of dying before the "bureaucratic involution" that had defused the revolutionary aspects of the revolution, he was still responsible for the repression that had followed from "democratic centralism."

Silone refused to be cowed by the prestige of the Russians. When Lenin took to the podium to criticize the Italians, Silone—responding in French and defending his colleagues—was called to task by Trotsky. At issue were the ramifications of the split with the PSI and the emerging dependence of the PCd'I on the Russians. So began a conflicted and discordant relationship with the Russians that was never to end, even with Silone's expulsion from the party a decade later. Even before his ejection, Silone was a difficult case for the Communists; in the "family album," his faded photograph is one that the party sought to purge since 1931, a page to be turned over quickly. He was to be banished from collective memory and, if possible, from history.

Silone always claimed to have viewed the Russians with a skeptical eye. What struck him most about the Russians was that "even in truly exceptional personalities like Lenin and Trotsky was an absolute incapacity to discuss with fairness any opinions contrary to their own." The dissident, by definition, was a traitor. The irony, which Silone did not fail to point out, was that self-proclaimed materialists and rationalists affirmed "the primacy of morality over intelligence." It reminded Silone of the heresy trials of the past.

In an interview after Silone's death, Camilla Ravera, another important party leader, recalled that in those early years of clandestine activity (1923–24) Silone was impetuous and quickly came to the notice of the Fascist police. He avoided all forms of rhetoric or demagoguery and was "ironic to the core." Without considering either his temperament or his precarious health, party leaders sent him on missions abroad. When the political waters had calmed down a bit, he was permitted to return to Italy; it was then that Ravera met Silone. She was struck by his seriousness. One day he appeared at party headquarters with the latest issue of the youth newspaper. Its headline read: "Shitty Work for a Shitty Salary" (*Al salario di merda, lavoro di merda*). Silone was incensed. "It's true that we must be severe with fascism," Silone said on that occasion, "but to be severe we must be serious and to be serious we need a serious language and not words thrown about like this." Ravera confirmed that Antonio Gramsci had been among the first to notice Silone's literary talents. "We must always remember," Gramsci admonished his colleagues, "that Pasquini [Silone's party name at the time] is not a politician but a writer. We must make sure that he does not lose the possibility to develop as a writer and not give him too many difficult tasks as a politician." Years later, Ravera reflected that Gramsci had been right all along and that perhaps the party had placed too much of a burden on the young writer. Ravera found Silone to be emotional, sensitive, but also affectionate, fraternal, and very cordial. She detected a thin skin on the young man from the provinces, perhaps intimidated by his urban and urbane intellectual colleagues: "Every little thing that was pointed out to him, every criticism, even if very benevolent, would immediately put him in crisis."

Originally allied with Bordiga, by 1925 Silone supported Gramsci as leader of the party. But a year later, Gramsci, notwithstanding his parliamentary immunity, was arrested by the Fascist police. (The public prosecutor at trial had demanded, "We must keep this mind from working for the next twenty years!" Instead, Gramsci spent the next decade in prison at work on his prison notebooks, published posthumously, and fundamentally changing the course of Western Marxism.) Years later, in an interview with the Italian journalist Enzo Biagi, Silone sketched a psychological profile of Gramsci that revealed their sometimes contradictory, and often ambiguous, relationship:

> I knew him well, but I haven't yet written or said anything about him. He cannot be defined in two sentences. He had a very intense inner life; at times he could even seem distracted or lazy. But all of a sudden, without any warning, while we would be discussing mundane subjects, he would begin to speak without telling us that he was about to say something of fundamental importance, which would force us to change our actions, revealing a new perspective on a problem. At first, he was a libertarian Socialist, not completely an anarchist, but almost; his enthusiasm for the Soviets and the motives he ascribed to them represented the freest form of liberty . . . His character? He could be cheerful or downright ferocious . . . but this often occurs in timid people. His infirmities [Gramsci was a hunchback and often ill] kept him from participating in meetings or large conferences; he therefore was not comfortable in public debate with his opponents. Behind the protection of the page, attack is easier. It goes without saying: He was very intelligent.

For Silone, there was a "fundamental ambiguity" in Gramsci, "two contradictory aspects of his thought" that bequeathed to the Italian left a contested legacy: the question of power, which vacillates between the libertarian and the tyrannical. Even his most ardent followers, Silone suggested, would recognize the necessity of "stripping Gramsci of an artificial *gramscismo*, to de-mystify him." To so nakedly criticize a figure who, by 1958, through the publications of his *Prison Notebooks* and his martyrdom in a Fascist prison had become the patron saint of Italian Marxists, was to court ostracism by the cultural hegemony of the political left.

On December 22, 1921, at the direction of the PCd'I, Silone took up a new position as editor of the party paper, *Il Lavoratore*, in Trieste. It was in that northeastern town that Silone first met Gabriella Seidenfeld. Since Camilla Ravera had "baptized" Silone as "Sereno," Seidenfeld adopted the name "Serena." Together, "Sereno" and "Serena" took up party tasks in the border city. Ravera noted that Gabriella Seidenfeld was one of the few who "understood him very well even during these strange emotional episodes."

Gabriella Seidenfeld, one of three sisters, had been born in 1897 in Fiume into an observant Jewish family of modest means, originally from Slovakia. "Pious people, timid before God, rigorously observant, believing in the coming of the Messiah." One day Gabriella's sister "the librarian" returned home with a biography of the Russian revolutionaries: Sofia Perovskaya, Vera Figner, and others. Finishing the book, the three sisters each burst out with the same declaration: "I want to be a revolutionary!" and soon after marched off to the local office of the Communist Party, declaring their intention to enroll. After listening politely—albeit with some amusement—to their confused speeches, an old comrade looked at them and asked with more than a touch of condescension, "Do you know what socialism really is?" "But of course," they responded in unison and were duly enrolled.

Notwithstanding her membership in the PCI, Gabriella managed to find work in a bank. With her two sisters in Rome and her mother's death, Gabriella found herself alone in Trieste with her aging father. On meeting her, Silone asked if she knew German. The Communist Youth International, which had its seat in Berlin, was looking for someone who was bilingual German-Italian and Silone thought Gabriella would be the right person for the job. In Fiume, Gabriella's situation was deteriorating rapidly. Twice the police searched her home and she was under surveillance at all times. So when Silone wrote to her from Rome, suggesting that she move to Berlin, she decided to accept. Seidenfeld's father died several years later, never seeing his daughter again. All her other relatives were eventually deported to concentration camps by the Germans in 1943.

After having worked a few weeks with Silone, Seidenfeld was able to offer a subtle portrait of the man:

> He was a solitary type, sickly, with sad eyes. Very intelligent. He told me of his life after the death of his mother in the earthquake, a mother whom he adored. He fled the seminary and wandered the streets of Rome, penniless, spending many a night at the Coliseum. He also had a long stay in the Santo Spirito Hospital. He had been a revolutionary since the age of fifteen, when he led a peasant uprising.

In a letter from Marseilles, Silone wrote to Seidenfeld on the occasion of her birthday in 1924, addressing her as *mia adorata vecchierella* (my adored little old lady):

> I wish I could be with you today to ask forgiveness for the way I have treated you, little martyr of my nerves, or at least I would like to write you beautiful things. But you know that I'm not expansive with words, not even with Romoletto, not even with grandmother. I have never written letters of compliments, nor love letters and not even letters of friendship, and I don't know which phrases to use. That's why I would have wished very much to be with you and I would have told you all the tender things I feel for you.

In March 1922, Silone was passing through Berlin on his way to Moscow. On his return to Rome, Seidenfeld joined him in the Eternal City. Later that year when Silone was appointed editor of *Il Lavoratore*, Seidenfeld accompanied him to Trieste, where he was arrested for the first time in December. Seidenfeld wrote of their life together there:

> It was a very agitated time; we were constantly attacked and molested by the Fascists and police. Once they searched everyone who was leaving the office of *Il Lavoratore*. Vanni Buscemi, at that time a great friend and in Trieste, was already walking down the stairs. He told

me he had a knife in his pocket and didn't know how to exit the building. We hid the knife in my thick hairdo and everything turned out well. When the Fascists stabbed the Hon. Gnudi, and we wanted to visit him in the hospital, we had to inoculate ourselves against smallpox. Gnudi was very happy to see us, but in the days following, many of us had to stay at home in bed with fever.

From Trieste, Sereno and Serena traveled to Berlin, where Silone worked with Münzenberg to send aid to comrades in Spain. In Madrid, the couple met many of the left-wing protagonists who would later play such an important role in the Spanish Civil War. Silone himself went to Spain disguised as a businessman and started writing for *L'Humanité* and *La Batalla*. With the coup d'état of Primo de Rivera in 1923, Silone was arrested. Put on a train to Barcelona and prison, Seidenfeld took a faster train, got off at a station ahead of him, and met Silone on his train, chained by his feet to an anarchist whom she described as *"molto simpatico."* After leaving him with a package of woolen clothing, Seidenfeld got off at the next stop, where, when she told the railway workers that she was the *"esposa"* of a political detainee, they took care of her. But on boarding a train back to Madrid, she was arrested by two police officers and, in possession of no official documents, sent to a women's prison. Since her companions in prison were for the most part prostitutes and petty criminals as well as illiterate, Seidenfeld soon became the prison's unofficial letter writer, of letters whose chief characteristic was their "unrepeatable contents." Three months later, she was released and expelled from Spain. On leaving the prison, she made her way to Paris and the only address she knew there: that of the Soccorso Rosso, the Communist Party's "Red Cross." As she was entering, Silone was just making his way out. So began their Parisian *soggiorno*, living in squalid hotels and eating at a "more than modest" restaurant in the Place de la Nation frequented by rowdy anarchists. When they could not rent rooms at a hotel because of a lack of money or proper documents, they were taken in by the daughter of an old Communard, Mini Devoyon on the rue Duris.

Improbable as it may seem, Silone first came across the writings of Dostoevsky only in 1923. Appropriately enough, he found himself at the time in a Spanish prison. The Communist International sent Silone to Madrid and Barcelona, where he became acquainted with the prisons in both cities. He once remarked that it was one of the happiest times of his life. When asked why, he responded, "because of the company." That company included a young Spanish nun in the infirmary of the Madrid prison. She lent him devotional books and listened—surely with trepidation for his eternal soul—to his Marxist ideas. When she discovered that the young, ill Italian was to be extradited to Barcelona and back to Italy, where he might perish in a Fascist prison, she delayed his departure long enough so that he missed the train for Barcelona. The military dictatorship of Primo de Rivera had imprisoned Silone, thinking him exceedingly dangerous. "My presence [in Spain] was, in fact, not motivated by tourism," Silone confessed thirty-three years later. The Cárcel Modelo di Barcelona (which was truly a model prison, Silone quipped) incarcerated a broad spectrum from the Spanish left: Communists, Socialists, syndicalists, separatists, and anarchists. "What magnificent men," Silone recalled. "In no other country of the world have I ever known men so admirable as the Spanish subversives." In Barcelona, Silone befriended an imprisoned doctor. Seeing an opportunity to economize, prison authorities dismissed the "official" doctor and permitted the "criminal" doctor to tend to the prison population. The good doctor decreed that for reasons of health, Silone had to spend mornings in the infirmary. There, Silone could read the many books and journals brought to him by his sympathetic friend. And there is where Silone first encountered *The Brothers Karamazov* and *The Idiot*. Those hours passed with the Russian writer were a form of liberation: "The narrow walls of the cell disappeared and I found myself thousands of miles from there, in an atmosphere that filled me with an anxiety never felt before." And there in the prison was where Silone encountered the Dostoevskian figure of a very young Spanish anarchist condemned to death, passing his time drawing caricatures of the Spanish generals. Complicating matters was an illustrious Catholic jurist who inconveniently pointed out to the authorities that minors could not be put to death under the Spanish legal code. During 1923, as controversy swirled around this young man and his fate, Silone befriended both doctor and anarchist. "Every morning, meeting that young man condemned to death in the doctor's office, what else could I speak of? Even thinking about it many years later, what wonderful days they were; certainly among the most beautiful of my life." Silone revealed the fate of the condemned man by acidly noting that the juridical dilemma was solved by deciding "to respect the law and wait until he reached the age of adulthood before hanging the boy."

Silone eventually was expelled from Spain, not to Italy but to Marseilles and from there eventually to Ventimiglia. He managed to recross the border into France, finally making his way to Paris again. The inexorable round of arrests, trials, deportations continued. When Silone was arrested in Paris, he was escorted to the Conciergerie, the same prison that had housed Marie Antoinette in 1792. After Silone was sentenced, his lawyer Berton confided to Seidenfeld: "Tranquilli should call himself Terribili; he was always interrupting me [in court] to say the most radical things."

Expelled from France, Silone and Seidenfeld made their way to the train station, where they were carefully watched by the police. They could not contain themselves and goaded the police: "You'll see," they said, "what will happen to you when we come to power!" "That day, Mesdames," replied one of the policemen, "we'll be with you!"

One day later, Silone and Seidenfeld were back in Paris, having again recrossed the border illegally. Their life was not without moments of absurdist comedy. To celebrate their return, Vanni Buscemi organized a meeting at the union hall in rue de la Grange aux Belles. To avoid detection and arrest, Silone had dyed his hair blond and purchased a blond mustache. During his impassioned speech against the bourgeoisie, the mustache threatened to fall off and Silone was forced to make his speech with one hand to his upper lip.

But more often, Silone and Seidenfeld found themselves at the juncture of history and contemporary politics. To commemorate the uprising of the Commune, they joined a crowd marching from the Place de la République to the cemetery of Père-Lachaise, singing all the way. At the cemetery, they placed red carnations, the symbol of the left, at the wall where the Communards had been executed. In Paris, Silone and Seidenfeld often worked at the offices of the French Communist Party's newspaper, *Humanité*. Already, he sensed a conflict between his political career and his literary aspirations. In a letter to Seidenfeld, Silone wrote, "What I want is to go plumb my fate [*andare fin in fondo al mio destino*], to write and tell stories; I have no other ambition."

In 1925, the PCI recalled Silone to Italy, where Gramsci charged him with the direction of the press office of the party. Seidenfeld soon followed him to Rome, where they took up residence in the Celio quarter of the city, not far from Piazza Venezia, where Mussolini would give his bombastic speeches from the balcony to wildly adoring crowds below. Seidenfeld and Silone were given the responsibility for "agitation and propaganda." But with the promulgation of the exceptional decrees of 1926, they were forced to move once again, this time to Genoa. Outside the port city, in the small town of Sturla, Camilla Ravera had organized a small hotel, the Albergo dei Poveri (Hotel of the Poor). Here Ravera and the others struggled to reestablish the Segreteria of the Centro Interno of the party. They had, though, an unwelcome guest: OVRA, the Fascist secret police, had managed to infiltrate the Albergo dei Poveri with a spy. Eros Vecchi, a spy code-named "Leo," betrayed Ravera and others to the Fascists; Silone managed to avoid arrest.

While Silone wrote articles for the party press, Seidenfeld and her sister (code-named "Nuvola") were responsible for maintaining contacts with party cells in Milan and Turin. Accordingly, "Nuvola" would leave each morning weighted down with newspapers, party memos, and directives, returning in the evening or early the next day. The work was dangerous, especially after the imposition of full dictatorship in 1926. Most damaging was the infiltration of police spies: The Albergo dei Poveri was quickly abandoned when a functionary of the Soccorso

Rosso, Guglielmo Jonna, revealed its existence to the Fascist police after his arrest in October 1927.

Silone and Seidenfeld were then sent to Basel, Switzerland, with much of the Centro Interno. Expelled once again, they made their way over the French border to Vaucresson, near Paris, where they rented quarters from an elderly Madame Carpentier, who still dressed in the Empire style and often spoke of having witnessed the siege of Paris during the Franco-Prussian War.

Early in 1928, Silone, again separated from Gabriella because of his work for the party, wrote her an emotional letter:

> I've just realized that today is January 13, the anniversary of the greatest misfortune of my life [the earthquake in which his mother perished] . . . I'm so sorry that I didn't know you before that January 13; you would have come to Pescina and we would have been truly happy. You would have met my mother and become friends with her and Grandmother. Thinking back on those times, I seem to be dreaming of things a thousand years ago. Little by little the memories become more confused. Fortunately I later met you, and it seems almost as though my mother has returned from the dead so as not to leave me alone in the world.

Seidenfeld's sister Barbara (code-named "Ghita") had married Pietro Tresso ("Blasco"). Originally an ally of Bordiga's, Tresso had the opportunity for long discussions with Gramsci during their stay in Moscow in 1922 and 1923 and eventually sided with the latter in the internal disputes of the PCI.

Tresso's and Silone's fates would cross in their eventual expulsion from the Communist Party. When Tresso was expelled, party bureaucrats emptied his home of documents, letters, false papers; Barbara Seidenfeld and Tresso were left with nothing more than a typewriter. Tresso returned to his trade as a tailor, but for Barbara, a *"rivoluzionaria per professione,"* the expulsion from the party was traumatic.

As a rapidly rising party functionary told her in words similar to those expressed later to Silone, "In the party you are everything; outside the party you are nothing." In their humble house on the rue Pierre Bayle in Paris, Tresso and Barbara Seidenfeld were visited by Trotsky's son, Lev, later assassinated in Paris in 1938. Silone, increasingly sick, requested and received a leave from the PCI in October 1929 and was ordered to recover in a Swiss sanatorium.

In 1949, Silone recalled an evening twenty-three years earlier spent with comrades hiding from the Fascist secret police in a small villa on the outskirts of Milan. Communist Party leaders and members had come to the inevitable conclusion that, with the passage of the so-called Special Laws, there was "no doubt about the intention of the dictatorship to exterminate every trace of resistance." Warned not to return home that evening, Silone found himself in the sparsely furnished villa with a half dozen colleagues. As there was only one bed, they pulled up chairs and, in the manner of Boccaccio's *Decameron*, agreed to tell each other their stories to pass the night away. It was a dark night of the soul for each of them, forced to examine their assumptions and conceptions of the revolutionary struggle. Realizing the danger, one warned the group, "It may be dangerous for any of us, including myself, while we're in the midst of the struggle, to examine the how and the why, to look back. At a certain moment the die is cast." But look back they did. One recounted how, that very day, he had walked by the famed La Scala opera house as patrons were waiting on line to purchase tickets, and, considering the current political developments, had "a strong impression of being in a group of madmen." A colleague, noting their own precarious situation having abandoned family and friends for a political ideal, responded, "It's not easy to know who the really crazy people are. Perhaps it's one of the hardest of all things to determine." One comrade who refused to relinquish his critical faculties in the face of ideology insisted that while committed to the revolutionary struggle, "I'd like to continue seeing things with my own eyes."

Silone, as usual, was quiet until they turned to him for his story. "That would be a long story," he demurred. Thinking of his vastly different background from the cosmopolitan intellectuals he was with, he protested that "some things, frankly, you just wouldn't understand." A German woman teased him: "Tell us your long, incomprehensible story," she said "Even if we don't understand, it won't matter. The most beautiful stories aren't always understandable."

As always, the answer was to be found in Pescina. Even as a young boy, Silone could neither understand nor abide the "grating, incomprehensible, almost absurd contrast between private family life—which at least appeared decent and honest—and social relations, which were very often hostile and deceitful." And although Silone promised his comrades that he would tell his story "without recourse to parables," he could not avoid relying upon such an anecdote.

He was only a child when he witnessed an event that revealed the heart of a savage society. One Sunday while in the piazza with his mother, the young Silone observed "a local young man of good family" let loose his vicious dog on a poor old woman leaving church. This "stupid and cruel spectacle" was not in retaliation for some real or imagined offense, but merely for the enjoyment of the young man. The woman was thrown to the ground and mauled, her clothes torn to shreds. The public humiliation was witnessed in silence by a good portion of the townspeople. While indignant, no one came to her aid, neither then nor later, when the woman foolishly decided to press charges and needed eyewitnesses to corroborate her ordeal. The young man, though, secured the services of a lawyer who bribed witnesses to testify that the old woman had provoked the dog. A judge acquitted the man and ordered the woman to pay the court's expenses. Some months later, when the very same judge was in the Silone home, he attempted to defend his decision. His mother listened politely, but when he left, she turned to her son and admonished him, "When you grow up, be anything you want, but don't be a judge." And in words that are well known to any child born in the Mezzogiorno: "Mind your own business." This warning was repeated to the young boy on every occasion: "Minding one's own business was the fundamental condition of honest and peaceful living."

It was not that the "sublime concepts of justice and truth" were unknown to the people. "Truth," "Justice," "Liberty" were often spoken of, and eloquently so, in public and on suitable occasions. But everyone, including children, was conscious of the fundamental deception. This state of affairs, Silone was careful to point out, did not rest on the ignorance or stupidity of the peasants. It was, instead, borne out by centuries of oppression and poverty (*miseria*). There was little to be done against such a "humiliating and primitive stagnation of the community's social life." A critical and perceptive mind "merely made it harder to bear." For everything was arranged "so as to teach children to submit and to mind their own business."

In the midst of Silone's long and drawn-out struggle with the PCI came the last act of his family tragedy: the arrest, imprisonment, and death of his only surviving sibling, Romolo. By 1928, Romolo was working in the Tipografia Artigianelli in Venice and was required to present himself weekly at the local police station to "sign in," enabling the police to keep track of the "subversive." On March 18, 1928, Romolo made a surprise visit to Don Orione, who noted that the young man was excited and nervous. Romolo then disappeared for some days. On April 12, a bomb exploded in Piazza Giulio Cesare in Milan, killing eighteen and wounding several dozen innocent bystanders. The bomb had apparently been meant for King Vittorio Emanuele III, who was to pass that very spot on his way to the Milan Fair. The police immediately rounded up 560 Socialists, anarchists, and Communists. Romolo had been missing from Venice since April 1, his absence duly noted by the police. When he was spotted at the Hotel Bellavista in Brunate, near Como, by carabinieri who demanded to see his papers,

Romolo told them the documents were in his hotel room. He fled from a window and a massive search immediately began. By the afternoon of the next day, he was found and arrested in a forest outside Montorfano. In his pockets, police found false identity papers and two sketches of a piazza that to the authorities seemed to be diagrams of Piazza Giulio Cesare. Romolo defiantly told the police that he had indeed been in Milan the previous day. This was enough for the police to declare that they had captured the "terrorist assassin." *La Stampa*, one of Italy's leading papers, headlined, "A Sensational Arrest in Como," and went on to write about "a strange individual with a Communist party card, a mysterious map, and doses of poison. Flight from a window and dramatic chase. Murky circumstances, denials and contradictions in testimony." A search of Romolo's apartment turned up nothing incriminating, but his situation nevertheless seemed dire. While being interrogated, Romolo was beaten, resulting in pulmonary lesions and three broken ribs. "If I get twenty years in prison," he said, "I'll consider myself lucky."

Silone, apprised of his brother's arrest from the newspapers, wrote immediately from Berlin:

> Dearest brother,
>
> Never before as now have I felt so strongly the bonds of fraternity that bind us together! I live, hour by hour, the entire lie into which chance has thrown you. I hope with you, hour by hour, I suffer with you, I resist with you. What I wish to tell you at this time you can imagine but, with the present conditions, is inexpressible. I assure you that everything will be done so that the truth of your innocence will triumph. In the meantime, be strong and patient. I embrace and kiss you with great affection.
>
> Your brother, Secondino

Don Orione hastened to collect all of Romolo's letters in an effort to work on his behalf. Showing one typical letter to his colleague Don Gaetano Piccinini, a friend of Romolo's, Orione pointed out the relevant passage: "I don't feel like a Marxist: I don't want to emigrate far away; I feel the Gospel in my heart, I don't want to be on the other side . . . Thank you for the good you have done me and the goodness with which you have guided me, and the evil you have kept me from. I have always followed your teachings! This though I feel: I could not eat a piece of bread without turning to share it with one who does not have any. And this comes all from you who always acted like a father." Someone who writes like this, Don Orione said to Don Piccinini, could not have placed a bomb for the king or killed so many innocent people. "I will defend the poor boy against anyone!"

Don Orione was indeed called to testify in the investigation and handed over all of Romolo's letters to the prosecutor in Genoa. The real perpetrators of the bombing were never discovered, but much evidence points to a radical republican wing of Fascists. Silone, by then in Swiss exile, anxiously followed these developments and decided to contact a police official in Rome, Guido Bellone. A handwritten document dated April 23, 1928, from Chief of Police Arturo Bocchini to Mussolini stated: "From Basel, Guido Bellone has received a telegram from Tranquilli Secondino—one of the Communist leaders—that announces his arrival in Italy. The colloquium that will follow could be interesting. I will keep Your Excellency informed." But five days later, Silone wrote to Bellone: "I canceled my trip to Rome following information from the Lugano police, according to whom I was wanted at every Italian border crossing. My friends, who were already against my returning to Italy, didn't want me to go . . . I will also write to you tomorrow; in the meantime, I want some assurances regarding my brother. Write to me through some Fascist relative (for example a member of the Fascio of my town) with trustworthy information, to an address that I sent to my grandmother." (A more detailed discussion of this correspondence is in chapter eight.)

In Pescina, Silone was assisted in his efforts by a cousin, Pomponio Tranquilli, and a precious few friends: Gianbattista Barbati and Vincenzo Parisse. Pomponio Tranquilli acted as intermediary between the two brothers, facilitating an exchange of letters, funds, and small gifts.

Pomponio Tranquilli often visited Romolo in his various prison cells: from the San Vittore in Milan to the infamous Regina Coeli in Rome, to temporary quarters in L'Aquila and Perugia (where the Communist Gastone Sozzi was tortured to death), to Romolo's final internment at Procida. For his troubles, Pomponio was arrested more than once. (Barbati and Parisse would arrange for secret safe houses for Silone when he returned to Pescina in the 1920s.)

Even Silone's grandmother was paid a visit by authorities. They wanted to know who was sending Romolo money and the provenance of the funds. In reality, Silone and Romolo had decided to sell some property, and the resulting transactions had been handled by Pomponio. The grandmother lamented her eighty-five years and poor finances in finding an attorney: "Who will now help poor Romoletto?" Here in Pescina, "no one thinks of defending Romolo's innocence." She charged Silone with finding "an honest lawyer" so that Romolo could be freed and she could die in peace.

Romolo was brought before the Special Tribunal for the Defense of the State, a Fascist judicial organ created to deal with anti-Fascist opponents. On Mussolini's orders, the tribunal changed its locale from Rome to Milan and passed a death sentence on Romolo.

Silone immediately began to organize an international campaign on his brother's behalf. Among those protesting Romolo's arrest were Henri Barbusse, president of the Comité de Défense des Victimes du Fascisme; Romain Rolland, winner of the Nobel Prize in Literature; and the British foreign secretary, Arthur Henderson, president of the Socialist International. Perhaps because of this attention, the regime dropped charges of attempted regicide against Romolo when it became apparent that he was not involved in the bombing. No less a personage than Arturo Bocchini, chief of police, realized that Romolo and the others held were innocent of the bombing. He intervened in the pretrial proceedings and so Romolo was spared the firing squad. Still held on charges of being a subversive, and defiantly claiming to be a Communist, he was convicted and sentenced to twelve years in prison. The official charges were membership in the PCI and possession of false identity papers. The map discovered on Romolo was not a diagram of Piazza Giulio Cesare in Milan where the bombing took place but of a piazza in Como where Romolo was to have met Luigi Longo of the PCI for instructions on fleeing Italy. As for the poison mentioned in the press accounts, this may have been a case of yellow journalism. Romolo had supposedly been instructed to commit suicide if captured. Why he would have been charged by the PCI to carry out such a rash act has never satisfactorily been explained.

The official verdict sounded more like an indictment of Silone than Romolo: "a dangerous Communist," "always maintaining control of the direction of the Communists," "clandestine publisher of incendiary, subversive, revolutionary material," "an influential functionary of the party." In 1965, Silone explained his own role in Romolo's travails, persuading his brother to illegally depart Italy and make his way to Switzerland. There, Romolo was to have enrolled at the Polytechnic in Zurich, at Silone's expense. Silone's proposal was transmitted to Romolo via Edoardo D'Onofrio, a Communist Party member. Since Romolo's request for a passport would surely have been denied, it was decided that Romolo would meet in Como with D'Onofrio, who would introduce him to Longo. It would be Longo who would arrange for Romolo's crossing the border into Switzerland.

There has long been a question of Romolo's "communism." Silone always insisted that his brother was not a Communist but rather an "anti-Fascist of Catholic upbringing." Romolo defined himself as a "Communist sympathizer" (*simpatizzante comunista*) in his testimony, but there is some question as to whether he claimed allegiance to communism as an expedient to leave the country, depending on the party's network to get him to Switzerland.

Alternative explanations for what unfolded further cloud the waters. Don Flavio Peloso, present director of Don Orione's Order of Divine Providence, has suggested that perhaps Romolo was merely bait in an intricate web woven to catch Silone. Peloso ventures two hypotheses: that OVRA, the Fascist secret police, set up Romolo to snare the more famous older brother and, more startling but hardly out of the question, that elements of the PCI, wanting to destroy Silone, sacrificed the younger brother.

By the time the sentence of twelve years was pronounced on June 6, 1931, Romolo had been in prison more than three years. He turned and denounced his court-appointed lawyer (his remarks, recounted in a letter to Silone, were redacted by prison officials). In Rome's notorious Regina Coeli prison, he had been tortured, suffering three broken ribs and pulmonary lesions. The abuse continued with his transfer to the prison in Perugia (July 28, 1931, to July 12, 1932) and finally the prison on Procida, the island midway between Ischia and Naples. Conditions there exacerbated the ill effects of torture. In mid-July 1932, when he appeared on Procida, the medical doctor on staff noted that Romolo suffered from "tuberculosis with frequent and serious hemoptysis" and that his general condition was "declining rapidly."

Like his older brother and so many before him, Romolo spent his time in prison reading. Fellow prisoners recall seeing him with the Bible, speaking of St. Francis and Don Orione. In a letter to his brother, he wrote: "Now, if I read Dante, I am able to understand his beauty, which previously I understood very imperfectly. I enjoy Petrarch and the other two: Tasso and Ariosto. Dante, Petrarch, et al.; I'm in good company, don't you think?" Responding to some advice from his older brother, Romolo wrote: "You said it well: one must endure and harden oneself. I desire nothing more than to become better, morally stronger, to free myself from every baseness, to be able to make any sacrifice for my ideas."

A devoted exchange of letters took place between Romolo and Gabriella Seidenfeld. In fact, it seems that in prison, Romolo developed a strong emotional bond with Seidenfeld. While letters between the brothers often carried a note of tension regarding a lack of funds and Silone's excuses about not sending more money, those between Romolo and Gabriella seem to have offered the young man a psychological and emotional anchor. Reading between the lines, one can detect notes of resentment toward Silone. "I have received much news from Pescina," Romolo wrote to Gabriella on September 13, 1930, "not by letter, but from a paesano who is here in prison with me." A week later, he strikes a darker note, hinting at a nervous breakdown: "I've always withstood [torture]; even when I suffered terribly, and didn't know what the devil might happen, I wasn't afraid . . . it wasn't enough to make me ask for pity." Or a month later: "Dear sister-in-law, I have received your check for 200 lire . . . But don't 200 lire seem really very little to you? They do to me."

Romolo's letters to Silone ranged from the mundane details of prison life (asking for a wool sweater and clean underwear, the perils of shaving with a rusty razor, lacking funds to pay for writing paper) to the poignant. In April and May 1931, Romolo was nostalgic for springtime in Pescina; memories of the town were both a comfort and a torment in prison. "I must make something of an effort to not think that outside it is spring, that in Pescina the cherries are blooming, that the fields are green, . . . all stuff that I wish to enjoy once again after three years in prison."

Conditions in the various prisons, combined with the effects of torture, spelled disaster for Romolo's health. Coughing up blood, he sent a letter whose tone was either mocking or despairing: "I was angry at myself because as a former athlete and soccer player, I shouldn't be subject to such incidents." In early September 1932, Romolo was admitted to the infirmary of the Procida prison with a raging temperature. From his sickbed, he sent a last letter to Silone asking for two sweaters. His tuberculosis worsened, and on October 27, 1932, he died. There is some indication that near the end, Romolo asked for, and received, permission to confess to Don Orione. Silone was notified by their cousin Pomponio, whose letter, written on All Souls' Day, assured the writer in Zurich that he would take care of the necessary arrangements to have a tombstone ordered. Romolo's grave, in the squalid prison cemetery, was marked by a simple cross. Silone, returning to Italy in 1944, attempted to exhume the body for a proper burial in Pescina, only to discover that during the war, the cemetery had been bombed; the grave and Romolo's remains had been destroyed.

Silone, convinced he was responsible for his brother's fate, spent the rest of his life in grief and guilt, haunted by his brother's ghost, tormented by the tragedy and especially by a line from one of Romolo's letters: "I have tried to act as I thought you would have in my place." Silone's first book, *Fontamara*, was dedicated to Romolo (and Silone's companion of ten years, Gabriella Seidenfeld). The writer was not above using his brother to make a point: In writing about how Italian writers had prostituted themselves under fascism (and every other political system in Italian history), Silone insisted they were all courtiers, and that any man who had any pride must decline the name of *littérateur*. "A young Italian intellectual, Romolo Tranquilli once asked me, 'How can we avoid this terrible fate?' I advised him, 'We must give ourselves body and soul to that class which is the mortal enemy of the present social system in Italy. That is the only way we can save ourselves from becoming bootlickers.' He took my advice. He wanted to become a worker, a printer. But he paid dearly for it. The government had him killed in prison."

Expulsion

"The life of a revolutionary," Silone wrote more than a decade after his expulsion, "is much more difficult, dangerous and full of pitfalls than that of a Nietzschean hero." It was dangerous, for example, to go forth into battle "without being completely truthful with oneself, down to the depths of one's soul."

In Silone's recounting of his experience as a Communist, the May 1927 meeting in Moscow of the Executive Committee of the Communist International is pivotal. Thinking that they had arrived late, Silone and Togliatti found themselves in the midst of a discussion denouncing Trotsky for his critical analysis of the situation in China and the drafting of a resolution to expel the Russian. When Silone naïvely asked to read the supposedly incriminating document, he was told it was not possible and was astonished to learn that no one of the Executive Committee had read it either. When the two Italians refused to condemn Trotsky for a document that neither of them had seen, the meeting was adjourned to the next day. The Executive Committee appointed the Bulgarian Vasil Kolarov to convince Silone and Togliatti. The two were invited for tea at the Hotel Lux that night. After admitting that he himself had not seen the document, but that "documents have nothing to do with it," Kolarov stated simply, "We have to choose . . . we're not in an academy here. Have I made myself clear?" he asked, looking straight at Silone. "Yes," Silone answered, "very clear." "Have I persuaded you?" asked Kolarov. "No," was Silone's reply. "Why not?" Kolarov wanted to know. "I'd have to explain," Silone concluded, "why I'm against Fascism."

The next day, when the two Italians still refused to condemn Trotsky, Stalin smiled and simply withdrew the motion from a vote. But Silone and Togliatti were astonished to read in a newspaper picked up the next day on the train ride back to Berlin that the Executive Committee of the Communist International had "unanimously" condemned Trotsky for betrayal.

For the next two years, Silone continued carrying out important tasks within the PCI but with increasing disgust. In the summer of 1929, he requested and was granted a leave of absence for medical reasons. It would be another two years before he was expelled and finally free.

Silone's expulsion from the Communist Party in June 1931 was the culmination of a long, drawn-out political and psychological battle that left an indelible stigma on his public persona and trauma on his private self. However, it does not appear that Silone was entirely innocent in the ambiguous and murky maneuvering of the PCI and its attempt to expel the three "deviationists": Pietro Tresso, Alfonso Leonetti, and Paolo Ravazzoli. Further complicating the drama was the fact that Tresso was Silone's brother-in-law, having married Barbara Seidenfeld. At the height of the crisis, Silone wished only "to disappear in silence."

The dispute revolved around the changing tactical and strategic thinking of both the Communist International and the PCI. Moscow ordered that social democrats were now to be referred to as "social-fascists" and that Communist parties were to increase their domestic networks in preparation for a soon-to-be-expected collapse of the bourgeois order. Tresso, Leonetti, and Ravazzoli disagreed, thinking the policy suicidal. Silone hesitated at first, refusing to take a clear public position. Writing from Switzerland on January 15, 1930, Silone (as "Pasquini") committed his position to a memorandum: Without explicitly aligning himself with Tresso, Leonetti, and Ravazzoli, and with an implied critique of the "socialfascism" theory, he agreed that returning to underground activity in Italy would be suicidal. Togliatti was furious, condemning Silone as an opportunist whose position would lead to a "liquidation of the party."

When it appeared that Silone was less than straightforward in his dealings with Tresso, Leonetti, and Ravazzoli, the PCI published excerpts of his letters, clearly demonstrating that while privately he agreed with the three, publicly he was criticizing them. Trapped by party intrigue and his own less-than-forthright declarations, Silone was openly charged with betrayal: "[Pasquini] should have the courage of a Communist. He should openly declare: 'I have betrayed the party.' He says it but doesn't say it. He confesses yet searches for an excuse." One critical point in the fiasco was the revelation that Silone sometimes had Gabriella Seidenfeld write and sign the incriminating letters to Ravazzoli, Leonetti, and Tresso. From Moscow, Ruggero Grieco wrote that "the party must conduct a pitiless campaign against the positions held by Pasquini." (It can be no coincidence that the party bureaucrat who investigates Rocco De Donatis in *A Handful of Blackberries* is named Ruggero.)

Silone's close confidant, Angelo Tasca, was expelled from the PCI in 1929. Accused of "right deviationism," Tasca was paying the price for criticizing the doctrine of "socialfascism," which held that the real enemy was not so much fascism (the orthodox definition was that fascism was a sign of the impending crisis of capitalism and therefore, in a bizarre way, to be welcomed) as social democracy. In this reading, the social democrats were guilty of diluting the revolutionary fervor of the working classes and, by so doing, strengthening Fascist regimes. Tasca had been a colleague of Gramsci's in founding the Ordine Nuovo movement in Turin. The latter emphasized the factory councils; the former, the trade unions. Tasca had joined Gramsci, Palmiro Togliatti, Umberto Terracini, and Silone in the Italian Communist Party in 1921 but almost immediately fought against Amadeo Bordiga's left-wing faction. A member of the executive committee of the PCI, Tasca clashed with the Executive Committee of the Communist International while in Moscow. His stance against the "socialfascism" thesis was the final straw: He was expelled in September 1929 and spent years in exile in Paris, taking French citizenship and moving increasingly to the political right—so far to the right that he collaborated with the Vichy regime as a journalist and radio commentator.

Until Tasca's collaboration with Vichy, Silone never abandoned him, and even then, Silone's criticism was muted. If Silone's "original sin" was his own collaboration with the secret police, he could not bring himself to condemn his friend outright. Instead, he wrote a moving commemoration after Tasca's death in March 1960.

Silone and Tasca found themselves on similar terrain: a rejection of state socialism, reform socialism, democratic socialism, and Marxist orthodoxy, and an attempt to reestablish the moral and ethical foundations of a humanistic socialism. They approached this task from different perspectives: Tasca returning to the writings of Marx and Engels and Francophone Marxism, Silone from a Christian socialism developing from the Germanic milieu of Zurich and contacts with Thomas Mann, Bertolt Brecht, Martin Buber, Stefan Zweig, Ernst Toller, Jakob Wassermann, and Leonhard Ragaz. Notwithstanding their different places of exile, Silone's and Tasca's intellectual itineraries were so similar that one Italian scholar has written about their parallel fates (*vicenda parallela*). The necessity of finding their respective voices in exile, in foreign lands, did not go unremarked by Silone. "The young people of my generation," he wrote many years later, "were forced to find an echo of their most intimate anxieties in foreign authors . . . and we wondered as to why there was such a silence regarding our contemporary problems in contemporary Italian authors. It was not just because of censorship, but rather self-censorship." For Silone, Italian writers from the Renaissance on, with precious few exceptions, were "an ornament of society," not an essential fact of reality. "The fundamental themes of conscience were avoided."

Between Tasca's expulsion in September 1929 and Silone's in June 1931, the two men exchanged letters between Paris and Zurich that would lay the foundation for a thirty-year relationship that ended only with Tasca's death. "Whatever decisions you make on the political terrain," Tasca wrote in March 1930, "you can count on my solidarity."

Much of their correspondence was devoted to helping each other find publishers, editors, and paying venues for their writings. Silone openly confessed to Tasca that he had undertaken his theoretical analysis of fascism for purely financial reasons, desperate for money. "Buying paper is already a sacrifice. For ten days, I haven't bought a newspaper." He dashed off *Der Fascismus* in a matter of weeks. Tasca had introduced Silone to Paul Nizan, the French writer and philosopher, but Nizan, under pressure from Maurice Thorez and the French Communist Party, managed to put Silone off. (Nizan would later resign from the party at the announcement of the Molotov-Ribbentrop Pact in August 1939 and was killed fighting at Dunkirk.) The French Communist Party had also pressured Henri Barbusse, editor of *Le Monde*, to fire Tasca from the journal. Silone was adamant that he would earn his living rather than be supported by the party. "Even at the risk of croaking (*crepare*), I want to earn my own living, like most men. At the beginning, it will be difficult, but I'll manage. If I don't, it means I'm inadequate to living." Yet he was still able to maintain his sardonic sense of humor. While waiting for a signed contract from Nizan for the fascism study (which never arrived), he could write with wry humor to Tasca that "eating every day is a necessary precondition to work." More seriously, they discussed Silone's impending expulsion from the party, which was technically delayed for some months because Silone had enrolled in the Swiss Communist Party.

On June 20, 1930, Palmiro Togliatti ("Ercoli") sent Silone ("Pasquini") a letter stating that the party had decided to ask Silone for a public declaration. They demanded that Silone publicly break with the three "deviationists" (Ravazzoli, Tresso, Leonetti); condemn Trotskyism; and state "absolute fealty to the party and the International." Togliatti's threat was not subtle: "I hope you don't want to follow the road the others have taken." Two months later, after failing to receive a reply, Togliatti tried again: "So far we have not received anything from you, neither a declaration nor even a suggestion of a declaration . . . The struggle against the opportunists, the enemies, and disintegrators of the party is something that is beyond any possible discussion."

To another party member, Romano Cocchi, Silone quoted Stendhal: "Dream of not spending your life in hate and fear." Silone boasted of having no fear "of any kind," only of a "horror of creating victims" with his expulsion. He asked Cocchi, "Don't you understand that your zeal is, at the very least, inhuman and sadistic?" Perhaps Cocchi did—belatedly—understand, for he later condemned the Molotov-Ribbentrop Pact and was himself expelled from the PCI. Arrested while fighting with the French maquis, he was sent to Buchenwald, where he perished.

In January 1931, six months before his official expulsion, the following declaration from Silone appeared in the Communist publication *Falce e Martello* (Hammer and Sickle):

Certain comrades have asked what is my position with regard to the Communist International and the PCI. To clarify this question I hereby declare:

1. That I am in agreement with the general line of the Communist International and PCI;
2. That I have never had, and have, nothing in common, neither politically nor organizationally, with the "group of three" [Leonetti, Tresso, Ravazzoli] expelled from the party, who have now passed over to the Trotskyist opposition;
3. That I condemn this group, their positions, and their activities, and am in solidarity with the struggle that the Communist International and the PCI carries out against them and against the Trotskyist faction;

4. That I accept without any reservations the discipline and the
   decisions of the Communist International and the PCI.

Togliatti and Ruggero Grieco struggled for more than a year to keep
Silone in the party; when it became obvious that their efforts would
bear no fruit, they turned to threats. Silone walked out of a meeting of
a commission chaired by Grieco to examine his case. During this session, Silone was accused of myriad offenses: a refusal to collaborate
with the current direction of the PCI; an inability to work with the
party apparatus; his "arrogant and impudent" bearing; the fact that he
burst into scornful laughter at every mention of the doctrine of "socialfascism"; that he was not an "internationalist" but an "Italian" and,
worse, a southern Italian; in fact, his *"contadinismo"* (advocacy of the
peasants) was a grave theoretical error. "These were the charges
against me," he wrote to Tasca, "but they probably won't be the public
charges against me in the act of expulsion. Those are not difficult to
imagine: traitor, deserter, etc." The only thing that Silone and the commission could agree upon was that he had a different ideology from
the party, that even his language was different from that of the party,
"that we speak and yet we fail to understand each other." But by the
summer of 1931, the case, as far as the party was concerned, was
closed. Silone was fully prepared now for the consequences. Fully conscious that one never freely resigned from the party but could only be
expelled, he wrote to Tasca that he now felt "ripe" for expulsion.

Summoned one last time before the PCI in July 1931, Silone admitted, according to the official party communiqué, to being an example
of the "political underworld," an "abnormal politician," and "a clinical
case." "There is no place in the ranks of the party," thundered the
announcement, "for softheaded intellectuals" such as Silone. The vote
to expel him was unanimous.

As Silone and Tasca discovered together, expulsion from the PCI
was both a blessing and a curse. As Silone had compared joining a revolutionary party to entering a monastery ("An outlawed revolutionary,"
says Pietro Spina, "is in the ideal state of a Christian in a monastery"),

he likened the "traumatic" situation of the ex-Communist with that of the ex-monk. Leaving the Communist Party, he wrote, "is like a small death" (una piccola morte). Ironically, Silone rediscovered what he had been seeking in the party—"a genuine rapport with others"—only after being expelled. With the passage of time, he could reflect on how he had misconceived politics. There were limits to what one could achieve through politics, "on that score I had no illusions." Equally important perhaps was his cynical conclusion that to work in politics "for any motive other than the pursuit of personal power must surely, I think, demand a certain measure of self-deception, of deliberately closing one's eyes to certain aspects of the truth." Again he turned to the metaphor of wolves in searching for answers. The fate of socialism, he wrote, was comparable to the hunter who went hunting for quail, only to find wolves. "In the struggle with the wolves, to save ourselves some of us were obliged to . . . rediscover our paleo-Christian heritage." The fate of Marxism convinced him that there was no revolutionary theory that could not be used for reactionary ends. What had survived of Marxism was its ideological critique, which was paradoxically both "a tragically cold technocracy" and "essentially humanist." But as History was the mother of Irony, Silone speculated that one day we would arrive at the aphorism that "Marxism is the opiate of the people." More than thirty years after his expulsion, it was still painful for him to recount that period in his life. The slow realization that the Soviet regime was the exact opposite of what it claimed (and what Silone believed it) to be came almost as a sickness, a medical crisis, as well as an intellectual one. When oppression, censorship, "absurd persecutions and ruthless tyranny" became obvious and no longer aberrations but systemic, Silone found himself in a "tragic dilemma." It was impossible to remain subject to such degradation but also impossible to cut the ties with men and women of good faith who were struggling against fascism.

"My entire world had collapsed," wrote Gabriella Seidenfeld on Silone's expulsion. She turned for help to Willy Trostel, secretary of the

Soccorso Rosso, and his wife, Käthe, but soon begged off to spare them the hostility of the party apparatus. (Trostel and his wife were later victims of Stalin's terror.) Seidenfeld eventually found lodgings in an apartment in Zurich put at her disposal by Albert Einstein's ex-wife, Mileva. Silone returned from Davos for a brief visit to Zurich, not completely cured, and to earn some money typed manuscripts for the Socialist libertarian Dr. Fritz Brupbacher.

Brupbacher was a physician ministering to the workers in Zurich. He had an international orientation and extensive contacts with Socialists, anarchists, Communists, writers, and artists. Originally a member of the Swiss Social Democratic Party, he was expelled because of his anarchist sympathies and joined the Swiss Communist Party in 1921. He had married Lydia Petrovna Kochetkova in 1901. With his companion, Paulette Raygrodski ("Russian women are one of my erotic fetishes," he once confessed), he scandalized Protestant Switzerland with bold advocacy of sex education, birth control, and abortion. At a conference on these matters in Rheinfeld, Brupbacher and Lydia were arrested and jailed overnight. On leaving the next morning, he reached into his pocket, extracted a five-franc coin, and left it on the desk of the warden as a tip.

Instead of paying Silone, Brupbacher offered his typist tea and biscuits; Silone would drink the tea and bring the biscuits home to Gabriella. In addition to the tea, Brupbacher supplied Silone with something far more precious: political cover to keep the Italian exile who possessed no official papers out of prison or safe from another round of expulsions. The good doctor's home was a welcome refuge for European anti-Fascists of all political persuasions. He was particularly attracted to the charismatic Italian and Russian anarchists and a great admirer of Mikhail Bakunin, whom he crowned "the Satan of the Revolution." In the Brupbacher home, Silone and Seidenfeld met the Hungarian count Michael Károlyi, who had turned over his vast landholdings to the Hungarian peasants to liberate himself from a sense of guilt.

It was Brupbacher who, in his inimitable style, arranged a "solution" to Gabriella Seidenfeld's precarious political status: marriage to a

Swiss citizen. Urging her to look through a photo album, the two settled on a Mr. Meyer, an elderly man "with a beard like Karl Marx," who, notwithstanding his devotion to bachelorhood, could not refuse a request from "Dr. Brup," as he was affectionately called. On the day of the wedding, bride and witnesses (Silone and Brupbacher) were left standing alone at city hall when the groom failed to appear. Brupbacher was not going to let his plan go awry: Two weeks later, he and his wife showed up at the groom's door, dragged him from bed, dressed him, and escorted him to the town hall. After the ceremony, they all retired to a local pastry shop. Thus Gabriella entered into a "normal" life as far as the Swiss authorities were concerned. In reality, she found an apartment rented out by two radicals and continued her conspiratorial life.

In January 1937, Gabriella was in Davos with Silone (where they rented two rooms in a pensione). On March 7, Silone abruptly ended their physical relationship, although the two remained lifelong friends. In keeping with his character, he gave no reason to acquaintances or even to Gabriella herself. Gabriella continued to live in Zurich, and when she opened a small bookstore, the Libreria Internazionale on the Langstrasse, Silone, with profits earned from the publication of *Fontamara*, lent her some of the money necessary to acquire stock. (The idea of the bookstore was his.) Thinking that the Italian emigrant population in Switzerland would welcome the diffusion of Italian literature and culture, the two were disappointed when the results proved "catastrophic." In the first few weeks, not a soul entered the bookstore. People came only on Sundays to purchase the tabloid newspapers; others asked only for the writings of Carolina Invernizio (a romance novelist whose books had been placed on the Index of Forbidden Books by the Vatican). One client would come in asking for books "that would make me cry."

Gabriella Seidenfeld had given Silone a chance to be reborn after the first terrible years of clandestine politics. In a letter to Gabriella on her birthday in 1924, Silone credited her with saving him from despair:

Two years ago, I was completely dried up, withered. Two years ago, such a letter would have disgusted me. To endure the horrible life I had previously lived, I had burned everything in me that was from Pescina: rural, from the seminary, familial, etc. To better endure, I had become deaf and dumb in spirit. Nothing mattered to me. What happened? My interior destruction had not been complete, neither physically nor morally. Then you arrived. Certainly, I am now no longer what I once was. I am physically reborn, that is, newly born. Even the desire to work has returned. Indeed, here's a curious fact: Reborn, I am returning to what I once was, that is, Pescinese. This should not displease you because at Pescina with Mamma I was truly a darling child, educated and so studious that Mamma was proud of me. At bottom, everyone has his own temperament and I realize that all I believe now I already thought at the age of fifteen. So that you, red Jewess [*ebrea rossa*], have brought me back to my spiritual condition when I entered into the seminary.

Nor had Silone forgotten Seidenfeld toward the end of his life. In the second codicil to his last will and testament, Gabriella was one of only four people other than Darina Silone who is mentioned. "To a small number of people, toward whom, for diverse reasons, I feel tied by affection and gratitude, I intend to leave some tangible sign of memory, unfortunately measurably limited because of scarce resources."

After his expulsion from the Communist Party, Silone was invited to join the Union Internationale des Écrivains Révolutionnaires and write for its review, *La littérature de la Révolution Mondiale*, but declined both invitations. (Publishing in French, English, German, and Russian, the union and its review were based in Moscow and Leningrad.)

By 1934, Tasca was urging Silone to return to active politics. "I propose to remain, as I am, independent of parties," Silone replied. Tasca shot back, surely thinking of the changed equation with Hitler in power, that while he too did not want to be ensnared in party politics,

"I think, though, that it is truly the moment to begin to draw on our experiences, which give us every right, except that of being silent." Angela Balabanoff wrote to him comparing the current situation of Stalin's show trials and the continuing civil war in Spain with the fate of the young idealist Cristina devoured by wolves: "The truth is so sad, as sad as the ending of *Bread and Wine.*"

On the Stalin show trials and the Zinoviev-Kamenev trial in particular, Silone's English translator, Eric Mosbacher, wrote to Silone that the whole Socialist movement suffers, noting that the New York–based Communist paper *Daily Worker* had issued a call to "shoot the vipers!" Just months after Fascist Italy's defeat of Ethiopia in 1936, Mosbacher had declined an offer to translate Marshal Pietro Badoglio's book about the conquest of Ethiopia.

Carlo Rosselli, leader of the Justice and Liberty movement, continued his earnest entreaties for Silone to rejoin the anti-Fascist cause, arguing that "it is necessary to de-provincialize antifascism and bring it in contact with the European public." Silone refused.

Notwithstanding his refusal to return to official party politics, Silone maintained close contact with many exiled left-wing intellectuals. To Balabanoff he wrote, "Give my regards to [anarchist Carlo] Tresca, whose name I have known since I was fourteen. Tell him that at the Ospedale degli Incurabili in Naples I was cared for by one of his sisters, a nun; she was a good old lady, cheerful, and not at all ashamed of having an anarchist brother."

There was to be no return to the fold, no return of the prodigal son. Try as he might, Togliatti failed in each and every attempt to bring Silone back to the PCI. In public, he was chastised, criticized, and denigrated. In his own hometown, where the local Communist Party cell had turned Romolo into a martyred saint, Silone was often derided and scorned. Some, in private, were sincere enough to admit that they had lost one of the party's best minds. But Silone had been one of the first to discern the ultimate fate of communism in the West and the Soviet Union. "After the death of Lenin, it appeared clear that the State was not going to escape what seems to be the fate of every dictatorship: the gradual restriction of the influence of those who participate in the direction and control of political power." Once the party had suppressed all rival political parties and established itself as the sole source of power, "every difference of opinion among the leaders was destined to end up with the physical extinction of the minority." Whether a tragedy of epic proportions or one of the many ironies of history, the revolution that had defeated its enemies "began to devour its favorite sons." The "thirsty gods," Silone realized, "permitted no truce. Marx's optimistic phrase about the natural decay of the Socialist State was revealed to be a pious illusion."

A decade after his expulsion, he could look back and recognize that in himself and in the movement "side by side with love and respect for man resided hate and contempt, and that a vocation for tyranny nestled next to the desire for liberty."

While he recognized it as a liberation—an "emergency exit"—his expulsion from the party was in truth, he wrote eighteen years later, "a very sad day for me, a day of mourning, of mourning for my youth. And where I come from, mourning is worn longer than elsewhere." He would not renounce his participation in the underground movement. Looking back after a half century of political life, Silone would reflect that "the rashness of my judgment was equaled only by my sincerity." He would later claim no "superior moral virtue" but only the "naïve spontaneity of the provincial subversive not yet corrupted by cold political calculations." And although during World War II and in the immediate postwar period he would collaborate with various currents of the Italian Socialist tradition, he remained aloof from party politics, never forgetting that liberty was dear to him precisely because of what he had "suffered to recover it." Silone never forgot the wounds he received in his participation in and expulsion from the revolutionary underground. But he recognized in those wounds a great source of strength for himself and others, like Tasca, similarly expelled. "There are many of us," he later wrote with defiant pride, "outside all parties and all churches, who carry these burning stigmata in secret."

THREE

WRITING in/and EXILE

In Switzerland I became a writer; but, more importantly, I became a man.

—SILONE, *Memoir from a Swiss Prison*

For a Communist denied by his party, it was difficult to find a home in the 1930s. Great Britain several times refused Silone permission to enter. "Finally, the English consulate has called to grant me a visa. The moral of the fable is this: If I was perhaps a Fascist, I would have no need to go to the British consulate for a visa; being an anti-Fascist, there is immediately the presumption that I am a scoundrel." France denied him permission to enter the country; his friend Léon Blum could not arrange permission even when he was prime minister of France in 1936. Evidently, in the eyes of the authorities, being an anti-Fascist was not a badge of honor, but rather a stigma.

Deprived of a passport, in poor physical and mental health, wracked by his conflict with the party and guilt over his relationship with Bellone, Silone settled in Switzerland in late 1929. He would not return to Italy until 1944. In Switzerland, he initiated a two-front "private war against Fascism" as well as a "fight against the danger of totalitarianism." It was in Switzerland that he became fully cognizant that "our fate depends on ourselves alone." Notwithstanding occasional arrests, harassment by the police, and more than one stint in prison, Silone became fond of the country. In 1940, in an autobiographical portrait, he wrote that he would like to spend the rest of his life in Zurich, which had become, in that time, "my second homeland: Here I have many friends, and where one has friends is one's true homeland [patria]. The day that Italy is liberated from the gentlemen who now rule her, I must naturally return there, I must live in Rome; but I am certain that I will live there as a sad Zurich refugee. What I like most about the Swiss, to tell the truth, are their defects. May God help the Swiss to keep them."

There is some indication that Silone turned to the new science of psychoanalysis in Switzerland. After the war, in an autobiographical essay, he compared his expulsion from communism to psychoanalysis: "One is cured of communism the way one is cured of a neurosis." He corresponded with (and was perhaps treated by) Dr. Ch. Strasser in Zurich. Dr. Strasser's stationery identifies him as a specialist in *Nerven und Gemütskrankheiten* (neuroses and depression). After thanking Silone for a copy of *Fontamara*, Dr. Strasser added ambiguously, "So far, I have kept you out of the rumors and gossip that has surrounded me and from which I intend to extricate myself."

In a letter to Romolo, written in Berlin, Silone complained about the inclement weather that "delays my convalescence, especially the treatment of nervous disorders." Letters to Gabriella Seidenfeld and Romolo in 1929 refer to serious mental or nervous disorders (*gravi squilibri nervosi*). The arrest of his brother, his increasingly acrimonious relationship with the PCI and the international organs of communism, and an exchange of letters with a Fascist police official were proving too much to bear. On August 7, 1929, he wrote to Gabriella:

I have been cured, that is, the psychoanalysis is finished . . . There is nothing else to analyze, everything is clear. I feel well. Now for the time that is called reconstruction: to reaccustom myself to normal collective life, forget the past, etc . . . Every symptom of phobia and fear has disappeared; I have a memory of past fears, but I am not afraid.

Assuring Gabriella that his doctor was competent and that the treatment wasn't very long (from an initial prognosis of six months to completion in three), he continued:

The important thing is that the analysis is finished, and that I am already at work, that I no longer have a crisis. We have a simplistic and infantile idea of psychological matters; they are made up of incredible minutiae that have their own importance. The unconscious has a tremendous slowness and laziness; it is unaffected by any influence, neither the will nor reason. One must be patient.

A year later, on September 1, 1930, he was still mentioning psychoanalysis in his letters to Seidenfeld. "I continue to go to the doctor. I am cured. But the doctor still finds in my dreams things of the past, which must be eliminated to be tranquil until I am ninety years old."

In Switzerland, Silone tried to make ends meet as a typist and a translator, even by teaching Italian. He began an affair with Aline Valangin, a pianist and psychiatrist (a former patient, then assistant, of Carl Jung) eleven years younger than he. Valangin and her husband, the successful lawyer Wladimir Rosenbaum, had created an oasis of peace and serenity for artists and writers at their home in Zurich and country estate in Comologno, dubbed "La Barca" by Silone, to praise its similarity to Noah's Ark. Valangin and Rosenbaum hosted intellectuals persecuted by the Nazi regime: Thomas Mann, Ernst Toller, Kurt Tucholsky, Joseph Roth. A contemporary writer penned this portrait of her:

The beautiful young lady who lives in the small, ivy-clad palazzo on top of the hill is regarded as a little strange or eccentric. The *sciora,** as they call her in the small village of Comologno in the Ticino, receives lots of visitors: men and women in outlandish costume, artists who laugh loudly and seem to have little respect for tradition. Hans Arp is among them, Ignazio Silone and Kurt Tucholsky, too. With some she takes trips to the countryside, with others she has love affairs. Everyone in Zurich knows her name; she is interested in all things new, exciting, and unconventional. Aline Valangin belonged to the most ardent initiators of the artistic avant-garde. She knew them all: James Joyce, Elias Canetti, Max Ernst, and Meret Oppenheim. And they loved this woman, her energy, her intelligence, and her boundless zest for life.

Silone spent much of his life in writing sporadic letters to Aline (the last is dated 1971). They were a strange mixture of banalities and searing images and words. One, from September 25 (no year, but from 1931 or 1932), slips, without any preamble or explanation, into two lines of the "Ave Maria":

I hope that in spite of the bad weather—here it is terrible—you had a good trip. I thank you for the letter from Florence.

    Benedicta tu in mulieribus

    Et benedictus fructus ventris tui . . .

Truly, we have no need to be together to feel ourselves one within the other [*per sentirci l'uno nell'altro*].

Bon voyage, dear, and be careful with the car.

On December 23, 1932, he penned a charming and irreverent alternative account of Genesis, recounting how Noah's Ark had been the scourge of Turks, pirates, and sharks, and how a certain "Remonda" of

*The Ago di Sciora is a rock formation in the central Swiss Alps.

Comologno had "acquired the rights" to the ark, which was subsequently brought to her villa, where it was colloquially called "La Barca."

> The spirit of the ark, the spirit of Noah, the spirit before the Flood, the spirit of human optimism, remains in the ark . . . It has survived the Flood. It will survive all crises . . . Today it attracts men of all races and religions. It does away with all differences between Chinese and Russians, between Italians and Germans, between Jews and Catholics, and even between Swiss from the Ticino and Swiss from Bern. Because the ark was built before Babel. Before the confusion of languages. Before the division of nations. The ark was at the beginning. The Beginning. And I assure you that humanity will finish with its beginning.

Silone was irresistibly drawn to the idyllic world Valangin offered but was tormented by his attraction to a "bourgeois" lover. Valangin reflected on their relationship nearly sixty years later in her memoirs:

> We wrote to each other often. How many words flew between us! But in fact, he was always reluctant in his love for me. Despite his intelligence he always saw me as a bourgeois, an enemy, in every sense as a pleasurable appendix without any importance. I could not really reach him. For sure, his feelings for me, such as they were, were passionate. He was more disposed to revealing his feelings in writing. I received from him letters that would have made any woman happy. A certain letter, very long, a kind of litany of love in which he praised me as the mother of sorrows, I sent back. I couldn't accept it, it was simply too much: too fantastic, too beautiful. And yet, I don't think it was just an exercise in writing; the letter was sincere, but it was the fruit of a particular state of mind [*stato d'anima*]. It didn't belong to me and so I wrote him. Other letters failed to make me understand him. It was not clear if he accepted or rejected our relationship. Probably he didn't know himself. He was always plagued by the idea that I had nothing to do with his world and his fate . . . This dissent of his

created many problems for me. His attitude was fickle: at times passionate adoration, at times superficial rejection. This hesitation seemed futile to me. I was absolutely sure of one thing: Except for him, there was nothing and no one. Everything that regarded him, regarded me as well. I was never so liberated, partaking in the burning present, and I would never feel so again.

Since Silone confessed to being unable to speak on the telephone (April 25, 1932), their stormy relationship can easily be reconstructed from their explicit correspondence, ranging from the banal to the erotic to the sublime. On April 11, 1932, from the Central Hotel in Zurich, Silone, in French, wrote that he would write her *un nouveau Magnificat*. He had a "Virgilian" motif in mind, "a variation on the ancient oration on disinterested love." But when Valangin suggested psychoanalysis for Silone's melancholy, he responded with ire:

> Instead of making love, you wanted to do psychology and have forced me, innocent that I am, to undergo psychology while I would have preferred to make love. I would rather abandon psychology and embrace love. If you only knew, my friend, how sweet, gentle, and terrible is love without psychology, terrestrial love, a goatlike [*l'amour chevresque*], animalistic love, that one does one, or two, or three, or ten times in a night without ever tiring, after the mind rests (after reason, psychology rests).

When Silone, who had rather traditional notions of gender relations and the "proper" comportment of adulterous affairs, heard rumors that Valangin had other lovers, including Rudolf Jakob Humm, he penned a long letter breaking off their relationship. "I cannot have," Silone crudely wrote, "a nymphomaniac as a friend." Claiming that his decision had nothing to do with jealousy, he insisted that he could not remain in a relationship where love led to "impoverishment" rather than "enrichment." His fury was unrestrained: "When you caressed me and kissed me, I had to turn my head so as not to smell your breath . . . It was as if a whitened sepulchre had opened. *Moritur et ridet* . . . Your words had the same perfume. Your lies had the same smell."

After he had learned of Valangin's relationship with Humm, Silone had left her house and walked along the banks of the Limmat River in Zurich, "feeling the seduction of the water." (As he would later occasionally do with his wife, Darina, vaguely threatening suicide.) When he returned to his rented room, for "the first time in fourteen years, I fell to my knees at the foot of the bed and I called for assistance of Life against death, against corruption, against chaos."

Although Zurich was home to a large emigrant Italian population, Silone was at first reluctant to assimilate into a new society and met socially only with Fernando Schiavetti and his family. Schiavetti, prominent in Italian republican circles, had fled to Switzerland in the wake of fascism. His daughter, Franca Magnani, recalled that Silone left her with a vivid impression on their first meeting in 1933:

> The man was tall, with brown hair and an olive complexion. He wore a strange black felt hat with a wide brim; it was unusual in that the top was reinforced with metal to form a kind of bowl. This framed his face in a strange manner that vaguely brought to mind a halo. The little boys in the town square would look at him and laugh . . . I did not like him at first, but I was soon intrigued. I was struck by his drawn out, muffled way of speaking, his cough—little coughs barely emitted but continuous, short, and hoarse—the incessant movement of his eyes and his blinking eyelashes that showed his moist eyes. His slow movements that reflected a cautious man. Silone's manner of shaking hands disturbed me. One found in their hand a limp, weak hand incapable of squeezing the other, as if he was lacking in strength.

Magnani recalled that the Swiss were surprised by the presence of Italians seeking refuge in their country. Italy's northern neighbors had insisted that *"Aber de Duce hät Ornig bracht"* (The Duce has restored order!) and that *"dass d'Italiener en Duce bruchet, d'Schwizer nöd"* (the Italians need a Duce, the Swiss don't). But with Adolf Hitler's rise to power in 1933, political dynamics and foreign relations changed radically in Switzerland. Magnani noted this at the cinema: When Hitler appeared in newsreels, the audience was "profoundly silent," scrutinizing him attentively, afraid. When Mussolini appeared, the audience would burst out in "liberating laughter": Italy simply wasn't taken seriously. Apparently, the Swiss and the Italian anti-Fascist exiles there had more sense than the French who, Magnani recalled in shock, took to the streets of Paris in 1936 chanting, *"Plutôt Hitler que Blum!"*

The scholar Deborah Holmes has recently demonstrated that Silone eventually established a complex network of colleagues, writers, intellectuals, and editors in Switzerland. Among the most noted were Thomas Mann and Robert Musil, but also important were his friendships with lesser-known men such as Leonhard Ragaz, a proponent of Christian Socialism, who later inspired the character of Franz the carpenter, derisively called "Agnus Dei" in *The Fox and the Camelias*. By all accounts Silone at first retreated into a melancholy exile, far from the glamour of Paris, the capital of Italian anti-Fascists. In the rather more austere setting of Zurich, Silone developed a reputation as a solitary and sorrowful man, broken in health and spirit. And yet his Swiss exile was a turning point in Silone's life; it afforded him an opportunity to be reborn, the promise of refashioning himself, of transforming himself from a Communist Party member into what Gramsci had first seen in him: a writer, first and foremost. The process of "reinvention" as Elizabeth Leake has called it, was a painful one.

It was in Switzerland that the "exile trilogy" of *Fontamara*, *Bread and Wine*, and *The Seed Beneath the Snow* restored Silone to physical and mental health. He called the three novels "the victory of my soul in its struggle against that which was vulgar and merely instinctive in my earlier life." Claiming that his books did not possess "great literary value," he admitted, "I myself know full well their formal defects." For

Silone, the exile trilogy was "human testimony" and he confessed that "there are pages in those books that were written in blood."

Fontamara

"Driven by homesickness, and by a passion for politics that could find no other outlet," thinking that he had not long to live, tormented by his position within the PCI and his relationship with Bellone, Silone retreated to a sanatorium at Davos, the Swiss alpine resort, and began writing what was to be the most powerful and influential work of anti-Fascist literature of the 1930s. It is an extraordinary achievement—sui generis—especially considering Silone's lack of formal literary and writing experience. He once described himself as one who did not write as a trade or profession but "obeying at all times a strong internal impulse, an authentic necessity." The result is there on the page in *Fontamara*. Thirty years later, reflecting on the genesis of the novel, he confessed that "writing for me was a need, a way to converse and to remember; to resuscitate in me memories of my people, to share a common sorrow." Memories of his infancy and adolescence were "my only strength, because in them there was a moral and I would even say religious source with which I could face and confront the adversities of life."

Begun in 1930 but not published until 1933, *Fontamara* is the story of a fictional town based on the older, poorer part of Pescina, farther up the mountain, inhabited only by the poorest peasants and without even a parish priest. "Ill and in exile in a Swiss mountain village," he wrote in 1965, "I believed that I did not have much longer to live, and so I began to write a story to which I gave the name *Fontamara*. I invented a village, using my bitter memories and my imagination, until I myself began to live in it."

Writing to Gabriella Seidenfeld (addressing her as "dearest wife" and signing as "your husband") while composing the novel, he told her that although the town of Fontamara is fictitious, everything that unfolds there is true to reality. And even though the setting is a provincial

Italian hill town, he endeavored to strip his writing of all folklore and colorful description. There were certain characters of *Fontamara* who were so alive, Silone wrote, that he found himself talking to them. "I believe they are the first peasants of flesh and blood who have appeared in Italian literature. I have never attempted, in writing, what I am now attempting." At night, he would waken and go to his desk to jot down notes; other times he found himself recuperating in the garden of the sanatorium at Davos and would have to run back to his room to edit a passage. "I have told you on other occasions," he continued to Seidenfeld, "that the time to produce for me had not yet arrived and that I always considered myself in a period of preparation. Now I believe that the time to produce has arrived. There is something new in me." Claiming that he was not worried about the judgment that others would render of the work, he boasted that "I have never been so sure of myself. I am certain that it will be a brick in the stomach of the southern Italian bourgeoisie." To Angelo Tasca, Silone confided, "I am working on a novel about southern Italian life . . . I am writing it because one can't say everything in political essays: There is always a part of reality that escapes."

The real protagonist of the novel is not an individual but a social class, the rural proletariat, the eternally suffering peasants, the much-despised cafoni. The peasants are the existential *primum* for Silone. Scorned in *Fontamara* as "flesh used to suffering," they are for the author the protagonist of contemporary history that most clearly reflects the human condition, the true children of the suffering Christ depicted, as in an ancient Roman graffito, as a crucified donkey.

Silone wrote most of *Fontamara* in a small pensione in Davos, so poor that he was forced to leave the manuscript, his typewriter, and a raincoat until he could return to pay the bill. When the book was finally published, not in Italian but German, in 1933, it carried a poignant dedication to "Romolo Tranquilli and Gabriella Seidenfeld." In his own personal copy, Silone inscribed the Latin from Lamentations 1:12: *"Videte si dolor vester est sicut dolor meus"* (See if there be any sorrow unto my sorrow).

The novel opens with an exiled Fontamarese living in Zurich returning home one evening overwhelmed by nostalgia, finding three fellow villagers awaiting him on his doorstep. Father, mother, and son are the survivors of a tragedy and recount their tale in turn.

The poor cafoni of Fontamara are subject to the eternally unchanging barren landscape and an indifferent if not hostile local aristocracy. Into this semifeudal world a new actor appears in the guise of the Contractor, representative of the Fascist regime in Rome. It has taken eight years but the new dispensation has finally arrived in Fontamara: The Contractor has easily absorbed the local village elites such as the priest Don Abbacchio and the old lawyer Don Circostanza and the petty aristocrat Don Carlo Magna. Into the millennial suffering of the peasants has arrived a new brutality.

Beginning with a cynical exploitation of the peasants' illiteracy, which gives specious legal claim to the diversion of a precious stream of water to the Contractor's land, the story unfolds of one peasant's dire plight to obtain a meager piece of land so as to be able to marry his sweetheart, Elvira. Berardo Viola was born, as his mother prophesied to everyone in the village, under a dark star. (San Berardo was one of the patron saints of Pescina; the Church of San Berardo had been irreparably damaged in the 1915 earthquake and consequently deconsecrated.) From passive resignation to primitive rebel and, finally, through his meeting with a mysterious underground man, to fledgling revolutionary, Berardo Viola is transformed by his condition. In the process, though, he brings down the wrath of the regime on the heads of his fellow villagers. In a final horrific orgy of violence, fascism reasserts itself in the town, and Berardo sacrifices himself in prison to the cause. Berardo's arrest, torture, and subsequent death in prison closely mirror Romolo Tranquilli's fate. And here surely Silone was trying to expiate his own sins in failing to help secure his brother's release and what he felt was his own complicity in his brother's martyrdom. (Berardo's death, which the Fascist police falsely attribute to suicide, also mirrors the death in prison by "suicide" of Gastone Sozzi on February 6, 1928. Sozzi, a fellow militant in the PCI, had suffered three months of torture; his death was a catalyst for Silone to begin a campaign condemning Fascist judicial procedures.)

Writing to a readership completely foreign to the world of Fontamara, Silone offers two cautions in his foreword: This is no picturesque, romantic lyric to a sunny southern Italy that exists only in the imagination of northern Europeans, and the reader is to be aware that although the dialogue may be written in formal, proper Italian, the reality took place in dialect, a universe away from the Italian learned in school. Related to the idea of a story translated from the dialect, Silone offers a model of writing and storytelling. If the former was almost unknown because of illiteracy, the latter was one of the arts of Fontamara, learned as children, sitting on the doorstep in the late afternoon sun, or around the fireplace in the long nights of winter, or by the hand loom, listening to old stories to the rhythm of the loom's pedal. "The art of storytelling—the art of putting one word after another, one line after another, one sentence after another, explaining one thing at a time, without allusions or reservations, calling bread bread and wine wine—is just like the ancient art of weaving, the ancient art of putting one thread after another, one color after another, cleanly, neatly, perseveringly, plainly for all to see."

The word "fascism" is not mentioned; when the peasants are forced to attend a rally, they are made to feel ridiculous when they insist on bringing along the banner of their patron, St. Rocco, to what turns out to be a political demonstration choreographed by the Fascist regime.

The novel ends with the self-sacrifice of the peasant Berardo as well as the woman he loves, Elvira. A final scene has the surviving peasants of a Fascist massacre gathered together to publish the first "cafone" newspaper, arguing over its title. Unknowingly echoing Lenin, Nicolai Chernyshevsky, and Tolstoy, they finally agree on a title that is also a plaintive cry for change. "They have killed Berardo Viola, *What Is to Be Done?* . . . They have taken away our water, *What Is to Be Done?* . . . The priest refuses to bury our dead, *What Is to Be Done?* . . . They violate our women in the name of the law, *What Is to Be Done?*"

After completing the manuscript, Silone wrote to Gabriella Seidenfeld that every period of a person's life must be judged according to the place it delivers you to. (Twice he uses the Italian word *destino*, "fate.")

Fate has decreed that, in order to express all the suffering of our age, I should know and experience all the miseries, all the shame, all the enthusiasms, all the defeats of our age; nothing that a man can suffer has been unknown to me. But if I am able to still live and recount the tale and if I can judge myself and if I can have pity for this poor human being, it's only because of you, dear. Without you, where would I have ended up? . . . *Fontamara* is no more than a first chapter . . . I wish to say *two or three things* before dying, things that no one else can tell and that fate has charged me to say. Two or three things that every worker, every peasant, every Communist, and every Fascist should think about, which every man should reflect upon. Two or three things about this damn world.

Getting the work published proved to be a daunting task. Since publishing it in Italy was impossible, Silone turned to his circle of foreign friends for assistance and advice. The manuscript was in the hands of Jakob Wassermann and scheduled to be published in German by Fisher Verlag, but Hitler's ascension to power in January 1933 precluded that possibility. Aline Valangin sent the typed manuscript to the exiled historian Gaetano Salvemini, then in Paris. Salvemini wrote back to Valangin that the work is "valuable," Silone "has much talent," and the author "has vividly felt the life of our peasants," but he spent most of the letter offering a critique of the novel: The use of the first-person narrative was clumsy; the writing was repetitious; the peasants appear "too stupid"; "certain obscenities are better off being suppressed or masked; naked and crude life is not art." Salvemini continued that "the rape of the girl is true enough but no one will believe it; they will say it's 'anti-Fascist propaganda,' and the work will lose any value." His advice was "to tell a lot less of the truth to be believed." His prediction of the book's fate was equally pessimistic: "A translation would be impossible; it is too far removed from the experience of those who are not Italian, and even to many Italians . . . It will sell very few copies because the Italians abroad read little, even less than Italians in Italy." For once, Salvemini was wrong. Tasca sent his encouragement from Paris: "My impression is less pessimistic than Salvemini's."

Notwithstanding Silone's precarious position with the PCI (he had not yet been formally expelled), the German Communist Alfred Kurella, a high-ranking member of the Comintern, read the manuscript and was impressed. When Silone was later expelled from the party, Kurella met with the writer in Zurich and brought a typewritten copy with him back to Berlin in search of an editor. Twenty-two years after its first publication, Silone could still remember with bitterness the "insolent" reply of Rascher, Henri Barbusse's German publisher (and future publisher of the complete works of Mussolini).

Just when it seemed that the manuscript was fated to languish, it was taken up by Nettie Sutro, originally from Bavaria, now resident in Zurich. Silone had met Sutro and her husband, the noted neurologist Eric Katzenstein, through the French poet Jean-Paul Samson. A conscientious objector during World War I, Samson had fled to neutral Switzerland. (He too would later translate several of Silone's works into French.) Many years later, Silone recalled with profound gratitude Sutro's "act of pure generosity" in translating the manuscript into German, perhaps because she had come to take pity on a manuscript that Silone had left in the pensione at Davos until he could pay his bill. At the apartment of Katzenstein and Sutro, Silone was introduced to Ernst Toller, Jakob Wassermann, and Martin Buber. The Austrian novelist Wassermann wrote to Sutro after having read the manuscript that it had "a Homeric simplicity and grandeur." He, contrary to Salvemini, was convinced that the book was destined for great fame. Silone's circle of friends urged him to publish Sutro's German translation, even at his own expense; they would pledge a certain number of subscriptions. With Aline Valangin a moving force, eight hundred subscriptions were secured and *Fontamara* appeared "at the expense of the author," first in a Swiss German edition by the Zurich publishing house of Oprecht. Silone recognized that even with eight hundred pledged subscriptions, which permitted Emil Oprecht to publish two thousand copies of the book, Oprecht was taking a political as well as a financial risk. Hitler and Nazism had recently come to power in Germany. In fact, the *Frankfurter-Zeitung* had planned to publish the work in installments starting in February 1933, but this was abandoned in light of the unfolding political catastrophe. But, as Pietro Spina recalls his grandmother saying, "when God closes a door, he sometimes opens up a window." The book was typeset by the Tipografia Cooperativa in Sciaffusa, and the Socialist typesetters there asked for neither an advance nor a guarantee of payment.

Since the publication of *Fontamara* coincided with the Nazi seizure of power, many German refugees found it in their hands as they passed through Switzerland, fleeing Hitler's regime. By the winter of 1933–34, the book had already made its way onto the Nazi blacklist: "to be confiscated even in bookstores and household searches." German refugees made the book known in the other European countries in which they settled, as well as in the United States, where a Hungarian Jewish pacifist, Rosika Schwimmer, received no fewer than a dozen rejection letters from American publishers to her proposals for an English translation. Sutro's translation was reprinted by the associates of the Universum Bücherei guild in Basel and serialized in fourteen daily and periodical publications in Switzerland between 1934 and 1935. A flawed American edition was finally published in 1934, and a much better English translation by Eric Mosbacher and his wife Gwenda David was published in Britain the same year. Mosbacher was perhaps Silone's best English translator and carried on a thoughtful correspondence with the writer for several decades. Jean-Paul Samson published a French translation in 1934, and an Italian edition was published the same year in Paris by the fictitious publishing house Nuove Edizioni Italiane. In reality, the Italian edition was printed by Imprimerie SFIE, a group of Italian anti-Fascist emigrant typesetters at 29, rue du Moulin Joly. The cover of this edition was graced by a woodcut engraving by Clément Moreau, pseudonym of Carl Meffert, who also produced the half dozen striking woodcuts for the English translation of *Viaggio a Parigi* as *Mr. Aristotle* in 1935.

Over the next few years, the book was translated into twenty-seven languages, including Dutch, Flemish, Polish, Czech, Hebrew, Portuguese, Spanish, Danish, Norwegian, Finnish, Croat, Romanian, Hungarian, Russian, and even Esperanto. During World War II, Jonathan Cape in London published a cheap edition of twenty thousand copies in Italian to be given to Italian prisoners of war. In late 1944, one of these copies ended up in the hands of the archbishop of Naples, Alessio Cardinal Ascalesi, who denounced the book from his pulpit. In London in 1942, the BBC transmitted a radio broadcast of *Fontamara*. By 2000, the book had sold close to two million copies. Three decades after the book had been published, Silone mused on its fate. He had been compared to Giovanni Verga and William Faulkner by foreign critics but confessed to having read Verga only after having written *Fontamara*. Conscious of (but in no way embarrassed by) his lack of formal literary training, "I hastened in search of books by these two illustrious authors" only to discover that "we had nothing in common: neither the sense of life nor our way of representing it." To the Sicilian writer, journalist, and anti-Fascist Giuseppe Antonio Borgese, Silone confessed that perhaps success had come a bit early in the wake of *Fontamara*, but that he wanted "to remain faithful to myself and to the reason that pushed me to write. Because as far as talented writers are concerned, Italian literature has had perhaps too many already and in this sense my contribution would be fairly limited; if, instead, I continue along my path, I will create *impure* art, but art that would count for something."

On returning to Italy in October 1944, Silone refused to hand *Fontamara* to any Italian editor or publisher who had collaborated with fascism. This curtailed his options, to say the least. It prevented *Fontamara* from being made into a film because Silone felt that the studios had been too accommodating with fascism. But *Fontamara* was finally published in Italy in 1945, serialized in *Il Risveglio*, a weekly journal published by the defrocked priest Ernesto Buonaiuti. A modernist priest, Buonaiuti was excommunicated in 1925 and lost his university position in 1931 for criticizing the Lateran Accords between the Fascist state and the Vatican and refusing to swear an oath of allegiance to Mussolini's regime. (Only eleven professors out of twelve hundred refused.) He later was forced to give up a chair at the University of Lausanne because he refused to convert to Protestantism. Buonaiuti recalled that *Fontamara* had circulated clandestinely in Fascist Italy and came as a revelation to artists who had matured "in suffering and hope." He felt the 1945 publication in Italy was a triumph and a definitive condemnation of that kind of poor and pale literary aesthetic or vain poetic fantasy intended to satisfy the taste of "spineless aesthetes and effeminate dandies" (*smidollati e cicisbei*). A year after Buonaiuti published *Fontamara*, he was dead. Silone was forced to recognize the realities of the publishing industry in Italy and, accordingly, *Fontamara* was first published in book form in postwar Italy by Mondadori in 1949. Translations continued apace around the world, including Slovenia, Serbia, Greece, Catalonia, and two editions in India (in Kannada and Bengali). A Turkish translation appeared in 1943; Japanese, 1952; Lebanonese, 1965; Afrikaans (South Africa), 1968.

The book's message, though, was not universally well received. Writing in an Italian literary review in 1973, an American professor at Florida State University noted how his deeply bourgeois white students had difficulty understanding *Fontamara*, while his black students, marked by a very different social and cultural history, were deeply moved by the novel.

Carlo Rosselli, writing to Silone from Paris on November 17, 1933, was effusive in his praise: "I have reread *Fontamara*. And my first impression has been greatly reinforced. It is a very beautiful book, the most beautiful Italian social novel." It was a "painful and stunning" book; more important, Rosselli made the critical point that it was the first Italian "social" novel in which the protagonist was not an individual but a social class, the cafoni, and a social condition: *la miseria*. Rosselli went on to say that he only recently discovered that the

Romolo Tranquilli who died in prison a year earlier was Silone's brother. "In the name of all anti-Fascists, permit me to send all my sympathy." A month later, Rosselli wrote again, proposing to publish Romolo's letters in his journal, *Quaderni di Giustizia e Libertà*.

Trotsky, whom Silone had met in his brief visits to Moscow in the 1920s, had read the book aboard the ocean liner *Bulgaria* in July 1933 during a transatlantic voyage. In a letter to Silone, the Russian revolutionary wrote, "In *Fontamara* passion is heightened to such a fever pitch that an authentic work of art is the result." Later that year, Trotsky repeated his private thoughts in a review in a Parisian journal and concluded, "From the first to the last line, this remarkable book is directed against the Fascist regime in Italy, its acts of violence, and its atrocities. *Fontamara* is not only a book of passionately political accusation; for in it the revolutionary passion is raised to such a height that it becomes a true work of art." Trotsky's "benediction" of the book opened the doors for Silone's appraisal in literary journals on both sides of the Atlantic: from the *Nouvelle Revue Française* to *Partisan Review* in New York. Silone, detecting an ideological dogmatism in Trotsky, judged a political collaboration impossible and declined an invitation from the exiled Russian to meet.

A fellow exile in Zurich, the German writer Bernard von Brentano, noted the book's revolutionary power: "One hundred rich men can beat a poor unarmed man, force him to kneel before them, humiliate and exploit him. The poor man seems lost. But it is not so. Look, reader, at the story of Fontamara, to see how freedom itself begins to write when everyone believes its defenders have been locked up for good." Graham Greene's review in London's *Spectator*, in which he confessed to a spiritual affinity with the Italian writer, paved the way for a positive critical reception on the part of English readers:

In *Fontamara* we are not concerned with eternal issues: we are down in the mud and the blood, the injustice and ignominy of the present. This story of an obscure Italian village [of] "about one hundred ragged, shapeless, one-floor hovels" is the most moving account of

Fascist barbarity I have yet read; it is told simply, in the first person, as if by one of the peasants: how the villagers of Fontamara were driven by suffering at the hands of the swindling landowners and corrupt administrators to a useless tragic revolt against the State. Only an old man, his wife and son have escaped abroad to tell the story to Signor Silone of how the Blackshirts came down to Fontamara . . . It should be read to its merciless end.

Almost four decades after the book first appeared, Silone responded to a series of questions from a student in Brescia, noting that "the entire action of *Fontamara* unfolds over the fundamental contrast between the still semifeudal psychology of the 'cafoni' and the irruption of new elements of exploitation and oppression. The contrast has tragic elements but comic and grotesque ones as well." When the student noted that the novel ends with a question ("What is to be done?") that has no answer, Silone corrected her: "It is a question that is in itself an answer. The Fontamaresi, before then, had never asked that question. The abuses and humiliations were considered a part of the natural world created by God. To begin to pose the question was already a liberation. (And in Berardo's sacrifice is the beginning of an answer.)"

Silone's German translator Nettie Sutro was also one of his most astute critics. In Silone's writing, "life itself is dressed in poetry," she wrote, "even if it presents itself in all its dark sadness." *Fontamara* unfolds with an inexorable necessity; one reads with a sense of foreboding, of fate hovering over the action. As Sutro noted, "Because all this is equivalent to a Greco-Roman tragedy, there is no place in it for sorrow or sentimental pity. Everything happens because it must. It cannot be otherwise, it can come about in no other way; and all the time one keeps staring at the next development in the story, as a sailor in distress watches the next wave that threateningly rolls toward him."

Silone often commented on how his characters went on living and evolving in his mind long after a novel was finished; hence his propensity to revisit and rework his books. When a new edition of *Fontamara* was to be published in 1960, he expressed surprise on rereading it:

"My embarrassment was not the result of comparing the book with the reality that I once more had before my eyes, but between the 1930 story and the developments it had undergone inside me during all the years in which I had gone living in it." Speaking in Rome to a group of students from Smith College in 1962 who specifically asked the writer about the various versions of his novels, Silone replied that in the rereading and subsequent "corrections" he was guided not by "the norms of beautiful writing [*bello scrivere*] but by my new way of seeing and feeling."

Unfortunately, because of Fascist censorship, *Fontamara*'s great success abroad was not matched in Italy. Even though it circulated clandestinely, most Italians remained ignorant of Silone until after the war. An episode involving the 1934 Nobel Prize–winning author Luigi Pirandello was telling: At a press conference in America before World War II, the author of *Six Characters in Search of an Author* was asked his opinion of Silone as the first question at a press conference. "Who is he?" asked Pirandello. "I never heard of him." Whether Pirandello was sincere in his ignorance or simply being politically astute, we do not know. It was not until 1949 when Mondadori put out a revised and corrected version from the Jonathan Cape edition that the Italian critical establishment began to take note. The young Guglielmo Petroni, who had spent time in Fascist prisons and whose memoir *The World Is a Prison* was a literary jewel, recognized that Silone was a writer for whom "the necessity of a deep consciousness of the moral figure of man was stronger and more necessary than for any other writer." The Communist literary establishment held back their firepower, thinking of Silone as the prodigal son who would eventually return.

Fascism

Their thinking was based partially on the vaguely Marxian overtones of *Fontamara* and on the orthodox Marxism in Silone's *Der Fascismus:*

seine Enstehung und seine Entwicklung (*Fascism: Its Origin and Develop-ment*), first published in 1934. Based partially on articles that had appeared in the official theoretical journal of the PCI, *Lo Stato Operaio,* Silone offered a three-part definition of the new political ideology. First, he defined fascism "chronologically": as a movement that arises in capitalist societies, at times of economic crisis, typically when the crisis is prolonged, and when both capitalist and workers' parties are incapable of filling the vacuum. Second, Silone described fascism "morphologically" (that is, by its shape, or phenomenologically): as "a broad political movement of the masses," typically with a nationalist ideology and petit bourgeois support. Third, Silone defined fascism "dialectically": as a movement that develops and changes. In particular, he contrasted fascism as a movement with fascism as a regime: "Fas-cism, the strongest movement that has ever emerged from the petite bourgeoisie, results in the open dictatorship of high finance and in an unprecedented repression of the petite bourgeoisie as a class." Fas-cism, Silone wrote, "was a counter-revolution against a revolution that never took place." It was "the elevation of nihilism to power." And combining political acumen with peasant wisdom, he warned in a later essay that "revolutions, like trees, are recognized by their fruits."

Sandwiched between the first two exile novels, *Der Fascismus* was a brutally stark work. As Silone confessed to Angelo Tasca, he undertook the task solely to earn a bit of breathing room, pay some bills, and afford him a few months' leisure to finish *Fontamara.* Written between 1931 and 1934, never published in Italian during its author's lifetime (indeed, he renounced the work and forbade its publication in Italy), it originally appeared in 1935. Translated into three languages (Croat and Polish in addition to the German), it did not appear in Italian until 1992 (in an unauthorized version); it wasn't until a decade later that an edition appeared with the blessings of Darina Silone. These Italian edi-tions were translated from the German, as the original manuscript had been lost in Silone's Swiss exile. Silone wrote several times that he felt his position on fascism was better explained in the subsequent *School for Dictators,* which appeared in 1938.

Employing a strict Marxist methodology and written in a polemical vein, *Der Fascismus* was the last remnant of Silone's party mentality. Its essence is distilled in an essay that appeared in an unorthodox journal Silone founded, *information*, as "Was ist Fascismus? Versuch einer Definition." It was published in Zurich by Emil Oprecht, who, with the success of *Fontamara*, had founded Europa Verlag, publishing some of the great works of the 1930s in German: Benedetto Croce's *History of Europe*; Bernard von Brentano's *Theodor Chindler*; Hermann Rauschning's study of Nazism, *Die Revolution des Nihilismus*; and Thomas Mann's journal *Mass und Werk*.

Notwithstanding the Marxist analytical framework of *Der Fascismus*, the PCI intervened with Paul Nizan, editor of Carrefour in Paris, to prevent its publication in French. That did not prevent Nikolai Bukharin from writing a positive review in *Izvestia* in May 1935. (Three years later, Bukharin would become a victim of Stalin's purges.)

The work is both a sociological study of the development of fascism as well as a study of class conflict in Italy. It is also a history of the workers' movement in Italy, its successes and failures. A major interpretive key was Silone's assertion that fascism arose more in reaction to reform, rather than revolutionary, socialism. His conclusion was that the political immaturity of the workers' movement in the immediate postwar period caused it to fail against capitalism and, in so doing, assisted the rise of fascism. Writing from the mid-1930s, Silone recognized that fascism could last years, even decades, but "that the victory of capital over labor could not be eternal. The future belongs to socialism. The future belongs to liberty."

After World War II, he occasionally returned to examining fascism in his essays. With its bombastic rhetoric, its climate of fear, and its insistence on servility, fascism had brought about an aggravation and acceleration "of the general moral decadence" in Italy. With its myth of Rome and claim to totalitarianism, fascism "deluded itself that it was purging the Italians of their skepticism with strong medicine." Thus, public life was "bristling with heroic sentiments" but failed to take root in people's consciences. While the "half-tragic, half-farcical nature of

Fascism facilitated its downfall," the end of fascism created the "unfortunate illusion" that the "moral infection of nihilism" that had inspired it had disappeared with it.

When the manuscript of *Fontamara* had been completed and as Silone established an editorial relationship with Oprecht, he conceived the idea of a new cultural review, *information*, whose inaugural issue appeared in June 1932. Rejecting any school of philosophy, any system of ideology, or any imposed orthodoxy, *information* attracted a heterogeneous group of artists, writers, designers, and architects. Although it appeared for only two years, it was a signal achievement for intellectuals of Mitteleurope fleeing the burgeoning Nazi movement in Germany and elsewhere. The inaugural editorial laid out a vision of modern life as "development, movement, change, struggle, contradiction, evolution, and revolution at the same time." Dialogue and dialectic were the forms that best established a link between thought and life conceived as "an incessant becoming."

The School for Dictators

Since *Der Fascismus* was undertaken both as a last expression of Silone's orthodox Marxism and for purely pecuniary reasons, Silone later disavowed it, although its most profound line is one he embraced for the rest of his life: *"La storia è sempre autocritica"* (History is always self-critique).

During the summer of 1937, after the successful publication of *Bread and Wine*, and while he was working on *The School for Dictators*, Silone was again deeply unsatisfied with the recent turn of political events. Urged to join the Italian Socialist Party, he confessed to a temptation, only to see it cooled by "the idea and a memory of what a party (every party) really is." As for his work at the time, "even if with good results, [it] gives me only mediocre satisfaction and I cannot successfully delude myself into making a virtue out of necessity."

When asked for his theoretical analysis of fascism, he would respond that readers should look closely at his satire in the form of a dialogue, *The School for Dictators*, composed between 1937 and 1938. The interlocutors are three: a certain Professor Pickup, founder of the new "science" of "pantautologia" (who bears an uncanny resemblance to Dr. Henry Kissinger) and adviser to Mr. W, aspiring future dictator of America; and Thomas the Cynic (Silone), whom they have sought out for his wisdom in all things political. (Silone's ironic epigraph for the book is *"Quam parva sapientia regit mundum"*: How little wisdom rules the world.)

Before introducing the two to Thomas the Cynic, the author amuses himself with the professor and Mr. W in polite discussion and debate on how best to bring about a dictatorship in America. Noting that there has been a "recent setback" in a possible dictatorship (an allusion to the 1936 reelection of Franklin D. Roosevelt), Professor Pickup (so called even in the original Italian) insists that he has made a scientific analysis of dictatorships and the two aspirants have made pilgrimages to the beer halls of Munich as well as Piazza San Sepolcro in Milan, the birthplace of Italian fascism on March 23, 1919. Silone warns him against excessive faith in a scientific theory of politics and offers a humanist interpretation of Machiavelli's theory of politics:

> Politics [for Machiavelli] were not immoral, but pre-moral or a-moral. He humanized political thought in the sense that he brought it down to earth from the theological clouds in which it had been soaring for centuries. He demonstrated its purely terrestrial foundations. He showed that politics were a purely human, historical product, the result of the energy, the virtues, the weaknesess, the vices of men . . . He broadened the conception of human liberty—that is, of human responsibility—that is, of human morality.

But simply aping Machiavelli would not be sufficient. "A deep knowledge of history," Silone warns the two would-be dictators, "makes fanaticism impossible."

Thomas the Cynic tells his pupils that fascism is indeed barbaric, not because it pits one class against another but because "it mobilizes and marshals all the relics of primitive barbarism that still survive in modern man, whether plebeian or aristocratic. It frequently succeeds in also contaminating many of its political opponents, who, struggling against fascism by fascist methods, become barbarians themselves, Red barbarians."

Long before scholars were writing about fascism as the aestheticization of politics, Thomas the Cynic points Professor Pickup and Mr. W to Gabriele D'Annunzio's seizure of Fiume after World War I as a "work of art, an empty rhetorical creation" behind which, however, were the "concealed fangs" of the Italian military. To this must be added a fanatical will to power. "The fascist leader's superiority over his opponents consists above all in this: that he aspires to power, only to power, and nothing but power. Whether he is on the side of the capitalists or the workers, the church or the devil, is a secondary matter to him. What matters to him is power." Thomas the Cynic sees fascism as a kind of metapolitics:

> Although a political movement, fascism succeeded from the first in avoiding the arena of struggle on which its opponents took their stand. On the latter it would have easily been beaten. Instead, without opposing program to program, without pledging itself to this or that organization of the state or society, it successfully applied itself to discrediting politics in general and political parties and programs in particular, thus reviving and transferring to the despised political scene many pre-logical and a-logical relics of primitive mentality which were slumbering in the masses and which the progress of civilization had covered with a thin exterior varnish without touching their deeper roots.

To his pupils' mistaken notion that fascism is dependent on a certain form of state, Thomas insists that fascism can exist without national traditions or the vaunted "corporations." The essence of fascism lies not in any of the institutions it may create. Therefore, you may have fascism in a monarchy or a republic. "The only thing fascism cannot be reconciled with is clear ideas . . . The only thing with which fascism is incompatible is discussion."

In a passage that echoes both Carlo Levi's idea that fascism perverts the sacred into the sacrificial to induce a holy terror and Emilio Gentile's later notion of fascism as the "sacralization" of politics, Thomas responds thus to Mr. W's query about the proper drug to induce a mass following:

> Nothing but an adequate liturgy. A religious and sacramental nothing; a pure, perfect, and disinterested nothing; the self-sacrifice of a life that in nostalgic moments rejoins its creator and returns to the unformed. The defeated in life, those for whom existence has no more meaning or value, who yet refrain from suicide because their despair is not yet purely individual, because they feel themselves buoyed up and spurred on by a vitality that needs to be employed for some unusual object, are the likely recruits for our contemporary impresarios of terror. Fascism for them is a kind of nihilistic drug . . . Fascism, with its violence, its terrorism, and its liturgy of death, was made possible by the war and the consequences of the war in certain countries, the bankruptcy of the bourgeoisie and the proletariat, of capitalism and anti-capitalism, of monarchies and democracy, of religion and atheism.

In essence, Silone's analysis of fascism is a synthesis of the sociology of the Frankfurt School with the psychoanalysis of Freud and Jung, grafted on to his own personal experiences sifted through a sieve of peasant wisdom.

The School for Dictators was accorded wide acclaim when it appeared on the eve of World War II. Some critics hailed Silone as a contemporary Machiavelli in forging a whole new way of thinking about politics. In the *New York Herald Tribune*, Alfred Kazin placed Silone in the pantheon of Machiavelli, Bodin, Grotius, and Montesquieu. More interesting, though, is Kazin's sense of a "modern melancholy" that suffuses the book. Irving Howe included an excerpt in his collection *The Essential Works of Socialism*. Writing in *The New Yorker*, the novelist and critic Niccolò Tucci pointed out that this was a dangerous book because "Silone knows too much."

Among those who nurtured Silone's image of himself as a writer were Robert Musil and the publisher Emil Oprecht and his wife, Emmie. Silone recalled that at their first meeting, in Zurich in March 1939, Musil pointed to Efraim Frisch, who had written an insightful review of *The Man Without Qualities*, and said, "He is the only one who understands me." And then, almost whispering, to Silone: "Unfortunately, not even I am able to understand myself." Musil was bitter about his Swiss exile, writing to Silone that "today they ignore us. But once we are dead they will boast they gave us asylum." To Emmie Oprecht, Silone wrote from the mountains of Sils Maria on January 2, 1934, that 1933 had been a "chaotic" year. But starting a new year in the mountains was a very good thing; he was now able to think and work and find some order and clarity in his life. The mountains were more congenial to his work, far from the distractions of Zurich. "Here I truly feel myself to be young and well. A new springtime in my life has begun."

By 1933, he had settled in Zurich at the home of Marcel Fleischmann at 53 Germaniastrasse. Fleischmann, a wealthy grain merchant turned art dealer, reveled in his patronage of emerging artists and writers, furnishing his home with an impressive library and contemporary works of art. He placed a wing of his villa at Silone's disposal. Years later, when Silone had established himself as a writer of international fame, he penned an extraordinary letter to his benefactor on his birthday. Typically, what he could not express in person, he committed to the page:

13 January 1941   To Marcel Fleischmann

My dear friend,

It is often the case, and it is easily explainable, that those who, deserving very little, receive the most, do not know how to express their joy and gratitude. At celebrations they remain near the stairs or at the edge of the table, silent, because words cannot express the inexpressible, happy only if their embarrassment does not attract any attention. Even so, if I write to you, my dear friend, it is not to express the inexpressible, but to hide behind a sheet of paper the words that emotion would prohibit me from speaking face-to-face. I do not know if you are aware that January 13 was, until my arrival in your house, always a day of mourning for me: the day in which, at the age of fifteen, I lost my family* and my house. When, as an orphan, leaving my native village, my grandmother spoke certain words to me, which, at the time, I thought were prompted by pity: "Very often," she said to me, "the good Lord closes a window and opens a balcony." I could not have known at the time that on this very same mournful day of January 13, a man was already born through whom, later, I was to rediscover my own home and abandon my nomadic life; I could not know at the time that the good Lord, in place of the window that was closing, already prepared a magnificent balcony for me. And since I have no merit, and there is no external reason, no tie of race or political solidarity, nothing in common that could sufficiently explain the hospitality that I enjoy in your house, your kindness toward me has the same character that is normally attributed to saints and whose greatest praise was written by the apostle Paul. Separately I will copy for you the small verses of the apostle that are a hymn to pure, trustworthy, patient, gratuitous love. I beg you to find the invisible signatures of all the other friends whom you have helped and who are now scattered in every corner of the world, the signatures of all those to whom, like me, you have given both the bread of your table and the courage to go on living.

Yours,

S. Tranquilli

---

*Silone sometimes conflated the deaths of his entire family in the earthquake, a point often repeated by biographers.

Silone divided his time between Fleischmann's home and the libraries and museums of Zurich or the Caffé Odeon, which attracted German and Austrian refugees from Nazism. Zurich, Silone discovered, was an ideal location to carry out research: In addition to the canton library, which was connected to the other cantonal libraries of Switzerland, he used the Zentralstelle für Sozialliteratur and the great Museumgesellschaft, open from morning to late at night, with its popular *salon fumoir* bringing together scholars for conversation, gossip, and, at least in Silone's case, an opportunity for romance. It was in the Museumgesellschaft that he would meet a young Irish student who would eventually become his wife, Darina Laracy.

As a consequence of his Swiss exile, Silone's antifascism and intellectual evolution was shaped far more by the German and Austrian emigration than the Francophile antifascism of Italians in Paris, Marseilles, or Toulouse. But Silone's difficult personality often led to friction and misunderstandings.

One of these difficult relationships was with the German refugee Bernard von Brentano. During the 1930s, Silone and Brentano saw each other almost every day, either at the Caffé Odeon or the reading room of the Museumgesellschaft, where both were members. Brentano's relationship with the other German exiles in Zurich was often strained: He chastised them for repudiating only Nazism, not Germany as well; they accused him of a hidden anti-Semitism and philo-Nazism. His conduct during the war estranged him from even Silone, who broke off their friendship. Silone thought him a tragic figure.

Another writer whose relationship with Silone was fraught with tension was Arthur Koestler, who met Silone for the first time in the mid-1930s. "I very much admired *Fontamara*," Koestler wrote in his autobiography, "and I wanted to meet Silone. I found him polite but very reserved, closed in himself, wrapped in an impenetrable fog of melancholy and depression. To my great disappointment, I was incapable of finding any real personal contact with him." Koestler recalled that he, Silone, and André Malraux were often grouped together by the critics as a kind of triumvirate of ex-Communists of continental writing.

Silone could never accept Koestler's rabid communism early on ("he was a fanatical Stalinist") nor his anticommunism after the war. When they found themselves, together with their wives, in a Roman restaurant in 1948, Koestler was put off by Silone's behavior. For the entire meal, the Italian writer buried himself in a newspaper and barely spoke a word. Koestler had failed to note what the critic R.W.B. Lewis perceived was "the sorrowful comedy" of their meeting: Koestler wished to meet Silone based on what he thought was common ground that Silone never shared with him; Koestler saw the rejection of communism as a joyous moment, whereas Silone always thought of his break with the movement as the great trauma of his youth.

Even with intellectuals and anti-Fascists much closer to his own way of thinking, Silone could be difficult. From his own exile in Paris, Carlo Rosselli tried several times to convince Silone to collaborate with a new anti-Fascist but non-Marxist movement, Justice and Liberty, based on Rosselli's heretical concept of a liberal socialism. When *Fontamara* appeared, Rosselli wrote that it was "a beautiful and painful book," the work of "an authentic writer." Rosselli recommended it to all anti-Fascists and anyone who sought "a reflection of humanity in a work of art," recognizing that the protagonist of Silone's novel was not an individual but a social category—the peasantry. No revolutionary program, wrote Rosselli, could ever be as effective and convincing as Silone's book. It was, in short, probably "the best Italian social novel."

Rosselli shared with Silone a conviction borrowed from Piero Gobetti that "fascism did not fall from the sky," nor was it inevitable. The reasons for its appearance and success could be found in the pre-Fascist past and the passivity of the political parties. Rosselli recognized in Silone a kindred spirit and in shared exile a correspondence began. Rosselli wrote urging Silone to participate in Justice and Liberty. Silone usually responded with affirmations of solidarity but pointing out that he had withdrawn from active politics and propaganda. Silone refused to write about tactics or political programs; his experience with the Communists was still too fresh in his mind. The expulsion from the party was a liberation, *"una vera fortuna,"* and "not even Christ could make me speak" on things better said by others. Instead, Silone agreed to write on cultural issues such as the historical problems of the Italian revolution or the general crisis of socialism, even if, as he himself admitted, the "schoolmarmish presumption and arrogance of a Leninist functionary" had marred his previous writings on these subjects.

More important, Silone had come upon a profound revelation: Not everyone wishes to be preached to, but almost everyone enjoys listening to a story. *Fontamara* had been read by hundreds of thousands of foreigners who would otherwise have never read a political treatise or a party tract condemning fascism. "Besides, there is a large part of reality that lives within me, which cannot be extricated except in fictional form and since this is not easy for one who is completely taken with party militancy, it is only right that he who is alone intervenes to reestablish the equilibrium and in solitude entertains himself with the phantoms of his interior world."

Rosselli responded to Silone: "I understand perfectly. Your experience in the party has been too serious and tragic to transcend your reservations. On the other hand, with your books you have served and continue to serve our cause with an efficacy that your modesty causes you to underestimate but that we appreciate for its real value." Rosselli recognized Silone's fate as tragic yet insisted on his collaboration, since *Fontamara* had served the cause of freedom better than all abstract theories. Silone contributed several short pieces to Rosselli's *Quaderni di Giustizia e Libertà* but retained his distance from active antifascism. Silone was much closer to Rosselli's position than has been acknowledged; when he returned to active politics during World War II, he wrote that "today [1942] the usual term, in Italy and abroad, to define our thinking and to distinguish it from traditional social democracy is *liberal socialism.*"

Viaggio a Parigi

At the request of a friend, Silone sent several short stories to a Swiss newspaper in 1934; these were published as *Die Reise nach Paris* that same year and promptly translated into three languages. Feeling the stories to be lacking in development, Silone refused to have them published in Italy after the war. They appeared in Italian only in 1999. The title story concerns a peasant named Beniamino whom some critics have seen as a version of Berardo of *Fontamara*. "The Fox" was the basis for the novel *The Fox and the Camelias*, Silone's only novel that takes place outside of the Abruzzo (in this case the Ticino canton of Switzerland). The five stories are sarcastic and satirical, with elements of surrealism and eroticism that Silone would soon abandon.

In the prison of La Santé in Paris, Silone came to know a young worker who had made a voyage to Paris traveling by rail in a dog crate. Having lost consciousness, the young man awoke at the Gare de Lyon. Attracting the attention of some gendarmes and lacking a passport, he was promptly arrested. After a brief stay at La Santé, he was sent back to Italy. This became the basis for "Viaggio a Parigi." Twenty years later, Silone was stopped on the streets of Rome by the young man, who took him by the arm and asked, "What, don't you remember me? I was the one who traveled in the dog kennel."

Viaggio a Parigi garnered the praise of readers as diverse as Béla Kun and Bernard Berenson. From Moscow, the Hungarian Kun had read *Fontamara* in Russian and now tried to have the short stories translated into Russian as well, to no avail. Berenson recounts in his postwar diary that he invited Silone to lunch at his villa only to have the Italian writer not say a word for the entire meal.

Bread and Wine

Although *Fontamara* has had more commercial success, most critics would argue that *Bread and Wine* (*Pane e vino*) is Silone's best work. The Swiss writer Rudolf Jakob Humm wrote Silone that "a book like yours is an equation of all the forces which govern the world." Silone, though, with his characteristic self-deprecation, claimed not to have been "deceived" by the book's exceptional and "to me entirely unexpected success," for he was "well aware that the success of a book can sometimes owe more to its defects than to its merits." Written in 1935–36 and published in Zurich (as with his first book, in a German translation) in 1937, it was followed by an Italian edition the same year and translated into nineteen languages. During World War II, the Allies printed twenty thousand copies of an imperfect edition to distribute among Italian POWs. A decade after the war ended, Silone's Italian publisher issued a new edition, sufficiently revised that Silone felt it necessary to switch the objects of the title and render it as *Vino e pane*.

Bread and Wine is the story of Pietro Spina, a Communist returning from exile to gauge the possibility of revolution in his native Abruzzo. Hunted by the Fascist police, he dons the robes of a priest, takes the name Don Paolo Spada, and is welcomed by the town of Pietrasecca (Dry Stone), a place where "it's impossible to do so much as draw a breath without being misunderstood" and so poor it cannot maintain a priest of its own. The townspeople are quickly convinced of his sanctity, even though (or perhaps precisely because) he refuses to carry out the duties of a local parish priest. Without meaning to, he eventually comes to see himself as more a priest than a militant Communist, questioning his long-held political beliefs, and gradually develops a passionate but platonic relationship with the young and idealistic Cristina.

To Cristina, he secretly pens his thoughts in a journal that revealed Silone's own process of self-analysis.

> The cause of my pain is the question of whether I have been faithful to my promise . . .
>
> Is it possible to take part in political life, to put oneself in the service of a party and remain sincere? Has not truth for me become party truth and justice party justice? Have not the interests of the organization ended up getting the better of all moral values, which are despised as petit bourgeois prejudices, and have those interests

not become the supreme value? Have I, then, escaped from the opportunism of a decadent Church only to end up in the Machiavellianism of a political sect?

A curious incident in Cristina's childhood would foreshadow her tragic end. Still an infant in her cradle, Cristina was left one winter's day in the sheepfold for the warmth it afforded. A wolf entered the sheepfold but left without disturbing either the sheep or Cristina, who joked self-deprecatingly that even the wolves didn't want her. Spina, unknowingly speaking as an oracle, foretells her fate: "Perhaps the wolf realized she was still a baby and decided to come back for her when she was bigger." When Spada/Spina flees from Pietrasecca in a snowstorm, Cristina, who has found the journal and discovered his secret longings for her, attempts to follow, only to be devoured by a pack of wolves in the mountain pass.

Earlier in the novel, a meeting with Uliva, a bitter party functionary, drives Spina to despair. Uliva insists that the party, now persecuted, will, in turn, persecute its enemies. When Spina replies that it is not their ideal, Uliva is withering in his reply: "It's not your ideal, but it's your destiny." Spina attempts a humanist response, "Destiny is an invention of the weak and the resigned," but Uliva has the last word: "You're intelligent, but cowardly. You don't understand because you don't want to understand. You're afraid of the truth." Spina comes away from their meeting deeply troubled. He is not surprised to learn that Uliva is later killed in a bomb blast that may have been an act of suicide.

A major figure in the novel is Don Benedetto, Pietro Spina's old teacher, now forced into retirement for his theological heresies and for refusing to bow before the Fascist regime. Don Benedetto represents for Spina (and Silone) an uncorrupted spirituality. Silone, through Don Benedetto, solemnly concludes that the essence of modern tragedy is that one doesn't become what one wishes.

Revealing his identity to an old school friend who is now a prominent local Fascist, Spina tells him, "We live the whole of our lives provisionally . . . Freedom is not a thing you can receive as a gift." To which the friend, thoughtful and troubled, replies, "You are our revenge. You are the best part of ourselves."

But the focus of attention since the revelation of Silone's correspondence with Bellone has been on the character of Luigi Murica, a party member. Murica has become ensnared into spying for the Fascist police and goes to Don Paolo Spada to confess. "An insuperable abyss opened up between my apparent life and my secret life . . . I became obsessed with the idea that my situation was irremediable. I felt condemned. There was nothing I could do. It was my destiny." Yet by an inexplicable stroke of luck, Murica went first to see Don Benedetto, who told him that "nothing is irreparable while life lasts, and that no condemnation is ever final." The good priest pointed out that "though evil must not of course be loved, nevertheless good is often born of it." Murica is told by Don Benedetto that he might never have become a man if not for the "infamies and errors" through which he passed. Don Paolo Spada, touched by this confession, offers one of his own and reveals his identity to Murica as the hunted Pietro Spina. Murica, now in possession of a very valuable piece of information that might save his life, refuses to pass this along to the Fascists, even under torture that leads to his death. His broken body is brought back to the town for burial, and as Spina enters the house Murica's father turns to the mourners and says, "He helped me to sow, hoe, reap, thresh, and grind the corn of which this bread is made. Take it and eat, this is his bread . . . He helped me to prune, spray, hoe, and gather the grapes of the vineyard from which this wine came. Drink, for this is his wine." When the grieving old man notes that it takes nine months from planting to reaping to make bread, and nine months for the grapes to ripen, Murica's mother notes that it takes the same nine months to make a man.

While the PCI and Communist intellectuals in other countries tried to ignore the work, the critical reception around the world was intense. Typical was Angela Balabanoff, who wrote to Silone: "Dear comrade, I don't know if I've read a book filled with such anguish and anxiety as yours since my adolescence." Rudolf Jakob Humm compared it favorably to Gogol's *Dead Souls*; Thomas Mann wrote that the book was the greatest expression of a consciousness—full of love—of the Italian people and an impassioned love of liberty. Stefan Zweig and Arturo Toscanini wrote to Silone of their immense regard for the book. Alfred Kazin called it "a compassionate parable."

On the back of an August 25, 1937, letter from Philip Rahv, editor of *Partisan Review*, inviting Silone to contribute to the magazine (Rahv notes his review of the recently published *Bread and Wine* in *The Nation*), Silone sketched a brief reply to those who had commented on the novel.

> Just another word to refute a rapprochement of *Bread and Wine* with the Russian literature that flowered during the czarist repression of 1906–07, commonly known as the literature of the "God-seekers" [*cercatori di Dio*; *bogoiskateli* in Russian]. Whoever reflects a bit will be persuaded that Spina is not, from any point of view, similar to those "seekers of God." Spina was moved to distance himself from religion by the prodding of purely ethical motives. The contrast between society—sustained and recognized by the church—and his sentiment of justice, of liberty, of human dignity was too great. The same spiritual forces that led him to communism distanced him from it when communism revealed itself to him, in its real politics, in an unacceptable form. Spina is never occupied by the metaphysical problem of the existence of God, and he has no nostalgia for Catholic dogma. The only impetus that torments him and goads him is an intuition of life in which the manner of conducting himself is completely at one with his moral sentiment.

Bread and Wine proved that *Fontamara* was not a one-book phenomenon; Silone could now consider himself a "writer." Yet just as *Bread and Wine* was being published to almost universal critical acclaim, he refused the mantle of professional writer. "I force myself not to be a professional writer . . . I wish to be faithful to the first impulse that compelled me to write and to safeguard my work from the degradation that professionalism always brings. I wish to stand guard and save myself from 'Literature.'" With characteristic irony and satire, he claimed to have no personal theory of art but admired those who did. He found them all valid, even when they contradicted each other. Nor should he be charged with negligence for failing to armor himself with a literary theory or ally himself with a literary school: "If, as a youth, I knew that I would become an author, then I certainly would have armed myself with a theory, but I became a writer by chance." In an essay published in English during the war in New York and London, he refused to give an explanation of his work because "a novel cannot be explained without being demolished."

In 1936, a group of exiled Italian intellectuals came together in Geneva for a new cultural initiative: the creation of a publishing house that would disseminate their work. Nuove Edizioni di Capolago took its name (suggested by Egidio Reale) from a similar publishing venture in the nineteenth century inspired by the exiled Italian patriot Giuseppe Mazzini. Its mission was to defend freedom of thought and to prepare for a post-Fascist Italy. Contributors were Socialists, Communists, anarchists, and republicans in the Mazzini tradition. Joining Silone and Reale were Gina Lombroso (daughter of the criminologist Cesare Lombroso), who published a memoir; Guglielmo Ferrero, whose novel *Gli ultimi barbari: Liberazione* was the inaugural volume of the house; Count Carlo Sforza, postwar ambassador to the United States; Gaetano Salvemini; and many others. Silone's own *Bread and Wine* and *The Seed Beneath the Snow* were first published in Italian by Nuove Edizioni di Capolago in 1937 and 1942, respectively. Securing funds proved discouraging. Silone recalled having "forgotten that in the best cases, the Italians would more easily offer their lives than their wallets." In 1943, along with Guglielmo Canevascini, Silone helped to establish the

Ghilda del Libro, which published, among others, the works of Elio Vittorini and Ernest Hemingway's *A Farewell to Arms.*

Like a seedling breaking through the snow, Silone, even from his Swiss exile, could discern the first stirring of a post-Fascist reality. If victory in Ethiopia and the acquisition of an "African Empire" in 1936 had been the apogee of Fascist popularity, Italy's intervention in the Spanish Civil War began the long process of disengagement and eventual resistance to the regime. In the church, in factories and schools, in offices and on the farms, the Italians—through their "intrinsic spontaneity"—were beginning to take advantage of the chaos of war and the manifest abject moral and political failure of fascism to delineate a new vision for Italy. Fascism was falling into the very abyss it had created for itself: a now unbridgeable chasm between the state and civil society. Italy, which had been the first to spawn fascism, was likely to be the first country to create a post-Fascist society. The situation would be unprecedented, for Italy had "never really known a true democracy."

The Seed Beneath the Snow

While *Bread and Wine* came to be seen as Silone's "mature" work (he was in his midthirties at the time of its publication), *The Seed Beneath the Snow* was not accorded the same critical reception. Silone, though, felt it was his best novel.

Written in Zurich between 1939 and 1940, and published—again first in German—in 1941, it contradicted the pessimistic and tragic state of European affairs at the time. In fact, it might be read as Silone's most hopeful work.

Pietro Spina, broken, disillusioned, on the verge of death, has returned after fleeing at the end of *Bread and Wine* to the countryside. Still hunted by the Fascist police, hiding in a stable with the company of only a donkey, he is discovered by the peasant owner and "sold" to his maternal grandmother, who nurses him back to physical and emotional health. He soon forges friendships with two odd characters,

Simone the Weasel and Infante, a deaf-mute. In the stable, Spina undergoes a painful transformation, which leaves him spiritually stripped bare. He recounts to his grandmother how, one day, he noticed a seed germinating just outside the door of the stable.

> At first I was afraid it was dead, but I gingerly used a bit of straw to move the earth around it and discovered a minute white shoot sprouting from it, a tender, living shoot of the shape and size of a tiny blade of grass. The whole of my being, the whole of my soul, Grandmother, concentrated around that small seedling. It worried me to death that I didn't know exactly what to do to give it the best chance of survival. I still don't know whether what I did was right or not, and I still worry about it. As a substitute for the protection provided by the stone that I had moved and to shelter it from the frost, I put a little earth on it, and every morning I melted some snow to water it; and I often breathed on it to give it some warmth. That clod of earth, with that small, weak treasure hidden inside it, alive though threatened by so many dangers, ended up acquiring in my sight the mystery, the familiarity, the sanctity of a maternal bosom. And since, for lack of anything else to drink, I too had to use the small amount of snow that I could gather through that opening, I tried to make sure it was as clean as possible, though there was always a slight flavor of wood and dung, a flavor of liquid earth, about it; and the result was that in a way that small seed and I lived on the same food; in a way we became real companions. I felt my life to be as fragile, as helplessly exposed, and as endangered as that of that small, abandoned seed beneath the snow.

Spina explains to his grandmother why he will refuse the pardon from the government that she so desperately tries to obtain for him. In the end, Spina—in the name of friendship that has now replaced ideology in his mind and heart—offers himself up as a sacrifice to the powers seeking his destruction.

World War II

Although Carlo Rosselli could not secure Silone's collaboration in the anti-Fascist cause before his assassination in 1937, Silone did return to active (or at least underground) political activity during World War II. After his expulsion from the Communist Party in 1931, Silone swore that he would not return to the world of politics. His status as a refugee in Switzerland and his registration with the Swiss Police for Foreigners expressly forbade any political activity. (The Swiss had instituted these antiliberal measures in order to avoid the wrath of Fascist Italy and Nazi Germany in a desperate attempt to maintain Switzerland's neutral status and prevent an invasion of the country.) But World War II changed Silone's mind and he slowly reentered the political struggle against fascism and Nazism by working with the PSI. He and a few others established the Centro Estero (Foreign Office) of the PSI in Zurich in 1940. From there, Silone worked with Allen Dulles of the Office of Strategic Services (OSS, forerunner of the CIA) in coordinating assistance to the anti-Fascist Resistance working within Italy (hence the later charges of "spying" for the CIA).

Even in "safe" Zurich, the war could touch Silone in odd ways. A Luftwaffe raid in London on September 15, 1940, hit a warehouse near Sir Christopher Wren's St. Paul's Cathedral. The cathedral miraculously survived, but the entire first print run of the English translation of Silone's *Bread and Wine* was destroyed.

In the midst of the war, he penned an eloquent manifesto titled "The Third Front." The document was both the first issue of what was to be the organ of the Italian Socialist Party in exile and a call to civil disobedience against the Fascist regime. While Stalin was imploring his allied counterparts Churchill and Roosevelt to open a second front in the West, Silone insisted on combating fascism on the third or domestic front. While the two military fronts might attack fascism and Nazism, it was this third, domestic front, according to Silone, that would be decisive in defeating the social and political conditions that had given rise to fascism. The military defeat of the Fascist powers was to be considered only as a prelude to the decisive struggles that would unfold on the third front.

On December 1, 1942, *Il Terzo Fronte* was published. It was a trenchant critique of the Fascist regime and a call to civil disobedience on the part of Italians still living in Italy. "Italians!" it begins. "Our nation is on the eve of grave and decisive events. Military defeat is on the horizon, and with it, also the end of the hated, corrupt, and oppressive Fascist regime, so ardently hoped for by millions of Italians. The Fascist dictatorship already totters on its base of mud tainted with blood. Its twenty-year reign is a fraudulent bankruptcy, a summary of failures: a failure of foreign policy; a failure of economic autarchy; a failure of the corporate state; a failure in educating the youth; and a failure in the formation of a new ruling class."

Silone reminded Italians that fascism had promised them an empire and instead had made Italy a colony of Germany; it had promised prosperity and had reduced Italians to beggars; it had promised social peace and fraternity between workers and owners through its sham ideology of the corporate state but had instead turned a blind eye to rampant corruption, cronyism, and the sacking of the public sphere in favor of a few wealthy "sharks." The Fascist regime had promised the restoration of the traditional values of Italian society but had dragged the people into the "barbarous cult of the swastika." Mussolini had thundered from the balcony of Palazzo Venezia in Rome that when taking to the skies, the Italian air force "would darken the sun" and that Italian tanks "would make the earth tremble." But when war finally came—war that the Fascist regime had glorified for twenty years—fascism sent soldiers to the front who, while brave and full of valor, were ill equipped, poorly dressed, malnourished, and under the command of the criminally incompetent. By now, with the military failures in Greece, Albania, and the Russian front (where Italian losses were frighteningly high and from where there were reports of cannibalism), all segments of the Italian population were conscious of the universal failures of the regime. It was time for the Italian people to reestablish those spontaneous ties of spiritual affinity that the totalitarian regime had attempted to smother. It was time for the Italian people to reclaim their human dignity, their honor as free citizens rather than degraded subjects, and to reassert their own natural rights.

Silone made it clear that the PSI insisted that freedom could not be granted from above by the Allies: "Our liberation can be accomplished only by ourselves." A democracy brought about by a coup d'état led by an elite "is not a real democracy." The democratic and liberal character of the future Italian state would depend on the extent of popular participation in the struggle against fascism. While not everyone could carry arms, everyone could participate in acts of civil disobedience. Silone was quick to point out that civil disobedience was not necessarily armed insurrection or the general strike; it was rather "a fact of individual conscience." Every honest citizen must feel a repugnance in collaborating with a hateful regime and its infamous war. Civil disobedience is, above all, "a transformation of the spirit, a refusal to acquiesce to a regime that is contrary to reason and conscience." It is accessible to all and, if practiced by a great number of people, a political weapon of immense potential, a weapon capable of paralyzing the repressive apparatus of the regime and hastening its collapse.

Civil disobedience meant ignoring laws, decrees, regulations; or, when this was not possible, applying the letter of the law if, in doing so, one produced a result contrary to that demanded by the regime. Civil disobedience meant not paying taxes, or paying late; it meant sabotaging munitions work, refusing to turn over crops to the state, running the trains late, resigning from the civil service or obstructing the oppressive functioning of the state from within, students and teachers refusing to participate in the numerous ceremonies that marked the academic calendar. In short, each category of citizen should find its own manner of expressing civil disobedience.

By bringing together the political problem of the country with a moral task, civil disobedience would synthesize the exigencies of thought with the responsibility for action. It would transform antifascism—which until that point had been mostly intellectual—into an enthusiastic spirit of sacrifice, an audacious conquering of freedom. Antifascism would then become conscious of its own power.

Silone was not without some sense of the difficulties involved. He knew that in a country dominated for two decades by dictatorship and a long history of conformism, civil disobedience "was a new fact in the history of our nation." The PSI was demanding of Italians something that was "unusual but not impossible." Ideally, it would "reveal the Italians to themselves." Individuals could find through civil disobedience an escape from the "fearful atomism" through which the dictatorship had enslaved the population; one would no longer feel alone; ties of friendship, solidarity, and fraternity, all smoldering just beneath the ashes, would create a free society. And recalling the sacrifice and assassination of Giacomo Matteotti and the Rosselli brothers, Silone cautioned that "there will be victims," but paraphrased one of Mussolini's more ridiculous aphorisms: It was "better to live one day as a man than a hundred years as a slave."

Not coincidentally, the same day that the manifesto appeared, a broadcast from Radio Moscow went out over the airwaves of Europe, revealing the existence of a small cell of Socialists working in Switzerland. This was a base betrayal by Stalin since the Soviets knew the Swiss police would now be forced to arrest Silone and his colleagues. Two weeks later, Silone and the entire staff of the Foreign Office of the PSI—consisting of a total of three others—were indeed arrested.

The first interrogation took place on December 15, 1942. Immediately afterward, Silone was concerned that since the questions (and his answers) had been in German, he may have been misunderstood. Perhaps this was merely an expedient to have him write a more persuasive defense of his position in Italian; for by 1944, Silone had spent almost fourteen years in Switzerland and his voluminous correspondence was sometimes written in German.

His first concern was to clarify his political ideology. Arrested under laws directed against anarchists and Communists, Silone protested. As he points out in his letter to the Swiss federal attorney general's office, "between us and the Communists there has been—and continues to be—a struggle with daggers drawn. The Communists consider us to be, with good cause, the major obstacle and danger for their movement to come to power in Italy." In fact, Silone had worked for some time to prevent the fusionist wing of the PSI, led by Pietro Nenni, to consummate a merger with the PCI. He pointed out, not without some bitterness, that the catalyst for his arrest and that of his three colleagues had been the broadcast from Radio Moscow. In this way, the Swiss Federal Police had rendered Stalin a very welcome service.

More important, Silone was eager to clarify his own brand of socialism. During the interrogations, his political philosophy had been described by the Swiss police as "social democratic." But this was equivocal. In the lexicon of the time, "social democratic," at least for Silone, meant a Marxist, centralized, statist socialism. In philosophy, his socialism sought to counter economic determinism with an ethical foundation; in place of centralization, federalism; in economics, replacing bureaucratic statism with a pluralistic system permitting freedom of initiative and the self-governing of the producers.

Silone took upon himself the burden of the accusations against the Foreign Office of the PSI. "I declare complete political and moral responsibility for the political direction and ideological turn carried out in the name of the Foreign Office." In particular, Silone confessed to having written the call for civil disobedience and the initiative to publish a newspaper with the title *The Third Front*. In order to protect other anti-Fascist Italian exiles then living in Switzerland, Silone claimed that this had been done only through his collaboration with members of the PSI in Italy.

Silone viewed imprisonment, "which I accept as evidence of my love of freedom," as a badge of honor, "as would any other decent human being." He accepted "the entire moral and political responsibility" of all activity carried out under the aegis of the Foreign Office of the Italian Socialist Party. While not doubting the integrity of the investigating officers, he charged them with failing to understand the political and historical context of his work on behalf of the Centro Estero of the PSI. And here Silone shrewdly used Swiss history to frame his defense. For the authorities were far too concerned with the technical aspects of the case rather than "the spirit that animates it." The fact that a group is forced to make use of certain "organizational tools" is not adequate proof of criminal intent. Where political freedom has been denied, as in Italy, all opposition parties were, by nature, heretical and "criminal." This was too important an episode to leave to future historians.

Surely the Swiss authorities recognized that Silone and his three colleagues were "resolute partisans of democracy and liberty." The police themselves had evidence—in the form of confiscated letters, testimony, and published works—that Silone was neither a Communist nor an anarchist, but a defender of liberalism and democracy. And here, Silone wrote, was the "paradoxical and painful consequence" of the police operation: Both the accused and the accusers "clearly fight for the same ideal, the latter to defend democratic institutions in their own country, the former to introduce those very same institutions in their wretched country." This was one of the many "painful contradictions" of wartorn Europe. It was "a tragic, objective, real contradiction," due to the unequal development of the various European countries. The Swiss had indeed been fortunate; they had a "miraculous" advantage over the Italians in that their confederation had been born 750 years ago, while true liberty and freedom had never taken root in Italy. Noting the absurdity of a struggle between the police of a democratic state and those working for democracy, Silone wryly noted his sympathy for the Swiss police: The most difficult role was not going to prison but imprisoning those who struggled for democracy.

In the present historical context of war, Silone argued that men of goodwill could no longer remain silent. As Yahweh said to the prophet Isaiah (42:14): "For a long time I have kept silent, I have been quiet and have held myself back. But now, like a woman in childbirth, I cry out." When God loses his patience and cries out into the soul of a man, one can only stand trembling in awe. The experience, Silone wrote, was not something that could be explained; it must be experienced to be understood.

Prison afforded Silone the occasion to reflect on his turbulent life. In December 1930, twelve years previously, Silone had been "a guest" in the very same prison. Looking back on the time he passed in Switzerland since then, he marveled at the transformation of his inner self. At the time of his first arrest, he was thirty years old, had just recently left the Communist Party, to which he had sacrificed his youth, his studies, and every personal interest. He was gravely ill and without any means of support, without family, and had been expelled from France and from Spain. He could not return to Italy. "I was," he confessed, "on the threshold of suicide."

That terrifying crisis, though, granted him salvation. Recalling a passage from Saint Bernard, Silone reflected on how there are men whom God chases, persecutes, searches out, and, "if he finds and grabs them, he mangles them, he tears them to pieces, he bites them, chews them up, swallows and digests them, and he creates them as entirely new creatures, creatures that are entirely his own." Reflecting on his own sufferings, it seems that he had that very same "painful and privileged experience."

"In Switzerland I became a writer; but, more importantly, I became a man." He had finally freed himself from the "Bolshevist nightmare." In his daily encounters with the free, democratic, and peaceful Swiss people, Silone had discerned something that he had previously thought impossible. Moreover, he rediscovered a "Christian and divine aspect to the very meaning of man's existence on earth," a meaning that he had glimpsed in early adolescence but that he had lost as he grew older. This "interior rebirth" corresponded with a rejection of any ambition or desire for power. "It appeared evident to me that the highest aspiration of man on earth must be above all to become good, honest, and sincere." His work as a writer had been "the testimony of this struggle of mine and its internal maturation."

Perhaps too magnanimously, he credited the Swiss for his "rebirth and resurrection." His moral debt was so great that he had no hope of ever repaying it. He could only modestly offer gratitude, nostalgia, love. Therefore, as dark clouds gathered over Europe and then war broke out, Silone, unlike many other European intellectuals, did not abandon Switzerland. Vaunting an invitation from the Association of American Writers and President Franklin Roosevelt himself, Silone proudly pointed out that "among the refugee writers then in Switzerland, I was the only one who did not abandon the country." He stayed not only because he had come to think of Switzerland "as my second patria, as the homeland of my spirit," but because he would have considered it cowardly. He would have been proud to defend the small country, if not as a soldier, at least as a writer, for it would have been "an honor to share the same fate of this free people."

Silone maintained that he had kept his promise to the Swiss Police for Foreigners not to engage in political activity. He kept his silence during momentous events: the Abyssinian War, the Spanish Civil War, the anschluss of Austria, the outbreak of the present world war. His silence derived not only from his promise to the Swiss authorities but also from an understanding of contemporary events that "superceded that of a superficial and simplistic politics" and that gave greater significance to "other causes, more profound, more concealed, more fundamental." His books until that point (*Fontamara, Bread and Wine, The School for Dictators*, and *The Seed Beneath the Snow*) were "the sincere expression of a man who remains radically opposed to fascism and to every form of dictatorship, but for human and ideal reasons that transcend those of political antifascism."

After this impassioned defense, Silone continued with an acute analysis of the Fascist regime and its present situation. He reminded the Swiss that from the very beginning of fascism, Mussolini had to contend with political opposition. To counter this opposition, fascism had acquired the consent of large swaths of Italian society: from the monarchists to the Catholics; from the industrialists to the major part of intellectuals; from a large stratum of the rural population to certain categories of workers. But sometime around the spring of 1941, a rupture seemed to have taken place. The "triumph" of the Ethiopian War in 1936 had marked the apogee of "consensus." But beginning with the Spanish Civil War and continuing with the "Pact of Steel," the Rome-Berlin Axis, and now the humiliating military defeats in Greece, Albania, and North Africa, that consensus had unraveled. "The latent contrasts within the heart of the dominant political class," Silone dryly noted, "have been aggravated." Accordingly, the Fascist regime had "entered into a phase of internal decomposition." By December 1942, the final outcome was "no longer in doubt."

Silone had come to this conclusion based on correspondence with Italian writers, intellectuals, and workers. Some had even managed to seek him out in his Swiss exile. They did so because they found in his books "an echo of their own intimate sufferings" and "a sublimation of that suffering in a modern, humane, and Christian conception of man, society, and the state."

Fontamara, Bread and Wine, and *The School for Dictators* had circulated clandestinely in Italy "because of the initiative of persons totally unknown by me." (Tellingly, Silone did not mention his Marxist-inspired *Der Fascismus.*) It was, Silone claimed, the repetition of an old phenomenon. "The Spirit blows where it chooses and *Habent sua fata libelli*" (Books have their own destiny).

Turning his thoughts to the postwar scene, Silone examined the question of whether Italy would finally choose freedom and democracy. Here he argued against the framing of the postwar settlement as a false dilemma: fascism or bolshevism.

The postwar fate of democracy and liberty, he argued, would be determined by the working classes. Silone had returned to active politics, breaking his promise to the Swiss Police for Foreigners, partly to prevent the fusion of the PSI with the PCI. Workers, activists, and writers had appealed to Silone to articulate their fear of the submersion of the PSI within the PCI. He acceded to the "categorical imperative of my conscience," which demanded he "translate the concepts of autonomy, responsibility, and dignity into a more immediate and comprehensible language." The goal was to "vaccinate" the Italians against the "Communist psychosis," which Silone defined as "a species of red fascism."

In a famous open letter of August 1936 sent to the editorial board of the journal *Das Wort* in Moscow, while the Stalin purge trials were unfolding, Silone vehemently criticized the Russian Communists for having betrayed the workers' cause: "What is the worth of your protests against the Fascist police and tribunals? What worth are all your magnificently eloquent tirades on the basic rights of man, on the dignity of man, and your defense of culture? What moral validity does your self-styled humanism have? . . . I am in fact convinced, and I have tried to express this in all my writings, that to resist fascism we have no need of material means, nor of arms, nor great bureaucratic apparatuses, but above all we need a completely new way of thinking about life and men. Without this 'new way of thinking about life and men,' we ourselves, dear friends, will become Fascists. I mean to say red Fascists. Now, I must tell you, I refuse to become a Fascist, and especially a red Fascist."

But the nature of the present crisis went beyond fascism, which merely pushed the underlying symptoms to the surface. There had always been a fatal flaw of the Italian nation-state since its unification in the nineteenth century: the failure to "bring together the political organization of the state with the real and living development of Italian society." The postwar order had not only to dismantle the present elephantine totalitarian state but, more difficult, substitute for it a political organization that is the direct expression of the people—"a state at the service of society and not vice versa."

In his first contacts with those who were fighting fascism in Italy, Silone saw a "spiritual hunger for truth." In particular, he recalled receiving a letter from someone in Italy: "I've been thinking of [these ideas] too, in secret, but . . . I was afraid that . . . they could be heretical." Silone pointed out that from the point of view of a certain Marxist orthodoxy, his ideas *were* "heresies, but heresies pregnant with life and painful truths."

Citing from memory passages from his letters to those in Italy, Silone crafted a new vision of socialism alloyed with the ethical and moral impulse of Christianity:

The pain provoked by the persecutions ceases to be a useless expenditure of energy when the pain, with the aid of conscience, is capable of renewing and purifying . . . The persecutions can be beneficial to socialism if socialism is capable of freeing itself from the dross that over the course of its development has been superimposed on its primitive spiritual nucleus and if socialism is capable of once again becoming a movement for liberty . . . Fascism has taken from socialism its negative and materialist aspect; fascism appropriated many things from socialism that seemed essential to socialism but were not. We must leave them behind. In traditional socialism there lived, side by side, one within the other, the two figures of Christ and Barabbas. Fascism (and National Socialism) has chosen Barabbas. It is the dictatorship of Barabbas, *imperium Barabbae*. We must leave Barabbas to fascism and recognize ourselves in Christ.

Silone argued that his socialism and antifascism were not "classist, materialist, or intellectual in origin" but "essentially ethical." The traditional bifurcation of socialism into warring camps of "reformism" and "maximalism" was now anachronistic. Reformism had failed because it wished to paint "a rosy veneer over a society whose crisis was organic and structural." The revolutionary maximalists had "dreamed of a gloomy and antihistorical apocalypse."

In place of the centralized state, Silone advocated a federal democracy as "the only form capable of assuring self-governance of the people." There would be no nationalization of industry nor a state-run economy, but a pluralistic economy allowing power to devolve to the workers, producers, and consumers through guilds, cooperatives, and unions. Silone considered this activity "an imposition of the exceptional circumstances" and the "irresistible obligation of my conscience" to combat the Communist attempt to conquer the Italian Socialist movement.

His arrest put an end to an episode of his life that "I myself have always considered accidental or transitory." He was not, nor did he wish to be, a politician "in the meaning ordinarily given this word." "I am, and I want to remain," he wrote, "a writer, tied to no other discipline except that which my thinking and conscience master." Once the investigation was closed, Silone predicted that he would return to his work writing what was to be the counterpoint to *The School for Dictators*, a work he had tentatively titled "The School for Liberty." "I will complete it in prison or an internment camp . . . the place is not very important. Perhaps prison, for my spirit, is the most propitious place." He knew that the most "vivid, living texts of Italian freedom have been written in prison": from the *Consolations of Philosophy* of Boethius to the books of Giordano Bruno and Tommaso Campanella. His arrest, which forced him to abandon politics ("a line of work for which I am not at all cut out"), had obliged Silone to return to the solitary pursuit of writing. Was it not, Silone asked, "a blessing in disguise"?

Silone was not above implying a sly threat in case he and his colleagues were actually put on trial. If that were to happen, he warned, it would be fascism on trial before public opinion. "It would be," he warned, "a most instructive trial."

Before ending this memoir, Silone had to deal with a painful subject, one that had caused him "sleepless nights." He was referring to the fate of the materials confiscated by the Swiss police. Among the papers were the names and addresses of anti-Fascists living in Italy. These had been kept against all rules of underground and conspiratorial life by a colleague whom, Silone argued, suffered from a particular form of mental illness: "archival madness."

Surely thinking of his own epistolary exchange with Bellone and the never-ending guilt it had implanted in his soul, Silone pleaded with the Swiss police to recognize the "tragic consequences" that would fall upon the Italian anti-Fascists if the Italian police came into possession of the names and addresses. These were "courageous men, convinced idealists, in whom the passion for liberty burns as in the purest heroes of the democratic revolutions. For the future of Italy and democracy, these are precious men." Silone, perhaps recalling his own experience, reminded the Swiss of "the diabolical means of penetration and corruption" used by the Italian Fascist police services in Italy and abroad.

He concluded by quoting St. Bernard: "I have spoken and freed my spirit," and asserted his utter sincerity. "I hope to be read not by a policeman," he wrote, "but by a man and a Christian. That he may receive my message as a Christmas gift. If he fails to understand it, perhaps those who a hundred or two hundred years from now search through these miserable papers will understand enough to seize a spark of the great struggle of our time."

He spent Christmas 1942 in prison. A few days later, in another round of questioning, Silone confirmed the existence of the Foreign Office of the PSI, that it consisted of a total of four people, that they were in communication with the Centro Interno or domestic office of the PSI within Italy, and that the four in Zurich were in possession of a Gestetner copying machine. When asked if he had any ties with "Italian terrorist groups," Silone was offended. External relations existed with the Swiss Social Democratic Party, the Swiss Socialist Party, the Labour Party of Britain, and the American Labor Federation. All these organizations (except the first) had sent the Foreign Office of the PSI approximately 50,000 Italian lire and some 1,000 Swiss francs. From various Swiss labor unions, the Foreign Office had received another 6,000 francs. All of the lire and some of the francs, Silone admitted, were sent to the PSI in Italy.

Silone then turned his attention to more personal matters, pointing out that he had suffered from tuberculosis in the past and that at present his health was poor, that the evening before (December 28), he had spit up blood and had a high fever. He acknowledged that he had been notified by the Swiss authorities that any further political activity would result in his expulsion from Switzerland and pleaded to be allowed a cure in the mountains, preferably at Davos, where he had written his first book, *Fontamara*. He promised to abandon political activity (a promise perhaps made in poor faith).

Suffering from a pulmonary hemorrhage and high fever, Silone was released from prison on December 30, 1942. Darina was waiting for him; together they went to Davos, where he was kept under surveillance and was again called in for questioning before the Swiss courts issued a sentence on February 11, 1943. Arrested supposedly in violation of article 299 of the Swiss penal code, the Swiss judge forged a creative interpretation of the facts. The article in question charged that it was a crime to use violence to challenge the public order of a foreign state or to advocate a violent overthrow of a foreign power. Arguing that the activities of Silone and his three colleagues at the Foreign Office of the PSI constituted "a grave threat to the external security of the Confederation," nonetheless he found that the activities were "effectively limited to an ideal preparation and a distribution of advice." That is, the call to civil disobedience was directed toward individual behavior and passive resistance and was "not an invitation to violence." The Italians were guilty of illegal political activity and Silone was officially to be expelled from Swiss territory. In light of his fame as a writer, his ill health, and the impossibility of expulsion (all Swiss borders had been sealed on account of the war), he was to be placed under house arrest. Silone would indeed get back to Davos, and he was to get medical attention. But his phone calls, correspondence, and visits would all be monitored and recorded by the Swiss police.

The "memoir from a Swiss prison" was drafted on December 17, 1942. As the Italian historian Lamberto Mercuri wrote in his introduction to the first publication of the memoir in 1979 (a year after Silone's death), the document details Silone's conception not just of his political faith but of writing and life as well. It is, in short, an "examination of conscience" of a major twentieth-century writer, one who struggled against two forms of totalitarianism but whose greatest battle may have been within his own soul.

Allen Dulles and the OSS

Silone was to find a problematic ally in his return to politics in Allen Dulles, station chief in Bern, Switzerland, of the Office of Strategic Services. Silone had been introduced to Dulles through the latter's secretary, Betty Parsons, a Quaker and a friend of Darina Laracy, whom Silone was dating at the time. Dulles introduced himself as "the special representative of President Roosevelt," not as a member of the OSS. Dulles often asked Darina about Silone's opinion on currently unfolding political events. Dulles even speculated to Darina about Silone leading a government in exile from Tripoli! There is no record of how Silone responded, but it is not hard to imagine his wry, ironic smile at such a suggestion. Dulles had reached Switzerland in November 1942, mere hours before the Nazis sealed the French borders. He established an outpost of the OSS in Bern from where he kept the Roosevelt administration informed about the precarious situation in Italy immediately after Mussolini's fall in July 1943 and was a forceful advocate of the Italian anti-Fascist Resistance. By gaining the trust of important figures in the Resistance, including the first postwar prime minister Ferruccio Parri, Dulles was successful in managing the surrender of the Germans in Italy.

Silone was given both financial support and, perhaps more important, a channel of communication to the Allies. The Bern office of the OSS allowed Silone to communicate with Count Carlo Sforza, the Allies' emissary to Italy. Through Dulles, Silone was able to secure funding from Italian Americans in the labor unions of the United States as well as support from Italians abroad like conductor Arturo Toscanini. (The maestro had been forced to flee Italy after having been attacked by blackshirts at Milan's La Scala for refusing to play the Fascist anthem *Giovinezza*.) Money from the United States would be funneled to the PSI but first "laundered" through Luigi Antonini (1883–1968), an Italian-American labor organizer. He joined the International Ladies' Garment Workers' Union in 1913, and from 1934 to 1967 he was ILGWU vice president. Antonini was founder of the Italian Chamber of Labor in 1913 and of the Anti-Fascist Alliance in 1922. He also was president of the American Labor Party (1936–42) and editor of *L'Operaia*, the Italian-language magazine sponsored by ILGWU Local 25. Another labor leader in the United States, Vanni Montana, cabled Silone through the Bern office that, if all the anti-Fascist parties were to break relations with the Communists, American labor and public opinion would more easily support the anti-Fascist Resistance. Montana had changed his name from Buscemi; unbeknownst to Silone, he was also a Fascist spy.

Dulles's involvement in Italian affairs led to the more controversial manipulation of the critical 1948 national elections in Italy. Silone's relationship with Dulles laid the groundwork for accusations in 1968, and more recently, that Silone was a spy for the CIA.

Silone was given a code number (475) and various aliases ("Tulio," "Frost," "Mr. Behr," "the Man from the Mountain," and, the most commonly used, "Len"). The relationship must have been fairly close because, as Neal Petersen notes, "With the war raging, Dulles found time to interest himself . . . in Ignazio Silone's search for a U.S. publisher." Silone, profoundly moved by stories that Italian peasants were sheltering Allied soldiers from the Nazis and Fascist militias, thought to write a screenplay for a movie. Dulles, struck by the "psychological value of such a movie as well as my wish to help 475," sought to have the material sent directly to Harper & Brothers publishing house in New York. Dulles even took some heat for advocating too insistently on Silone's behalf. When Silone requested from Assistant Secretary of State Adolf Berle that the United States publicly denounce the Italian monarchy and call for its liquidation, none other than "Wild Bill" Donovan admonished Dulles that the OSS was to avoid the appearance of carrying out activities of a political nature.

More concretely, Silone—even from his Swiss exile—supplied critical information concerning the situation in Italy. For example, Silone informed Dulles that the Allies' insistence on Italy's "unconditional surrender" along with Nazi Germany was counterproductive. It was a propaganda coup for the Fascist regime and "is being used to paint a somber picture of the result of the Italian defeat; that is, extreme poverty, servitude, territorial mutilation." "Len" went on to suggest a revision of strategy: "Unconditional surrender" would be modified to signify a refusal to compromise with Mussolini and apply to the Italian people, who would be protected by the Atlantic Charter; the precise conditions of the postwar settlement would be applied by the United Nations to reflect the degree to which the "Italian people themselves help toward the victory of the democracies." There would be neither a Soviet-styled nor an American system imposed on Italy after the war; the future political regime in Italy would depend "exclusively on the free will of the Italian people." Silone tried to impress on Dulles that "from the earliest days Italian history has contained traditions of free-dom that are adequate to inspire the choice of political regime when Fascist dictatorship collapses." Silone recommended that the Allies use Count Carlo Sforza as a conduit to the anti-Fascist Resistance in Italy. Silone and others were desperate that the Allies not force them to deal with Marshal Pietro Badoglio or the king, "who have compromised with fascism," for this would lead to a bloody revolution and would preclude the possibility of restoring to Italy a true democracy. In the spring of 1943, Silone informed Dulles that the major anti-Fascist par-ties were willing to foment strikes in Italy itself.

Silone's information to Dulles could be surprisingly specific, as when he suggested that partisan forces could unite in a military action aimed against the Axis rail line through the Brenner Pass. This sugges-tion, just two weeks before Mussolini was overthrown in the summer of 1943, would prove to be prescient, as German forces overwhelmed the Italian peninsula soon after. Silone even broached the daring idea of an invasion of the Abruzzo by Yugoslav partisans, crossing the Adri-atic and landing in Pescara. In a dispatch from Bern to Washington, D.C., on July 12, Dulles cabled that Silone "states that the insurgents could hold out in the Pescara region for some time; the large stone bridge halfway between Pescara and Rome could be blown up causing the single rail line to Rome to be cut. Since there are no Italian troops stationed in this section at the present time, he believes that arms could be dropped safely and substantial numbers of insurgents estab-lished there." The militarily risky and politically suicidal project was wisely dropped.

Dulles provided Silone with a conduit to Adolf Berle; as Allied forces made their way through Sicily, Silone requested from Berle that anti-Fascist workers be permitted to "take over Fascist corporations and that publication of Socialist newspapers be authorized in Italian territory occupied by the Allies." A few days after King Vittorio Emanuele III deposed Mussolini and installed Pietro Badoglio as the new prime minister, Silone, writing to Dulles on behalf of the PSI, denounced the king, who had failed to preserve constitutional rights on October 22, 1922, and who did nothing to avert war on June 10, 1940. "Badoglio's role is to sacrifice Mussolini, to save the throne and Fascism, and lastly, to prolong the war. There is nothing but rapid failure in sight for this maneuver. The Italian people want an end to war, they want an end to dictatorship." Dulles concluded, after conferring with Silone and "other competent sources," that "the unanimous opinion was that unless the Badoglio government brought peace immediately, on any terms, the government would be promptly discredited." Furthermore, Silone convinced Dulles that "if we desired to support the Italian people," it would be necessary that the Badoglio government be liquidated in favor of one with no previous Fascist connections and no Fascist attributes."

By 1944, with an end to the war in sight, Dulles and his colleagues were already thinking of the postwar situation in Europe, as was Silone. Eager to reinforce his anticommunism, Silone sent a message to anti-Fascists in London through Dulles arguing against Pietro Nenni's proposal to fuse the Socialists (PSI) with the Communists (PCI). The newly created Italian Socialist Party of Proletarian Unity (PSIUP), created for the express purpose of preventing the fusion of the PSI and PCI, and its new party organ, *L'Avvenire dei Lavoratori* (The Future of the Workers), were committed to the principles of democracy and federalism. The postwar period offered an opportunity for a vast reordering of Italian society. To Count Sforza, Silone wrote that "it is impossible to win the peasants to the democratic cause unless there is a strong alliance in southern Italy between the Partito d'Azione and the Socialist Party for the liquidation of the latifundists and the establishment of a republic." More than six decades later, there is still debate and controversy over Silone's relationship with Dulles and the OSS, but a dispassionate review of these documents should lay to rest at least this aspect of the caso Silone.

In the darkest days of World War II, when Europe was largely under Nazi occupation and the Battle of Stalingrad had not yet ended, Silone discerned something that seemed counterintuitive: a seed beneath the snow. Speaking to intellectuals and ordinary folk who had sought refuge in Switzerland, he wrote in November 1942 for *The New Republic* that "many things which had been dispersed, buried and forgotten are returning to life."

Silone always harbored warm feelings for his exile in Switzerland. Nearly a quarter century after having returned to Italy, now a famous writer, inundated with requests for interviews from foreign journalists, American scholars, and Italian students seeking advice for their theses, Silone wrote that at times like these, "My nostalgia for Switzerland becomes irresistible."

Silone's Swiss exile had offered him a destination after passing through the "emergency exit" of his expulsion from the Communist Party and a refuge in which to develop as a writer. With no formal literary training, he spent much time in exile deeply immersed in European literature, especially French, Russian, and Middle European. He gave much thought to his craft. Among the handwritten documents in the archives is a revealing page—titled "Confessione"—listing a series of elements to consider in crafting characters in his writing. These ranged from the expected categories of "Look," "Manners," "What they believe," and "What they think" to more complex considerations such as "their directions in decisive moments" and "the most profound strata of their being and the contradictions derived." The character of every protagonist, Silone continued, must follow from an ensemble of data:

a) *Their manner of acting even (above all) in minor episodes and revelatory scenes*

b) Their manner of speaking

c) Their manner of hiding themselves

d) Their manner of wanting to appear something they are not

e) Episodes recounted by others

f) Confession

g) Judgments (true or false) of others

When he began writing in the 1930s, Silone considered "a book once published belonged no longer to the author but to the public." But he found that even after finishing a novel, having it published and read by millions of people, the characters continued to live and evolve in his mind. Hence, on returning to Italy in 1944 and considering the reprinting of *Fontamara, Bread and Wine,* and *The Seed Beneath the Snow,* he discovered to his surprise that his characters had changed. He began a process of whittling away the extraneous elements of plot and development. For example, in the original version of *Fontamara,* the saintly Don Benedetto, Pietro Spina's old schoolteacher, is assassinated by Fascists who poison the sacred wine of the Eucharist. In the postwar edition, this episode, while based on a real event in Italy, was deleted by the author because he thought it too melodramatic. Silone's editing of his novels might be likened to Michelangelo's conception of sculpture: Remove excess marble to reveal the trapped human figure within. Silone the writer removed all that was superfluous to the interior development of his characters. The result was a sparer—but more intense—body of work.

If Switzerland was where Silone matured as both a man and a writer, it was also there that he was to meet a woman under unusual circumstances, a woman who would remain at his side for the rest of his life and with whom he had a tempestuous and ambiguous relationship.

FOUR

DARINA

Better to read a writer than to meet him.
—*DARINA LARACY*, after meeting Silone for
the first time

Darina Laracy and Ignazio Silone
were a study in contrasts: she tall,
extroverted, proud, self-assured,
confident, and radiating a luminous
presence; he shorter, introverted, quiet,
often morose, full of doubt, restless, taciturn, a dark star.

One day Darina's father, who had lost a leg in World War I, brought
home the English translation of *Fontamara*. Darina, then seventeen,
who had been taught to read by age three by her paternal grandfather,
inquired about the book only to be told by her father that although it
was a beautiful book, "it's not for you." (The first edition of *Fontamara*
and the first English translations had several brutal scenes that Silone
edited from subsequent printings.) Darina, though, knew where her
father kept books that "were not for her" and devoured *Fontamara* in

one sitting. From the book's jacket, she learned that the author was an Italian anti-Fascist exiled in Zurich. A few years later, she would find *Bread and Wine* as well as *The Seed Beneath the Snow*; these, though, she did not have to read in secret.

Born in Dublin on March 30, 1917, Darina was one of four daughters and educated in Catholic schools by nuns. Tall, with auburn hair, she was a striking woman. Eighty years later, she was still bitter about how the nuns treated her and her sisters, rejecting "the superstitious nonsense I heard from ignorant priests and nuns." Their main concern, it seemed, "was to get it into my head that Protestants went to hell." Not surprisingly, at an early age she decided she would secretly be a Protestant. At the same time that she developed a wish to attend Alexandra College, a Protestant girls' school in Dublin, the archbishop of the city suddenly discovered a new mortal sin: Catholic parents could not send their children to Protestant schools. (The archbishop, she noted scornfully, was later implicated in a pedophile scandal.) Thus, by decree, she was condemned to a school where the nuns were "stupid, bigoted, ignorant, and to a large extent obsessed by sex." At the age of twelve, when she was found by the curate of the local parish to be reading Pascal's *Pensées* as she walked along the street to school and reported her to the mother superior, Darina coolly responded to both that "if God gave us intelligence, it is an insult to him not to use it." Naturally, there was scandal. Three years later, she was reading a biography of Father Charles de Foucauld, whom she would later introduce to her husband. During her first year in college, she devoured all the works of Jacques Maritain and took up the Russians, mostly Dostoevsky, and began to approach the mystics, beginning with Meister Eckhardt. One gets the impression that in her autobiographical writings (all unpublished) she sought to establish an intellectual résumé equal—if not superior—to Silone's. In interviews, she was often irritated that her husband refused to acknowledge that it was she who had introduced him to Charles de Foucauld and, later, Simone Weil.

Darina Silone maintained an enduring, though complex, relationship with her native Ireland. The trauma of the Troubles and the terrorism of the IRA were only part of the reason she criticized Irish parochialism her entire life. As early as age four (or so she claimed), Darina looked to India in search of a different "truth." As a child reading about the Black Hole of Calcutta and the first rebellions of 1857, she wrote, "The curious thing is that I felt myself on the side of the rebellious Indians. Thus was born in me an interest in India that became a passion for my entire life." Later, she called India her "elective affinity." She renounced both her Catholicism and her Irish heritage, giving up her Irish passport for a British one ("which did not deprive me of Yeats's poetry"). The atmosphere of religious bigotry and political hatred in which she grew up forced her, in conscience, "to become a heretic at the age of seven."

If her relationship with Ireland was fraught with the desire to flee its conformity yet embrace its culture, her relationship with Italy was more straightforward. In 1924, when she was seven, Darina Laracy read of the assassination of the reform Socialist member of the Italian parliament, Giacomo Matteotti. "I understood that Mussolini had had him killed because Matteotti was for liberty. I began to hate Mussolini; I cut out a portrait of Matteotti from a newspaper and pinned it to my wall next to my bed."

Matteotti inflamed Darina politically; Dante inspired her in other ways. She was "thunderstruck" by the Florentine poet, and acquaintances sometimes came to her mother worried after having seen the young girl talking to herself on lonely walks in the countryside outside Dublin, reciting Dante from memory. In a passage that strikingly echoes Silone's own autobiographical accounts, she recalls:

> During my school years I was continually punished for my obstinate friendship with the pupils from what the nuns called "the poor school," that is, free elementary school. They were dressed in rags, and their shoes, when they had shoes, were broken. I preferred their company, walking along the street to school, to that of my "legitimate" companions. The nuns considered my behavior as a form of "class betrayal."

Earning a degree in languages in Dublin, she then traveled throughout Europe, studying in France, Germany, Venice, and the Università per Stranieri in Perugia. In Zurich, she washed floors in exchange for Russian lessons. She was an omnivorous reader, "but my quest was solitary: I could not shock, I could not wound, and even later my contemporaries seemed terrified of hellfire, in which I did not believe because no good God could have invented it."

After her father had been wounded in World War I, Darina became a fervent pacifist and devoured the war's trench literature and poetry, particularly struck by Wilfred Owen and Siegfried Sassoon. During the summer of 1935, at age eighteen, she traveled to Germany to learn the language. In preparation for study there, she read Willi Münzenberg's *The Brown Book of the Hitler Terror*. When her father sent her money to purchase a camera, she immediately walked into a "Jewish" store whose window was emblazoned with *"Gute Deutsche kaufen nicht hier"* (Good Germans don't buy here). An avid reader of the London *Times* and carefully reading posters plastered with the ranting of Julius Streicher's *Der Stürmer* on the walls of German cities, Darina was fully conscious of what National Socialism meant for Germany and Europe. Some Germans were fascinated by her Nordic beauty. In Freiburg, she was introduced to university friends. One of these "good Germans," after speaking to Darina of his fiancée in Munich, jumped to his feet, clicked his heels together, and proposed to her on the spot. When Darina demurely inquired about his fiancée, he responded, "But she's a brunette, not an Aryan type like you!" Instead of accepting the gallant marriage proposal, she consoled herself by purchasing a copy of Joyce's *Ulysses*, then banned in Ireland.

With the Fascist hymn to the Ethiopian War, "Facetta nera,"* ubiquitous throughout the country, Darina spent the summer of 1936 in Italy, studying Italian. From Italian newspapers, she read of Franco's attempt to overthrow the Spanish republic. Returning to Dublin, she

---

*"Little Black Face" was an anthem sung by Italian soldiers promising a young Ethiopian girl the blessings of "Roman" civilization.

learned of a student friend who had gone to Spain in defense of the republic. Meanwhile, she failed to hide her disgust of Ireland, which sent a legion of Blue Shirts to aid Franco; on their departure from Ireland, they were blessed by Irish priests in their battle against "godless atheism."

Having won a scholarship to study at the Sorbonne, she traveled to Paris in October 1938. Her first stop was at the embassy office of the Spanish republic, where she offered her services to the Loyalists. Half a century later, she could still recall her conversation when a consular official inquired about what services she could offer the republican cause:

"Anything, except killing."

"Do you know Spanish?"

"No, but I can learn it quickly."

"Can you drive a car?"

"No, but I can learn quickly."

"Can you be a nurse?"

"No, but I can at least learn a little quickly."

"Mademoiselle, the best thing that you can do for the republic is to speak about our cause with your friends here in Paris."

Kristallnacht and the final dismemberment of Czechoslovakia forced her to a painful conclusion: Pacifism was no longer a possibility. Upon meeting a French Jesuit priest who had been interned in Dachau, she concluded that Hitler could be defeated only by force of arms. A planned trip to Krakow for September 1939 was put off at the announcement of the Molotov-Ribbentrop Pact. Then September 1, 1939, and "the world changed forever."

On June 10, 1940, when Mussolini declared war on France, Darina found herself in Milan. Ignoring her family's pleas to return home, she went instead to Rome and wrote for the *Herald Tribune* and the International News Service. Often she was the only woman present at the daily news conferences held by the Fascist press service Agenzia Stefani. Her first and only question at a news conference concerned the bombing of Coventry, an episode that led to the transformation of the city's name into a verb when an Italian official proclaimed: "Yes, we want to *coventrize* many English cities." The audacious question and its even more audacious answer found their way into many American newspapers the next day. Italian police harassed her, and the German Gestapo in Italy insistently sought her collaboration; she turned them down, but only after three ominous attempts to embroil her in espionage. In an hourlong telephone conversation, the Gestapo agent reassured her that spying "wasn't like the movies" and inquired, "Do you like diamonds? No? Furs then? Everyone has his price. The Pope has his price . . ." Some days later, meeting at a Rome café, the agent told her that her newspaper office "was full of spies" and warned her, "Something terrible will happen to that young man in Milan." That young man died a week later. "Now do you believe us?" the Gestapo agent asked menacingly.

She was pressed by John McCaffrey of the British SOE (Special Operations Executive, or military intelligence) to answer 253 questions about Italy. In June and July of 1941, McCaffrey was persistent in his amorous pursuit of Darina; when she continually refused his advances, he responded by denouncing her as a Nazi spy. Not to be outdone, OVRA opened a file on her. Expelled by the Italian government, she was on a train headed for Bern the day Germany invaded Russia. The Fascist secret police had her followed in Switzerland.

Working in the Museumgesellschaft in Zurich one day in December 1941, she was noticed by Silone. The library had heat, a welcome relief from the cold, and had hosted both Karl Marx and Lenin in the past. Silone first noticed the pile of books at her side dealing with Mussolini. Darina was trying to write an essay pointing out the contradictions in Mussolini's past public pronouncements as a Socialist and official Fascist policy. Ironically, when Silone inquired about her, British intelligence agents warned him that she was a spy. Silone was intrigued but did not approach her directly, instead sending a note to her to meet him at Fleischmann's villa for tea. "Dear Signorina, I have heard much spoken of you from my editor [a blatant lie, as Oprecht did not know Darina at the time] and it would give me great pleasure to make your acquaintance. You can come to visit me next Tuesday for tea at 4:00 p.m." Either Silone did not believe British intelligence or, perhaps wryly amused that she may very well have been a spy, was curious. As the episode in chapter eight with the Italian Fascist spy Platone will demonstrate, Silone was more than able to hold his own in their company.

Silone and Darina met privately for the first time at Fleischmann's villa on Tuesday, December 9, 1941, two days after the Japanese attack on Pearl Harbor, which apparently did not come up in conversation. In fact, there was almost no conversation at all. What little was said was spoken in Italian. Darina was overwhelmed by Fleischmann's luxurious villa and the original paintings by Picasso, Modigliani, Matisse, Cézanne, and Braque. Silone made Darina wait for thirty minutes in the parlor; she passed the time petting a large German shepherd guard dog. Silone, watching this scene unobserved, was entranced: The dog was usually ferocious around strangers. (Silone later confessed that he himself had at first been terrified of the dog.)

Dressed in a muted blue velvet jacket, Silone made no effort to help Darina feel at ease. She, for her part, was enormously self-conscious of her own threadbare clothes and worn shoes. Having just read Silone's dark satire *The School for Dictators*, she was convinced that he was an active member of the Resistance and volunteered her services. Silone, perhaps still not convinced she was not a spy, refused to accept her offer and the conversation languished. When Silone asked why she agreed to meet him if she had nothing to say, the visit ended prematurely. Darina immediately wrote to her parents of the visit, a letter intercepted, opened, copied, and diligently filed away by the Fascist police.

After their first awkward meeting, Silone suspected Darina was a spy; Darina found Silone a frightful bore. "Better to read a writer," she thought to herself as she left, "than to meet him." She had an unpleasant impression that Silone enveloped himself in figurative "peacock feathers." Yet he pursued her and she allowed herself to be pursued. "He fascinated me by telling stories the way a peacock displays his most beautiful feathers. Silone's noble feathers were made of stories of every kind."

Two more diverse people could hardly have come together in these circumstances. They did, however, share a disenchantment with the Catholic church. Darina soon confessed to Silone that although born an Irish Catholic, she no longer considered herself part of the church. She was not willing, though, to renounce Christianity. Christ, she once wrote, was "the spiritual leader fate had allotted to me." Surely Silone recognized himself in her as a "Christian without a church." But Darina refused to recognize Christ's divinity; for her, Shakespeare, Michelangelo, and Mozart "were my conceptions of the divine." It took Darina almost a lifetime to be convinced of Christ's divinity, and that revelation occurred, paradoxically, in a Hindu temple in India. "In that single moment of revelation," she later wrote, "I knew at last that Christ was divine."

After somehow assuring himself that she was no spy, Silone put Darina to work translating documents and essays. Revealing that he was indeed involved in the Resistance as head of the Centro Estero of the PSI, he asked her to translate the letters of Rosa Luxemburg for publication in Italian. She agreed: "I did quite a lot of work for the Centro Estero (translating from English and German) but of course never dreamed of compensation, though I was pretty hard up at the time. I mean, no one got any money out of it." Darina Laracy had proved herself to Silone. Giving her a copy of his novel *Der Samen unter dem Schnee* (*The Seed Beneath the Snow*), in November 1942, he inscribed it "To my companion Darina: *Unum in una fide et spe: libertas*" (United in a single faith and hope: freedom).

With Silone interned in Davos for six months at the beginning of 1943, Darina made "several expeditions" to Bern to meet with Allen Dulles of the OSS. OVRA learned of Silone's work in the Centro Estero by opening Darina's letters to her parents in Ireland. Her attempt at hiding his identity by referring to him as "S" obviously failed.

By early 1943, the Fascist police had augmented her file, noting that in Zurich she "lived a rather modest and morally correct life" (appar-

1. **Pescina after the earthquake of January 13, 1915** "Most of the dead were still lying under the ruins . . . and at night the wolves came." (Courtesy Romolo Tranquilli Jr. and the Centro Studi Ignazio Silone, Pescina)

2. **Romolo Tranquilli (1904–32)** "I could not eat a piece of bread without turning to share it with one who does not have any." (Courtesy Romolo Tranquilli Jr. and the Centro Studi Ignazio Silone, Pescina)

3. **Silone in Davos, Switzerland, 1930**
"I wish to say *two or three things* before dying, things that no one else can tell and that fate has charged me to say." (Courtesy Centro Studi Ignazio Silone, Pescina)

4. **Silone with Gabriella Seidenfeld** "My interior destruction had not been complete, neither physically nor morally. Then you arrived." (Courtesy Centro Studi Ignazio Silone, Pescina)

5. **Silone in Switzerland, 1935**
"In Switzerland I became a writer; but, more importantly, I became a man." (Courtesy Library of Congress)

6. **First page of** *Fontamara*
(Courtesy Internationaal Instituut voor Sociale Geschiedenis, Amsterdam)

7. **Darina and Ignazio Silone in the study of Marcel Fleischmann's villa in Zurich, August 1945** (Courtesy Centro Studi Ignazio Silone, Pescina)

8. **Darina Laracy Silone** "Silone was—under certain aspects—a mystery even to me." (Courtesy Centro Studi Ignazio Silone, Pescina)

9. **Silone beneath a banner of the PSIUP (Italian Socialist Party of Proletarian Unity)** The PSIUP was "a chaotic amalgram . . . a sad epilogue." (Courtesy Maria Moscardelli, www.amici-silone.net)

10. **Silone at home reading a newspaper created by the children of Pescina, echoing the last line of *Fontamara*: "What is to be done?"** (Courtesy Centro Studi Ignazio Silone, Pescina)

11. **Silone's study in Rome** "There are pages in those books that were written in blood." (Courtesy Centro Studi Ignazio Silone, Pescina)

12. **Silone at the fountain in Pescina** "If the spring is not clear, I refuse to drink." (Courtesy Centro Studi Ignazio Silone, Pescina)

Mi piacerebbe di
essere sepolto così,
ai piedi del vec-
chio campanile di
San Berardo, a Pe-
scina, con una
croce di ferro ap.
poggiata al muro
e la vista del Fu-
cino in lontanan-
za.

13. **Codicil to last will and testament** "I would like to be buried like this, at the foot of the old bell tower of San Berardo in Pescina, with an iron cross against the wall and the sight of the Fucino plain visible in the distance." (Courtesy Centro Studi Ignazio Silone, Pescina)

14. Silone's tomb in Pescina
"I have no fear of dying, only of not being conscious when the moment comes. It's the last moment of life, the most solemn of all: I don't want to miss it." (Courtesy of the author)

15. Fountain in Pescina
"They were all thirsty, but they could not all drink at once." *Fontamara* (Courtesy of the author)

ently the police were unaware of the full extent of her relationship with Silone) and that she worked as a journalist, using her knowledge of English, French, Italian, and Russian. In Davos, she taught languages in a school that sheltered Jews who had somehow evaded deportation to Dachau. There, they were working toward degrees that would permit them to study medicine and then practice later in what was to become Israel. It was these exiled Jews who, on the morning of July 25, 1943, told Darina of Mussolini's fall from power.

The Swiss police were diligent, arresting her on June 22, 1942. To their demand that she open her door at seven in the morning, she responded that no decent woman would open a door to an unknown male. The Swiss police, polite to the extreme, withdrew and returned with a female officer. Darina, reading Pascal, put down her book and was taken to the canton barracks in Zurich, the same prison that Silone had occupied earlier and would occupy again in six months' time. She was subjected to an absurd interrogation. Pointing to a letter from Silone on how to catch a squirrel, the police insisted this must have been code for political espionage. In truth, it was in fact about how to catch a squirrel. Finally, after four days of interrogation and Darina's threat to stage a hunger strike ("Considering the quality of the food there it would have been very easy"), she was released with profuse apologies. Before leaving the prison, while getting her fingerprints and photo taken, she was asked if she was a movie star. Silone, playing the part of the jaded ex-prisoner with good humor, found the whole episode very amusing. The Swiss police, for their part, found a new respect for her: "The signorina's morality is beyond reproach and she possesses an unusual intelligence." They were, though, according to a letter from Darina to her parents, "permanently scandalized by my lipstick."

The Fascist secret police were more ominous in their work, while McCaffrey of the SOE informed the Russians, who then broadcast the vital information regarding the Centro Estero on Radio Moscow.

Silone's own intimate knowledge of Swiss prisons was not without some comic scenes. Most curious was an earlier visit in December when his reputation had already been established with the publication of *Fontamara*. Prison authorities, noting the prisoner's fame, had loosened regulations to permit an unlimited supply of food, clothing, and flowers. Soon there was no more room in his modest cell, so Silone politely asked permission to share his Christmas bounty with the other prisoners; permission was granted. All his fellow prisoners were extraordinarily grateful, except for one. Silone entered his cell: "Good morning. May I offer you a rose?" "What?!" the astonished prisoner roared. "A rose," replied Silone, who had not been informed by the guard that this prisoner had just killed a flower vendor. "A rose. May I offer you a rose?" The prisoner looked at Silone, who, unlike the others incarcerated had been allowed to keep collar, necktie, belt, and shoelaces and so appeared to the prisoner to be a "civilian" and not a fellow "criminal." Silone placed the rose on the table and left the cell, while the murderer glared at it as though it were a bomb. The next day, in court, the flower killer turned to the judge: "Your Honor, thank you for the rose." The judge, understandably, erupted in a fury. It appears the accused may have avoided a verdict of murder with a ruling of "mental incompetency."

Silone and Darina finally returned to Italy in October 1944, flown to Naples on an American military plane made available to them by Dulles. Descending the steps from the plane, Silone bent down and kissed the ground. The two passed the night in the royal apartments in Caserta, guests of the Allies. Silone spent the next day on the large terrace overlooking the Capuana plains covered with golden vineyards, never tiring of the scene. With tears in his eyes, he kept whispering to himself: "What a beautiful country!"

On their arrival in Caserta, Silone immediately drafted a report that eventually made its way to the desk of President Roosevelt. Never one to mince his words, Silone began with a blunt warning: "The Allies are showing themselves incapable of establishing free and peaceful democracies in Europe." Roosevelt's public statements promising punitive measures against German industrial giant I. G. Farben—responsible for war matériel and supplying the extermination camps—

were "a ray of light amidst confused and contradictory policy," but the press had given little publicity to them. The democratic European revolution must be supported by the Allies. "This does not mean a radical and total form of Socialism but series of structural changes analogous to Roosevelt anti-trust measures." If Americans were in Europe representing the interests of the cartels and trusts and monarchical restoration and the Catholic clergy, the "result will be chaos and the birth of future Hitlers." For their part, the Italian and Swiss Socialist parties would insist that the British Labour Party call a conference of all Western European Socialist parties to confront the public with the "problem of democratic revolution in Europe." The fate of democracy in Italy, Silone insisted to his American colleagues, was bound to the labor movement. "If movement falls mainly in Communist hands, hopes for political democracy will vanish." The fusion of the PCI and PSI "would imperil hope of democratic regime." For the moment, Silone wrote, the danger of fusion had faded. "Work and bread to the masses indispensable. Freedom propaganda to homeless, starving men ironic." The current Allied relief programs were not the best solution to the elementary needs of the people. Italians, Silone insisted, must be given "legal responsibility to help themselves." Finally, he called upon the Allies to promote the formation of a constituent assembly with widespread local autonomy, for a "future democratic state will arise built by a political class with capacity for local government."

At dusk, the exiles left by car for Rome, where they were placed in a luxurious apartment in the fashionable Parioli district. But the brutal reality of the recently ended German occupation of the Eternal City hit home, literally. Answering the door one day, Silone and Darina were confronted by an elderly woman and her daughter, both dressed in black mourning, humbly asking entrance into their former home. They were the widow and daughter of General Giuseppe Cordero Lanza di Montezemolo, an aristocratic and distinguished officer who had joined the Allies and the Resistance, been captured and tortured by the Nazis in the infamous via Tasso prison in Rome, and finally executed in the notorious Fosse Ardeatine massacre in March 1944. (The

Nazis killed 335 innocent men and boys in retaliation for a partisan attack that killed 33 German soldiers the day before.) Visibly moved by the simple dignity of the two, Darina and Silone insisted on leaving the apartment immediately, going first to the Genio hotel (with no running water or electricity) and then to the Plaza (where composer Piero Mascagni had died). They lived on what Marcel Fleischmann had lent them before their departure from Switzerland.

Settling in Rome, Darina broached a subject that the two had studiously avoided until then: marriage. On the few occasions when Silone consented to discuss the possibility, Darina had expressed a wish to wed in Switzerland; Silone insisted on Rome. They were married in a civil ceremony at the Campidoglio on December 20, 1944. Although both were estranged from the Catholic church and did not agree to a religious ceremony, husband and wife attended Christmas and Easter Masses either in the church of Santa Maria Maggiore or Santa Prassede, not far from their apartment. Silone also made trips to the municipal records office in Rome and tangled with the notoriously inefficient bureaucracy to legally change his name to "Ignazio Silone." But as with everything else about Silone, this was a more complex turn of events than might appear at first sight. Two years earlier (1942), while still working for Allen Dulles and the American OSS and using various pseudonyms, but using Secondino Tranquilli for his political writings, he wrote that "after years of using false papers and borrowed names, it is odd suddenly to reacquire one's original name. This name can easily seem stranger and more unreal than the others we have used, since it brings back the years in which we were not entirely ourselves."

Darina believed that Silone married her seeking happiness, but that, in the end, "he was not capable of finding happiness." He was, she thought, suffering not only from depression but perhaps schizophrenia as well. At times, he could be "horrible," even when not in a depression; "he had no talent at all for human relationships." He could often be cruel, as when he would not permit her to renew her passport or when he was casual about his extramarital affairs. He sometimes told people, "I couldn't leave the poor, mad thing." With a frankness and steely resolve in her voice, Darina admitted that her marriage to Silone was "difficult."

They had no children, and Silone was casual about his adultery, seeming not to care that he wounded Darina deeply. This further muddies the already murky waters of his state of mind and persona. Perhaps Silone was victim of the traditional Madonna/*puttana* complex in which women fall into only one of these two categories. Where, then, did Darina fit into this schema? Some have even maliciously suggested that Silone's own mother, after the death of her husband in 1911, was forced into semiprostitution, destroying her in her young son's mind even before the earthquake of 1915 killed her, but there is no evidence of this.

Other than a brief homosexual scene in the early short story "Viaggio a Parigi," there are no overtly erotic passages in Silone's oeuvre. He had a "repugnance" for what he thought was a "fashion" for eroticism taken up "not only by wary scribblers who pander to the bad taste of the public, but also by writers of talent." Perhaps Silone was here thinking of Alberto Moravia? "In my opinion there is nothing more false than to justify the literary commercialization of eroticism in the name of freedom, while I remain convinced that it cannot be countered efficiently by censorship or any other bureaucratic means, only by the disgust that springs from a serious and profound sense of life."

Ignazio and Darina Silone lived in Rome for the entire period of their marriage. He would not contemplate living anywhere else. Like many adopted Romans, he could be withering in his appraisal of other Italian cities. Referring to tourist-favorite Florence, he once asked the American scholar R.W.B. Lewis, "Why do you live in that dusty backwater?" Lewis, who taught literature at Yale University, had fought in Italy during World War II, and had come across Silone's early novels while stationed in the Abruzzo, considered himself a "belated Florentine." He wryly describes how, while writing a long essay on Silone, the

Italian writer decided to accept an invitation for a traditional American Thanksgiving dinner with Lewis and his wife, Nancy, in Florence. This visit, announced with Silone's customary succinctness by the simply stated telegram ARRIVE THURSDAY AFTERNOON SILONE, "threw us into something of a turmoil; it was uncertain our oven was big enough for a turkey." The Thanksgiving dinner confirmed Lewis's original impression of Silone's "quizzical, darkly amused Abruzzese mind."

Silone and Darina had many differences. She had an innate love of animals. Silone, like many people from the countryside, had no particular love for animals, except donkeys, and refused her many requests for pets. It became a point of contention that Silone tried to defuse by sending her a photo of a teddy bear in March 1952 with the following on the reverse:

My dearest,

My best wishes for your birthday brought to you by this teddy bear. But, as you well know, he is mute, it's only an image. If, though, you welcome him warmly and you look at him for a while, you will clearly feel that one ineffable thing [*quell'unica cosa indicibile*] that he is charged with making you understand.

Yours, I.S.

Darina remained Silone's most important collaborator for their entire marriage. One scholar has detected a maturation and fuller development of his female characters between the three "Abruzzo" novels written before 1944 and their subsequent revisions after the war. In the postwar rewrites, the female protagonists are more developed, are more central to the plot, and have their own dynamic function lacking in the earlier versions. One cannot help thinking that the indomitable personality of Darina Laracy might have something to do with this fuller development of the female protagonists. Her first major work was translating Silone's first play, *Ed Egli si nascose* into English as *And He Hid Himself*. When she casually commented that she thought he was a better novelist than playwright, he was furious.

Silone's concept of the theater had been formed by the itinerant players, the so-called *guitti*, who traveled to small towns like Pescina, setting up a makeshift circular stage in the town's piazza, illuminated by
acetylene torches and with almost no props. The guitti, influencing the
filmmaker Federico Fellini as well, were often considered the least
accomplished actors as far as the formal recitation of lines and the
classic repertoire were concerned; what attracted Silone was their use
of dialect and their absolute refusal to be bound by formal scripts.

Darina was a fine translator of Silone's work into both English and
French. He, though, resisted all her attempts to teach him English; she
called his aversion to English "a fetish." For the entire period of their
marriage, Darina chafed in the intellectual and cultural shadow of her
husband. She published an English translation of Beniamino Gigli's
memoirs (finding the opera singer a rather distasteful person) and
translated some of Silone's later works into English. She was a friend
of Indira Gandhi, Martin Buber, and Leopold Sédar Senghor, the cultural and political proponent of "negritude." It was only after Silone's
death, which she somehow sensed as a belated gift of liberation, that
she then threw herself into various political and cultural movements
and repeatedly visited India.

As a widow, Darina spent some time in Ireland, surrounded by
"sixteen unexpectedly delightful nephews and nieces." Although she
complained that she oftentimes could not tell nieces from nephews
("they all dress the same way and have the same sort of unisex
hairdo"), she reveled in her newfound family life. Somewhat wistfully
she wrote to Mary McCarthy that "I realize that I haven't lived in a 'normal' family for a *very* long time and find that the experience is somehow helping me to become a 'normal' person again."

Although she confessed that even she, who knew Silone best, could
never fully plumb the mystery of his identity, Darina did come to
understand something about her husband's enigmatic and exasperating personality, including his need for her nurturing concern. "Often
he would seek refuge from a difficult situation by claiming to be ill,
and then he would really become sick."

They eventually settled into an apartment on via Villa Ricotti. In Darina's own words, it was a "poky, horrible little flat where no sunlight ever comes, rented from INAIL [the National Institute for Worker Safety], in the dreary and squalid district of Piazza Bologna." Even this modest apartment somehow found its way into the spying scandal. When a press conference was held in New York City to announce a sensational scoop, one person inquired why, if Silone had been spying for so long, did he not—like others in the pay of the Fascists—build himself a villa? (The most infamous example was Curzio Malaparte's beautiful house on the island of Capri.) The response, "He possessed a magnificent villa in the most luxurious section of Rome," made those who knew the apartment laugh out loud. During the time Silone was a member of the Chamber of Deputies working in the Constituent Assembly in 1946 crafting a new constitution for Italy, he was offered an apartment but was horrified when Darina pointed out the fine print in the original contract: After twenty years of paying a mortgage, they could own the property outright. "No, it's impossible!" Silone raged. "Me, a capitalist? Never!" They returned to a modest hotel with no electricity or running water. After some time, they moved to the relatively "luxurious" Plaza hotel. The couple refused a large apartment on via Barberini; instead, spurred by curiosity, Darina decided to take a look at an odd offer: the confiscated villa of Giuseppe Bottai, fascism's minister of education (1936–43) and mayor of Rome (in which capacity he promulgated and enforced anti-Semitic legislation). Bottai had been one of the more courageous members of the Fascist Grand Council to vote against Mussolini on the evening of July 24–25, 1943. (Il Duce was removed from office on the twenty-fifth by King Vittorio Emanuele III.) Bottai managed to avoid the firing squad for his vote against Mussolini (something that Galeazzo Ciano, Mussolini's son-in-law, did not) and fled to join the French Foreign Legion. Amnestied for his fighting against the Nazis, he returned to Italy in 1947. Darina was fascinated by the villa: There were trompe l'oeil books on trompe l'oeil bookcases behind which was an extensive (and very real) collection of liquor.

My first thought on entering the apartment on via Villa Ricotti to interview Darina Silone was that I was trespassing into Plato's Cave. This feeling has haunted me for years as I sought to distinguish between "truth" and the shadows thrown upon the back wall of that cave. Not that I ever felt Darina Silone was insincere or seeking to hide embarrassing details of their life together; on the contrary, she was quite open in her remarks and willing to answer difficult questions. But I had a sense that memory here could be a tricky ally in writing a biography. Most interviews were broken in two by a pause for a delicious Indian lunch, prepared and served by Darina's domestic aid, Shanta (who had a degree in economics), beneath a signed photograph of Indira Gandhi, a dear friend of Darina's.

Darina had often said publicly that she considered it her life's work after Silone's death to act as custodian of his work and memory. Yet in interviews she could be frank and even a bit mischievous. Once, when commenting—not for the first time—on Silone's resistance to learning English and his difficulty with the language, she said, "He had trouble understanding and pronouncing certain English words; words like *truth*, for example."

Darina had invited me for an interview with warm words of praise for my first book. Our first meeting in the Silone apartment in Rome, though, was not an overwhelming success. Silone's dark study remained off-limits, a sort of sanctuary where I was not invited to venture. A surreptitious peek revealed it decorated with memento mori: There were photos of Romolo, Benedetto Croce, Martin Buber, Gaetano Salvemini on his deathbed, Lazar Shatzkin (a Russian Jewish friend who had committed suicide), Simone Weil, and Piero Della Francesca's *Resurrection*. When Darina asked whether I spoke French and I answered truthfully that I did not, I caught a glimpse of disappointment in her eyes. She said she valued her meetings with Indira Gandhi more than those with writers such as Hemingway, Koestler, Gide, or Mann. Silone's 1942 call for civil disobedience, Darina claimed, was inspired by her introducing Silone to Mahatma Gandhi's ideas.

In another interview, Darina Silone was ambivalent about her husband. She claimed that the PCI did not attempt to bring him back into the fold and adamant that although Silone had met Carl Jung in 1935, he did not undergo psychoanalysis in 1929 as many articles and biographical essays repeat. Silone himself was to offer evidence that—if he did not undergo psychoanalysis with Jung—he was familiar enough with the Swiss doctor's theories to offer an essay to Angelo Tasca for his journal *Monde*. Darina Silone was far more forceful and convinced on this matter than the spying affair: She confessed that it was all a murky business.

Darina insisted that Silone's sexual relationship with Gabriella Seidenfeld ended as early as 1930 and that Silone had often been unfaithful to her, but they remained close. Silone's relationship with Seidenfeld was, understandably, a source of tension between him and Darina. In fact, when *Fontamara* was first published in Italy after World War II (by then Silone and Laracy had wed), its original dedication to Seidenfeld and Romolo was omitted. This has caused one scholar to argue that Silone was engaged in an act of erasing his brother's fate from memory, but the real reason was more venal: Darina had insisted that Silone drop Gabriella from the dedication, and Silone, caught in an unpleasant situation, decided to omit any dedication. When Darina Silone donated Silone's archive to the town of Pescina, she could not help but pen a note to add to Seidenfeld's typescript memoir, "Le tre sorelle": "largely rewritten and fictionalized [*rimaneggiato e romanzato*] by I.S. . . . there are many inaccuracies that I have not attempted to correct."

In a final series of interviews before her death in 2003, Darina reflected on her husband's ambiguous character and the most recent scandal. Having devoted the years after his death to a concerted effort to track down his papers and organize his archive, she spent her own last years grappling with the possibility that her husband had been a spy. "I am becoming aware—not just in this difficult situation—that the real document is the entire life of a person. It is necessary to give some space, a more ample sense of things, otherwise one runs the risk of losing that which is most important, the thing that is truer [*la cosa più vera*], the sense of the whole." Silone, she continued, "was—under certain aspects—a mystery even to me, but it is precisely this *mystery* that I wish to respect and believe to have done so by standing by him until the end and beyond, dedicating myself to his work."

In the summer of 2003, she suffered a stroke. Don Flavio Peloso, a follower of Don Luigi Orione who was called to her deathbed at a Rome clinic, asked if she wished to receive the last rites, and she said yes. With her right side paralyzed from the stroke, she made the sign of the cross with her left hand. Just before she died she had a dream in which she saw Silone calling to her: "Come." "Wait, I'm not yet ready," she replied. She soon slipped into a coma and died on the evening of July 25. She was eighty-six. A small Christmas *presepio* (nativity scene), given to her by Don Peloso, was at her bedside. After cremation and a simple service at the Prima Porta cemetery in Rome, her three sisters scattered Darina's ashes over the Sea of Ireland. Once asked what she thought about life, she responded simply that it was an "ethical adventure."

FIVE

The PROBLEMS of POSTFASCISM

Many of us have remained prisoners of an anti-Fascist mentality and even a pre-Fascist mentality, but the very difficult problems that we must solve are those of postfascism.

—SILONE, Speech at Salerno, November 1945

Before the flames of World War II were extinguished, Silone turned his attention to a postwar Europe. As early as 1944, he was already arguing that "our problems now are those of postfascism." A decade later, he would warn that fascism might have been defeated, but the seeds of the "moral infection of nihilism," which had been responsible for its birth, were "planted in people's consciences." Central to his concern was the desire to make clear to the Western Allies that fascism was not synonymous with the Italian people. The corollary to this argument was the necessity of reestablishing or, more accurately, establishing a true and representative democracy in Italy for the first time. Beyond the confines of Italy, Silone set his

sights on that grand dream of nineteenth-century idealists and visionaries, the formation of a united Europe.

In February 1944, Silone was appointed editorial director of
L'Avvenire dei Lavoratori, the bimonthly journal of the Italian Socialists
in exile in Zurich. The journal's motto was an echo of Silvio Trentin's
movement in Toulouse, Liberare e Federare, "to liberate and to feder-
ate" (or bind together) Europe. While editing the journal, Silone also
collaborated on the Socialist newspaper *Libera Stampa* in the Ticino.
As editor, he continued to resist Pietro Nenni's proposal to fuse the
PCI and the PSI. The foundational principle was that socialism's intellectual, cultural, and political prospects were not fulfilled in Marxism.
To the contrary, as Carlo Rosselli had argued in the 1920s and 1930s,
socialism had to find the courage to divorce itself from its Marxist vari-
ant and return to what it had been originally: an ethical and moral
protest. Silone added his own perspective to Rosselli's theory. If
Rosselli argued that a liberal, humanistic socialism was founded on
the twin pillars of "Greek rationalism [liberalism] and the messianism
of Israel" [socialism], Silone countered that a contemporary socialism
could free itself from a suffocating Bolshevism only by reviving a new
religiosity, "a socialism founded on certain Christian certainties." At
the same time, contemporary socialism would have to paradoxically
look back to the modernity of the nineteenth-century French anarchist
Pierre-Joseph Proudhon and the federalism of his contemporary, the
Italian anarchist Carlo Cattaneo.

His former Communist colleagues could not let such a critique
pass unchallenged. The editorial for the December 1943 issue of the
PCI's *Lo Stato Operaio* (published in New York because of the war) took
a moment from celebrating Palmiro Togliatti's fiftieth birthday to criticize Silone, recalling his expulsion in 1931 and calling Silone and others "a group of capitulators, demoralizers, double-faced cowards." Even
now, twelve years after his expulsion, Silone was once again mistakenly
branded a "Trotskyist counter-revolutionary."

Nine months after he assumed the editor's post at *L'Avvenire dei*

Lavoratori, the newspaper was temporarily shut down as Silone and Darina made their way back to Italy in October 1944. The new editor, Guglielmo Usellini, who reopened the newspaper in February 1945, put Silone in contact with the director Luigi Comenici for the purpose of exploring the possibility of a film based on *Fontamara*. Silone, eager to return to Italy after fifteen years in exile, could find no time for the film. Instead, he turned his attention to the first face of a war-ravaged Italy: the city of Naples.

As dusk fell on the evening of October 12, Silone, accompanied by Darina and flying with the old Socialist deputy Giuseppe Emanuele Modigliani and his wife, Vera, on an American military plane, landed at the Capodichino airport in Naples. In an interesting twist of historical fate, the pilot was Serafino Romualdi, a longtime labor organizer in the United States, now proudly wearing the uniform of his adopted country. Romualdi, born near Perugia the same year as Silone, was compelled to abandon Italy for America in 1923 because of his opposition to fascism. In July 1941, Romualdi had visited Argentina, Uruguay, and Brazil, where as a representative of the Free Italy Committee he directed a campaign to enlist the Italian population in those countries to the side of the Allies. He also worked closely with the Committee for the Political Defense of the Continent, whose main objective was to counteract the activities of Nazi and Fascist agents.

Romualdi had joined the Office of Strategic Services in May 1944 and was handpicked by Allen Dulles to pilot the plane. We don't have a record of Silone's conversation with Romualdi (probably difficult over the roar of the plane's engines), but Silone and Darina did witness a poignant scene at the airport: Modigliani, with his imposing beard evoking an Old Testament prophet, tired from the long trip that had begun early in the morning at Annecy, was sitting on the sidewalk waiting for the military car that was to pick up the small group. A woman spotted him, clearly an exile but so full of human dignity that she practically knelt in front of him. This scene "gave us the impression," Silone later wrote, "that we had not fully understood the significance of what was happening. In that old man with the great beard, she had seen *Padreterno* [God] defeated, humiliated, a power dispossessed."

Although he didn't learn of it until much later, a few days after their return to Italy a peasant revolt broke out near Pescina in Ortucchio. On October 16, peasants armed with nothing more than farm tools demonstrated for the distribution of the fertile land of the Fucino plain. The carabinieri shot into the crowd, killing one Domenico Spera (ironically, *spera* signifies "he who hopes") and wounding eight others. On May Day six years later, another peasant revolt near Pescina, this one in Celano, was put down with violence. Prince Torlonia had at his disposal not only the carabinieri but also the local police, communal guards, and die-hard Fascists. The demonstrators threw stones; the authorities responded with bullets. Three peasants were killed. The violence led to a debate of the land question in parliament where, on February 7, 1951, a decree was passed effectively dismantling the Torlonia estate and distributing the land to local peasants. Less than twenty years after the publication of *Fontamara*, the peasants' millennial cry of "land to those who work it" had become a reality.

Other endeavors were not as successful. Silone's first order of business in Rome was a meeting with the leader of the PSI, Pietro Nenni. In his diary, Nenni recounted the meeting as being very warm and affectionate with a clearly emotional Silone. Nenni claimed that Silone wished to make it clear that he considered Nenni the leader of the PSI, he agreed with the task of unifying the PSI and the PCI, and he placed himself at the services of the party. If the PSI could find no place for Silone, he agreed he would go back to writing. Nenni made note of three points: Silone reminded him that his brother Romolo had died in a Fascist prison as a Communist; that Angelo Tasca's descent into collaboration with the Vichy regime convinced Silone to rein in his anticommunism; and that a policy and politics of fusion between socialism and communism was the only way to avert a third world war.

In truth, either Nenni misunderstood or Silone was insincere. While the fusionist program seemed imminent—on November 7, 1944, the party daily newspapers *Avanti!* for the Socialists and *Unità* for the Communists published a single, combined issue commemorating the twenty-seventh anniversary of the Bolshevik Revolution—Silone, Modigliani, and Giuseppe Saragat continued to work against a fusion of the PSI and the PCI.

Both Socialists and Communists saw Silone as critical to their cause. For their part, the Communists decided to hold their fire. Togliatti declared that "it depends entirely on him. We will attack him if he attacks us." When Silone returned to the Abruzzo for the first time since his exile, the PCI of Avezzano organized a reception in his honor with the Communist cell of Pescina given a place of honor at the ceremonies. In the strategy of the PCI, peace with Silone was necessary to forge an alliance with the Socialists. Besides, the official line went, Silone was no longer really a Marxist; he had degenerated into Christian spiritualism and mysticism but was to be respected as an elderly relative with dementia is to be respected at family gatherings. When Ruggero Grieco offered an olive branch in the form of an invitation to join an "Alliance of Democratic Writers," Silone refused, thereby earning the wrath of PCI intellectuals. Writing in early 1945 to the still-exiled Gaetano Salvemini, who was then teaching at Harvard University, Ernesto Rossi concluded that if Silone and Modigliani had not arrived in Rome when they did, the Socialists would have fallen into the Communist "embrace."

In the voting on June 2, 1946, to create a Constituent Assembly and decide on a republic, Silone was elected a representative of the Abruzzo on the PSIUP list, receiving 929 votes in Pescina. He spent much of his time fending off innumerable requests for the notorious "letter of recommendation" that would magically open doors to the coveted *posto*, or fixed employment for life. One 1946 document reveals that there were, though, more humble requests. A schoolteacher from Pescina wrote to Silone describing the plight of her students, most of whom had no shoes for the winter. After a shipment of shoes arrived, her poignant letter, with the signatures of her students and their mothers and their profuse thanks, found its way to Silone's office in Rome.

To the Honorable Ignazio Silone,

The distribution of the shoes has been carried out. You cannot imagine the joy of the parents for such a blessing received for their children. With a soul profoundly moved and grateful, we send blessings and thanks to you and your dear spouse. Sending their affectionate greetings, in testimony of your kindness, through their individual signatures,

[Here followed the humble signatures of thirty women from Pescina.]

It was one of the few pieces of correspondence from his political career that he kept in his archive. But the pettiness, venality, and corruption of the postwar period sent him into a serious despondency and he refused to stand for the pivotal election of April 18, 1948, which ushered in decades of Christian Democratic rule. He did return once more halfheartedly to the electoral fray as a candidate for the PSDI (Italian Social Democratic Party) in June 1953 and was resoundingly defeated.

Meanwhile, "post-Fascist" Italy stumbled early and badly. When King Vittorio Emanuele's choice to replace Mussolini, Marshal Pietro Badoglio, resigned in June 1944, the veteran moderate Socialist Ivanoe Bonomi took his place. Bonomi would last one year, his fall engineered by both Socialists and Communists two days after the liberation of Italy from Nazi occupation (April 25). In June 1945, Ferruccio Parri of the Action Party attempted to pull Italy out of its Fascist past. A compromise candidate, Parri had fought valiantly in the underground Resistance. When Pietro Nenni was proposed as prime minister, the Christian Democrats vetoed the idea, so Nenni and the liberal Manlio Brossi became vice prime ministers; Palmiro Togliatti of the PCI was named minister of justice; and Alcide De Gasperi, who sought refuge from the war in a Vatican library and was now head of the Christian Democrats, was given the Ministry of Foreign Affairs. But before the end of the year, sabotaged by the conservative Christian Democrats, Parri fell from power.

Silone, though, was already thinking and writing about the problems of postfascism. In July 1944, a legislative decree created the High Commission for Sanctions Against Fascism. Directed by the veteran liberal diplomat Carlo Sforza, the commission was actually composed of four separate entities: one was charged with the administration of property confiscated from the Fascists; another was to sequester profits from Fascists; a third to prosecute prominent Fascist party officials; and the fourth, under the Communist Mauro Scoccimarro, to purge Fascists from the government. A week before the liberation of northern Italy, Silone, by ministerial decree, was nominated to the central committee for the purge of Fascist journalists. Torn by a desire to sweep Italy clean of its Fascist past but wary of a commission that was in danger of fomenting its own inquisition (or perhaps mindful of his own murky past with Bellone), Silone wavered for two weeks. With the memory of Stalin's purges of the 1930s still fresh in his mind, on his forty-fifth birthday, May 1, 1945, Silone resigned from the commission. But nearly a year later, he cryptically wrote in the PSI newspaper that "we should not pretend that the work of the purge has left everyone disappointed."

Another postwar phenomenon he criticized was the ubiquitous presence of so-called anti-Fascists who, until July 1943, had supported Mussolini's regime. As in France, where after the liberation, suddenly everyone claimed to have participated in the maquis, the ranks of the Italian Resistance suddenly seemed to be overflowing. Nor was Italy to be saved by Marshall Plan dollars. In a June 1945 speech broadcast over radio, Silone insisted that "the Truth could save us," but his adamant and intransigent stance on many issues was seemingly naïve when the postwar period was to be shaped by questionable compromise and political intrigue.

Indeed, an article published in the Socialist daily *Avanti!* on October 27, 1945, caused an uproar in Italy. Titled "Superare l'antifascismo" (Overcoming [or, Going Beyond] Antifascism), Silone argued that it was necessary to detach Italian life from the negative attitude of antifascism and orient it toward solutions for a post-Fascist Italy. Two weeks later, in a speech in Salerno, he charged:

Many of us have remained prisoners of an anti-Fascist mentality and even a pre-Fascist mentality, but the very difficult problems that we must solve are those of postfascism. Most of us lack this post-Fascist mentality; what is missing, in fact, is the intellectual and moral foundation to overcome fascism and confront—with a unified agreement of will—the problems of welfare and liberty that are at the root of our current needs. If we are not cognizant of this, we will be ruined; not only the ruin of a personal anti-Fascist politics, but what is far more important, the ruin of the country.

A related problem was what to do with ex-Fascists. Almost alone on the left, Silone warned against pushing the ex-Fascists into the embrace of neofascism. Caught between two radically different currents—one that advocated a total purge of former supporters of Mussolini's regime and one that advocated a quiet absorption of former Fascists into the body politic—Silone was left stranded. "Let us leave the dead to bury the dead," he said, "and let us pose before public opinion in Italy the real problems of today and the future, inviting Italians to argue among ourselves about these problems."

Three years later in an interview with Giovanna Santostefano published as "Umanesimo tragico di Silone," he confessed that antifascism had always "gotten on my nerves" and that "there have been and there are still Italians who know only how to be anti-Fascists and Italians who know only how to be Fascists. Italy has no need for either the former or the latter."

In January 1946, Silone and Pietro Nenni, who had spent most of the last decade battling each other over the fate of the PSI and whether or not it should fuse with the PCI, traveled together to London, guests of the British Labour Party, to informally discuss the peace treaty being drafted between Italy and Britain. Darina accompanied them as translator. Silone, who had immensely enjoyed the airplane flight from Switzerland to Naples in October 1944, was so terror-stricken by the mirror-smooth English Channel that he spent the short voyage in their cabin. Italy's new ambassador to Britain, Count Nicolò Carandini, hosted a dinner for the Italians to introduce them to Prime Minister Clement Attlee and members of the British government. After the first course, Silone rose from the dinner table, bowed formally, and apologized: "Gentlemen, excuse me; I have an important engagement." He left, to the surprise of all present. What could have been more important than the first, tentative exchanges after war? In truth, Silone and his English translator Eric Mosbacher slipped away to watch an Arsenal soccer match.

Silone's behavior was quite different for another visitor. The Labour Party had reserved rooms for Silone and Nenni at a modest hotel, but Ambassador Carandini had reserved a room at the embassy for Nenni, and a room for the Silones at the Savoy Hotel. There, George Orwell paid them two visits and invited them to dinner. During the war, Orwell had worked on a BBC production of *Fontamara*. Later, he adapted Silone's short story "The Fox" for radio as well. An Orwell biographer proposes that Silone's story influenced the English writer's conception of *Animal Farm*. To spare Silone embarrassment at his poor English, they spoke in French.

Silone was instrumental in the creation of yet another left-wing party, the Italian Socialist Party of Proletarian Unity (PSIUP). When Nenni's candidacy as prime minister was rejected by the Christian Democrats, the Socialists were furious and moved closer to adopting Nenni's fusionist proposal. Together with Giuseppe Saragat, Silone embraced the motto "*Unità sì, fusione no.*" With the fall of the Parri government in December 1945, Sandro Pertini resigned as head of the PSI, to be succeeded by Rodolfo Morandi. It was Morandi who, in order to be convinced to take on the lead role in the party, had insisted that Silone become editor of the party newspaper *Avanti!* Editorship of the paper at a time when fusionists and autonomists were at dagger points was a precarious intellectual and political balancing act. From Harvard University, Salvemini wrote to Ernesto Rossi encouraging the latter's entry into the PSI to support Silone against Nenni. But Salvemini had enough wisdom to see that "Silone doesn't have the qualities of a practical and cunning political man but he is a splendid moral and intellectual figure."

The crisis came in April 1946 at the party congress in Florence, where Silone hardly spoke at all. That spring, Vittorio Emanuele III, in a desperate attempt to save the Savoy dynasty and the monarchy in Italy, abdicated in favor of his son, Umberto, who darkly hinted at a coup d'état. On June 2, Italians went to the polls to decide on a Constituent Assembly that was to remake the laws of Italy, draft a constitution, and determine the fate of the monarchy. The results were not promulgated until three days later. By a narrow margin, Italians had decided to reject the monarchy and become a republic (the vote in the south had a majority voting to keep the monarchy). Silone, elected to the Chamber of Deputies, wrote the lead editorial for a special edition of *Avanti!* that was on the newsstands one hour after the results were known. The vote to end the monarchy was

> an act of life, an act of good health, an act of liberation, an act of creation, a new form for a new reality. It is a birth: a presence, a revelation, an apparition, something that has come from afar and will go far. But it is also, and above all, an act of modernity: Italian society has liberated itself from a parasitic superstructure of feudal origins and it has liberated itself primarily through the efforts of the working class, which are the principal motive forces of every true progress in our era; and for this reason we are little inclined to tolerate the rhetorical, classical, or Risorgimental reminiscences or we tolerate just that little bit that is permitted standing by the crib of a newborn, speaking of the dead . . . It is the happiest day in the long history of our country.

Of course, no event could live up to such fervent desires, and Silone soon came to realize that the republic, much as it may have wished to, could not so easily disentangle itself from more than two decades of fascism. Nor could Italy and the Italians so easily shed their culpability.

The hopes raised by the PSIUP were soon dashed. In an autobiographical essay he wrote of the "sad epilogue" of postwar Italian socialism. The PSIUP, in particular, was a disappointment. "Instead of the hoped-for free and ardent Socialist movement, open to all the new forces that sprang forth from the war and the Resistance, it was a chaotic amalgam, under the tutelage of the Communists," paralyzed by the debate between "fusionists" and "autonomists" and then torn to pieces by the "inevitable and disastrous schisms." Once again, Italian socialism had lost a golden opportunity.

The Ghost of Francesco Zauri

It was May 1946 and Silone was busy working in the offices of *Avanti!* on via Gregoriana in Rome. The convention of the PSIUP had just been held a month earlier in Florence, and Silone was struggling to keep socialism free from a fusion with the PCI. A staffer approached and said a vagrant with a wild beard and long hair was in the reception area asking for the esteemed writer. Silone, wary, hesitated but finally agreed to meet the *barbone*. Standing before him was Francesco Zauri of Pescina, the man unjustly accused of murder nearly half a century before. On behalf of Zauri's illiterate mother, Silone had penned her letters to the incarcerated son. The young Silone came to be convinced of the man's innocence, even though the consensus of the town was unanimous: Zauri was indeed guilty and there was no more to be said about the affair. Unknown to anyone else, including his parents, Silone struggled to translate a mother's concern and anguish into letters that could pass the prison censors.

Zauri had been condemned in 1898 and sentenced to ten years' solitary confinement and life imprisonment. As his fictional counterpart, Luca Sabatini in *The Secret of Luca*, pointed out, the difference between life with the general prison population and "existence" in solitary confinement was greater than the difference between life in prison and freedom. It was only in 1908 that Zauri was permitted correspondence with his mother, who approached Silone with the customary deference of the illiterate poor when dealing with the town's bourgeoisie. He read the prisoner's letters out loud to Zauri's mother and carefully penned her replies. Silone was overwhelmed with the burden, tormented by his responsibility, buoyed by a certainty of Zauri's innocence, proud of his secret, and quietly thrilled to have been asked to assume such an important task.

Now, nearly a half century later, the true murderer had given a deathbed confession, complete with details that were known only to the perpetrator. Zauri was released from the prison on the island of Elba at three in the morning, told he was pardoned (to which he angrily protested, pointing out that being pardoned assumed guilt, whereas he had been proven innocent), and sent on his way with a hundred lire in his pocket. He made his way to Piombino and was given a train ticket for Pescina via Rome. Sitting in his third-class compartment, Zauri could think of only one name: Secondino Tranquilli, the young boy who had so earnestly and scrupulously written on his mother's behalf. By one of those inexplicable twists of fate that are more characteristic of nineteenth-century romantic novels than real life, Zauri had met Romolo Tranquilli in prison. At the mention of the surname, Zauri struck up a conversation with Silone's brother and was later told that Secondino was no longer a student in Pescina but a world-famous writer by the name of Ignazio Silone. Discreetly tapping the shoulder of the train passenger in front of him, Zauri asked if the gentleman might know of a certain Ignazio Silone. And again, with an improbable novelistic twist, the passenger replied that Silone lived in Rome and edited the Socialist paper *Avanti!* Armed with this information, Zauri presented himself at the editorial offices as a specter from another world.

Silone took Zauri home to Darina, who saw before her a veritable Rip Van Winkle. After washing and shaving and changing his clothes, Silone, along with Darina, took Zauri to an open-air lunch in a trattoria. To Darina's question as to what most struck him as different after almost a half century in prison, Zauri responded dryly, "the women." She wondered aloud how he managed to survive a decade in solitary confinement. Before their insistent staring, he apologized for eating with his hands, as five decades of meals without a knife or fork had left him unable to use proper utensils. "I asked your mother what importance my opinion had, since I was still just a boy," Silone told Zauri. "Because you're still innocent," the mother had replied. But "from that moment on, though, I must confess," Silone confided to Zauri, "I began to doubt my innocence and that of the world."

Permitted only two texts in prison, Dante's *Divine Comedy* and the Bible, Zauri had memorized entire passages, including Canto 33, regarding Count Ugolino's tragic and barbarous end. When Silone begged to know why Zauri had refused to defend himself, the old man simply smiled and said sadly, "I'm sorry; I can't say why, I can never say why."

Zauri eventually made his way to Pescina a broken man, the townspeople refusing to welcome him back. Begging his bread, every so often boasting that he had been given a sweater by the great writer Ignazio Silone, he died a mere two years after gaining his freedom. For a decade, Silone was haunted by Francesco Zauri. Inquiring about records of the trial from officials in Avezzano, he was told in 1949 that the court documents had been destroyed in an Allied bombing raid during the war. Silone's torment was only partially exorcised with the publication of *The Secret of Luca* in 1956.

In July 1956, a month after the proclamation of the republic, Silone resigned as editor of *Avanti!* His farewell editorial, "Autocritica," did not spare the Socialists or the Italians from some severe criticism. The modern mass political parties, he wrote, were perhaps the worst possible vehicle for democracy. Constituting an oligarchical trust, they suffocated the spontaneity of social and political life, placing obedience to the party line above the most demanding moral imperatives of the individual conscience. Echoing Massimo D'Azeglio's famous remark after the unification of Italy—"We have made Italy; now we must make

Italians"—Silone implied that fascism had been defeated but the Italians had still not yet constituted themselves as "post-Fascists." As the Constituent Assembly began its work to craft a constitution and new legal and political foundations, "everything is open to debate. Even ourselves."

The Socialists continued their suicidal propensity, dividing once again. By now there were three major Socialist parties: the once-venerable PSI, the PSIUP, and the PSLI (Socialist Party of Italian Workers). Postwar Italian politics, in Silone's eyes, was incapable of fostering the moral, ethical, and cultural regeneration necessary after the horrors of Auschwitz and Hiroshima. (Silone did not place these two on the same moral plane; he meant only that war generated moral catastrophes all around.) An incident at the PSI's national congress in the summer of 1945 was emblematic: Nenni had announced from his political pulpit a policy of *politique d'abord* ("politics above all else," a phrase adopted, ominously, from Charles Maurras). Silone was indignant and outraged, believing the policy to be not only reactionary but even immoral. Before politics there were certain fundamental truths; there was culture, there was history, there were the people. Thirteen years later, in an open letter to the leader of the leftist Republican Party and editor of the literary journal *La Nuova Antologia*, Giovanni Spadolini (later the first postwar Italian prime minister not from the dominant Christian Democratic Party), Silone proposed an alternative to Nenni's formula: *societé d'abord*. Silone had already discerned the suffocating power of the political parties in Italian society that subsumed all of culture under their oppressive weight, crushing civil society.

So disillusioned was Silone by politics that he declined the plum invitation to be ambassador to France, instead deciding to launch another cultural journal, *Europa Socialista*. In an attempt to resuscitate European socialism, Silone invited writers and politicians from all the various Socialist currents in Italy (there were at least a half dozen) as well as European writers of such stature as André Malraux. Binding them all together were three threads: The failure of the Socialist movement in Italy was caused by its inability to distinguish itself from the Communist Party and to imitate the evolution of the Socialist Party in France, Belgium, or Switzerland; "culture" could not be subsumed under "politics"; and the grand project of European socialism after the war must be the political unification of the Continent.

In October 1946 at the Teatro Eliseo in Rome, leading Italian intellectuals such as Luigi Einaudi, Gaetano Salvemini (recently returned from exile in America), Ferruccio Parri, and Piero Calamandrei convened a conference on the prospects for European unity and peace. For Silone, it remained to be seen if the "revolution of our time" would be able to synthesize the necessity for collective well-being and the cultural values of the past. In the twentieth century, bureaucratic collectivism and "*tecnocrazia*" threatened the "insuperable values" of ancient Greece, Christianity, and the liberal revolutions of the seventeenth and eighteenth centuries. "If we do not make 'Europe,'" Silone concluded, "our generation will have to consider itself a failure." He often returned to this political and moral imperative in the immediate postwar period. "Together with the social question, the unification of Europe is the fundamental political task of our generation. If we do not solve this problem our generation can consider itself an historic failure."

Late winter and early spring of 1947 saw yet another political crisis unfolding for the new republic. Prime Minister Alcide De Gasperi presided over a coalition government that included the Christian Democrats with the PSI and PCI, all in uneasy alliance. These latter two practically came to blows over the contested article proposed for the new constitution formally recognizing the Lateran Accords, which strengthened the position of the Holy See and established Catholicism as the official religion of Italy. Surprisingly, Togliatti and the Communists voted to include the accords while the Socialists were vehemently opposed. De Gasperi, that wily politician, took advantage of the split to dismiss both from the governing coalition. In their place, he invited the liberals and neo-Fascists.

By 1948, Silone was disillusioned with the state of Italian politics. It had become apparent that the aspirations embedded in the Resistance as a second Risorgimento, finally uniting Italians, would fail. He refused to stand as a candidate in the April election but did not retire from the electoral fray. He challenged Nenni to a public debate on the merits of joining the PSI with the PCI, but the debate never took place. Four days earlier, Silone had delivered a speech in Milan that argued for the formation of a third party between the PSI and the PCI while recognizing that modern mass politics could not escape from its inherent sterility. It was a tragic and vicious circle: A political solution was necessary but from institutions that were structurally and intellectually incapable of offering real solutions.

"We are surely the people who have been defeated more than anyone else," Silone lamented in Milan. He had believed that it was possible to remain within the traditional parties and transform them from within; he had the illusion that it would have been possible to avoid the division of Italian politics into two warring camps, one under the protection of America, the other under the patronage of the USSR; he had the illusion that the church might play a political role in the new republic different from its traditional one. All in vain. Most bitter was his disillusionment with the political parties. One no longer joined a political party because of a certain view of the world. The mainstream parties now had to promise social welfare, a job from which one could not be fired, and vacations for one and his family. The modern mass political party had become, for Silone, nothing more than a surrogate for the paternalistic state.

Thirty years later, the writer Geno Pampaloni recalled the speech and its effects. Silone rose and began to speak, slowly, in a low voice with frequent coughs that reminded listeners of his battle with tuberculosis. But what most struck his listeners was that out of an "inexorable recognition of defeat," Silone derived not resignation or despair but, on the contrary, "a liberating force of faith, a corroborative strength."

In the spring 1948 elections, Silone opposed the PSI tactic of alliance with PCI, and when the results were tabulated, he was shown to have been prescient: The DC won with 48.7 percent of the vote, over-whelming the combined PSI-PCI list with 30.7 percent. Within the combined list, the Socialists managed only 42 seats in the Chamber of Deputies as opposed to 141 for the PCI; two years earlier, those num-bers had been 114 for the PSI and 109 for the PCI. It was, in short, a catastrophic defeat for the left and a humiliation for the Socialists. Things would only get worse: On July 14, an attempt was made on Togliatti's life as he was leaving the Chamber of Deputies, and the nation appeared to be on the brink of civil war.

Silone increasingly turned his attention away from domestic poli-tics to European affairs and signed the manifesto "Europe, Culture, Freedom" drafted by the historian of antiquity Gaetano De Sanctis and promoted by the philosopher Benedetto Croce. While a Socialist dep-uty in parliament, Silone never neglected his contact and work with various cultural entities in Italy and Europe. One that was close to his heart was the Amici dell'Università, of which he became president. The "friends" of the university included such prominent intellectuals as the liberal historian Guido De Ruggiero, Guido Calogero, Carlo Antoni, and the Jewish architect Bruno Zevi. Based on the premise that a university education should be available to all and not just a cul-tural, political, and economic elite, it sought to open higher education to all Italians. Likewise, the Teatro del Popolo project, founded with Darina, organized for workers and students. This was to be not only a theater with lodgings for actors but also a foundation offering courses in the history of music and the stage. In 1949, Silone was called upon to testify as a character witness for Giovanna Berneri, the widow of the assassinated anarchist Camillo Berneri. Giovanna had been arrested and charged, along with her companion Cesare Zaccaria, with advocat-ing birth control and promulgating *"propaganda contro la procreazione."* Silone wrote to the presiding judge in Naples that Giovanna Berneri led a life of selfless sacrifice and criticized the vestige of anachronistic laws left over from the Fascist regime's demographic campaign known as the "Battle of the Births." (Berneri was acquitted.)

"Emergency Exit"

Silone's essay "Emergency Exit" first appeared in English in Richard Crossman's collection of essays, *The God That Failed*, in 1950. (The essay would lend the title to a collection of autobiographical essays in 1965.) The five other essays in Crossman's anthology were by former Communists or Communist supporters, including Arthur Koestler, Richard Wright, André Gide, Louis Fisher, and Stephen Spender. Silone chose as an epigraph for the essay a line from Dante's *Divine Comedy*: "*Non vi si pensa, quanto sangue costa*" (They think not how great the cost of blood).

The essay, delineating Silone's early enthusiasm for communism, his rise through the ranks of the party, and his subsequent bitter disillusionment, sparked a fierce international debate and ignited a firestorm of protest and recrimination with his old comrades in the PCI. The essay had already appeared in its original Italian in the journal *Comunità* in the fall of 1949. Consequently, when *The God That Failed* appeared in early 1950, Togliatti was prepared. Writing in the PCI daily newspaper, Togliatti offered an explanation of how Silone had been expelled from the Communist Party and "the psychology of a renegade." Using his usual nom de plume, Roderigo di Castiglia, Togliatti argued in another essay that Silone's criticisms, as part of "the six that failed," were "enormous stupidities" that could be believed only by a public composed of "idiotic sheep." The six writers were, according to Togliatti, tainted by "an abyss of corruption and degeneration that seeks to present itself with a mask of intellectual refinement."

Not content with disparaging Silone and the other five contributors of *The God That Failed*, Togliatti expended considerable energy in criticizing all Italian intellectuals of the left who failed to recognize the historical infallibility of communism. Benedetto Croce was defined as a "blasphemer against humanity," while Gaetano Salvemini was not to be taken seriously. (The Fascists took him seriously enough to destroy his home and library and force him into exile.) The journalist Vittorio Gorresio was "a cockroach" and liberal intellectuals "pygmies of the cold war." No one escaped Togliatti's wrath, including the writers Italo Calvino, Alberto Moravia, and Cesare Pavese. Togliatti accused Pavese, who had spent the 1930s translating American literature (Dos Passos, Hemingway, Faulkner, and others) and suffered a period in confino, or domestic exile, of "not being able to make himself either an American or a Communist." (Pavese, distraught over his failed emotional life, would soon commit suicide in a dismal hotel room in his native Turin.)

Two years after the publication of "Emergency Exit," Silone received a scathing letter from Natalia Sedova Trotsky, the Russian revolutionary's widow, then still living in Mexico. Addressed to "dear Comrade Silone," the letter charged Silone with moral cowardice for failing to speak out sooner. "Your report makes a truly startling revelation, made known to me now for the first time." Natalia Trotsky's letter is a series of pointed questions: How was it that Silone had kept hidden all these years the truth concerning the supposedly "unanimous" resolution passed by the Executive Committee of the Communist International in condemnation of Trotsky? She bitterly reprimands Silone for speaking the truth of what happened at the May 1927 meeting of the ECCI twenty-two years too late. If Silone had made known the truth of what had transpired at the meeting in 1927, "or even in 1930 [sic] when you broke with the Communist Party," the revelation would have made "a tremendous impression." It would have served as a blow to the diabolical Stalinist bureaucracy; possibly it would have "saved many workers from that fatal disease that has undermined the entire working class movement." Trotsky, his widow pointed out to Silone, "would have known how to utilize the amazingly long-suppressed information."

Natalia Trotsky was all the more indignant because Silone had been one of "the very few who had the intellectual honesty" to refuse to vote against a document that no one had seen (Trotsky's criticism of Stalin's policy in China, "Problems of the Chinese Revolution," published later). Silone, she pointed out, had seen the Moscow trials for what they really were; he had, to some degree, defended Trotsky in 1937.

Why then this delay? "Is it possible that there is some good explanation for this conduct on your part? I think you owe to yourself and to others, as well as me, an explanation of this strange 'oversight.'" There is no record of Silone's response.

All this was part of a cultural war raging in postwar Italy. In 1948, Communist intellectuals had met in Wroclaw, Poland, and the following year in Paris. Organized by the Cominform, the Partisans for Peace organized the World Peace Council in 1950. Non-Communist intellectuals responded by creating the Congress for Cultural Freedom the same year. The Central Intelligence Agency noted at the time that leadership of the CCF had been assumed by "two eloquent Europeans" with very different views: "Although both had penned autobiographical essays about their breaks with the Party for a new book titled *The God That Failed*, they represented the two poles of opinion over the best way to oppose the Communists. Koestler favored the rhetorical frontal assault, and his attacks sometimes spared neither foe nor friend. Silone was subtler, urging the West to promote social and political reforms in order to co-opt Communism's still-influential moral appeal." Peter Coleman, in his history of the CCF, recounts how the founding of the organization pitted the "pugnacious and energetic cold warrior" Koestler against Silone, a "gentle socialist moralist." There was bound to be friction between the two, as Silone could never abide Koestler's womanizing (although the Italian was not exactly a monk) or his rabid anticommunism. If Picasso went to communism "as one goes to a spring of fresh water," Koestler opened the second volume of his memoirs by agreeing with the Spanish artist, but then adding "and I left communism as one clambers out of a poisoned river strewn with the wreckage of flooded cities and the corpses of the drowned." Silone's anticommunism was always tempered by the realization that there were millions of men and women in various Communist parties around the world sincere in their desire for political, economic, and cultural liberation. At the founding convention of the CCF in Berlin in 1950, as Silone took the podium, Koestler passed a note to a colleague: "I have always wondered whether basically Silone is honest or not.

Now I know he is not." When the congress was over, Koestler approached Silone and admonished the Italian for acting like an Abruzzese cafone. Silone thought Koestler was a "cosmopolitan gigolo."

In contrast, Silone's relationship with CCF Secretary-General Michael Josselson was based on mutual respect and admiration. Even the CIA noted their close relationship: "In Josselson's eyes, Silone seems to have won his debate with Koestler." Josselson, born in Estonia and educated in Berlin, had immigrated to America and served in World War II and in the State Department and was a founder of the Congress for Cultural Freedom. (Like Silone, he was rumored to have ties to the CIA; unlike in Silone's case, the rumors were true.) When Josselson died in January 1978, eight months before the Italian writer, Silone and Darina sent a telegram (in French) to his widow, Diana: "An unforgettable loss of a noble, heroic, and extraordinary friend."

At the conference, Silone took to the podium with such luminaries as Benedetto Croce, John Dewey, Karl Jaspers, Jacques Maritain, and Bertrand Russell in the audience. Silone had been reluctant to attend the inaugural congress, telling Darina that he suspected it was an American State Department "operation." Refusing to submit to or encourage any sort of fanaticism, Silone urged his fellow writers to prevent the CCF from becoming merely an organ of propaganda. The CCF was to be an encounter of free men and women, writers and artists, who refused to renounce their "supreme duty of freely speaking the truth." Rather than being among those who beg for their freedom, they were to grasp their own freedom. Silone's critique was not directed solely at the countries that had fallen behind the Iron Curtain: He fully recognized the pitfalls in the Western democracies. Learning from bitter experience that freedom was neither a natural right nor immutable but painfully acquired and maintained at great personal and collective price, he warned that "a democracy that, in the name of maximum efficiency, imitates the methods of totalitarianism, acts like the man who, through fear of death, commits suicide."

In a community of ex-Communists who extolled their inflexibility and refusal to accommodate their former comrades, Silone stood out for his insistence on dialogue with Soviet and Eastern European writers. The writer Giuseppe Antonio Borgese, representing the American delegation and writing in Milan's *Il Corriere della Sera*, noted the prevalence of ex-Communists in the CCF and warned that this was its fatal flaw. The former Communists, like Koestler, may have abjured the letter of Soviet Marxism, he wrote, but they retained the "spirit of its totalitarian crudeness." Except Silone. He was, according to Borgese, a "rare case," a Communist in name only, with "a gentle and free soul, in the ancient meaning of the words," impossible to assimilate into such company.

At the closing session of the second congress in Brussels on November 3, 1950, Silone delivered one of his most powerful speeches: "Habeas animam!" Against the absolutism of the seventeenth and eighteenth centuries, liberalism posited the concept of habeas corpus. For Silone, the twentieth century could respond to the depravities of totalitarianism only by counterposing *habeas animam*: the right of each person to his or her own soul. If, in the past, certain colleagues could be accused of a lack of imagination and foresight, now it was time to charge them. "If you still have ears, you have a sacred duty to listen." How could intellectuals remain silent when faced with the twin abominations that had afflicted and still afflicted Europe: fascism and the forced labor camps in Siberia? European intellectuals had failed in the first instance, but how could they again remain silent with the voices emanating from the frozen wastelands of Siberia? Before this "monstrous and diabolical reality," our "gravest words sound weak, pallid, banal, and inadequate." Even though our lexicon for describing man's suffering under tyranny had been tragically augmented during the past three decades, corresponding to our ability to torture and destroy human beings, it was still unable to delineate its significance. What language do we use in describing the deaths of ten to twelve million forced laborers? And perhaps what was the worst part of the horror: It was legally instituted and considered simply part of the normal bureaucratic, legal, and political system. Reflecting for a moment on those vast cities populated by slaves in Siberia, Silone could see a contemporary parallel to biblical stories of inhumanity and the ancient and desolate images of profound human suffering that so enraged the prophets. Citing Isaiah ("All that was human in him would be abused and offended"), Silone also referred to Stalin's victims as the paschal lambs whose cries are heard by no one but who atone for the sins of the modern world. This was the "tragic degeneration" of the Russian Revolution and it contained a "tragic lesson for us Socialists." The relationships between the forms of production and the culture of a society are more complicated than imagined; it was, evidently, possible that a system of collective production could lead to a system of "collective cannibalism." Yet Socialists should not yield their ideal to such a system. Although it was no longer possible to struggle for a simple repeat of the liberal revolutions of the seventeenth and eighteenth centuries—for the task was now immeasurably more complicated and difficult—it would be a mistake to forget or deny the political and spiritual victories of the past. That would be to hand totalitarianism victory.

> Many claim that our epoch will be defined in history as that which discovered the disintegration of the atom, but the Russian trials are revealing the existence of another invention, no less important: the technique for the disintegration of the soul. Perhaps we are not in a position to judge which of these two inventions is the more dangerous. One threatens the physical order; the other threatens the spiritual order. Both endanger the survival of the human species on earth.

Silone discerned in the Moscow show trials before and after the war a new (im)moral question: How did the Russians manage to get so many to condemn themselves? The "diabolical secret" that many had speculated upon was as well hidden as the secrets of the atomic bomb. Yet its results were all too clear: the complete annihilation of the self, of persons who, in earlier periods of history, could well have withstood the tortures and depravity of the czarist and Nazi regimes. Thus, the Russian trials posed moral, ethical, and spiritual questions that we were not prepared to answer. Before them, men and women of good faith must not only reaffirm the centuries-old right of habeas corpus, but given the threat now to be confronted, also must go beyond that to a more universal yet more simple and more radical demand: the vindication of the sacred and inalienable character of the human soul. *Habeas animam* meant nothing less than the right of every creature to his or her own soul.

In October 1950, François Bondy and Georges Altman of the Congress for Cultural Freedom met with Silone in Rome. The purpose was to introduce the CCF to three different circles of intellectuals: the liberals gathered around *Il Mondo*, the Socialists writing for Adriano Olivetti's *Comunità*, and the left Christian Democrats of *La Via*. Bondy and Altman were disappointed: The liberals of *Il Mondo*, inspired by Benedetto Croce's fierce anticlericalism, distrusted the Catholic church more than they did the Soviet Union; although several Socialists privately expressed support, the *Comunità* group was not enthusiastic; the Christian Democrats seemed the least interested. Nor were meetings with individuals more fruitful: Alberto Moravia, for example, was focused more on the threat of neofascism than the advance of Soviet totalitarianism.

Despite the less-than-enthusiastic reception, the Italian Association for Cultural Freedom was established a year later. A federation of almost a hundred different groups, it was held together by a manifesto written by Carlo Antoni and signed by such luminaries as the film director Roberto Rossellini, the former Communist and editor of *Il Politecnico* Elio Vittorini, Gaetano Salvemini, the art historian Lionello Venturi, and the writers Eugenio Montale, Guido Piovene, and Mario Soldati. Silone and Nicola Chiaromonte also signed on.

Josselson and others in the CCF were not optimistic. There was friction in the Italian association that was perhaps insurmountable: its innate anti-Catholicism. Croce was an honorary chair and Salvemini shared with the idealist philosopher a reputation as a mangia-prete. Vladimir Nabokov noted in a June 1954 letter to Josselson that the Italians were "drug addicts of anti-Fascism," a charge that Silone, in his own way, had made nearly a decade earlier.

A Handful of Blackberries

In his 1951 essay "Il sale nella piaga" (The Salt in the Wound), for the inaugural issue of a new journal proposed by Valdo Magnani and Aldo Cucchi, Silone pleaded for the creation of a socialism in Italy and Europe that was neither the mild reform socialism of the past nor the nihilistic state socialism of Stalinism. The key to this was a psychological rebirth for many Communist intellectuals into free men and women. Magnani and Cucchi were willing to undergo this painful process of rebirth, having lost faith in the USSR and Stalin, turning in their party cards and resigning from the PCI. They were immediately labeled agents of Western imperialism and subjected to a campaign of vilification. The big guns of the party, including Togliatti, were turned upon them. Their experience, recounted in a cowritten book, *Crisi di una generazione*, painfully stirred up memories for Silone of his own expulsion from the party two decades earlier.

When Togliatti traveled to Switzerland in 1930 to convince Silone not to allow himself to be expelled, Silone heatedly asked, "Don't you realize that one day the Soviet archives will be opened and then all this filth [*porcheria*] that is happening—with which we too are involved—will come out?" To which the ever wily Togliatti responded dryly, "If that's what is worrying you, I can reassure you: No important decision in the Soviet Union is put into writing." After the war, Togliatti had said (and written) that there could be no evidence of the Soviet massacre of Polish officers in the Katyn forest during the war because "a piece of paper with the order to execute the Polish officers will never be found." But in fact, the order—with Stalin's and Lavrenty Beria's signatures—was indeed found.

In early September 1951, as Italians were returning from their summer vacations, Silone was peripherally involved once again in a polemic with Togliatti. This was precipitated by an essay by Elio Vittorini in Turin's paper, *La Stampa*, in which he declared he was leaving the PCI. Vittorini compared his departure with that of Silone's twenty years earlier, both based on a crisis of conscience. Togliatti responded in the guise of Roderigo di Castiglia in the PCI's *Rinascita,* with some surprising praise for Silone:

> Vittorini compares himself with Silone. He is morally wrong because he is a good-for-nothing, but he is wrong for another reason as well. When Silone left, that is, when he was expelled from our ranks . . . the event counted for something. Silone helped us, by debating and struggling, in substance, not only to see many things deeper and better but also to recognize a human, determined, singular type of hypocrisy, of disloyalty, before certain facts and men. But Vittorini is useless.

Togliatti's fury was compounded a year later when Mondadori published *A Handful of Blackberries,* Silone's first postwar novel. Not only was the main character, Rocco De Donatis, clearly Silone's alter ego, but the obstinate Oscar, a PCI official referred to as the "blindfolded mule," is a thinly veiled portrait of Togliatti. The PCI was withering in its criticism. Typical of the Communist literary establishment was Carlo Salinari's review appearing in the party newspaper, *L'Unità:* "He might be an anti-Fascist . . . but he is certainly no writer . . . Holy Mother of God,* he is just a bad provincial lawyer . . . He has failed in every aspect of his life . . . Politician? No. Writer? No. So what will he have him do, this poor man?

Two weeks later, Salinari rubbed salt into the wound:

> The fundamental characteristic of Silone as a writer is impotence. He is incapable, with words, of creating a sentiment, a character, a milieu. There is always something false, calculated, insincere that prevents him from submitting to the rhythm of the narrative. His humor is as forced as that of a seminarian, his characters are as rigid and clumsy as marionettes, their state of mind is registered with the warmth and passion of an accountant; his landscapes are irremedia-

---

*Madonna santa, a rather odd term to use in a Communist publication.

bly banal and imitate stereotypes . . . The impotence of his entire personality is reflected in the writer.

Salinari used the occasion of the new novel to dismiss Silone's entire oeuvre. Going back to *Fontamara*, Salinari recalled his initial reaction to Silone's writing in 1933: "I considered him in good faith a Communist. I read him, therefore, in the proper state of mind, but I was greatly disillusioned . . . I had the same impressions, naturally aggravated, in reading this last novel." The PCI's *Rinascita* accused Silone of depicting the Soviet Union as one large concentration camp and the party as one of persecutors, delinquents, and gloomy, sinister figures. Even the Socialists weighed in with Giuseppe Petronio's review, in which he judged the novel "a failure, an ugly political gesture, and a useless artistic action." Emilio Cecchi was more perceptive, noting that Silone's success abroad and his relative critical failure at home were a scandal. Cecchi suggested that there was a fundamental problem of criticism: Either all the foreign readers and critics were mistaken, or the Italian literary establishment could not see the splinter in Silone's eye because of the beam in its own. *A Handful of Blackberries* for Cecchi was surely Silone's "most committed" novel and, he concluded, could be compared in many ways to Hemingway's *For Whom the Bell Tolls*. Eugenio Montale wrote that "Silone is one of the very few Italian novelists we have who have something to say and who know how to say it with the right means." (Among Silone's possessions was a copy of the book inscribed to Darina: "My dear, these humble blackberries as a viaticum for the journey in America.")

Silone was never the ideological equivalent of a Koestler; the Italian simply could not swing from committed Communist to rabid anti-Communist. Gustaw Herling, who had firsthand experience of Stalin's gulag, recounts how one time he convinced Silone to meet with a former Communist, the Polish poet Adam Vazyk, who had left the party in 1955. Throughout their meal together, Vazyk used a particular expression: "When I was a Communist, that is, when I was mentally ill . . ." Silone was offended and let Herling know it. "I was once a

Communist; I am not ashamed of it, and I write about it." Like Benedetto Croce, who also passed through a Marxist phase and later in life remarked that he was a better man and philosopher because of it, Silone felt that his Marxist past was not something that could or should be disavowed. Like Carlo Rosselli, Silone insisted that Marx had gained entrance to the pantheon of modern thinkers who have transformed our consciousness of the world, such as Kant, Darwin, Freud. No one could argue that Marxism was not a necessary tool for a proper understanding of the world; no one could escape Marx's influence. Silone agreed with Croce that the introduction of Marxism into Italy represented a moral and intellectual rebirth. Antonio Gramsci had remarked that "everyone is a bit of a Marxist, without being aware of it." While recognizing that Marx was undoubtedly part of modern consciousness, that the ideas and precepts of Marxism had embedded themselves in the psyche of contemporary society, Silone felt that the evolution of Marxism during the last decades of the nineteenth century and the first decades of the twentieth century had made it an obstacle to the emancipation of the laboring classes. The task for modern Socialists, according to Silone, is not to deny Marx but to emancipate themselves from his thought.

With little faith in ideology, he had even less faith in formal political parties. Yet in the last years of World War II and the immediate postwar years, he clung, perhaps naïvely, to a faith that a "spiritual polyphony" could be possible in the Italian Socialist Party. In truth, that spiritual polyphony was more an ideological cacophony as the Italian Socialists found ever more reasons to divide themselves into splinter groups and perpetuate the degenerative disease of the Italian left, political suicide.

A political party as envisioned by Silone could never survive in a modern nation. He had been influenced by his experience in Switzerland, where it seemed that the average citizen was far more involved in the daily workings of the parties and the cantonal government. For Silone, the modern mass political party had degenerated into rhetoric and proclamations, not discussion and debate.

Aldo Garosci, himself an anti-Fascist exile and later historian of the *fuorusciti* (anti-Fascist exiles), rendered his opinion on Silone: "I wouldn't have had him guiding the movement because he had a very strong streak of irony. Other than that, Silone was worth more than any of us." As Herling points out, Silone's irony did not disintegrate into nihilism; instead, it was synonymous with a critical spirit, an independence of judgment, and a "sharp and cutting humor" that although evident in his correspondence was less obvious in the novels.

It was readily apparent that Silone could not function as a traditional politician. An episode in 1951 clearly demonstrated to him that he was incapable of fulfilling the desires of his constituents. On returning to Abruzzo for a convention with the workers and peasants of the Marsica in Sulmona, not far from his hometown of Pescina, Silone dedicated his speech to outlining a vision of a new type of politician, one who would make available to the citizenry the tools necessary for education, labor, and culture, instead of the ancient conception of the politician as protector and provider of letters of recommendation. The crowd applauded warmly but, at the end of his speech, Silone was overwhelmed by his listeners with private requests for a "favor" for a son, brother, or nephew. "This made me realize," he wrote later, "that the only thing I could do was not act as a [traditional] deputy, so as not to engage in such practices." This was to be the basis, in part, of the character of Andrea Cipriani in *The Secret of Luca*. Not surprisingly, Silone fared dismally in the elections of 1953, losing his seat in the Chamber of Deputies to the Communist Party candidate. In Pescina, where the local Communist Party cell had named itself in memory of Romolo Tranquilli, Silone was jeered and received a mere 320 votes, roughly a third of the votes he had garnered in 1946. Although in one sense devastated by his loss, he perhaps recognized it as another "emergency exit." "You believe you go into politics to carry out some reform, while at the ministry there are all these old Fascists who force you to do what you don't want to do, so that in the end, you are their prisoner." But perhaps equally true was what he confessed in an interview: "I was not really fit to carry out political activity in the normal sense of the word.

For politics in that sense, I had no aptitude." It was Darina who continually reminded him after these political defeats that he was, above all else, a writer, a goad to the conscience (*un pugno alla coscienza*). With the 1953 loss, Silone left active party politics for good. A decade later, he could still be bitter about mass politics in Italy. "There are many childish things about contemporary Italy," he lamented, but also tenacious distortions from the past. The Italian parliament was a hopelessly incompetent and barren arena where political parties ruled their fiefs not very differently from organized crime bosses or Renaissance condottieri. Parliament was not the culmination of politics; in fact, Silone considered "this excessive importance" given to elections a sign of the "decadence of democracy."

Herling recounts how one day he came across a particularly troubled Silone. Apparently, Silone had spent the day making the rounds of the various offices of the political parties in Rome and had come home in a state of profound depression. He recognized that the modern mass political party—of whatever ideology—had become a voracious machine to acquire and devour funds and was divorced from the everyday lives of its constituents. Silone had discerned the first inklings of what was to explode in the early 1990s as Tangentopoli, the massive corruption scandal that brought down the major political parties in Italy. "In my day," Silone would recount nostalgically, "everyone made his contribution to the party and when there was something to discuss, we all went to a tavern to drink a glass of wine." Surely Silone could not have forgotten that ideological debates within the PCI could and did lead to expulsions, exile, and even assassinations, yet he stubbornly refused to forget that the life of the underground political radical also could summon forth moments of sublime companionship and *amicizia*.

On one thing many of his associates could agree: Silone could not rein in his biting sarcasm. Herling recounts in his diary that when Silone was introduced to Edward Ochab, the president of Communist Poland, Ochab's face lit up and he said, "How happy I am to personally meet you! I devoured your books in the prisons of reactionary Poland before the war." To which Silone responded with his characteristic deadpan delivery, "I am flattered, Mr. President. Since that's the case, couldn't it be possible to reprint my books in the progressive state of which you are the head, if not for the readers in prison, at least for those who are free?" In 1956, reflecting on the role of intellectuals in European society, Silone commented, "I have never been tempted by the ivory tower, even though I have been told that it has no lack of tranquillity and pleasant warmth."

America

After twenty days on the steamship,
we landed in America;
we lived on the bare ground,
we feasted on bread and dried fish;
we had tough work of it, but
we made Italy, built her cities.

Silone never entertained the vision of America that had sustained many Italian intellectuals and workers such as the Turinese writer Cesare Pavese in the 1930s. For Pavese, America was a wild and free land, a bit savage but mercifully free of the burden of history and individual self-consciousness shouldered by Europeans. In language and subject, American writers embraced a freedom that was lacking in Europe. Translating John Dos Passos, Hemingway, Sherwood Anderson, Whitman, and others into Italian, Pavese developed a personal mythology about America, a topography of political, sexual, and spiritual liberation. Not so for Silone. Although he felt strongly attached to Italian immigrants to America, especially those from the Abruzzo, America in his mind was decidedly an ambivalent and contradictory place. For the peasants of the Abruzzo—indeed, for the peasants of the Mezzogiorno—America had acquired in their minds the status of a myth. Letters and remittances from relatives convinced them that America was truly a country whose streets were paved with gold. But for Silone, America represented a rootlessness and a propensity for corruption and solitude that could not be overcome.

Although Silone prided himself on his supposedly flawless French and passable German, he refused Darina's repeated entreaties to learn English; he equally resisted America. A letter from Anthony Buttitta of the Federal Theatre Project for New York during the Depression cemented Silone's negative image of the New World: "America is no land to come to. It's disappointing . . . America is a crude, stumbling boy. Behind every tall building, every monument, [there is] envy." But for every negative image of America, Silone received a communication such as the following from the Reverend Cornelius Greenway of the All Souls Universalist Church on Ocean Avenue in Brooklyn, who read *Bread and Wine* "with tears in my eyes and with floodlights in my heart rekindled." Or a letter from Carmelo Zito in San Francisco: "No conventional platitudes: I too am a Calabrese cafone who ran from the mountains of Aspromonte to escape the wolf. I feel myself to be your brother, one of many such brothers who one day will answer the call from all the corners of the world. My friends and I pass your books amongst ourselves hand to hand like the sacred books of antiquity."

In *Bread and Wine*, a local peasant travels to America only to find himself nothing more than a beast of burden for another Italian immigrant who has changed his name from Carlo Campanella to Mr. Charles Little-Bell. Whenever the new immigrant would complain about the low wages or brutalizing labor, Mr. Little-Bell would tell him to "sciatàp" (shut up). This would be the only English word the peasant immigrant took back with him to Fontamara and he repeated it on every possible occasion, so often that the fellow villagers took to calling him "Sciatàp." For Silone, America silenced its immigrants. Those who somehow became successful, like Mr. Little-Bell, known as the *prominenti* among Italian immigrants, were, as described by Sciatàp, "a cursed race that reveled in the sorrow of poor people." At the tavern, he is asked what there was on the famous Forty-second Street. "The pleasure [*divertimento*] of the rich folk," he replied, closing his eyes and sniffing the air. "Beautiful women who walk around, perfumed women." While Sciatàp and the others imagine America as a sensual paradise of perfumed women, Silone was repulsed by what he saw as its open sensuality and vulgarity.

Of the few returning immigrants who found some success in America, Silone noted that they returned unchanged; only now they were able to succumb to the eternal tendency toward envy and build themselves grand mausoleums so that—at least in death—they were "equal" to the town's gentry and lords. In *Fontamara*, the peasants remark that the Impressario, the representative of the "new dispensation" (i.e., the Fascist regime), had managed to acquire enormous wealth in a short period of time. The peasants, in their cynical wisdom, said that "he had discovered America in our part of the world." Perhaps unfairly, for them the easy and unscrupulous acquisition of wealth was synonymous with America.

As Ferdinando Alfonsi (himself a displaced Abruzzese and former professor of Italian at Fordham University) has perceptively discerned, Sciatàp's moral abasement derived not from an inherent natural condition but from his contact with Italian Americans who, in their desperate striving for wealth and "sickened by the American dollar," had lost any qualities of human compassion and comprehension, or morality and moderation. America, therefore, was a land that dehumanized its immigrants by their attachment to material things, to wealth. America is a land of solitude, destructive of the sacred sentiments of friendship, understanding, love, and family. In *The Seed Beneath the Snow*, the simple, Christ-like figure of Infante is confronted by his father, Giustino, recently returned from America, having lost both an arm in an industrial accident and all his money after being swindled by fellow Abruzzesi. Giustino, humiliated by his experience, beats his son mercilessly, so brutally that Infante, in self-defense, murders his own father. America, for Silone, is responsible for the patricide.

American readers embraced Silone. His books were critical and commercial successes before they were accepted in Italy. *Fontamara* was adapted for the New York stage as *Bitter Stream* in 1936, and a year later *Bread and Wine* was a Book-of-the-Month selection, beating out John Steinbeck's *The Grapes of Wrath*.

When, in 1936, a new American edition of *Fontamara* was to be published, it was to contain a letter by Silone to Italian immigrants in America, especially those from the Abruzzo. The "Note to the Present Edition" in a letter to Girolamo Valenti, a trade union leader and editor of the anti-Fascist newspaper *La Libera Stampa* in New York, began by saying that if the book didn't already have a dedication, Silone would have been happy to dedicate it to the Abruzzesi immigrants in America, many of whom he knew personally and who were far from their homeland for the same reasons that had pushed Silone to emigration. (Here Silone was wrong: Most Italian immigrants in America were fleeing the abysmal economic conditions in the Mezzogiorno, whereas the writer had fled for political reasons.)

For those who found themselves far from Italy, *Fontamara* represents "a recent echo of what our country has suffered and still suffers." (Fascism is never mentioned by name in the book.) But more important than the terrors of any particular regime, readers in America would find something more tragic: "our inhuman destiny on this earth."

Silone noted that besides the original German edition of *Fontamara*, the book had been translated into French, English, Spanish, Portuguese, Russian, Polish, Hebrew, Czech, Hungarian, Romanian, Croatian, Danish, Dutch, Norwegian, Flemish, Slovenian, and even Yiddish. As he was writing to the Italian Americans, notice came that in India the book would soon be translated into Bengali. "Such a vast interest in the history of a small Abruzzese village, which in reality does not even exist, cannot have a literary explanation." Nor was the book's success due to politics. Silone noted with pride that the book had been criticized by Fascists as well as Communists. Silone realized the secret to the book's success only when he discovered that certain translations had encountered difficulties with the censors. The authorities in Poland and Yugoslavia, for example, refused to believe that this was a book originally written in Italian but rather was an elaborate ruse that was actually exposing the reality of some forsaken Polish or Slavic village. Many in Galicia and Croatia had seen in Fontamara their own village and fate. For Silone, this could only mean that Fontamara, "this invented Abruzzese village that doesn't even exist in Abruzzo, is a reality in every country." (A curious document in the police archives shows that the Fascist authorities had sent an expedition to the Abruzzo to track down this "Fontamara.") "Everything that you recount in *Fontamara*," the Indian translator had written to Silone, "happens right here, with us, every day."

So if *Fontamara* has any value, Silone continued, it was that it demonstrated the universality of the human condition of the peasants. Suffering is the same in all countries. "Beneath the rags of folklore there is above all the same human creature who sweats blood in bestial labor, who is oppressed, defrauded, exploited, derided, kept in ignorance by a dominating class that is ever more rapacious and parasitic." Silone's deepest hope was that every Italian laborer would ponder this truth as he finished reading the book. Knowing that their deep love of country and native towns was exploited by the prominenti, they could still combine a love for the *paese* (city/country) with a compassion for their fellow workers around the world suffering the same fate. The real task before us, Silone wrote to the Italian Americans, was to dig beneath the colorful folk costumes and customs, the regional and local dialects, the age-old rivalries and the traditional feasts, where they would find a greater imagined community of workers around the world. Only in recognizing the terrible shared sorrow of the memories of their native lands could they fully realize their humanity. "That sorrow, which is like a deep and bloody wound in the heart of every one of us southern Italians abroad, is not something individual and particular, but a great, universal sorrow. It joins us in fraternity with Negroes, Indians, Romanians, Poles, Portuguese, Slovenes, Jews, and all the others." It is only in overcoming "our inherent modesty" (*vincendo il nativo pudore*) and simply and truthfully recounting a universal story that we are telling our own story. "This is the message of *Fontamara*.

This is its secret truth. You will be faithfully and truly Abruzzesi, Pugliesi, Calabresi, Siciliani, only if you are courageously rebels and internationalists."

Fontamara did not affect only Italians in America. As the historian John Patrick Diggins has noted, "After *Fontamara*, no American writer of social conscience could remain indifferent before Italian fascism." In 1940, Sumner Welles, acting on behalf of Eleanor Roosevelt, offered Silone a visa for the United States; Silone thanked him but refused. Even so, Silone's outspoken denunciation of Senator Joseph McCarthy in the early 1950s and his support of the civil rights movement landed him on the State Department's list of "undesirable" visitors. At the urging of Darina and others, he finally accepted an invitation to the United States in 1963. The visit both confirmed and challenged Silone's image of the country. Falling ill, he was taken to George Washington Hospital in Washington, D.C. From his hospital bed there, he wrote to Nicola Chiaromonte with his customary blend of irony and satire:

> All things considered, I am happy to have come; I now understand how important it is to see certain things. The part of the trip that I have had to renounce (California) was merely tourism and so I'm not very sorry. I'm more interested in speaking with the people than in seeing panoramic vistas. I am forced to stammer in English with doctors and nurses who know no other language. As an Italian, I have been asked to accept condolences on the death of Pope John XXIII.

Introduced by the philosopher Sidney Hook, Silone spoke at Columbia University to a packed lecture hall, warning intellectuals young and old of the two most insidious temptations of their vocation: nihilism and idolatry. The first was defined by its "rhetoric of boredom, nausea, and the absurd" (surely a not-so-veiled criticism of Alberto Moravia, Jean-Paul Sartre, and the early Camus); the second, by "an unconditional acceptance of totalitarian dogma, whether of the right or the left." But Silone was no puritanical defender of the old aesthetic order; he praised Michelangelo Antonioni's film *La Notte* and Camus's *The Stranger* as truly great works of art, "imbued with a serious existential analysis."

Silone was honest in his criticism of America. He often used the pages of his journals to denounce American imperialism, McCarthyism, and censorship. In July 1952, he published a note of protest drafted by the American section of the CCF against a decision by authorities in Washington to deny a visa to the writer Alberto Moravia. Silone was particularly sensitive to the issue of race; in fact, he often used the pages of *Tempo Presente* to denounce racism in the "advanced" countries and its influence in maintaining colonial empires. In 1948, he had met with Richard Wright on the publication of *Native Son* in Italy. At a conference in West Berlin in June 1960 celebrating the tenth anniversary of the CCF, in addition to noting the various fomenting crises (repression in Poland and Hungary, post-Stalinist Russia, developments in Mao's China, and a criticism that elections did not seem to be forthcoming in Castro's Cuba), Silone denounced apartheid in South Africa and made particular mention of the burgeoning civil rights movement in the United States. "The General Assembly expresses its deep admiration and sentiment of fraternity with the youth of the United States, men and women, white and of color, who struggle to eliminate the barriers of segregation and who fight for the right of all to participate in the privilege of citizenship in a democratic society." American officials took note: At least one biography claims that Silone was refused a visa to the United States because of his position on civil rights.

In 1964, it came to his attention that a black man, Edgar Labat, was on death row for having raped a white woman in Louisiana in 1950. While in prison, Labat had begun a correspondence with a white woman, Solveig Johansson, a widow with a young child, in Stockholm, who had become interested in his case. On learning of the correspondence after four years, prison officials in Angola, Louisiana, confiscated the letters and banned any further contact between the two, citing an existing rule that "correspondence is not permitted unless the correspondents are of the same race." When pressed, the ban was upheld not because of race but because of an unspecified law in Louisiana that "limits access to condemned prisoners." Perhaps thinking of Romolo in Fascist prisons for four years and how much (or how little) his own letters may have relieved his suffering, Silone drafted a letter signed by Denis de Rougemont, chair of the CCF, the philosopher and sociologist Raymond Aaron, the sociologist Edward Shils, Manes Sperber (who left the German Communist Party in 1938), former mayor of Bombay Minoo Masani (imprisoned for two years for his leading role in the Quit India movement), and the scientist and philosopher Michael Polanyi. They found the entire scenario "shocking."

> Though the origin of the ban would seem to be the fact that Mr. Labat is a Negro and Mrs. Johansson a white, the larger significance lies elsewhere. What is at stake is a fundamental issue of cultural freedom—the freedom of one individual to correspond with another. The recent history of the world has provided us with too many tragic examples of similar kinds of censorship—families cut off from families, prisoners held for years in a circle of total silence—to allow this symbolic event to go unchallenged. We firmly believe that any section of that area which thinks of itself as "the free world," and particularly in the United States, where the present racial situation lends a somber overtone to the whole affair, such infringements can and must be looked into and corrected wherever and whenever they arise.

(Labat was eventually removed from death row and, in August 1966, the Fifth Circuit Court of Appeals in New Orleans ordered him released, citing that his trial had been prejudged by an all-white jury.)

Silone's influence could even be felt far from the literary circles. The journalist and critic Nello Ajello recounts how, on visiting a

Navaho reservation in the United States, he was questioned about Silone. Evidently, the Italian writer's works had struck a chord with those Native Americans.

Curiously, it was America that brought Silone to the defense of another leftist Italian intellectual, Pier Paolo Pasolini. When his 1966 essay "Altra America" appeared in *Paese Sera*, Pasolini was criticized by many leftists in Italy. Although Pasolini was very different from Silone, in the Communist, atheist, homosexual Pasolini Silone recognized a kindred anticonformist spirit. "To discover what is being born new and authentic in American society, Pasolini has had the courage to overcome the old European sociological schemata and to look around with a clear vision [*occhio nudo*]. The pacifist and nonviolent demonstrations in which he took part made a deep impression on him and left him with an irresistible feeling of fraternity. Those demonstrations were no flash in the pan but transformed those who participated in them."

In June 1969, three years after his initial trip, Silone was back in America for the thirty-fourth annual PEN conference, where he continued a public battle on behalf of the Soviet writers Andrey Sinyavsky and Yuly Daniel. Sinyavsky and Daniel had been arrested in the fall of 1965 and charged with "anti-Soviet activities." Silone wrote a manifesto calling for their release, signed by Italo Calvino, Alberto Moravia, Carlo Bo, E. M. Forster, W. H. Auden, Saul Bellow, Mary McCarthy, Arthur Miller, Norman Mailer, and Günter Grass, among others. The trial of February 1966 witnessed the extraordinary scene of the two writers declaring their innocence to no avail: They were sentenced to seven (Sinyavsky) and five (Daniel) years in Soviet labor camps. The verdict had been handed down by the Soviet Supreme Court: There could be no appeal.

Four months later in New York, as head of the Italian delegation of PEN, along with Ugo Stille, Paolo Milano, Piero Chiara, and Mauro Calamandrei, Silone charged his fellow writers with moral laziness and failure to speak out on behalf of the Soviet writers. He was particularly incensed with left-wing writers such as Pablo Neruda who refused to condemn the trial. Neruda responded: "I thought that the time of the Cold War was over, but here is an eminent colleague who has rudely awakened me from my dream." After having traveled widely in Socialist countries, "which capitalists define as totalitarian," Neruda continued, he found happy writers and unhappy writers. "But I must add," he concluded, "the happiest writers I have found in the socialist countries." Silone asked how a writer could be happy in a country where the state had absolute and arbitrary power, controlling every aspect of the lives of its citizens, which could decide what is beautiful and what is not, or what is true and what is false.

Silone always seemed to be fleeing something or someone. Guglielmo Petroni recalled a trip to Paris for a conference of the Congress for Cultural Freedom, during which Silone was feted by Gide, Faulkner, and others. When Petroni found himself seated in the audience next to a man known to have been a Fascist spy and in the company of the Rosselli brothers just before their assassination in June 1937, Silone, from the stage, was horrified and sent Petroni a hasty note: "Change your seat immediately." Petroni recalled the incident with some amusement, but there remained a disturbing sense that Silone always felt tormented, "almost as though there were a shadow over his face." He was used to behaving as "someone who is fleeing peril and must constantly watch over his shoulder."

SIX

COLD WAR CULTURE

*The final struggle will be between
Communists and ex-Communists . . . One
cannot fight communism without having
assimilated all the good it contains.*
—*SILONE*, "Emergency Exit"

A s early as 1942, Silone was contemplating his role and responsibility as a former Communist
activist and intellectual in a postwar Eu-
rope. In "The Situation of the 'Ex,'" he outlined a cultural and intellectual program for former members of the various Communist
parties—men and women who had been expelled as heretics from the
Marxist church. In a way, they could consider themselves fortunate.
They had escaped the monstrous Moscow show trials and the labor
camps of Siberia; they had avoided the fates of Voja Vujovic, founder
of the Communist Youth Group in Yugoslavia (assassinated); Lazar
Shatzkin, leader of the Russian Communist Youth Movement (suicide);
Andrés Nin and Camillo Berneri (both assassinated by Stalin's agents

in Spain); or the general secretary of the Communist Youth International, Willi Münzenberg, whose hanging in a forest near Marseilles in 1940 appeared to be a suicide but was perhaps the work of Stalin's secret police. Again, Silone compared the situation of the ex-Communist to the ex-monk. And the exes had "a painful duty to perform." It would not be pleasant to admit "mistakes, stupidities, and moments of hysteria"; it would be agonizing to "relive those nightmare years, even in memory." At a time when the Soviet Union was bearing the brunt of the Nazi assault on Western civilization, Silone would insist that the ex-Communists had to "bear witness." They were "directly involved" and "could not remain silent." They were "both martyrs and mercenaries, fighters for liberty as well as inquisitors, rebels, and police spies." What were they to say to the world? "Simply the truth." Truth was not the "scandalous revelations" devoured by the sensationalist press but "the tragic reality which lies behind the façade of Communism."

On March 5, 1953, the world learned of Stalin's death. By September, with the emergence of Nikita Khrushchev, the shock had still not worn off the PCI. By the end of 1953, the feared Lavrenty Beria, chief of the secret police, had been reported executed and the first signs of a thaw emerged. Stalin's death released some party members from a trance; others, such as Togliatti, refused to countenance an anti-Stalin backlash. To Anita Galliussi, who had briefly been Togliatti's secretary in Moscow, Silone gave this piece of ambiguous advice when she and Giulio Seniga left the party in the summer of 1954: "Friends, remember that a militant outside the party is like a foot outside a shoe: every kind of deformity is possible."

A few weeks after Stalin's death, Silone received an invitation from an obscure graduate student at Harvard University to write for *Confluence*, a journal of foreign affairs that carried essays from both liberal and conservative scholars such as Ralph Ellison, Arthur Schlesinger Jr., McGeorge Bundy, and Russell Kirk. The editor, Henry Kissinger, had come across "Emergency Exit" in *The God That Failed* and declared it "the only compassionate and human statement among a galaxy of technocrats and manipulative intellectuals." Whether he was referring to Silone's fellow contributors in that collection or a wider range of thinkers was not clear.

In February 1956 at the Twentieth Congress of the Communist Party of the Soviet Union, Khrushchev made his infamous "secret" speech denouncing Stalin, his crimes, and the "cult of personality" that had developed around the former Soviet leader. A few months later, Soviet tanks crushed the rebellion in Hungary. Silone fired off essays at a furious pace and traveled throughout Europe challenging leftist intellectuals to face the truth about the Soviet Union. He founded a new journal created to give voice to the Hungarian uprising, the *Giornale Ungherese d'Italia*, published in Italy, in Hungarian, by Hungarians.

In light of Khrushchev's speech and the invasion of Hungary, the PCI sent Giancarlo Pajetta to answer questions from journalists and attempt some damage control at a news conference. Pajetta had been born in Turin in 1911, joined the PCI as a youth, spent eleven years in Fascist prisons, and been released upon the fall of Mussolini in July 1943. Leaving prison, he immediately joined the anti-Fascist and anti-Nazi underground and participated in many military operations. At the news conference, the questions from the journalists were becoming pointed and difficult. Pajetta found himself in an embarrassing position, increasingly under hostile fire. Finally he lost his patience and erupted: "What do you want from us? After all, our comrade Silone denounced these things a long time ago!"

In March 1956, Silone was in Venice to welcome four writers from the Soviet Union who had been invited by the Société Européenne de Culture. The SEC had been formed in 1949 by Umberto Campagnola to foster a dialogue between Western and Soviet intellectuals. Silone was joined by Stephen Spender, Jean-Paul Sartre, and Maurice Merleau-Ponty. The Soviets sent officials who had, among other things, persecuted Boris Pasternak and Andrey Sinyavsky, and refused to publish Alexander Solzhenitsyn's *Cancer Ward*. Poland sent the writer Jaroslaw Iwaszkiewicz and Yugoslavia sent their ambassador to Paris, the essayist and poet Marko Ristić. Accompanying Spender, Sartre, and

Merleau-Ponty, the West was represented by the Swiss theologian Karl Barth and the Italians by Guido Piovene, Giuseppe Ungaretti, and Carlo Levi. The Soviet writers were "escorted" by a government official, in continuous contact with the Russian ambassador in Rome, who never left their side. Silone refused to play the part of the gracious host, and in his speech lamented the disappearance of the great Russian tradition of nonconformist literature. His most pointed question—why had the revelations of Khrushchev's "secret" speech at the Twentieth Party Congress not been incorporated into Russian literature?—left the Soviet writers speechless. Thus began what was to be an "impossible dialogue" with Soviet writers, best reflected in Silone's acrimonious exchange with Ivan Anissimov.

Deeply disappointed with the meager results of the Venice meeting, Silone and Maurice Nadeau, editorial director of the journal *Lettres Nouvelles*, organized a second encounter in July of that same year in Zurich. Joining Silone and Nadeau were Georges Bataille, then editor of *Critique*, Stephen Spender, Nicola Chiaromonte, and Jean-Paul Samson. But the Zurich meeting was as much a fiasco as the Venice encounter. While Silone approached the Soviet writers in a spirit of fraternity, seeking to hear from them what men and women liberated from terror had to teach the West, he was met with either bureaucratic pleasantries or stony silence. While Silone called for nonconformity, individual decisions, and safeguarding the rights of the intellect, he realized that the Soviet writers were still trapped in the intellectual nightmare fostered by Stalin's "culture czar" Andrei Zhdanov, even though Zhdanov had been dead since 1948.

Before leaving Zurich on September 28, 1956, Silone drafted a series of questions for the Soviet writers, hoping that on their return home, temporarily freed from the censors, they might begin an honest and open exchange. Confessing that the West was often misinformed about circumstances in the Soviet bloc, Silone prefaced his questions with assurances that they contained no evil intentions and no ulterior motives and made himself available to answer any questions they might have about the West.

Silone's first question: In light of the Russian writer Mikhail Sholokhov's speech at the Twentieth Party Congress, when he denounced recent Russian literature as a "literature of dead souls" because of party directives, were cultural directives still emanating from the state? The second question asked whether there had been any literary or artistic works that had been cited as "abuse of the cult of personality and a violation of Socialist legality." The third query was whether, in light of the "thaw," it was now time for the Soviet public to become acquainted with works by independent Socialists from the West. Hinting at the recent dark history of the gulag system, Silone asked his counterparts if it was time for them to make available works by authors in the West who had direct experience of the "objective reality of the recent past." He cited specifically the works of Alexander Weissberg (*Hexensabbat*), Józef Czapski (*La terre inhumaine*), Elinor Lipper (*Eleven Years in Siberia*), and Gustaw Herling (*A World Apart*). "If you are not familiar with these books," Silone asked slyly, "would you like me to ask the publishers to send them to you?" Silone's last question was whether the changes that had been applauded and embraced in Hungary, Poland, and Yugoslavia had been equally accepted in Russia.

Silone had his first response not from Anissimov but from the Russian tanks that rolled into Hungary on November 4, 1956. Later that month, from the pages of *Tempo Presente*, he publicly added a question to the list: "What do you think of the massacre of Hungarian workers and intellectuals carried out by your army?" Anissimov took three months to reply to Silone's provocation; his letters were reprinted in two issues of *Tempo Presente*. But as Silone made clear, the supposed "dialogue" between East and West was fundamentally flawed. A true dialogue demanded that the interlocutors were free in word and thought. Anissimov's letters (the first dated January 5, 1957; the second, April 3) convinced Silone that they were not. "Under these circumstances, Mr. Anissimov, you are correct: Dialogue between us is not possible and would have no sense. Censorship demands you to play the role of a person feigning deafness."

Anissimov and other Soviet writers shackled to the state were not the only targets of Silone's pen. His speech at the March 1956 congress in Venice, "The Writer Against the State," had Sartre (seated in the audience) in its sights as well. In arguing that "the writer belongs to society and not the state," and that a resignation before unpleasant facts rendered both culture and intellectuals "a dead language, a sepulchre," Silone had in mind the French writer's defense of the Soviet Union and his recent attempt to explain away Khrushchev's "secret" speech a month earlier. Sartre's flaw, according to Silone, was caused by an "ideological hypertrophy" that forced him to reduce everything to "two irremediably opposed camps." Sartre's vision, therefore, violently distorted reality (*fa violenza alla realtà*) and was mistaken from any vantage point: political, economic, sociological, ideological. Sartre's sectarianism, according to Silone, made him appear a "victim of the neophyte's zeal." Comparing the vast panorama of socialism to the development of Christianity, Silone argued that the movement simply could not be reduced to the Manichaean vision proposed by Sartre and others. Echoing what the heretical Rosselli had written in the 1920s, Silone insisted that socialism could not be equated with Marxism; "one can refute Marxism and accept socialism." More critically, no raison d'état could be identified with man's fate.

Sartre was dumbfounded by the critique, which would only intensify after the invasion of Hungary later in the year. With striking sarcasm and irony, Silone again besieged the French philosopher in *L'Express* and *Tempo Presente*: "Just as no well-raised child is permitted to contemplate the nudity of his mother, no good Western Communist is permitted to see Russia as it really is. Sartre, who is a libertine existentialist, is still not resigned to this, but for true Communists it is a rule that is beyond discussion. In the place of critical inquiry, they have for some time substituted the cult of a certain number of fetishes."

Silone was convinced that Khrushchev's speech revealed more than just Stalin's past crimes. Stalin, in Silone's interpretation of the unfolding events, was being recast as a scapegoat. The "Man of Steel" would be sacrificed to ensure the continuity of the Soviet system. But neither the condemnation of the "cult of personality" nor the "rehabilitation" of thousands liquidated as traitors and "enemies of the people" would resolve the fundamental political problem that lay at the base of the Soviet state. Abandoning the grosser forms of political and cultural oppression that Stalin had inaugurated and perfected in a so-called thaw was merely a palliative of little importance, even if such "reforms" were announced with great demagogic flair. The secretary-general of the Communist Party may change, he may surround himself with more collegial and less brutal followers, but this would in no way change the anachronistic character of the Russian dictatorship. Sooner or later, Silone predicted, "we will witness other episodes similar to Khrushchev's speech while the underlying crisis remains."

On December 7, 1956, Silone's response to Sartre's stance on the invasion of Hungary appeared as "The Lesson of Budapest" in the Parisian *L'Express*. Mocking the French writer's stance as master of *engagement*, Silone satirically asked to whom Sartre felt committed after having criticized Khrushchev for revealing and condemning Stalin's "cult of personality." And Sartre was emblematic of a whole community of Western intellectuals who "preached the most absolute faith in Stalin and his dictatorship in the West. You have put at the service of Russian propaganda your prestige as writers, philosophers and dramatists." Now these same intellectuals expressed shock at Russian tanks invading Hungary. But Silone would have none of it. "No one has deceived you; you deceived yourselves." A rare figure such as the French writer Vercors had the honesty to confess: *"It is not true that we knew nothing."* The worst tyranny, Silone commented bitterly, is one of words.

The search for truth could not be subordinated to the interest of class, party, or state. Silone mocked Sartre for his facile teleology: A true writer, Sartre argued, can identify only with progress; progress, in the modern age, is identified only with the working class; the working class, in turn, is identified with the Communist Party; the Communist Party is identified with the Soviet Union, which is identified with History. Hence the intellectual who is "against" any of these entities is against History. "The true revolutionary spirit," Silone contended, "prefers to seek differences, not identities." And in a devastating image he pointed out their "cruel awakening": These intellectuals "thought they were marching with the youth of the world, in the vanguard of History, while actually they were nothing but flies decorating a hearse."

Sartre was not the only leftist intellectual singled out for criticism. It had now been seven years since Silone's "Emergency Exit" had first appeared, and he did not let pass an opportunity to revisit Togliatti on the page. Togliatti had "known the temptations of heresy" but had forsaken them for "the necessities of his career." One of the few from the interwar period to have survived Stalin's purges, Togliatti had revealed a propensity for being "cynical, pitiless, and cruel, especially against intellectuals who do not allow themselves to be tamed." And while Silone could admire Antonio Gramsci's "philosophy of praxis" as a "philosophy of human activity which leaves many doors open," he was to challenge the "special cult" that had developed around the sainted and martyred Sardinian. Although the authorities in Moscow had discerned "serious heresies" in Gramsci, the wily Togliatti had managed to wrestle a special dispensation for Gramsci's thought (but only in Italy).

Still, after all the crimes, after all the false steps, after all the bitter disillusionments—from the purge trials of 1936, to the Molotov-Ribbentrop Pact of 1939, to the present crisis in Hungary—Silone refused to see these events as evidence that the left was morally bankrupt. He insisted that there were men and women of good faith in the ranks of communism. A "new era" had dawned in the Communist world and it began not with Khrushchev's speech but with a little-known strike by the slave laborers in the gulag camps at Vorkuta. There, in 1937, Stalin exterminated the last of the Trotskyist opposition. Three years before the Soviet invasion of Hungary, inmates staged a massive uprising. The cracks in the system were there for all to see: "The Russians we have always loved," Silone cheered, "are beginning to awaken: the grandsons of Herzen, Tolstoy, Bakunin, and Vera Figner; the students who distribute forbidden books according to the noble tradition of underground activity; the farmers who hide and feed those who have escaped from detention and exile." But Russia was only a symptom. There were no longer "geographic frontiers of peace, liberty, and truth. These frontiers are within every country and within every one of us." The lesson of Budapest, Silone concluded, was to learn the truth from the people, "even hidden truths, and make ours known to them."

The Fox and the Camelias appeared in May 1960, dedicated to Marcel Fleischmann, and is often considered one of Silone's "minor" works; even his publisher, Alberto Mondadori, thought so and registered his disappointment with its author. But *The Fox and the Camelias* is now read by some as part of Silone's "confession" regarding his relationship with Bellone. The story takes place in the Ticino Canton of Switzerland, the only novel that unfolds outside of Abruzzo. There, Daniele, a Socialist, is the son of an Italian expatriate who has returned to his father's farm. Daniele is involved in the anti-Fascist underground, and his assistant on the farm, Agostino, is an exiled anti-Fascist. Daniele would like his elder daughter, Silvia, to marry Agostino, but the girl is enamored of a young man who is taken into the house after an automobile accident. This "victim," named Cefalù (like the city in Sicily), turns out to be a Fascist spy. On entering Daniele's studio, Cefalù realizes the father is an anti-Fascist and flees. Daniele and Agostino are torn by the need to protect others in the underground and their desire not to wound the love-struck Silvia. Days of intense anxiety are resolved when it is discovered that Cefalù has committed suicide. This gives consolation to both father and daughter that the man chose suicide rather than betray the father of the girl he loved. The ambiguous depiction of Cefalù, who carries out a selfless and even noble gesture, confused many readers. But just as Silone could never be a virulent, hate-filled anti-Communist, so too he could see the humanity on the "other" side. In an interview with the journal *Encounter* (the English counterpart to *Tempo Presente*), Silone said that "when I look at a fascist I naturally view him as a human being." In the wake of the spying scandal, some have suggested that just as Silone painted a self-portrait as police spy in Luigi Murica, he confessed to his role in the character of Cefalù. In truth, Silone saw himself more in the character of the mild-mannered Christian-Socialist carpenter Franz, nicknamed "Agnus Dei," based on the Swiss theologian and proponent of Christian Socialism, Leonhard Ragaz.

On August 21, 1963, while most Italians were enjoying their traditional summer vacation at the beach or in the mountains, Palmiro Togliatti died of a cerebral hemorrhage in Yalta. (He too was on vacation with his companion, Nilde Iotti.) The wily Togliatti had managed to survive four decades as leader of the PCI, making it the largest communist party in Western Europe. Although at times he had been more conservative than the party base (he had chartered a postwar alliance with conservative political allies and argued successfully for the inclusion of the Lateran Accords into the new Italian constitution), his death was met with an extraordinary deluge of praise. Silone could not remain silent. In *Tempo Presente,* he criticized what he called the "*laudatori funebri*" for going beyond the prescribed norms of praising the dead. Silone argued that a figure like Togliatti had no need of party propaganda to claim a place in history. Togliatti had tried, without success but with apparent sincerity, to keep Silone in the PCI in 1931. For that Silone was grateful, and no matter how vitriolic their differences later, he never thought of Togliatti as a personal enemy, just as he did not conceive of Mussolini as a personal enemy. But it was necessary to combat the "irrepressible mythmaking impulse" of the party apparatus. (Ironically, Silone himself was to be a beneficiary of a smaller but no less devout impulse after his own death.) In pointing out the obscenity of the operation, including the recounting of a fictional episode where Togliatti supposedly escaped death during the Fascist "March on Rome" in October 1922—an episode that Togliatti had once confessed to Silone was made up out of whole cloth but necessary to maintain the heroic image of Communist resistance to fascism—Silone did not intend to denigrate the memory of his old comrade but to unveil the mechanisms that permit a political party to bring about the apotheosis of a human being.

The death of Togliatti and the naming of Luigi Longo as the new secretary of the PCI led some to believe that a new era was arriving for the party. Silone dissented. Hopes for a different sort of party were "unjustified illusions" because the PCI was a fragile colossus. "The reform of communism," he solemnly wrote two years later, "will not take place." Even the evolution of Eurocommunism in the 1970s was not enough to overcome Silone's skepticism on the ultimate fate of the movement. On reading a history of the Italian Communist Party by its official historian, Paolo Spriano, he felt a sense of "self-alienation."

Emergency Exit

In 1965, Silone published a collection of autobiographical essays, using the 1949 "Emergency Exit" as anchor and title. As with *Fontamara* and *Bread and Wine*, it thrust the author back into the cultural and political arena. His publisher, Mondadori, refused to take on the book; instead, it was published by Vallecchi in Florence. For the thirty-sixth edition of the Premio Viareggio, one of Italy's most prestigious literary awards, *Emergency Exit* was excluded from consideration, thereby igniting yet another caso Silone. The exclusion had been paved by negative reviews by Communist literary critics such as Luigi Russo and Carlo Salinari. An anonymous j'accuse appeared in one of the country's leading literary journals denouncing the trading of votes that was common on literary juries and calling Silone the bête noire of the Viareggio. The writer troubled the conscience of all those who, "degrading the toga of the impartial judge, annually maneuver within the Viareggio panel to affirm, without any concern about the means, Marxist supremacy in the field of culture."

Today recognized as one of the most important memoirs of the twentieth century, the book acted as a catalyst for a reexamination of the caso Silone. The regret of many Italian intellectuals was that they came around to the book and its author so late. Carlo Bo attempted a "rehabilitation" of the writer and began the process of auto-critique on behalf of left-wing literary critics when he pointed out that the vast gulf between Silone's reputation abroad and his slights at home depended on Italian leftist critics who were not able or not willing to appreciate a "writing that did not hide its moral roots." The most clamorous change of opinion was voiced by the dean of Italian journalism, Indro Montanelli, in the pages of the nation's most influential daily newspaper, *Il Corriere della Sera*. Montanelli had been a devoted Fascist, serving in the Ethiopian War. He was the first to offer an outright confession that he had misread and misinterpreted Silone for three decades. When Silone was in exile, Montanelli thought him to be a "professional anti-Fascist," having found in others' aversion to the regime "a comfortable shortcut to success" with books denouncing fascism. Montanelli had thought Silone disagreeable (*antipatico*), but it was only now that the Italian journalist realized it was because of his own mistakes and not those of the writer. "He was not the character I had imagined," Montanelli conceded; "in fact, he represented the flagrant contradiction." As a human document, Montanelli wrote of *Emergency Exit*, he knew of none other that was as noble and passionate. "A Dominican [severe] with himself, Silone is a Franciscan [compassionate] with others and therefore resistant to involve others in his own self-critique. There are no recriminations or accusations. There is one accused: Silone; one judge: his own conscience."

Giancarlo Vigorelli wrote that certain passages of *Emergency Exit* cried out like pages from Kierkegaard, Dostoevsky, and Tolstoy. For Vigorelli, the publication of the book would put an end to Silone's "second exile"—this one in Italy.

Christian Democratic literary critic (and later senator for life) Carlo Bo also penned a mea culpa after the publication of *Emergency Exit*. Bo returned to the book after the scandal of the book's neglect by the Viareggio jury. In a bitter essay, "Hanno avuto paura" (They Were Afraid), he offered an insight into the mentality of the Italian literary establishment and the larger society. Silone had been excluded from the Viareggio just as he had been excluded from "our concerns and our daily reflections because his case disturbs us but above all because to confront him would require another commitment and would end by colliding with our entire intellectual and spiritual framework." Better, then, to leave him aside, ignore him, or at most offer him some minimal honor and continue to treat him as a "secret guest" (*un ospite segreto*).

The jury for the Marzotto Prize in its official announcement stated: "We know of no other work today where sorrow and poverty have spoken a more powerful and sincere language than in these pages." In his acceptance speech, Silone could not resist unleashing his stinging irony. Referring to the "by-now boring question" of why his works were so appreciated abroad but neglected in Italy, Silone slyly reminded his audience, "My books were not publishable in Italy, because—I don't know if everyone remembers—back then there was fascism and my books were not exactly benevolent toward it." He then addressed the theory that his books were popular abroad because they were published with the help of foreign governments hostile to Italy. "That would be an offense against the truth. The truth is the opposite . . . I have been expelled from every European country in which I lived, including Switzerland, where I was permitted to remain (for some time interned) only because there was no other country that was disposed to accept me."

When the book was translated into English by Harper & Row in 1968, it generated considerable comment and praise. Bertrand Russell was typical. When asked to identify his favorite Italian authors and artists, Russell rounded up the usual suspects: Dante, Petrarch, Leonardo da Vinci, Machiavelli, Leopardi, but he concluded: "Among living writers I very much admire Silone." In December 1968, Irving Howe wrote that if given one thousand anonymous books and only one of Silone's, he would be able immediately to pick it out. "His every word seems to have a special quality, a stamp of fraternal but undeluded humaneness." To Howe, it was truly a mystery that literary criticism "with all its solemnity, had not been able to understand Silone."

And in comparing Silone with Orwell, and acknowledging the latter's superiority as an essayist, he held that Silone was the better novelist.

The question must be asked why it was only with *Emergency Exit* in 1965 that Silone finally was accorded the kind of critical recognition in Italy that he had enjoyed abroad. Perhaps it was Silone's autobiographical account of his personal purgatory through class betrayal, abandoning the church, membership in the party, and his eventual expulsion that shamed Italian intellectuals.

The novelist and critic Luce d'Eramo discerned three broad periods of Silonian criticism: The first, from 1945 until about 1950, was marked by silence; the second, from around late 1949 until 1965, was when the caso Silone was first posed; the third, which she called the "recognition phase," unfolded with the 1965 publication of *Emergency Exit*. While the Communists struggled with Silone, Catholic critics, before the Second Vatican Council, often considered his writing bordering on "Protestant" and failed to engage him. Silone's books acted like the proverbial grain of sand in the eyes of Italian critics who were often forced to reconsider their initial critical stances on Silone, so much so that in the end, they oftentimes placed into discussion the very act of reading itself. There was a tendency to place Silone's oeuvre in the context of "exile literature," and, the exile being over, their concern with his writings was subsequently therefore to cease. Alfred Kazin remarked in his "Italian Journal" from Rome on September 3, 1947, that "it is almost impossible to find one of Silone's books . . . In Italy, Silone is considered a bad writer, more a politician than a writer." For Kazin, this was because of "Silone's love of the people which cannot be appreciated by the Italians."

As early as 1945, the American critic Edmund Wilson had paired Silone with Malraux. The Catholic writer Michael Harrington also placed Silone with Malraux and Koestler in a 1955 essay correct in seeing Joachim of Fiore as a main inspiration but perhaps less convincing when he writes that Silone was the "Robert Frost of the Abruzzi."

On Intellectuals

If Silone was severe in his moral judgment of his fellow politicians, he was no less critical of his fellow writers and intellectuals. As president of the Italian section of the PEN Club, his speech at the International PEN Congress in Basel in 1947 echoed across Europe and deep into the Soviet Union and was subsequently published as "Sulla dignitá dell'intelligenza e l'indegnità degli intellettuali" (On the dignity of intelligence and the unworthiness of intellectuals).

When asked to explain his concept of "intellectual" in the Parisian magazine *L'Express*, Silone offered a Gramscian definition: "all those who contribute to the formation of a critical consciousness within their era." Perhaps thinking of Sartre and others in Italy and Germany, Silone took intellectuals to task for conceiving of themselves as an elect caste entrusted with a guiding role in History. For Silone, being an intellectual was a function and a personal vocation, not the imposition of an ideology or doctrine.

He was, as pointed out by several biographers, "*un intellettuale scomodo,*" a troublesome intellectual. He has even been compared to a modern Don Quixote astride a sharp and stinging pen. This trait was recognized by Giovanni Spadolini, historian and professor of history at the University of Florence between 1950 and 1970. The Florentine Spadolini, twenty-five years Silone's junior, was editor of Bologna's daily newspaper *Il Resto del Carlino* (1955–68) almost exactly coterminous with Silone's editorship of *Tempo Presente*. In 1962, after years of prodding and pleading by Spadolini, Silone finally agreed to collaborate and write for *Il Resto del Carlino*. This would give him a venue different from the novels or *Tempo Presente*. In fact, as Spadolini confessed years later, the only way he could get Silone to write for a "bourgeois" daily was to pay him enough so that he could keep *Tempo Presente* afloat.

On September 11, 1949, Silone delivered the opening speech to more than five hundred distinguished writers at the PEN Club in Venice. With W. H. Auden, John Dos Passos, Stephen Spender, and

Julien Benda in the audience, he argued for the privileged role of the writer in contemporary society but warned that it was not enough that writers not submit to the power of the state, not succumb to being mere vassals of those in power. Recognizing the temptations of totalitarianism, he charged that writers and intellectuals had a moral obligation to resist the corruption of mass media and communications.

An incidental item in a newspaper caught Silone's eye in the spring of 1950. Fifty-two anti-Communist Russian refugees who were being held in the Fraschette displaced persons' camp fifty miles southeast of Rome had gone on a hunger strike to protest their imminent repatriation to the Soviet Union. The hunger strikers were protesting the "pressure of the Soviet authorities" who had gone to the DP camp trying to "persuade" them to return to the Soviet Union. The strikers claimed that the official Soviet repatriation mission in Rome was making daily visits to the camp and trying to indoctrinate them with communism. The refugees were the pathetic remnants of eighty-three Russians whom Italian authorities had seized at the end of World War II. Soviet authorities were demanding their repatriation as "war criminals," and evidently the refugees had some idea of the executions that were then taking place in the USSR. A Roman tribunal examined their cases individually and "acquitted" them.

Silone's abiding interest in the role of the European intellectual fostered enduring relationships. For Czeslaw Milosz, "Silone and Camus feed our hope in human fraternity." Silone recognized that Milosz's *The Seizure of Power* was not about the struggle for power but rather the struggle for love.

Perhaps nothing better expresses Silone's stance regarding intellectuals than his differing relationships with Albert Camus and Jean-Paul Sartre. (It might not be too difficult to see the Sartre-Camus debate reflected in the Togliatti-Silone relationship.) Along with Carlo Levi, Alberto Moravia, Elio Vittorini, and other Italian writers, Silone had contributed to Sartre's *Les Temps modernes*, but the French intellectual's increasingly strident defense of Stalin in the early 1950s put an unbearable strain on their relationship. In the inevitable rupture between Sartre and Camus, Silone had no doubts on whose side he would find himself. In Camus, Silone saw a possible escape from contemporary nihilism. In his earlier works such as *The Myth of Sisyphus* and *The Stranger*, Camus had posed the subject of suicide clearly and sympathetically. "Dying voluntarily," Camus writes in *The Myth of Sisyphus*, "implies that you have recognized, even instinctively, the ridiculous character of that habit, the absence of any profound reason for living, the insane character of that daily agitation, and the uselessness of suffering." The antidote to "this lonely sense of the absurd," writes Silone, "is offered by compassion." Just as Silone could not quit the Communist Party—although its policies disgusted him, it was composed of men and women of good faith and sincerity—so he would agree with Camus in *The Rebel* that although "the world in which we live disgusts me, I feel a solidarity with the men who suffer in it."

Their friendship was strained when Camus refused to denounce French tactics in the war with Algeria, but their relationship was such that when Camus went to Stockholm to accept the 1957 Nobel Prize in Literature, he said that the award should really have gone to Silone instead. Both from outside the traditional literary establishment, both physically from the periphery (Camus from Algeria, Silone from Pescina), both having suffered from tuberculosis, both sharing an awareness that nihilism was the virus left behind by totalitarian ideologies, even after their defeat: Camus and Silone felt a fraternal affinity that was shattered upon the French writer's death in an automobile accident in 1960.

Silone's relationship with important Italian intellectuals was no less fraught with tension. When Pietro Nenni was named recipient of the Stalin Peace Prize in 1951, Silone urged Nenni to refuse (Pablo Picasso had been so honored a year earlier). Instead, Nenni traveled to Moscow to accept the award, only to return it in disgust after the events in Hungary in 1956 and donate the $25,000 to victims of Soviet repression. When asked about the possibility of spreading socialism through interventions like the Soviet Army in Hungary, Nenni replied bitterly that it was like burning down your house to fry an egg. Two years later, the prize (now renamed the Lenin Peace Prize after Khrushchev's speech at the Twentieth Party Congress in 1956) went to Danilo Dolci, the "Gandhi of Sicily." Silone tried to persuade Dolci to decline, but Dolci too accepted and used the funds for his various projects in Sicily. Silone then sent the sociologist a scathing letter, pointing to Nenni's gesture and concluding with an admonition: "In every spiritual vocation, the most dangerous temptation can be that of efficacy. Do you recall the speech made by the Grand Inquisitor? Do you not see what the Catholic church has been reduced to? The great difficulty is for us to remain faithful to our own intuition of what is good, without renouncing it to effectiveness."

Tempo Presente

In April 1956, Silone embarked on a literary and cultural project that was to consume his time, energy, and intellectual vigor until 1968. In a letter of October 11, 1955, to Nicola Chiaromonte, Silone outlined his conception of a new type of journal that would serve as a "clearing" for an exchange of ideas and articles "and nothing more." There was to be a critique of the current "infatuation" with former Prime Minister Giovanni Giolitti (famously labeled by Salvemini as the *ministro della mala vita*) and the corresponding "infatuation" with Antonio Gramsci. "To describe our method or our ideal, I would avoid like the plague any mention of the words 'liberal' or 'liberalism.' They are terms that have, in Italy, a conventional historical meaning of which no one can strip them, and to use them with their original meaning or in the American sense today, we would create useless misunderstandings with our readers." He and Chiaromonte were named editors of *Tempo Presente*, which was to accompany the Congress for Cultural Freedom's other literary journals: *Preuves* in France, *Encounter* in England, *Der Monat* of Germany, *Cuadernos* in Spain and Latin America, and *Forum* in Austria. Mediating between the two writers, with their vastly different personalities, was the editor in chief, Vittorio Libera. Silone the novelist was primarily concerned with politics and social life, as reflected in his column

"Agenda." Chiaromonte, primarily an essayist, touched on more universal problems, less on contingent concerns. "They were different," Gustaw Herling observed, "but they complemented each other." Both could be taciturn, gloomy, closed off from colleagues and loved ones. Both found the writing process difficult. But when they finished an essay or put an issue to bed, they would emerge from the editorial offices content, relieved, as though a cloud had been lifted from above their heads. They might even have been described—briefly—as happy.

Chiaromonte had been a colleague of Carlo Rosselli's in Giustizia e Libertà. A 1932 Chiaromonte essay in Rosselli's journal mapping out a "morphological affinity" among fascism, Nazism, and Stalinism caught Silone's attention. A meeting with the Russian-born Andrea Caffi moved Chiaromonte to a libertarian critique of fascism and communism, influenced by the Russian anarchist Proudhon. Writing that "the essence of fascism is the negation of politics," thus creating the "necessity to think outside of politics," Chiaromonte's position was similar to Silone's. For Chiaromonte, a revolutionary elite would have to be not only professional and passionate but also skeptical, tolerant, and humane, and would be drawn from the bourgeoisie, the artisans, the peasants, and the proletariat. Equally intriguing for Silone was Chiaromonte's equation "fascism = death." Writing as "Sincero" in the *Quaderni di Giustizia e Libertà*, Chiaromonte insisted that *"la morte si chiama fascismo."* The progressive moral, social, and political degeneration of Europe since 1914 had culminated in a new form of politics; Europe was now reaping what it had sown. Chiaromonte was clear in his denunciation of the liberal state before fascism: Mussolini had simply replaced one form of "totalitarianism" with another, for the liberal state had fostered a conception of the nation-state as a "myth of salvation."

Chiaromonte had been struck by the power of *Fontamara*. Writing from his exile in Paris, he praised Silone's sense of the reality of the peasants' "universe" and told Silone that he could write a new *I Malavoglia*, Giovanni Verga's 1881 realist saga of poor Sicilian fishermen (later made into the 1948 neorealist film *La terra trema* [The Earth

Trembles] by Luchino Visconti). An example of both Silone's biting humor and his accurate reading of peasant culture can be found in a 1929 memorandum he wrote to party officials. Remarking on the party lexicon, he noted: "*Plenum* in my town means a pregnant woman." Hence, a party document titled *Silvia:* Decimum Plenum of the Communist International* would signify, for the peasants, "Silvia, the tenth woman impregnated by the Communist International." Surely Silone would have agreed with Chiaromonte's contention that "for us Italians, socialism began in the twelfth century with Joachim of Fiore and things have remained more or less at that point."

Silone and Chiaromonte had first met in Switzerland in 1934. They shared a pessimism regarding the isolation and demoralization of the anti-Fascist movement among both intellectuals and workers. One of the first to arrive in defense of the Spanish republic, Chiaromonte abandoned his pacifism and flew in what Enzo Bettiza dryly called "the antiquated flying coffins of the Malraux squadron." The figure of Scali, the art historian who reads Plato at the front in Malraux's *Man's Hope*, is based on Chiaromonte. During World War II he was just one step ahead of the German invasion of France, making his way to the United States via Toulouse and North Africa. By 1941, he was in New York, in the company of Mary McCarthy and Dwight Macdonald and writing for *The Nation, The New Republic, Partisan Review,* and *Politics*. In postwar Italy, he, like Silone, found himself either unable or unwilling to participate in the modern mass political parties. A "libertarian stoic" (Peter Coleman), a "Renaissance man" (Leo Labedz), a "sulky son of the earth" (Enzo Bettiza), Chiaromonte refused to write of "the Masses" and "History," instead focusing on the contingencies of history. In his essays on Stendhal, Tolstoy, and Pasternak, Chiaromonte argued that history was better understood through the imaginative fiction of writers than the systems of historians or philosophers. Chiaromonte was subtly slaying a sacred cow of leftist thinkers: the Hegelian concept of a rational History, comprehensible through a

*Code name of Camilla Ravera.

Marxist historicism. History, Chiaromonte wrote, proceeded not by following Hegelian dialectics but haphazardly, with false starts and unexpected stops, refusing to bend to human schemata.

Chiaromonte befriended Malraux and flew in the latter's air squadron during the Spanish Civil War but was not reticent in criticizing Malraux's "cult of action" and obsession with force. Nor could Silone forget that Malraux, in his role as editorial director at the French publishing house Gallimard, had refused to publish Boris Souvarine's critical survey of the Russian Revolution and Stalin's legacy. The book, which Silone read and reread many times, was, according to Malraux, a good book, a great book, perhaps even a book of truth, yet it was not yet politically possible to publish it in France.

Chiaromonte had met Camus in Algeria in 1941 and the two immediately became friends, bound by a common dark vision of the world. On Camus's death two decades later, Chiaromonte penned a moving tribute to the French writer, focusing on the opposing drives of sweeping history and the seemingly powerless individual. As Chiaromonte saw, this did not necessarily lead to nihilism but to a possible "solution": the rebel who resists in order to maintain his own clear conscience.

Even before their collaboration on *Tempo Presente*, Silone and Chiaromonte had maintained an exchange of letters devoted to exploring themes and topics dear to them both. When Silone sent Chiaromonte the typeset manuscript of *A Handful of Blackberries*, Chiaromonte questioned the title ("I hope you find one more expressive, this one doesn't express well enough the essential subject of the book") and whether or not to include the story of Elinor Lipper. Lipper's memoir of eleven years in Soviet concentration camps had struck a profound chord with Silone.

In April 1956, the first issue of *Tempo Presente* appeared, with essays by Silone ("Ideologie e realtà sociale") and Chiaromonte ("La situazione di massa e i valori nobili") and contributions from Albert Camus, Alberto Moravia, Gustaw Herling, Leonardo Sciascia, Isaiah Berlin, Alexander Weissberg, Jean Daniel, and others. There was no acknowledgment of support from the CCF on the masthead of the journal.

Silone's commitment to supporting writers and artists was exemplified in his friendship with Gustaw Herling. Born in Kielce, Poland, in 1919, Herling had studied literature at Warsaw University and had read Silone's *Fontamara* before the war. He joined the anti-Nazi Resistance in 1939, was sent to Soviet-occupied Lvov, was arrested by the NKVD in March 1940, and spent two years in the gulag system. That experience became the basis for his memoir, *A World Apart*, which described the inhuman gulag universe a decade before Solzhenitsyn's *A Day in the Life of Ivan Denisovich*. In 1942, he was released from the gulag and fought for General Wladyslaw Anders's Polish Army in Italy, seeing combat at Monte Cassino. After the war, he remained in Italy, first in Rome, where he founded and edited the literary and cultural journal *Kultura*, then in Naples, where he married Croce's daughter and lived until his death on July 4, 2000. Herling noted that after the war, the Polish government refused to grant permission to publish Silone's works, "condemning him to nonexistence, like in Orwell's *1984*."

Herling, a great admirer of Italy, was not reticent in penning trenchant critiques of Italian culture. He often criticized Italian writers for being too concerned with style and literary flair to write works of moral and ethical weight. Silone, in his mind, was an exception. Although he found the Italian writer "taciturn and a bit surly," they became friends. Herling made the trip from Naples to Rome once a month to collaborate with Silone and wrote for every issue of the journal's twelve-year run. Herling found Silone a loner (*un solitario*) with the closed and serious temperament of an Abruzzese peasant who finds himself in cosmopolitan Rome. Chiaromonte marveled that the "taciturn" Abruzzese so easily confided in the Polish writer. Herling recalled an encounter with Silone when he was lamenting his fate as a Polish exile in Italy. "He looked at me with astonishment and said, 'I too am an exile: in my own country.'"

For Herling, Silone's best work was *The Secret of Luca*. "He was truly," Herling remarked in an interview late in life, "a man who did not speak much and who knew how to keep a secret."

In Rome at the Accademia di San Luca in November 1996 to commemorate the fortieth anniversary of the founding of *Tempo Presente*, Herling recalled his great emotion on arriving at the editorial offices of the journal in via Sistina, across the street from where Gogol wrote *Dead Souls*. In the afternoons, the editorial offices would come to life and everyone would contribute to the ongoing arguments, debates, and discussions. Herling recalled one afternoon's work being interrupted by a visit from a captain of the Guarda della Finanza, Sergio Quinzio, timidly asking if he could contribute something to the journal. Silone invited the captain to submit an essay. Captain Quinzio had meditated much on Holy Scripture and wished to write about morality and religion. Eventually he retired from the Guarda and spent fourteen years living isolated in the Marche and writing about religion and theology. His first book, *Diario profetico*, was published (1958) just as his first essay in *Tempo Presente* appeared.

Quinzio, like Herling, haunted the editorial offices for the next decade. Twelve years after Silone's death, he confessed that "the man always remained a bit difficult to understand. Behind that disarming smile that was so characteristic of him, he remained in a sense a peasant, wary, not completely explicit. Certainly, there was in him an authentic Christian sensibility deluded by the institution [of the church], a delicateness, a profound perception of the human dimension." But Quinzio also discerned a hardheaded practicality, a peasant-bred pragmatism. Later, in *La speranza nell'Apocalisse*, his last book, Quinzio dedicated the final chapter to Silone, critiquing Silone's self-definition as a "Christian without a church, a Socialist without a party." But in Quinzio's tragic Christianity, in which he delineated a "defeat of God," he was perhaps closer to Silone's tragic humanism than he acknowledged.

For Herling, the appearance of Quinzio in the editorial office of *Tempo Presente* was in no way atypical: No one and no idea was to be summarily dismissed, even if in military uniform. But Herling could not hide the bitterness of their experience with the journal. After the cold war, it was not uncommon, Herling said, to hear people from all over the political spectrum praising *Tempo Presente* as the most vivacious, stimulating, and independent journal. "But back then, in an atmosphere of intellectual conformity, of bad faith, of disinformation and moral torpor," the journal was greeted with "hostility if not repulsion and gnashing of teeth, accompanied by the usual stupid label 'a product of the cold war.'" For Herling, a refugee from Nazi Poland and the Soviet slave labor camps, the journal was "a natural port" and a "gift of fortune."

Herling was fully cognizant of his own image in the minds of most Italian intellectuals of the left. "I was just an eccentric, a strange personality who had got it into his head to play the exile, to flee from a country in the East that was making gigantic strides toward a radiant future." Some considered him to be a Fascist; others thought him simply mad. In fact, in the late 1950s, the Communist newspaper *Paese Sera* advocated expelling Herling from Italy. It was only a fortuitous encounter with Chiaromonte and then Silone that allowed him to work and write in Italy. Everything was fodder for debate; in the editorial offices or the local bar where they might retire for a coffee, "there was no taboo."

Tempo Presente marked an important point in the culture of postwar Italy, but its birth was difficult and its life marked by intrigue as well as intellectual brilliance. Writing to Chiaromonte in the summer of 1956, after the first issues had appeared, Silone lamented, "It is, unfortunately, difficult to do anything without trickery or deception." It was common for Italian Communists of the late 1950s and 1960s to solemnly swear that they "wouldn't soil their hands" with the review only to discover, in conversation with them, that they had read every issue with great care.

The first year of *Tempo Presente*'s publication presented the journal with the Hungarian crisis. Workers' demonstrations in the summer were followed by outright insurrection in the fall. In late October and then again in early November, the Soviets intervened, the second time with tanks crushing demonstrations (and demonstrators) in the streets. Imre Nagy was arrested and brought to the USSR, where he was executed two years later. The Soviet invasion precipitated a crisis within the PCI with hundreds of intellectuals and thousands of rank-and-file members quitting the party.

Nor was *Tempo Presente* averse to antagonizing the established national powers in Europe. In the fall of 1960, Silone and Chiaromonte published a "Declaration on the Right to Insubordination," signed by 121 European intellectuals, regarding the civil war in Algeria. "The cause of the Algerian people, which contributes in a decisive manner to the end of the colonial system, is the cause of all free men." Authorities refused to permit publication of the statement in France.

When Boris Pasternak was forced to renounce his Nobel Prize in Literature in 1958, Silone responded by sending copies of *Doctor Zhivago* to all the branches of the AILC. Pasternak's novel had been published by the left-wing publishing house Feltrinelli in Milan a year earlier, notwithstanding the pressure brought to bear by both the PCI and the Soviets. In the pages of *Tempo Presente*, Silone and Chiaromonte published verbatim the Union of Soviet Writers' condemnation and expulsion of Pasternak. "It was," Herling reported, "one of the most important moments of the journal."

But in 1966, rumors began circulating that the Congress for Cultural Freedom and its journals were being funded by the CIA. For the next two years, Silone and Chiaromonte struggled to keep *Tempo Presente* alive, but it was an exhausting endeavor. From a CCF conference in Paris in the spring of 1967, Silone wrote to a friend that the rumors were again in the newspapers. "In the past we had always indignantly denied any such accusation. Now the executive director of the movement [Josselson] has confessed the truth: For several years the funds came from so-called foundations behind which was the notorious CIA." There were renewed accusations that Silone had been a spy for the CIA. Silone once again became the focus of scandal, innuendo, rumor, and political vendetta. For those in power on both sides of the Atlantic, he was a dangerous character. While SIFAR (Italian military intelligence) had warned authorities in 1957 that Silone was an informant for the American embassy, responsible for "underground anti-Communist initiatives," American intelligence thought him a subversive leftist. So rooted was this fear that the FBI asked no less than Ronald Reagan to spy on the supposed Italian spy!

This was not Silone's first inkling of the provenance of the funds coming from the Congress for Cultural Freedom. Ebe Flamini, secretary of the Italian branch of the CCF, recounts that in 1959 she was pressured by the novelist John Clinton Hunt to publish material in the Italian association's bulletin. "He came from America and I told him to his face what I thought of American policies and the CIA, which for me were equivalent to Soviet politics. Then I resigned." Even earlier was an episode recounted by an assistant, Antonietta Leggeri: "One evening a very upset Silone told me of having received an offer of money from some American trade unions. Smashing a fist on to the table, he was furious and added: 'Do you know who's behind this? It's the CIA!'"

Silone was now trapped by his own past. During World War II he had indeed "collaborated" with the OSS, not as a spy but to offer advice and information to defeat fascism, rebuild Italy, and prevent a Communist victory. As director of the Centro Estero of the PSI in Zurich, he did indeed receive funds (from the OSS) that had been "laundered" through American trade unions. Although it may be hard to believe since it was the precursor of the CIA, at the time, the OSS was considered a "leftist" organization ("*Oh, So Socialist*" was the witticism among more conservative intelligence agents both in America and Britain). And it was the OSS that flew Silone and Modigliani to Italy in October 1944. Yet a careful reading of the hundreds of documents now available on Silone's relationship with the OSS demonstrates quite clearly that he was no spy.

There is no evidence that Silone knew that funds for *Tempo Presente* originating from the CIA were being laundered through the CCF. He may have suspected; he may even have entered into a Faustian bargain, preferring not to ask and not to know. When Silone finally inquired about the source of funds for the Congress for Cultural Freedom, he was reassured by Sidney Hook: The money was from an American millionaire, Julius "Junky" Fleischmann. Ironically, the CIA was funding a journal that condemned many aspects of American society from McCarthyism to Jim Crow segregation to American intervention in Vietnam and South America. Even a cursory examination of the journal reveals its biting critique of American domestic and foreign policy. And although Darina claimed it was simply because he never applied for one, Silone, until 1963, had been denied a visa to visit the United States. Paradoxically, in Italy, Silone was an agent of the CIA; in America, a dangerous, subversive leftist.

As it was, the journal was always short of funds, even with money coming in from the CCF, and so Silone and Chiaromonte closed the offices on via Sistina in 1968. Silone remained bitter the rest of his life over the demise of *Tempo Presente*. It had represented for him a way out, another "emergency exit" from the internecine struggles over culture and politics in postwar Europe. "Silone loved this journal like nothing else in the world," recalled Giovanni Spadolini. Looking back, Silone and Chiaromonte could point with pride to the extraordinary galaxy of writers they had published: from the Calabrian Corrado Alvaro to Hannah Arendt; from Raymond Aron to Isaiah Berlin; Italo Calvino and Jorge Luis Borges; Albert Camus and Danilo Dolci; François Fejto, Ennio Flaiano, and Carlo Levi; Czeslaw Miloscz and Elsa Morante; Alberto Moravia and Guido Piovene; Ferruccio Parri and Ernesto Rossi; Denis de Rougemont and Gaetano Salvemini; Leonardo Sciascia and Stephen Spender; Angelo Tasca and Giuseppe Ungaretti; Leo Valiani and Franco Venturi; Elio Vittorini and Tommaso Landolfi.

Silone resigned from the CCF in 1967. As Darina Silone pointed out thirty-three years later, Silone had been an unwitting pawn in the cold war, a fact that threw him into an "incredulous despair," perhaps recalling—without anyone else knowing, not even Darina—his past with Bellone. Silone "cannot be said to have had any relationship with the CIA at all," she wrote, "because until the spring of 1967 he did not know that it was funding the Congress for Cultural Freedom."

(Repeated requests, through the Freedom of Information Act, to examine CIA records relating to Silone were politely answered with forty-one pages of previously released documents. Of this material, only one page, consisting of four paragraphs of 150 words and several errors, concerns Silone. The CIA "can neither confirm nor deny the existence or nonexistence" of further documents, based on section 6 of the CIA Act of 1949.)

Although *Tempo Presente* had folded, Silone's relationship with Chiaromonte had not. Silone's continued ostracism from the lofty realms of the Italian literary establishment was noted by Chiaromonte, who discerned the real reason behind it: "Your problem as a writer is always a problem of simplicity and truth that completely isolates you from the world of the *'letterati'*: lucky you." When asked to contribute an essay to a volume in honor of Silone, Chiaromonte elaborated on this theme of Silone as "a writer as isolated as he is eminent." Silone's distance from the established literary firmament meant that, with the passage of time, his originality was increasingly pronounced. In a literary age marked by artifice, ideological posturing, and an aggressive courting of the latest fad, Silone simply wished to be a writer of eternal truths, much like Chiaromonte's beloved nineteenth-century Russian writers. Silone's characteristic irony was inseparable from his concept of justice; it was also to inform his belief that the roots of socialism were to be found in Christianity. For Silone conceived of socialism as sharing the poverty, misery, and suffering of the peasants that led inevitably to not only their resignation but also their sarcasm and cynicism, as well as their eternal aspiration for a simple and concrete justice. Silone's cafoni are neither romanticized nor forced to carry the burden of being the vessel of History. Their "truth" is rustic and inarticulate. That truth remains while all else is transitory, transient. That truth is based on necessity while the rest is ambiguous and arbitrary. It is a truth that is humble, not triumphant; from the outside it may seem "monotonous, stubborn, closed in on itself." It is this search for that which is permanent that nourishes the roots of Silone's religiosity and, in consequence, his socialism. Although Chiaromonte knew that

Silone had described himself as hunted down by God, Chiaromonte sensed that the Abruzzese writer was "a Christian who seeks, not one who has found." What exactly was he seeking? "The sense of that which, through the turbulent changes of our time, endures and is worthy of enduring."

Notwithstanding the Italian literary establishment's silence and even scorn regarding Silone, it was not above using him for its own ends. Silone became president of the PEN Club in Italy (the futurist poet and literary provocateur Filippo Tommaso Marinetti had been president until Mussolini banned PEN in Italy). By nominating Silone, Italian writers and critics, many of whom had arrived at a comfortable arrangement with the Fascist regime, could ease their conscience and their way back into the postwar literary scene. Silone was above moral reproach, thus lending some much needed moral stature to Italy's postwar cultural stance. Italian writers were eager to avoid the fate of their German counterparts. Even with their nomination of the morally impeccable Thomas Mann, the Germans were originally prevented from participating in PEN by the objections of French and Israeli writers.

If Silone could ask impertinent questions of the Polish president and publicly chastise France's greatest living philosopher, he could also place his considerable prestige at the service of those outside the realms of official power. One such person was Danilo Dolci. A writer from northern Trieste trained in sociology, Dolci had somehow got the outlandish notion of assisting the most miserable and downtrodden peasants and fishermen of Sicily. After he was arrested in February 1956, it soon became apparent that the judges were in no way willing to dismiss the trumped-up charges and that the authorities were preparing what would amount to a political trial. When Dolci was denied the provisional freedom on bail before trial, the public was outraged.

Although Silone had retired from politics, he could not retire from cultural politics. He accepted a position as head of the jury of the

Venice film festival of 1954. The festival exploded into an abrasive confrontation between the supporters of Federico Fellini's stark and haunting *La Strada* and Luchino Visconti's luscious *Senso*. In their Solomonic decision, the jury awarded the prize to Renato Castellani's *Romeo and Juliet*. It's not known how Silone voted.

The independence of India and the French wars in Indochina and Algeria turned his attention to the problems of colonialism, racism, and Europe's waning empires. Even before World War II had ended, Silone had called for the liberation of subject peoples and the dismantling of Europe's colonial empires. "Colonialism," he wrote to Rudolf Jakob Humm in 1957, "is a wretchedness [*un'abbiezione*] that every intellectual must condemn." But he recognized that a Western (and particularly American) desire to dissolve colonial empires based on the idea that "free people produce and consume more" was to be replaced by a financial colonialism no less (and perhaps more) insidious. One of the thorniest problems of the era was precisely how to "assist the former colonial peoples in such a way as to not endanger their economic and political independence." He was also willing to lend support to such figures as Diego Rivera in a campaign against nuclear war.

He was often prepared to say things that others perhaps were not prepared to hear. He criticized French intellectuals for their support of the Algerian War. In Israel to accept the Jerusalem Prize for literature in 1969, he asked permission to speak on the current situation.

We defend the right of Israel, but we are and intend to remain lay people [*laicisti*] and internationalists. The ethnic heterogeneity of the population of all countries is an irrefutable argument against national or confessional states that reduce the minority to second-class citizenship. We hope that certain aspects of domestic Israeli policy are provisional, due to the transitory necessity of defense. We have no hesitation in declaring the fundamental right of the Israeli people to a unified, national life, in peace and harmony with the men of other origins and faiths . . . The Hebrew people have had a destiny incomparable to any other . . . Israel has been formed through an organic bond of nation, tradition, and land and it would be blindness to deny it. Christianity is unfortunately guilty if this historic event has only come about with such tardiness . . . Fortunately, Catholicism has in recent years begun to become conscious of the fact, but perhaps some time is still needed before it arrives at a complete mea culpa without any mental restrictions.

While not hesitating to criticize the Catholic church, he also felt a need to speak on behalf of those displaced by the creation of the new nation:

Our meeting here is based on the relation of peoples and not of States. But a duty toward sincerity stronger than any caution induces me to speak to you of the Palestinian refugees. You know better than everyone else the most unhappy fate of the Arab refugees of this land, aggravated and pushed to the extreme limits of desperation by the political exploitation of nearby countries and the immense hypocrisy of the United Nations. Many of us hope that the Israeli people, who have known such bitter sorrow, will eventually propose an equitable and generous solution to this sad situation.

More personally for Silone, in February 1954, he heard of the plight of the peasants in a small Sicilian town who were protesting the lack of water for their fields and homes. Mussomeli, an ancient town whose Arab origin is revealed in its name, was under the control of the local Mafia chieftain Calogero Vizzini. In a scene that could have been drafted directly from *Fontamara*, three women and a child were killed while protesting.

As television was making inroads into Italian society and culture in the 1960s, Silone could not remain unconcerned. In 1961, he declined the political plum job of director of RAI, Italian state television, just as he had declined the offer to be Italian ambassador to France. (RAI would eventually be split into RAI 1 under the direction of the Christian Democrats, RAI 2 for the Socialists, and RAI 3 for the Communists; all three offered ample opportunities for political patronage and corruption.) Although RAI would go on to produce dramatic performances of some of Silone's novels, he was not so cowed that he could not criticize the state monopoly or television in general. Two years earlier, when RAI had broadcast a special on Italian history in the twentieth century, Silone, as president of the AILC, had fired off a letter to the president of RAI, complaining of the depiction of the early years of the Fascist regime and its defining crisis, the assassination (in 1924) of the reform Socialist deputy Giacomo Matteotti. What most offended Silone and the AILC was the "a-critical and un-nuanced acceptance of traditional hagiography," which the director had appropriated directly from Fascist propaganda, "using the same photographic and cinematographic documents and even the very same trite slogans" put into circulation by the regime to exalt Mussolini and the regime.

When the people of Berlin woke up one morning in August 1961 to find their city cut in half by the wall, Chiaromonte and Silone published Willy Brandt's anguished cry of protest in *Tempo Presente*. Joined by Raymond Aron, Denis de Rougemont, Jorge Luis Borges, Stephen Spender, and others, Brandt's appeal, based on the Declaration of the Rights of Man and Citizen, was published in the bulletin of the AILC. A society that forced millions of its citizens to flee elsewhere, that prevented people from fleeing, that blocked flight with barbed wire and concrete walls, bayonets and rifles, treating its people "as though slaves fleeing from prison," was surely a failed society.

Equally fatal to the Soviet system was its lack of irony. Speaking with Alexandra Kollontai, the former people's commissar for social welfare and Soviet ambassador to Norway (and thus the first female ambassador in the world), in Moscow in 1922, Silone noted that she had "acquired her sense of irony in the West, and she used it only in conversation with Westerners." Kollontai was a fierce internal critic of the Bolsheviks and challenged socialism's continuing patriarchal oppression of women, but her critique was effectively muted, first by Lenin, then by Stalin.

More tragic was the case of Lazar Shatzkin, leader of the Russian Communist Youth Federation. Silone met him in Moscow in the early 1920s and described him as one of his best friends. One day they were walking together in Red Square and came across Lenin's tomb (still a wooden structure at the time). The Italian was touched by the young Russian's lament that he had been born too late to participate in the revolutions of 1905 or 1917. Silone sought to console his friend by assuring him that "there will be other revolutions . . . There'll always be need of revolutions." The Russian inquired—whether with skepticism or hope is difficult to determine—"What kind of revolutions, and when can we expect them?" Silone pointed to Lenin's tomb, which attracted long, interminable processions of poor peasants every day: "You must admit that this superstitious cult of his mummified body is an offense to his memory and a disgrace to a revolutionary city like Moscow." Silone facetiously proposed a little revolution of their own with some gasoline and a bonfire of Lenin's tomb. Shatzkin was horrified and, trembling with fear, begged his friend not to repeat the suggestion to him or anyone else. Togliatti had once suggested—and Silone agreed—that in judging a regime it is very important to know what it finds amusing. Ten years after their encounter by Lenin's tomb, hounded by Stalin's police in the Great Purge, Shatzkin committed suicide.

Even during World War II, Silone was already challenging one of the myths of the cold war: that in countries where all the means of expression were monopolized by the state, men and women could no longer think freely and courageously. "The truth," he claimed paradoxically, "was the contrary." The most burning thoughts of freedom arrived from the countries in which there was no longer any freedom. The human mind would not permit itself to "be transformed into a machine. Liberty and human dignity are concepts that will never perish." In Bread and Wine, Silone—through Pietro Spina—had argued:

One can be free even under a dictatorship on one simple condition, that is, if one struggles against it. A man who thinks with his own mind and remains uncorrupted is a free man. A man who struggles for what he believes to be right is a free man. You can live in the most democratic country in the world, but if you are lazy, callous, servile, you are not free, in spite of the absence of violence and coercion, you are a slave. Freedom is not a thing that must be begged from others. You take it for yourself, whatever share you can.

In 1954, Silone had submitted to a "40 Questions for . . ." interview, and his answers were a combination of sarcasm and sincerity. Asked why he wrote and what he offered his readers, Silone responded simply, "to communicate . . . and to give a bit of companionship." His ideal readers were men and women who were "solitary, worried, and disposed to reflection." When asked about literary critics, he smiled and offered that in this world "there is a place for everyone." As to their influence on his work, he answered with a single word: "none." His favorite novelists were Cervantes, Tolstoy, and Giovanni Verga; his favorite painter, the Fauve and Expressionist Georges Rouault. When asked if he might return to active political life, he solemnly answered, "If freedom were endangered." As to the most important personal encounters in his life, they were Don Orione, Antonio Gramsci, Leon Trotsky, and Leonhard Ragaz. The most important Italian historical figures were Joachim of Fiore, St. Francis of Assisi, and Tommaso Campanella. From their own epoch: Simone Weil. He confessed to a belief that a third world war would create the premise for a fourth and that he had no belief in the idea of inevitable progress. Was man a free and responsible agent? Man could be responsible "only insofar as he is free." He did not believe in a perfect political order or in the possibility of perfect laws or institutions. As to the possibility of a Christian state: "It would be a contradiction in terms." But a Christian society was one in which love substituted for laws. His concept of a Socialist revolution was one in which present economic and social obstacles were eliminated to permit the freedom of men and women. Would man then be happy? Not necessarily. Ancient concerns would survive and new ones would arise. Freedom could not come about without certain socialist measures. This was not the case in the Soviet Union, where socialism did not exist but rather its contrary: "capitalism of the State." He denied being a pessimist as he was often portrayed. "I have faith in man who accepts sorrow and who transforms it into truth and moral courage," he concluded. "I think that from the tremendous polar night of the labor camps of Siberia there may come forth Someone who will return sight to the blind." "Someone?" the interviewer demanded. "Who?" "His name," Silone answered, "doesn't matter."

In 1953, Silone, as a former member of parliament, sent an inquiry concerning Romolo to Carmelo Camilleri, former vice commissioner for public safety in Milan at the time of the fatal bombing in 1928. Refusing to confirm at the time the "official" inquest that Communists and anarchists were responsible for the deadly bombing, Camilleri was eventually removed from the police force and sentenced to five years of confino because of his contacts with Italian anti-Fascists. In 1953, Camilleri was president of the national union of retired police officers. From his office in Rome, Camilleri sent Silone a report that revealed "without any evasiveness, the truth about the assassination attempt in Milan and places the martyrdom of your poor brother Romolo in its true light," affirming the police's first suspicion that dissident Fascists were behind the bombing.

Thirty-three years after Romolo's death, Silone was still adamant in maintaining some control over the narrative of his brother's arrest, trial, and death. When Don Gaetano Piccinini, also from Pescina and taken in by Don Orione after the earthquake, wrote an article commemorating Romolo, Silone responded with a stinging letter, outlining eleven misstatements. These ranged from the relatively harmless (Romolo was four years younger than Silone, not seven or eight; Silone never attended university; Romolo entered into Don Orione's schools at the *ginnasio* level, not the elementary) to the more substantive:

Romolo was sentenced to twelve years in prison, not six. More seri-ously, Silone was offended that Piccinini seemed to downplay the grav-ity of Romolo's predicament. Silone reminded the priest that the Special Tribunal for the Defense of the State, on Mussolini's orders, was transferred from Rome to Milan especially to pronounce a death sentence on Romolo. It was only after the tribunal was presented with irrefutable evidence that Romolo had not been in Milan at the time of the bombing that they were compelled to convert the original charge of attempted regicide to membership in the PCI and change both verdict and sentence. Most disturbing for Silone was the complete lack of con-text in Piccinini's reconstruction of events: The priest's "euphemisms" and "abstract allusions" failed to convey to the reader the reality of the Fascist regime and left Silone with "a great sadness." Although he detested those who rallied over the corpses of the dead, why, Silone asked, couldn't the good priest "call things by their proper name"?

Calling things "by their proper name" had become Silone's literary touchstone. Although he briefly experimented with surrealism and symbolism in some early short stories, he soon came to reject both the florid conservative style of the Fascist period as well as the more exper-imental writing of the European avant-garde. Silone's realism was his only method of "bearing witness" to the lives and tragedies of the Mezzogiorno.

SEVEN

The PAINFUL RETURN

*I cannot imagine a life that does not
contain within itself a radical antithesis.*
—SILONE, "Fiction and the Southern Subsoil"

The art of storytelling, Silone once remarked with a smile, is similar to the culinary arts: When the pasta is al dente it is time to remove it from the stove. Similarly, it is necessary to learn when to *stop* writing. Silone found this particularly difficult. Like any writer, he came to live with his characters and often found it difficult to send them out into the world of readers. In a letter, he criticized the literary agent and translator Barthold Fles as one who "talks too much. Unfortunately, he knows only the Old Testament, and not the New, where it is written that after death, one must offer up an account of all useless words." While sensitive to the necessity of knowing when to stop writing, Silone confessed to being unable to "give up our quest for understanding."

In his last two decades, after the publication of *The Secret of Luca,*

Silone spent less and less time on active politics and withdrew to a more contemplative life. "Certainly not because of any misanthropy," he insisted. "Those who know me know that I am very sociable." He criticized what he saw as a never-ending Italian "literary carnival" of prizes, pageants, and paparazzi. Convinced that the highest and only dignified ambition a writer could cultivate was to "be and remain oneself, not to alter one's voice," he advised young writers "not to sing in falsetto, not to wish to be something they were not."

He was drawn to the simple spirituality of St. Francis of Assisi and the modern order he inspired, the Little Sisters of Father Charles de Foucauld. Added to this was a deep and abiding interest in Simone Weil. Although Silone never publicly acknowledged it, it was Darina who introduced him to both Weil and de Foucauld. Although he was less inclined to travel, he was in Paris in 1957 for the Congress for Cultural Freedom when he visited the mother of Simone Weil. Thus, the seed was planted for an idea that was to bear posthumous fruit in *Severina*. (It was to Weil's mother that Camus, on his way to claim his Nobel Prize, had confided that it was really Silone who deserved the award.)

For Silone, the death of historian Gaetano Salvemini in Sorrento on September 6, 1957, was cause for reflection on a passing epoch. Salvemini had been born in Molfetta, in the province of Bari, the eldest of nine siblings. In the earthquake of 1908, Salvemini saved his own life by standing in the architrave of a window but lost a sister, his wife, and five children. In a letter to the idealist philosopher Giovanni Gentile, he painted a self-portrait that could also describe Silone: "I move ahead, work, give lectures, prepare conferences, and throw stones at those who do not seem honest or sincere to me. People think me strong . . . In truth I am a miserable wretch, without home or hearth, who has seen the happiness of eleven years destroyed in two minutes. I have here on my table a few letters from my poor wife, my sister, and my children. I read them little by little. I seem to hear their voices. And after having read a few, I stop, because a desperate sadness overwhelms me, and I want to die."

Salvemini was buried beside his beloved students Ernesto Rossi and the brothers Carlo and Nello Rosselli, in the Trespiano cemetery overlooking his adopted city of Florence. In November 1957, a commemoration was held in the Teatro Eliseo in Rome. (The Eliseo had been the first theater in Italy to stage Arthur Miller's *Death of a Salesman* and *A View from the Bridge*, both directed by Luchino Visconti.) Organizers had billed the tribute "Il socialismo della povera gente" (the socialism of the poor), and Silone, picking up on the theme, took the podium, describing himself as a "cafone from Pescina" come to pay tribute to the "peasant from Molfetta," both outside the official Socialist parties, both intimately tied to a lost world of peasant values. "His speeches fell upon the ears of the deaf," Silone said mournfully, "but it is likely that the socialism of the poor and the oppressed, being rooted in the hearts of the honest and in their thirst for justice, will not be extinguished." Salvemini, a die-hard mangia-prete, had surprisingly requested on his deathbed to be buried with a simple crucifix. In Salvemini's work and final gesture, Silone discerned a kernel of truth: the essentially religious nature of socialism. Although Salvemini had ceased to believe at the age of eighteen (approximately the same age as Silone), he forced himself to follow "the moral law of Christ," a Christ refigured in the sorrowful expressions of Silone's own peasants.

In the early fall of 1958, Silone found himself surrounded by boring politicians and intellectuals in Vienna. From there he wrote to a friend that he would soon go to Rodi for an international conference of third world leaders, hoping that "they will be less political" than their European counterparts. Composed mostly of the leaders of the newly independent countries of Asia and Africa (among them India, Pakistan, Israel, Egypt, Tunisia, Nigeria, and Indonesia), the Rodi conference was grandiosely and hopefully titled "Representative Governments and Public Freedoms in New States." Silone's speech was just as much a warning to the new states as it was a critique of contemporary events in Europe. The return of Charles de Gaulle in the face of the Algerian uprising was of particular importance: Those arguing for Gaullism as the lesser evil would eventually regret their weak argument. The "investiture" that de Gaulle had secured from the French parliament was seen as the "chrism" of democracy. (Silone's use of the ecclesiastical term signifying "gift" was not casual.) "How can we forget that most totalitarian governments had the same consecration?"

Decades before the word came into common usage by political scientists and journalists, Silone described Italy as a "*partitocrazia*," that is, a society that thinks itself a democracy but where real power lies not in parliaments or representative institutions but rather in the executive committees and subcommittees of the various political parties that parcel out the spoils of the state among themselves.

The year 1959 was dedicated to his last novel and the only one set outside the Abruzzo, *The Fox and the Camelias*. From the Swiss canton of Ticino, Daniele must decide how to deal with a Fascist spy who has penetrated both his study (where compromising papers were kept) and his daughter's heart. The novel was an expanded version of a short story that had appeared in the collection *Viaggio a Parigi*. On the first Thursday of May, Silone made a trip to the town of Cocullo (population five hundred) in the Abruzzo, famed for its sacred procession in which a statue of St. Domenic is carried through the town covered with live, writhing snakes. The townspeople were honored to have such a distinguished person attend their feast, but Silone was dismayed at how the sacred and pagan aspects of the original feast had already been commercialized and abused. Silone was sardonic, feeling that the original meaning of the snake-covered saint had been lost.

The so-called economic miracle in the Italy of the late 1950s and early 1960s and its accompanying consumerism often were subjects of Silone's essays. He cautioned against an "irrational exuberance" in the wake of material prosperity.

> The social conditions of the southern Italian peasant are in a phase of rapid transformation, as in Italian society in general. I am of course satisfied . . . I wouldn't say, though, that the new situation is Paradise

on Earth . . . There are no reforms that can substantially modify the problematic character of the human condition: the contrast between the collective and the individual, between society and the State, the imbalance between sorrow and the search for happiness.

With most of the myths of communism laid bare—from the liberating spontaneity of the proletariat to the power of class consciousness to the inevitability of progress to the cleansing power of violence—Silone became more concerned with what he called the "sphinx of affluence" in Western societies as more and more people bowed down before the gods of consumerism. Silone often bitterly commented on what Thorstein Veblen had pointed out as the conspicuous consumption of a savage society. "Many respectable people can go without food to diet, but not to feed a starving man."

While postwar Europe had been disillusioned with the "myth of Progress," it had to deal with an unexpected prosperity sooner than anyone had anticipated. No political party in the West could ignore "the categorical imperative" of prosperity. The paradox was "the spectacle of human beings who have reached the last stages of personal alienation even though all their wants are satisfied." The most distressing aspect of a materialist and prosperous society, for Silone, was the loss of all spontaneous generosity, where social relations tend increasingly to be dominated by consumption rather than production. How could sociologists, writers, or politicians explain the grotesque paradox of a nation like Italy, obsessed with soccer betting pools and the lottery, a nation that used *cafoni!* and *morto di fame!* as derogatory exclamations yet which embraced St. Francis, the "poor man of Assisi," as its patron saint? This was the "sphinx of affluence." On another occasion, he noted that in a very precise and not paradoxical sense, it was capitalism that destroyed private property, not socialism.

Christmas 1961 found Silone and Darina in the Near East, first for a conference in Beirut, then traveling to Jordan and Damascus. In Jerusalem and Bethlehem, Silone was struck by the bitter antagonisms among the various Christian sects. At Yad Vashem, the memorial to the Jews exterminated in the Holocaust, Darina, overcome with emotion, knelt to kiss the ground. Silone, as usual more reticent, did not imitate her gesture. After meeting with the Samaritans, a Jewish sect that today numbers fewer than one thousand souls, and leaving a small donation, husband and wife took a cab from Jerusalem to Jericho, passing by Bethlehem. The arid, dusty, naked landscape caused Silone to withdraw into one of his melancholy moods.

He appeared less in public, and his lifelong aversion to conferences and conventions approached a mania. In a 1970 letter to Don Piccinini—like Silone and Romolo, taken in by Don Orione after the 1915 earthquake and educated in Orione's schools—Silone refused an invitation to participate in a radio commemoration of their beloved teacher. His reasoning was bizarre: "Dear Don Piccinini, I am sorry to say that I cannot accept your invitation to tape a commemorative radio program on our dear Don Orione. For some time now, I have renounced entrusting my thoughts to the radio. It is a diabolical machine, an irremediable form of alienation." And then, with his usual mordant humor, and expecting his own demise in the near future, he concluded sardonically: "I'll explain it better personally to Don Orione."

To the journalist Annibale Gentile, who had invited Silone to Avezzano in celebration of Natale del Fucino, Silone dryly replied that "by instinct I am allergic to celebrations." Yet he could still be moved by personal experiences as when he sent a telegram to Teddy Kollek, mayor of Jerusalem, thanking him for introducing Silone to S. Y. Agnon. Silone called that introduction to Agnon, winner of the 1966 Nobel Prize in Literature, "a great privilege and an unforgettably moving experience." Agnon's death in 1970 caused Silone "a profound sense of bereavement." Agnon's books for Silone recorded "a world now vanished."

Georges Rouault

When asked in an interview to name his favorite painter, Silone answered without hesitation: Georges Rouault. Rouault was perhaps the most tortured religious painter of the twentieth century, similar in some ways (though not politically) to the German Expressionist painter Emil Nolde. Rouault was born in the cellar of the family home as the neighborhood near the Père-Lachaise cemetery was being bombed by government troops in the 1871 Paris Commune uprising. Rouault's father was a disillusioned follower of the Catholic democrat Félicité Lamennais, who sent his young son to a Protestant school. In 1903, Rouault was one of the founders of the Salon d'Automne. He was poor for most of his life—his work was kept out of the public eye by an eccentric patron/dealer. It was not until 1937 that forty-two of his paintings were shown at the Exposition des Artistes Indépendants. In November 1948, he dramatically burned more than three hundred of his old works in a public auto-da-fé. In the days after World War II, the Museum of Modern Art held a retrospective of his work; another followed a year later at the Tate Gallery in London. Honored late in life, promoted to the rank of commander in the Legion of Honor, he was given a state funeral when he died in 1958.

For Silone, Rouault's paintings captured the raw emotional power of life with all its misery and hope. Silone was particularly attracted to Rouault's continuing depiction of the Holy Countenance. When Silone wrote that he would happily spend his life writing and rewriting the same book, the way medieval artists painted the face of the Lord over and over again, always the same yet always different, surely he must have had Rouault's paintings in mind. The French painter's Christ is sometimes depicted mocked by Roman soldiers, sometimes alone, always with a mournful visage, as if reminded of man's capacity for cruelty to his fellow human beings. Silone often spoke of Rouault and the influence the French painter had on his own work. Although he never wrote about Rouault, all his friends knew of his appreciation for the painter and often gave him birthday presents of Rouault prints and reproductions. For Silone, Rouault's paintings were an antidote to the so-called economic miracle and resulting consumerism of the 1960s and 1970s.

The Story of a Humble Christian

Silone increasingly took to thinking and writing that humanity's situation (if not fate) was tragic. There were many times when loneliness and anxiety goaded him to remember with "sharp nostalgia the paternal home, with its old order, peace, and security," but he refused to permit a "love of comfort" to prevail over a "love of truth."

For much of the 1960s, Silone, accompanied by Darina, sought out the convents of the Little Sisters of Father Charles de Foucauld as well as lonely monasteries in Abruzzo. The impetus was as much a spiritual anxiety as a desire to do research that would culminate in *The Story of a Humble Christian*. Charles de Foucauld (1858–1916), born in Strasbourg, had a religious transfiguration at age twenty-eight and devoted his life to both contemplating the Divine and actively assisting the most miserable and outcast members of society. Although de Foucauld had been born into an aristocratic family, no doubt Silone felt an affinity with the French boy who was orphaned at age six, lost his faith at age sixteen, and then lost his grandfather, who had functioned much like Silone's maternal grandmother, at age twenty. Although his grandfather had left the young man a small fortune, it was soon squandered. Much like St. Augustine, he lived a dissolute life and was last in his class at cavalry school. Like that other "fool of God," Antoine de Saint-Exupéry, he felt called to the desert and left for Tamanrasset in southern Algeria in 1907 and spent time in North Africa, learning both Arabic and Hebrew. In 1886, establishing himself in Paris, he set to work on his book *Reconnaissance au Maroc*, recounting his travels across Morocco disguised as a rabbi (shades of Pietro Spina/Paolo Spada). When he visited the Église St. Augustin, he experienced a revelation and began to think of himself as a "fool of God." Two years later, he made a pilgrimage to the Holy Land and chose to model his life on

Jesus ("the hidden life of the poor and humble worker of Nazareth").
He spent most of the rest of his life in North Africa, developing an
appreciation for Islam, ransoming several slaves, and translating the
Gospels into Tamachek, the language of the Tuareg. In December 1916,
he was assassinated by members of the Tuareg (even though they had
once saved his life when he fell ill). His rule established both the Little
Sisters of Sacré-Coeur and the Little Brothers in 1933 and, in 1939, the
Little Sisters of Jesus. It was this last that attracted the attention of
Darina, who introduced the group to Silone as well as the writings of
de Foucauld (who was beatified on November 13, 2005). De Foucauld's
motto and daily prayer, *"Mon Dieu, si vous existez, faites que je vous con-
naise"* (My God, if you exist, let me know you), expressed a view different from Silone's. Silone had written that, far from being similar to the
"seekers of God" in Russia who went in search of the Divine, he tried
to hide from a seeking God, only to be found and "devoured."

Now Silone traveled throughout Abruzzo, visiting monasteries,
convents, libraries, churches in trace of his ideal Christian, the late-
thirteenth-century hermit Pietro Angelerio da Morrone. From his hide-
away in the Maiella mountains, Morrone was brought news that he
had been named pope by the College of Cardinals. In order to prevent
the papacy from falling into the hands of the powerful Caetani or
Colonna families, the cardinals in their divinely inspired wisdom
chose the humble servant Pietro. When the delegation arrived with the
news and a noble white horse to bring Morrone to Rome, he insisted
on riding a donkey instead. At the local church, what is now the basilica of Santa Maria di Collemaggio, in August 1294, he was crowned
pope and took the name Celestine V.

Pietro da Morrone had been born ca. 1215 (at least half a dozen
towns claim the honor of his birthplace) and in 1235 retreated to Monte
Pallano, where he lived in a cave dug out with his own hands. His reputation for sanctity was such that he was forced to retire to Monte Morrone and the almost inaccessible peaks of the Maiella, seeking solitude
from crowds of devout Christians. In 1294, the conclave at Perugia
named him pope. After only a few months as Vicar of Christ, aston-

ished and dismayed by the extraordinary corruption of the church, Celestine V resigned the papacy on December 13, thereby earning Dante's eternal wrath as *"colui che fece per viltade il gran rifiuto"* (he, through cowardice, who made the great refusal). His successor, Pope Boniface VIII (Benedetto Caetani, also finding a place in Dante's *Inferno* for simony), had him imprisoned in the Castello Fumone, near Anagni. For two years Celestine survived, dying in May 1296.

Silone retreated himself, to the less spartan quarters of a hotel in Rocca di Cambio in the Abruzzo. There he completed his second play, *The Story of a Humble Christian*. With his beloved Celestine buried nearby in the basilica of Santa Maria di Collemaggio, the writer immersed himself in the world of Christian hermits and Franciscan monks, and the theology of Joachim of Fiore—so much so that they started to permeate his dreams. Silone was especially moved by the landscape, a topography that lent itself to hermitage and meditation. The Maiella range and the mountain for which it is named had a strange fascination for him. "For us Abruzzesi, the Maiella is our Mount Lebanon." Its sacred character is, not surprisingly, tied to a local tradition of cursing and swearing. "They summon it in their hour of need to give them strength to react against life's many adversaries," one writer has recently noted. "Maiella takes its name from the goddess Maja who, after years of searching for her son, ended her days there. Maja was a harsh deity yet loving and gentle with her children. The primitive churches and hermitages present in even the range's most inaccessible valleys and gorges are a constant reminder of the spiritual importance of these peaks which, wherever you are in the area, seem to fill the horizon. So close, you could reach out your hand to touch them. Yet the closer you get the farther they seem to recede."

Silone decided to make a pilgrimage of sorts to the hermitage of Sant'Onofrio, on the Maiella, where Pietro da Morrone had escaped when the delegation from the papal enclave tried to find him and tell him that he had been elected pope. From there he could see the ruins of the house of Ovid, the Abbey of the Holy Spirit, and some buildings of a prisoner of war camp; in short, a palimpsest of the pagan, Christian, and contemporary history of the Abruzzo. When he met an old peasant gathering herbs on the mountain, they fell to talking and the old man asked about St. Celestine, he not being one of the more popular saints. For what graces or favors was he known? When Silone answered with solemnity, "Celestine can help us in avoiding the temptations of power," the old peasant burst into laughter but then gravely commented, "Then he's not a saint for us poor people; he's for the priests." Silone found this wandering among the monasteries, hermitages, and peasants more fruitful for his research than days spent in archives and provincial libraries.

In was in this landscape that Silone set out to tell the story of a poor Christian caught between his sincere faith and the corruptions of power. For Celestine, as for Silone, Christ was infinitely more than the institution of the church. By the summer of 1967, between Rocca di Cambio, Rome, and Pescasseroli, he had completed the manuscript and sent it on to his publisher. "I am fairly satisfied," he wrote to a friend. "In a few days I shall return to Rome . . . and return to my usual life, except that in the meantime I have become very old."

A first draft of the play had contained an explosive revelation, which was deleted from the published version. Silone had given this first draft to Diego Fabbri, who was shocked to read that Silone had uncovered evidence that Celestine V had been assassinated (his skull had been crushed). "What an ending!" Fabbri had blurted out to Silone. "You have one of the most extraordinary endings in drama." But Silone observed Fabbri with "that clear and slightly sad smile of his." Silone rewrote the ending, refusing to use the evidence as a finale, refusing to "cause scandal." The published version was more subtle:

CELESTINO: Will you restore me to my children?

BONIFACE VIII: How dare you hope for that? No, no. You will receive instead the punishment you deserve.

CELESTINO (makes him a deep bow, resigned, and answers gently): I will pray for you.

In a sort of epilogue ("The Mystery of the End"), Silone alludes to Celestino's grim fate through the words of one of his followers.

> FRA GIOACCHINO: Tell me, what will they do with him? What do you think?
>
> FRA TOMMASO (slowly, hesitantly, almost stammering because of his inner dismay): It's probable they'll offer him some further compromise. And there's no doubt he will refuse. And then I'm afraid they'll kill him . . . And then, then they will make him a saint. We mustn't try to understand. The destiny of some saints, while they are alive, is one of the most profound mysteries of the Church.

Pope Paul VI, having read the play and been asked his opinion, ambiguously replied that it was written "with great serenity."

It seemed as though with the publication of *Emergency Exit* in 1965 both the public and the literary establishment were now ready to accept Silone. *The Story of a Humble Christian* was a critical and commercial success, with Mondadori publishing thirteen printings in three years. Never one to chase awards, Silone found himself showered with them late in life. Honorary degrees from Yale University (1966), Toulouse (1969; the official citation mentioned the anticipation in his work of "May 1968"), and Warwick (1972); the Jerusalem Prize in 1969; the Ordre National de la Légion d'Honneur (1973); Cavaliere di Gran Croce (1982). In 1976, he was nominated for the Nobel Prize in Literature; two years later, his name was again among those being considered.

In September 1968, Silone won the Super Campiello literary prize. The ceremony in Venice could have been a scene from Fellini's *La Dolce Vita* with Gina Lollobrigida presiding at the magnificent Teatro Verde on the island of San Giorgio. The only actor missing from the mise-en-scène was the author himself, at home recovering from yet another bout of illness. To prevent another "scandal" from erupting by his absence, which he did not want to be interpreted as a snub or protest, he availed himself of an offer from RAI to tape a message to those assembled in Venice. But he couldn't resist a sardonic comment: "I didn't feel well enough to be there," he said in the interview, "but I didn't want to be rude . . . So I have made use of this TV, which, even though it is an annoying medium, at times can be a great help."

In the cataclysmic year of 1968, nothing—at first glance—might have seemed farther from the streets of Paris than *The Story of a Humble Christian*. Yet Silone was astute enough to see a connection between 1968 and the thirteenth century:

> If the idea of utopia has not been extinguished either in politics or religion, it is because it responds to a profound need rooted in man. There is in the conscience of man a restlessness that no reform and no material well-being can satisfy.
>
> The history of utopia is therefore the history of hope that is always deluded, but a tenacious hope. No rational criticism can uproot it, and it is important to recognize it even under different connotations.

Interviewed by a student a year later, Silone expressed sympathy and solidarity with the young protesters. "In the depths of my soul, the demonstrations fill me with joy. In them, in their most serious element, I recognize the same impulse that, as a youth, pushed me into the fray. That which is most disgusting in the society in which we live is its bad faith [*malafede*]."

Irving Howe, in his intellectual autobiography, recalled how—although from a vastly different background—he had been drawn to the work of Silone. Howe wrote mainly about nineteenth-century European novelists and "that group of twentieth-century writers who had gone through the ideological traumas of our age. No more, for instance, than Silone could avoid the subjects that had chosen him, could I avoid his work once it had chosen me. That in a final reckoning he would not be counted among the great writers of the century I knew quite well. It hardly mattered. I wrote about his books because his questions were also mine."

During the 1960s, Silone traveled less and stayed closer to the apartment in Rome. His daily schedule seldom varied: He walked every morning to the post office in Piazza Bologna to mail his letters and purchased several newspapers and journals on the way home. He passed the rest of the day in his study, reading the newspapers and journals, writing letters, and oftentimes receiving students and scholars who were studying some aspect of his work. No one was turned away. To those who lamented his withdrawal from public life, he responded that his solitude was only an exterior one: "I no longer speak at meetings and I have a certain repugnance for conferences. Life is too short to waste it chattering. But ever since I limited my public appearances, I feel less alone than before. It's when I work in my studio, with the door closed and the phone off the hook, that I really feel like I am communicating with others."

Late in life, Herling asked Silone when he first became conscious of his vocation as a writer. Silone, visibly moved, responded immediately: It all began when he was a child, sitting beside his mother the weaver, listening as the women told Bible stories and simple tales of human events, often tied to the history of the small town. Those two things— the slow, careful, patient process of the weaving and the fate of ordinary human beings—had fused in Silone's imagination. "I have always aspired," he confessed, "to a writing capable of evoking the life of my fellow townspeople, of the peasants; a compact prose, simple yet dense." That writing was extraordinarily difficult. When engaged in a novel, the process was terrible and sometimes terrifying. He would retire to his study for hours, not emerging as he struggled with haunted landscapes and complex characters. He could find no distance between himself and his characters and once wrote that even after he finished a novel (an act he considered arbitrary), the characters continued to live in him, maturing, changing, constantly evolving. Those characters— Berardo Viola, Pietro Spina, Andrea Cipriani, Rocco De Donatis, Daniele, Celestino V, and even Luigi Murica and Severina—were born from his own suffering and need for redemption, a redemption that could not be found in either socialism or orthodox Christianity.

Herling came away from their conversation in a contemplative and somber mood. From the dark apartment on via Villa Ricotti near Piazza Bologna, Silone moved with difficulty, and the task of simply rising from a chair took great effort. The lines in his face bore the traces of enormous fatigue, Herling wrote in his diary, yet it had been "enriched by the slow distillation of his thought." Between *Fontamara* and *The Story of a Humble Christian*, nearly forty years of time and experience had intervened, yet they barely registered because Silone had insisted on *quello che conta davvero* (that which really counts). "It is like a stone that is sculpted day by day by a stream of running water and indifferent to the gurgle of novelty, fashion, ideological rhetoric, political demagogy, and intellectual coquetry that the stream carries away." Herling was surely correct in discerning Silone's steadfastness in the face of varying ideological and literary currents, but he could not have failed to taste the bitterness of that stream.

On Suicide

Although he once claimed that it was "one of the many things that I could not understand," Silone was haunted by thoughts of suicide and death much of his life: the death of siblings to disease and accident, a father's early death from tuberculosis (a fate that seemed reserved for the son as well), a mother who perished in an earthquake, a last remaining brother dying in prison. Plagued all his life by ill health, he was told by his doctors in 1930 that he had not long to live. Tormented by melancholy, depression, and thoughts of suicide, he had written *Fontamara* so that he could die among his own people. In the short story "Letizia," about a professional weeper, a trade traced back to antiquity in the Mediterranean world, she asks the narrator, who has returned from a Swiss exile, how they weep in that northern country. When he reveals that some of the dignified Swiss women are too proud to show tears, Letizia gives him a sorrowful look. "'You know,' she said after she had thought it over for a moment, 'I am very poor and not in a position to do anything for you; but I want you to promise me one thing: I want you to promise me that you will come back here to your own town to die. I'd love to weep over your corpse.'" The author considered it "the greatest sign of affection she could have shown me."

Around Christmas 1950, just after the inaugural conference of the Congress for Cultural Freedom, Silone again apparently contemplated suicide. He opened the essay "The Choice of Companions" with a meditation on the too-numerous suicides of talented writers in the twentieth century. Considering the more significant expressions of the sense of "bewilderment, boredom and disgust" produced by the times, Silone thought not so much of the works of Heidegger, Jaspers, or Sartre but to the suicides of Sergei Esenin, Vladimir Mayakovsky, Ernst Toller, Kurt Tucholsky, Stefan Zweig, Klaus Mann, Drieu La Rochelle, F. O. Matthiessen, Cesare Pavese, and others. "What a mournful band of spirits they are, listed together this way."

Silone warned against easy generalizations and facile psychoanalysis. "How can one possibly know for certain what private despair drives a human being to take his own life?" The suicides could not be tied to a particular political or social structure; they had taken place under Fascist, Nazi, Stalinist regimes as well as the democracies of the West. Neither the triumph of revolution nor a belief in the trajectory of History could save these souls. The religious and humanist traditions of the West were also unable to prevent their deaths. Linking all the disparate individual causes—whether political persecution, exile, personal isolation, physical suffering, disease, or "abnormality"—Silone found "the same confession of anxiety and desperation over the difficult struggle to live, and, in the last analysis, its uselessness." It was this sense of nihilism—first defined by Nietzsche—that had overwhelmed not only the intelligentsia but popular and working culture as well.

Nietzsche's definition of nihilism was different from that proposed by Ivan Turgenev in his novel *Fathers and Sons* (1862) or in Mikhail Bakunin's anarchism. Modern nihilism was a form of solipsism in which one identified the good, the just, and the true with one's own interests. "Nihilism," Silone wrote in 1954, "is the deep conviction that there is no objective reality behind faiths and doctrines and that the only thing that counts is success." Postwar existentialist literature and philosophy had clearly portrayed the predicament: "Every tie between man's existence and his essence has been broken. Existence is bereft of any meaning which transcends it." The antidote to this "lonely sense of the absurd" could be found not in politics or religion but in friendship and compassion. Silone's response to this contemporary disease was in his last work, *Severina*, left unfinished at his death.

Even though Silone managed to overcome the despair leading others to suicide, he could still recognize the profound pain that was not uncommon in his part of the world that often led people to the local insane asylum. "I still have painful memories of departures," he wrote late in life, "of people leaving our native village for that sad refuge . . . The journey was considered a one-way passage." Family members would attend the departure as if at a funeral, while the townspeople, in order to spare the afflicted family more shame, would discreetly witness the drama from behind doors and shuttered windows. Once, while attempting to visit one of the inmates, Silone and a colleague came across an elderly fellow whom they took as the *portiere* (doorkeeper). He claimed to be a schoolmate of the writer. While Silone went off to find a doctor who told him his friend was going through a "critical phase" and advised against a visit, the elderly "doorkeeper" had whispered to the other visitor that he had been expecting Silone to be confined in the asylum "for some time" and that the "delay was incomprehensible." The old man was no doorkeeper but an inmate himself who had been anticipating Silone's arrival for years.

The consolations of religion were not forthcoming. A "return" to the church was impossible, even after the "aggiornamento" inspired by Pope John XXIII in calling for the Second Vatican Council (1962–65). At the time, Silone and Darina had opened their apartment in Rome to a flood of priests, nuns, monks, and theologians, many of whom confirmed a fierce internal struggle over the direction of the church. Silone was deeply moved by the peasant pope (Angelo Roncalli had been born on a farm near Bergamo in northern Italy) who, in his first act as Christ's Vicar, went to Rome's most notorious prison, Regina

Coeli (Queen of Heaven). During the Fascist regime and Nazi occupation of Rome, Regina Coeli had "hosted" many of Silone's anti-Fascist colleagues. Now it was home to common criminals. Pope John XXIII, with his beatific smile, said simply—and not without a touch of irony that Silone must have found delightful—"Brothers, since you could not come to me, I have come to you," and shocked the prisoners and the conservative hierarchy by declaring, "Here we are in our Father's house."

In the slight opening of the church to modernity, Silone could see some common ground. If the church embraced doubt, "it would find me, the old Communist, the dissident, the preacher of autonomy and freedom, of social humanity, entangled with ancient doubts." And yet he confessed to "an irrational, almost magical certainty: that life is not absurd, that life signifies, must signify, something."

After a last trip to Corfu in 1976, Darina and Silone did not travel far. In the 1970s, they began to vacation in a former villa converted to a hotel in Fiuggi, not far from Rome and Silone's doctors. Silone was so enamored of the place that he often extended his vacations while Darina returned to Rome to attend to household matters and mounting medical bills. In 1977, she took advantage of one of Silone's extended stays in Fiuggi to repaint, recarpet, and redecorate the entire apartment, something that was not possible when her husband was home as he detested any fuss, disturbance, or change. He either failed to notice the apartment's transformation on his return or, more likely, refused to compliment Darina on a job well done. In his defense, one might note that his mind was consumed with *Severina*.

Simone Weil and *Severina*

Found among Silone's notes for his last work is an ambiguous line from Spinoza's *Ethics*: "Fear cannot be without hope nor hope without fear." It was not the first time Silone had turned to the heretical Jewish philosopher from Holland. At the time of the Hungarian uprising in November 1956, Silone quoted Spinoza in his editorial for *Tempo Presente*, adopting the philosopher's motto: "I have made a ceaseless effort not to ridicule, not to mourn, not to scorn human actions, but to understand."

Silone had experimented with at least a half dozen different titles for this last work: *Vita d'una suora, Destino di una suora, Vita di una donna, Destino d'una donna, Vita d'una cristiana,* finally settling on *La speranza di suor Severina* (The Hope of Sister Severina), which was shortened by Darina to *Severina.* Could it be that in naming his protagonist, Silone might have been musing on his own name and fate? On Silone's presentation at the town hall to have his birth registered, the mayor had suggested his own name, Severino, when Silone's father's first choices were rejected as "un-Christian." Instead of taking the mayor's name, the town clerk's was used.

Severina is the contemporary story of a young nun who refuses an order from her mother superior to give false testimony in court after a worker is killed by police in a political demonstration. In his insistence that moral conscience is far superior to mere obedience, Silone was consciously echoing the Hebrew prophets. If the prophets had first articulated this new moral imperative, Silone discerned it as well in Spinoza and, most powerfully, in Simone Weil. This motif was to be most fully developed in *Severina,* completed after his death by Darina. But the idea ran like a thread throughout his entire oeuvre.

For Silone, assiduous reader of the Old Testament, the Hebrews represented an unprecedented moral example: absolute fidelity to human conscience through time and historical experiences such as exile, slavery, oppression, the Crusades, the Inquisition, totalitarianism, and attempts at extermination. Yet curiously, there are only two Jewish characters in Silone's fiction, both found in *A Handful of Blackberries*: the Austrian Jew Stern, "a timid, courteous, bearded little man, garbed in black," and his precocious daughter. When the inhabitants of the roadside inn are told that the word *"stern"* means "star," they name the daughter Stella (Italian for "star"). Stern and his daughter had arrived in Italy from Vienna after the anschluss. Scheduled to be deported to an extermination camp, they were instead sent to the roadhouse inn by a humane Fascist police officer.

Silone, a political exile himself, sensed a fraternity with the Jews (he often liked to recount the story of the Holy Family's flight from Herod), and Stern is a sympathetic character. For the peasants of Abruzzo, the two Jews are the personification of a persecuted race, one that had become the scapegoat of humanity. Their presence creates two theological problems, touchingly human and absurd. When the elderly Stern is close to death, Zaccaria, the ornery old bandit in charge of the roadside inn, sends for the local priest, Don Nicola. Upon arriving in the middle of a snowstorm, after having been threatened with an attack by the ferocious mountain wolves, Don Nicola discovers that the deathbed scene belongs to old Stern. When Zaccaria, citing the ancient laws of hospitality, insists that the priest administer the last rites, Don Nicola refuses because of the old man's Jewish faith. The argument threatens to escalate into violence until an agreement is finally reached: Zaccaria's wife, Giuditta, is dispatched to the deathbed to inquire if old man Stern wishes to receive the last rites. She returns with his answer: He would prefer to die "in the religion of his ancestors," but remembering a talk with Don Nicola about the brotherhood of all men, would like to speak one last time with the priest about the subject.

Entering the room, Don Nicola finds Stella reading to her father from the Torah: "Our fathers trusted in Thee; they trusted and Thou didst deliver them. They cried unto Thee and were delivered; they trusted in Thee and were not confounded." When Stella falls asleep, Don Nicola takes her place reading from the Book of Job. Don Nicola is then charged with a solemn task:

> "Forgive me," said the dying man. "I leave my daughter in your charge."
>
> "Have no fears for her," said Giuditta.
>
> "She's not of your religion," added the dying man. "Will you respect her?"
>
> "Do you doubt it?" answered Zaccaria.
>
> Signor Stern repeated his question, turning his eyes to the priest: "Will you respect her?"

"We shall love her," answered Don Nicola.

"I'm sure of that," murmured Signor Stern. "I know you. You're good people, warmhearted people. But will you also respect her?" . . .

Toward midnight old Stern revived, but Don Nicola was not fooled; he knew it was the rally that often precedes death.

"Do you really believe," Signor Stern asked Don Nicola, "that there is some meaning in it all? Are you sure?"

Then he said: "Now tell me about our being all children of the same Father."

This deathbed request comes to haunt Don Nicola when he is confronted by his parochial, bigoted spinster sister, Adele, to address the growing dual scandals of having an unbaptized person (Stella) in his parish, and the even more scandalous relationship between Stella and Rocco De Donatis, Silone's alter ego. The growing tension between brother and sister finally explodes one night as they sit down for the evening meal.

"I'll appeal to the Bishop," she said vehemently and furiously. "The scandal can't go on."

"What scandal are you talking about?"

"Your laziness about the Jewess."

"In what way? You mean there's a scandal that there are other religions in the world besides the Catholic religion? But that's an old scandal . . ."

"What are you doing to enlighten her and guide her?" pursued his sister in a nagging voice. "What have you done up to now?"

"Very little, alas," confessed Don Nicola . . . "Love is the best catechism. For the rest, faith is a matter of Grace."

Brother and sister continue their verbal parrying, with Adele accusing her brother of blasphemy and Nicola increasingly vigorous in his defense of his position and Stella's right to her own conscience. In one of Silone's few direct references to the Holocaust, Don Nicola challenges his sister:

> "Stella was driven by violence from her home and her country," Don Nicola went on, taking courage. "I can't be silent any longer, you must listen to me. She was hunted out of that Catholic country. By violence. Now she is here with us, an orphan. But hundreds of thousands belonging to her faith are at this very moment being persecuted, robbed, massacred, burned alive. According to my humble but irremovable way of thinking, a man with any sense of charity and decency, in the presence of that forlorn little being, can only feel ashamed and be silent."

(When a friend and colleague asked me about Silone's writings on the Holocaust, I was forced to concede that, surprisingly, he had written little or nothing on the subject. Perhaps he thought that in the face of such horror, he, as a writer and a Christian, could only remain "ashamed and silent.")

As Adele admonishes him not to forget that he is a Catholic priest, Don Nicola shoots back that he cannot forget that Stella is also a human being and that a "war of extermination" is being fought against her and her people. Their epic confrontation reaches a climax when Adele insists that the Lord abandoned the Temple and that their religion is false, to which Don Nicola responds, "And what if it is?" The spinster flares up "like a match" and asks if her brother has gone mad. In truth, Don Nicola finds himself standing on the very brink of two sins, heresy and indiscipline, the first as a Catholic, the second in his capacity as priest.

A *Handful of Blackberries*, then, is the story not only of Silone's estrangement from the PCI through the figure of Rocco De Donatis, but also of Silone's estrangement from the church through the figure of Don Nicola. De Donatis and Don Nicola, who had been inseparable as boyhood friends, took different paths yet ended up in the same place, together at novel's end, the former expelled from the party, the latter leaving his shrew of a sister and following De Donatis in his wanderings.

While the Jews did not figure prominently in his fiction, Silone was sensitive to the contemporary plight of Jewish intellectuals, especially in the Soviet bloc. He thundered with rage in a January 1957 letter to the Russian writer Ivan Anissimov about the fate of Isaac Babel. The Jewish writer had given a speech at the first Congress of the Soviet Writers' Union in 1934 in which he declared that he was fast becoming a master of a new literary genre, "the genre of silence," and a year later he addressed the writers and artists of the West at the International Congress of Writers in Paris. During Stalin's purge, his mentor Gorky died under mysterious circumstances. (Was he really, Silone asked Anissimov, poisoned by the political police?) Babel was arrested in the spring of 1939 and executed in January 1940, although the official Soviet version, passed on by the Russian Jewish writer Ilya Ehrenburg, was that he perished in a labor camp. Of the long line of Jewish writers condemned and killed under the grotesque charge of "cosmopolitanism," "I have only these names: D. Bergelson, Perez Markisc [sic], Itzik Feffer, Der Nistar, Moshe Kulbak; but what of the others?" Silone even cites an essay by Bernard Turner in the Tel Aviv journal *Di Goldene Keyt* (The Golden Chain), "With Jewish Writers in Siberia," in which he mentions, among other things, the rumor that Ehrenburg was an informer for the Soviet police.

Accepting the Jerusalem Prize for literature in 1969, Silone recalled, "During my exile in Zurich, I came to know and befriend many Jews, of every social condition, and with some of them I have remained tied all the rest of my life. I will never forget their accounts of suffering and sorrow." Through these Jewish refugees, he came to know a few words of Yiddish. His favorite, which he used in response to those who questioned his traveling to Israel to accept the award in the wake of the 1967 war, was "nebbish." "I could not have found an Italian word that was more precise. *Nebbish* is a marvelous word, untranslatable, mutable according to the voice and the attitude of the speaker; it is an authentic philological jewel."

Silone's encounter with the life and work of Simone Weil presented another fundamental turning point in his life, so important that two biographers refer to her as "a second life companion" (*una seconda compagna di vita*). But even here, Silone could not bring himself to admit that it was Darina who had introduced him to the tragic figure of Weil.

"It was not easy," Darina recalled in an interview shortly before her death, "to give gifts to Silone." On its publication in 1950, she gave her husband a copy of Simone Weil's *Attente de Dieu*. Judging by his copy marked by different pencils revealing many readings, "I think it was one of the most successful gifts." Silone went on to devour all of Weil's work, keeping her books on his nightstand, along with a Bible and a German translation of the Old Testament completed by his old friend from Switzerland, Martin Buber.

Not all contemporary writers shared Silone's enthusiasm for Weil. Susan Sontag criticized Weil's "anguished and unconsummated love affair with the Catholic Church," her "Gnostic theology of divine absence," her "ideals of body denial," and her "violently unfair hatred of Roman civilization and the Jews." But to André Gide, Weil was the "most spiritual writer of this century"; for Camus she was "the only great spirit of our times." T. S. Eliot called her "a woman of genius, akin to that of a saint." The critic Leslie Fiedler described her as "the Outsider as Saint in an age of alienation."

Weil (1909–43), like Silone, suffered from tuberculosis, succumbing to the disease (and self-imposed starvation) at the age of thirty-four in England, where she had fled the Nazi occupation of the Continent. Weil had been born in Paris to an assimilated Jewish family and studied with the French philosopher Alain. Her experience as a factory worker radically transformed her into a follower of Marxism and pacifism. One suspects that her popularity with some European thinkers was based—at least in part—on her critique of Judaism. T. S. Eliot wrote in his preface to a volume of her essays that "she was intensely Jewish, suffering the torments in the affliction of the Jews in Germany; yet she castigated Israel with all the severity of a Hebrew prophet. Prophets, we are told, were stoned in Jerusalem: but Simone Weil is exposed to lapidation from several quarters." Jewish writers, for their part, detected in her a classic case of Theodor Lessing's "Jewish self-hatred."

Silone, I believe, interpreted Weil's work as a creative and radical Jewish rejection of idolatry in all its forms, a position that constitutes the very heart of prophetic monotheism. In this sense, Silone and Weil both find themselves reinforcing Carlo Levi's meditation on man's inability to liberate himself from a primal dread, resulting in accepting sacrifice in place of the sacred and embracing fear in exchange for freedom. In "The Choice of Companions," Silone quotes Weil's *Shadow and Grace*: "One must always be ready to change sides in the name of justice, the great refugee from the camp of the conquerors."

Silone noted that Weil had discerned what had already been implied by Engels: the naturally oppressive nature of modern industrialization, no matter what class owned the means of production. Marx's colleague had once written that above the gates of every factory there should be written "Abandon all hope, ye who enter here." Weil, less dramatically, had simply noted the humiliation and suffering endured by the workers, whether in capitalist or Soviet factories.

For Silone, Weil occupied an intellectual position in the West equal to Camus, Orwell, and Sartre. Weil was not so much a revelation as the discovery of "a spiritual itinerary" very similar to his own. Shortly after having read *Attente de Dieu*, he wrote an essay for the Swiss journal *Témoins* in which he argued that the crisis of the age was both moral and religious. Metaphysics and religious dogmas had lost all relevance and the spiritual drama of this unknown French Jewish intellectual was also "our own." And while one cannot claim that Severina = Weil, nonetheless it is clear that the figure of the young initiate shares many of Weil's traits. Darina, who pulled the novel together from Silone's notes after his death, was clear: "If Silone had not encountered Weil's thinking, I don't believe he would have been able to create the character of Severina in that last desperate attempt to communicate his last message." In order to complete the manuscript, she immersed herself in Weil's work and biography to be able to better imagine Severina. Darina paid particular attention to those passages in Weil's books marked by her husband. Among his notes for the novel, Darina found this: "The sense of life according to Severina: love truth." It was this shared itinerary that pushed both to refuse all illusions and to embrace the moral duty of recognizing a painful and sorrowful reality without falling victim to inertia, skepticism, or nihilism. On the contrary: "It was precisely this love of truth, intimately joined to a love of justice, which forced Silone and Weil to act positively and courageously."

Simone Weil had read Silone. Selma Weil, her mother, confirmed that her daughter had been profoundly affected by *Bread and Wine*. Silone had made a pilgrimage of sorts to Paris to visit Selma, whom he met with Boris Souvarine, Robert Schuman, and a young French scholar who was to write a biography of Weil, Simone Pétrement.

It was Pétrement's two-volume biography of Weil, published in 1974, that may have planted the seed for Severina in his mind. After reading the biography, Silone wrote to a friend that "the two volumes have done wonders for me. Thanks to them I have begun again to write a little. And they have convinced me that there exists a communion of souls."

In failing health, physically frail, conscious of losing some of his mental and creative powers, Silone retreated into painful memories and nostalgia. He was well aware of how memory could deceive and recalled a story about Tolstoy's writing of *War and Peace*. It seems that when the Russian writer was composing his great novel, he heard of an old peasant who had witnessed Napoleon's invasion of Russia. After much searching, he found the old fellow, who promptly told him that the French emperor was "as tall as a giant with a great white beard." Tolstoy smiled, thanked the peasant, and returned to his writing.

Silone often thought of Pescina, Romolo, Switzerland. Just before he died, he spoke candidly about his brother: "The loss of my mother in the earthquake was a terrible pain, but it was caused by a natural calamity. The imprisonment and death of my brother have remained my personal torment, because they would not have happened if it weren't for me. That's why I rarely spoke of Romolo. It's a type of pain that is difficult to communicate."

Occasionally he would make a painful return to his hometown, traveling by train, often at night. Anyone who has made the trip by train can still recognize Silone's description of 1965: "Through the glass I could see the countryside, preserved for many years like a *presepio* [crèche] in my memory, coming toward me: the stony little fields and the dark, bare, deserted mountains. I saw the little stations appear and disappear, their doors and windows bolted, their walls falling down. In the darkness I could tell the peasant origin of the men and women in the compartment by the bitter smell." These brief returns to Abruzzo and Pescina tormented Silone with a biting sense of nostalgia and loss. "It is not easy to return to the place of one's childhood as a grown man, if one's thoughts have never broken away from it during one's absence and if one has continued to live through imaginary events there. It can even be dangerous." Typical were the obligatory receptions of ordinary citizens and public officials that were often waiting for him, causing him much anxiety. As a politician for a time in the early 1950s and a world-renowned writer, Silone was expected to embrace publicity and contribute to the bombastic rhetoric of these occasions. Instead, he felt "burdened with the saddest possible memories" and often fled or avoided the receptions altogether. The disappointed townspeople, he later learned, attributed his strange behavior to extreme political intransigence and a morbid misanthropy.

On his daily walk to Piazza Bologna to mail letters and visit the local newspaper kiosk, he was a rather pathetic figure. "When, as occasionally happened, I caught a glimpse of him on the streets of Rome," the novelist Antonio Debenedetti told Michael P. McDonald, "the sense of solitude that clung to him was overpowering." He was increasingly remote and brusque with Darina, often silent for days. After one such period he noted that "for me it is a good experience, not unpleasant," and perhaps thinking of his beloved Celestine, "but it is too late to flee to the mountains."

Early in 1973, Silone received another of the innumerable requests for an interview. As usual, he was torn between a desire to reach out to new readers and his natural hesitancy as well as physical infirmity. Unlike many other writers, Silone came to his craft rather late. "I was already thirty years old when I realized that writing books was for me the only possible activity in the conditions I had been reduced to. I found myself a political exile in Switzerland, completely isolated, without a real and true profession, and besides, with an intense internal burden that gave me no peace or rest." The unforeseen and unforeseeable success of *Fontamara* made him a writer. Now, forty years after that first book appeared, Silone could discern a thread that tied the books together, even if he could not say that they all corresponded to a preordained plan. They have in common that which binds the children of the same mother, "even if they demonstrate external differences in height, coloring, or even intelligence. Every book of mine corresponds clearly to a necessity of mine . . . every book was an immensely tiring work and at the end of each I repeat what many mothers say after giving birth: 'That's it, I don't want any more.' But the laws of life prevail and others arrive." Even though some critics had defined him by the environment of his books as a "southern" writer or a "peasant" writer, Silone insisted that the dominant theme of his work was elsewhere: the fate of Christianity in a society that was, essentially, insincere (*in malafede*). That which tied him to the poor was not their psychology, not their ideology, but the situation they occupied in society, the position to which they were bound, even after the so-called political revolutions of the last two centuries. For this reason "I think a writer must never place himself in the service of a state, nor an ideology, but must remain faithful to the humbled and the oppressed."

He proudly claimed allegiance to no system of philosophy, no ideology, no orthodoxy. "I think that all ideological systems inherited from the last century are at present in crisis, as is the society that gave birth to them, which is not to say that they do not contain some partial truths." All metaphysics had lost their "proofs." Still, "I have remained a Socialist . . . Only socialism can create a true democracy." His socialism was close to that of the anarchist Proudhon; his conception of "man" came from the popular Christian tradition of the Abruzzo.

In the foreword of the 1960 edition of *Fontamara*, Silone wrote that if it were in his "power to change the mercantile laws of literary society, I might well spend my life perpetually writing and rewriting the same story in the hope of at last understanding it and making it understood, just as in the Middle Ages there were monks who spent their whole lives painting and repainting the Savior's face, always the same face, yet always different."

His last years were, according to Darina Silone, "sad, agonizing, and cruelly unproductive." He often thought about his past, but without taking Darina back with him in his thoughts. Once, they were visiting the Pieve di Corsignano, a twelfth-century church near Pienza where Pope Pius II had been baptized, with Iris Origo. "When we came out we saw on the rough grass besides the church a group of cold, scrubby seminarians who . . . were kicking a ball about. Silone stood still in silence, with his hands in his pockets. The sun went down, it grew colder and colder, and Darina suggested repeatedly that we would all like to go home. When at last we got Silone to the car, I said to him, 'Were you looking at the sunset?' 'No,' he replied, "I was watching my youth.' "

In one of Silone's last public interviews, Gino De Sanctis found a man who "hid behind the allusion of a smile." Seeking to read the author's face, De Sanctis found a grave, almost sad visage, one "completely permeated by a doubting grimace" yet moved by "a hidden source of humor." The answers to the questions he had asked in his novels and essays were still to be answered, still to be sought out. Ill and sensing his own end, Silone remarked that it was quite possible that when answers to those questions would be found, he might no longer be around to hear them. "But who knows; it might very well be that the questions themselves, instead, are the answers." One thing was certain: At the advanced age of seventy-two, he was returning to the radical questions he had posed to himself at age fifteen, to a radical Christianity that had little or even nothing to do with the institutionalized Catholic church. His political commitment, his youthful militancy in the PCI, his encounters and dissension with Russian Communists, Fascist persecution, exile and the hatred of Communists, his literary fortune—all of these, he now realized, "were well-meaning distractions from those famous unanswerable questions." With the passing of years and much suffering, he had arrived at a point of indulgence and an understanding of everyone; perhaps it was already a rapprochement with "love and death."

At the Hour of Our Death

"I have no fear of dying," Silone once confided to Darina, "only of not being conscious when the moment comes. It's the last moment of life, the most solemn of all: I don't want to miss it." In October 1977, he was admitted to the Pio X clinic in Rome. Doctors there failed to properly diagnose the kidney disease that would eventually contribute to his death. In a letter to Mary McCarthy, Darina mentions the medical mistakes as "the grisly horrors of Rome." Silone became increasingly difficult with his doctors and especially with Darina. Fifteen years of mistaken diagnosis culminated in a "fatal mistake" in October 1977, causing him much needless suffering. Darina had sought for years to take Silone to Geneva, but it was only in March 1978, when Silone himself realized that his doctors in Rome had abandoned hope, that he permitted Darina to make the necessary arrangements. Although Silone showed signs of improvement, abandoning the black cane given to him by their devoted Sardinian housekeeper and writing daily, Swiss doctors had told Darina that an operation was, by this time, too dangerous for the patient. In Geneva, Silone regained some measure of lucidity and productivity. On August 12, 1978, Darina even wrote McCarthy that he was regaining his health in "miraculous ways." Yet in ten days he would be dead.

Darina had confessed to McCarthy that she intended to use *Severina* to keep Silone alive. More practically, she revealed that upon return from a trip to India just after Easter 1977, she finally discovered the full implications of their disastrous finances. Darina then made it a point over the next year and a half to protect Silone from any knowledge of their precarious situation. (McCarthy sent Darina some money—at least two checks were waiting for Darina when she arrived in Geneva.) "I have to consider his dignity and have not yet decided to beg for him from friends. I did discuss . . . the possibility of appealing to some zillionairish source but still can't bring myself to do it. I am trying still to find a dignified solution."

In an extraordinary seven-page handwritten letter after Silone's death, Darina mysteriously confided to McCarthy that she had been suffering from a yearlong hand injury "acquired, let us say, in Silone's service." It was the writer, activist, and photographer Dorothy Norman who had first passed along to McCarthy that Ignazio and Darina Silone were in grave financial trouble.

Their financial situation was "indeed desperate," as she confessed in a letter to McCarthy. McCarthy was instrumental in securing a grant of $5,000 from the Ingram Merrill Foundation, which arrived just after Silone died. (Upon the death of his wealthy father, the American poet James Merrill established a foundation to assist writers and artists.)

Kidney failure was causing irreparable damage to the arteries in Silone's brain. Although he seemed to recover somewhat, Silone sensed the inevitable. "How many years lost," he lamented to Darina. Now his thoughts turned, not for the first time, to the management of his archive and papers. So concerned was he about the future *sistematizzazione* of his written legacy, correspondence, and papers that he insisted that he and Darina travel on different planes for their many voyages.

From the Clinique Général in Geneva, Silone granted a final interview in July. When asked about Solzhenitsyn's speech at Harvard University criticizing the West's materialism, he replied, "I greatly admire Solzhenitsyn, even if I do not always agree with him. It is not true that spiritual strength today survives only in the East." Shortly before his death, he was asked if he was nostalgic for his Abruzzo. He shrugged his shoulders. "My Abruzzo can be anywhere." He did have several months of mental lucidity in Geneva and "his joy when he realized that he was retrieving his mental and creative faculties was unforgettable." But the doctor told Darina that now there was no hope, the brain lesion was too deep. They could keep him alive artificially, but Darina knew that Silone would not want that. Upon reflection, she asked the doctor to keep him alive long enough so she could make arrangements. Writing to McCarthy, Darina described the scene: "He was writing up to the last moment—frantically, as if to finish what he was doing. It was a beautiful day but he was so intent on writing that he refused both his customary siesta and his walk in the garden." Suddenly, around 6:30 p.m., "very calmly and slowly, he put down his pen and carefully lifted the writing table away from him." Moving to an armchair, he sat down "and said very clearly and distinctly, in *French*—I don't want to quote the exact words because I haven't told them to anyone, I want to write about them one day—that everything was finished now, that he was dying. So he *did* have the moment of consciousness of death that he had always wanted." In another version of this scene, Darina recounted how the personnel of the clinic had brought him his supper but not hers; he was concerned. While eating, he simply moved the table away from himself and made his way to an armchair and clearly and loudly said, *"Maintenant c'est fini. Tout est fini. Je meurs."* Darina wrote that Silone died as he wished: "with dignity and conscious." But he lingered almost four days. Darina, when she took his hand, felt that he seemed to respond; the doctors and nurses told her it was only a reflex. Silone opened his eyes only once, on hearing the doctor call his name several times. His heart finally gave out at 4:15 the morning of August 22, 1978. A dying patient's final words in a foreign language, the doctor told Darina, was something he had never witnessed before. She, remembering an old promise, recited the Our Father at his deathbed. On the desk in the room lay the pages of his unfinished *Severina*.

Italian president Sandro Pertini, who had called from Rome a month earlier to ask about Silone, sent his condolences: "With Ignazio Silone's death we have lost one of the most representative figures of the struggle for freedom, for democracy, for social justice; a noble, rigorous, inflexible democratic conscience of contemporary Italian culture. I express my great sorrow for this loss that wounds the entire Nation." Telegrams and condolences arrived from all over the world, from every corner of Italian political and cultural life, perhaps the most poignant from Aline Valangin and Francine Camus. But in truth, Silone had been as alone in death as he had been in life. As he explicitly requested, his body was cremated and the ashes brought to the cemetery of Pescina and placed in the family chapel. There was no religious ceremony, only the recitation of some passages of his work (as he specifically requested, without a microphone). A year later, a rough-hewn tomb was crafted from the rocks of the mountain and his ashes were laid to rest overlooking the place he never really left.

In November 1978, three months after his death, Darina was still outraged that the incompetence of Silone's Italian doctors had failed to spot uremia while the doctors in Geneva had diagnosed it on the first day of his stay at the Clinique Général de Florissant. Swiss friends paid the clinic and the funeral home. Darina returned to Rome, frantic about how to repay the debts that were piling up at a rapid rate. A royalty statement from Harper's in New York, Silone's American publisher, granted Darina the princely sum of 10¢ for the first half of 1978; another, from Stockholm, stated that Silone owed them money. Their insurance company refused to pay for the clinic's medical bills on the grounds that Silone was dead. Silone had put all the first editions of his novels in storage in the garage; by the time Darina went to find them, they had been destroyed by dampness and mold. A year earlier, their apartment had been robbed (Darina suspected the portiere) and the few things she had of value had been stolen. Darina was worried about "people stealing even more of his things than have already been stolen." She hated the apartment in Rome, "everything here is horrible and macabre." Their beloved Sardinian housekeeper had died just four days before Darina had left Rome to join Silone in Geneva. Darina could not go to Pescina (an enmity had sprouted long ago between the Pescinese and Darina). "I am (with a few exceptions)," she lamented alone and frightened in their dark apartment, "experiencing the Italians at their worst."

Darina maintained a ferocious watch over her husband's literary and personal estate. She spent the rest of her life in two pursuits: requiting her love of India and promoting Silone's literary and ethical reputation with a missionary's zeal. She often fled Rome for India: "I simply had to *clear out* of Rome," Darina wrote to McCarthy, "disappear, before I lost the remnants of any sanity. I need it all, such as it is." For Darina, Silone's death was his final gift to her. "Despite everything," she wrote six months later, "his death was and still is a very great gift to me. In Geneva he had changed, become extraordinarily *sweet* and—at last—very close to me." For that gift, Silone had charged her, verbally and in writing, with the care of his immense archive, "and in this," she wrote defiantly, "I am determined not to fail him."

Silone had stipulated in his will that his archive and editorial correspondence were to be administered by Darina with the understanding that they be made "available to future scholars," preferably in an American university. But the Italian government immediately declared Silone's archive part of the "national heritage," thereby erasing any chance that they would be removed from the country. In one of the documents making up his last will and testament, he bequeathed all his possessions and wealth (such as it was) to Darina. More important, his rights (and royalties) as author went to her. On her death, these would revert to the city of Pescina for "cultural purposes" such as a communal library and scholarships for worthy students.

Silone spent his life seeking utopia in two currents of history: Christianity and socialism. For him they meant the same thing: an attempt to find redemption through liberation of the body and the spirit, and freedom from oppression and injustice. He took up both crosses, mindful of his many painful stumbles (despair, betrayal, Bellone, adultery, contemplating suicide) yet was left with hope. He approached his end if not with a firm conviction, at least with a living hope that men and women of good faith would share in a third age of humanity as announced by Joachim of Fiore: governed by neither church nor state, without coercion, a sober, humble, benign, and egalitarian society entrusted to spontaneous charity among men. Our only hope, he felt, lay in the peasants, the much-maligned cafoni, and their spiritual brethren in poverty all over the world: not so much in a particular political or spiritual program but rather in an acute awareness of a moral tension that animates their daily lives. In an interview shortly before his death, he confessed, "I am a Christian in my own fashion."

In April 1977, when Silone's Rome doctors had told Darina privately that he had not long to live, she found the following document in his desk, in an envelope addressed to her.

At the hour of our death

(Creed) I trust that I am unfettered by any consideration of the opinions of my fellow men or any other ulterior interests in declaring that I do not wish for there to be any religious ceremony, either at the time of my death or afterward. This is a sad and serene decision, thoughtfully considered. I hope not to wound or disappoint anyone who loves me. I feel that I have sincerely expressed, at various times, all the duty I feel toward Christ and his teachings. I recognize that, initially, it was selfishness in all its forms, from vanity to sensuality, that led me to stray from him. Perhaps the loss of my family at an early age, poverty, my physical infirmities, and certain natural pre-dispositions toward anguish and desperation facilitated my errors. It was however through Christ, and his teachings, that I recovered, even as I maintained my distance from him. Several times, in painful circumstances, I have simply fallen to my knees in my room, without saying anything, with only an overwhelming feeling of aban-donment; a few times I recited the Lord's Prayer; once or twice I remember making the sign of the Cross. But the "return to the fold" has not been possible, even after the "modernizations" of the recent Vatican Council. I have already given an explanation for failing to return, and it is sincere. It strikes me that over the course of cen-turies there has been constructed a theological and liturgical elabora-tion—historical in origin—upon essential Christian truths that has rendered them unrecognizable. Official Christianity has become an ideology. It would be a violation of my deepest beliefs and nature to declare that I accept it; and if I did, it would be in bad faith.

"In his will," Darina revealed in 2000, "Silone asked that all his per-sonal correspondence be destroyed, and I, for my part, destroyed it, without regret because I knew that no one could ever understand it." Many years after his death, Darina reflected that there were aspects of his personality that always remained a mystery to her, she who knew him best. She sent flowers to his grave in Pescina three times a year: May 1, August 22, and All Souls' Day, November 2. Among his notes to *Severina* she found two fragments in a shaky hand revealing his increas-ing concern about his own end. One, from Rainer Maria Rilke: "O Lord, grant each his proper Death." The other, from Benedetto Croce, was more irreverent: "When it comes, may it at least surprise us at work."

Silone had embraced Carlo Rosselli's dictum that "the only serious way to be anti-Fascist is to be heretical." It had cost him severed ties with his family; immersion in and then expulsion from a radical, out-lawed political movement; the postponement of his true vocation as a writer; and infinite sorrow. As Irving Howe perceptively noted, "Everything Silone wrote was motivated by rebellion against social injustice and . . . by a need to define the condition of humanity for those who had chosen to rebel." But that heroic stance has been undermined by some dark shadows of Silone's past, which have only recently come to light.

EIGHT

"SILVESTRI"

Everything conspires to confuse.
—the Fascist spy *ALDO SAMPIERI* on Silone

Silone's life and literary career were often marked by bitter controversy. The first was his expulsion from the PCI in 1931; another was his scandalous (mis)reception by the literary establishment in Italy; late in life he was (again) accused of collaborating with the CIA. When, in March 1996, the Italian historian Dario Biocca presented archival documents implicating Silone as a former Fascist police spy, another caso Silone exploded in literary, political, and cultural circles.

The documents are letters purportedly written by Silone—some signed "Silvestri," others not—to a high-ranking Fascist police official in Rome, Guido Bellone. Biocca's bombshell was primed by a scoop two days earlier when Italy's most authoritative daily newspaper published his initial findings. A month later, an official of the Central State Archives leaked a letter that he had surreptitiously removed from the files to a rival newspaper in Rome. The letter is a powerful and poignant document that testifies to a political and emotional crisis. Most scholars have now accepted the authenticity of this letter (as have I). Biocca was eventually joined in his research by fellow historian Mauro Canali, a specialist on the Fascist secret police. For more than a decade, in Italy, France, Britain, America, and elsewhere (even Japan and Afghanistan), a tidal wave of ink has been spilled in a heated and often acrimonious debate: Are all the documents authentic and, if so, what is their significance in revising our conception of Silone as a moral exemplar of the twentieth century, committed to fighting both fascism and communism?

The spying charge is not new. Seemingly forgotten in the current controversy is the fact that for decades Silone had been accused of spying for the Fascist secret police. A day after Silone's death on August 22, 1978, the Italian journalist Giorgio Bocca wrote that he had met Silone late in life (1972) but was aware that accusations of all sorts had been raised against the writer. "There were already continuous slanders against him," recalled Bocca, "during the armed resistance: [that he was] a traitor, a social democratic friend of the CIA, an informer for [the Fascist secret police] OVRA." Or, as University of Cambridge scholar Robert Gordon has dryly written, Silone has so often been accused of spying—either for the Fascists or the CIA—"that he risked being turned into a spy for all seasons and for all sides."

The earliest charges date back to World War II. In the Silone Archive in Florence there is a curious document, undated (but from 1946) and approximately the size of a large postcard. It reads in full:

Press Collect Via ITALRADIO
Gottfried TIMEINC New York
    Director of TIME has stated that the text, charging T [Tranquilli] with personal responsibility for betraying Socialists to Italian police has been a misunderstanding. The necessary correction should be made clear that it was a question of Communist policy to denounce to the public all Socialists as betrayers of the cause of social justice and labeling them enemies to be treated like the Fascists.

Fifty years later, in 1996, Biocca's claims were initially met with skepticism, incredulity, and outright shock. The battle lines were quickly drawn. Biocca and Canali, along with a host of Italian journalists and some historians, were labeled "*colpevolisti*" (those believing Silone to be guilty), while Silone's defenders were called "*innocentisti.*" Silone's supporters claimed at first that the documents were forgeries. The Fascists were not beyond such tactics. A short story by Bruce Cutler demonstrates the ingenious and creative tactics the Fascist police could devise. A young student and partisan must undergo a rather unorthodox "Final Examination":

He's lucky.

He's a young partisan who has been captured, not by the German SS, who have just arrived at the outskirts of Naples, but by the Fascist police.

He undergoes the usual beatings. The police commissioner holds an adjunct professorship in the university law school, and after a few hours, hearing that the young partisan is a university student, he steps in and personally takes over the interrogation. After three days of questioning, the young partisan still remains silent, so the police commissioner makes him an offer. He tells him that this will be his "final examination." To complete it, he must choose between two alternatives. One: if he betrays the hiding places of his comrades, he will be sentenced to death. But the sentence will not be carried out; he will live, and eventually have his freedom. If the young partisan chooses this alternative, the police commissioner promises to plant false documents in the files proving that the information came from other sources. In this way, his reputation will remain untarnished, and in an anti-fascist victory, he will be in line for all the honors due a hero of the resistance.

On the other hand, if the young partisan refuses to give him the information about his comrades, the police commissioner tells him he is confident that in a few days, as a result of the terror caused by the arrival of the German SS, all his comrades will be rounded up.

After which, they will be shot. Then the commissioner will plant "proof" that it was information from him which had betrayed his comrades and thereafter everyone will look upon him as a traitor and spit on his grave.

It is for him to choose. Which will it be? The young partisan asks for a day to consider, and goes back to his cell.

Sixteen hours later, he hangs himself.

Cutler's vignette—besides its masterful compression of pathos and tragedy in a mere eighteen sentences—forces us to reconsider the status of documents in the archives and the role of memory in the reconstruction of historical narratives. As Jacques Derrida has pointed out, the archive is the locus where memory, history, fiction, technology, power, and authority all intersect in increasingly complex ways. The very word "archive," from the Greek "*archeion*," connotes authority and origin, a commandment and a commencement. As users of some European archives can attest, archivists often seem to conceive of themselves as custodians whose vocation it is to prevent the uninitiated from having any profane contact with the sacred texts. In Silone's case, because of a national privacy law, many of his personal papers from the last forty years, deposited by his wife Darina Silone at the Fondazione di Studi Storici "Filippo Turati" in Florence, cannot be consulted by scholars. The question of the malleability of history and the manipulation of memory has been the subject of several fine scholarly works. Most impressive, for both the methodological questions it raises and its eloquent style, is Alessandro Portelli's examination of the Ardeatine Caves massacre outside Rome.

Creative as the Fascists may have been, most scholars have either abandoned or rejected the defense that the letters are forgeries. This, though, does not resolve the myriad questions raised by the documents. Having seen the letters, I had to conclude that at least some do appear to be in Silone's handwriting. But even those documents that appear to be written by Silone are not signed, often have no addressee, and might not be interpreted as spying reports. Several letters are definitely not in his hand, referring to "Silvestri" in the third person. In examining some of the documents, the handwriting expert Dr. Anna Petrecchia of Rome has concluded that they are "all different from Silone's other handwritten works . . . [The writers] are two different people."

The recipient of these letters was Guido Bellone. Born in 1871 in Florence, Bellone was a career police official at the Questura (police headquarters) in Rome who, in the wake of World War I, had been assigned to combat political subversives in the nation's capital. In 1926, he was reassigned to the Ministry of the Interior and his brief as inspector general of the political police extended to surveillance of domestic and foreign radicals. He was considered an expert on the various left-wing political movements and charged with politically delicate missions abroad. As one scholar has aptly framed the story, Bellone plays the role of the shadowy yet omnipresent and omniscient bureaucrat, mysterious and pervasive, while the narrative of the spying scandal is a cross between Dostoevsky and Kafka, between *Crime and Punishment* and *The Castle*.

If Silone was indeed a spy, he was extraordinarily audacious. In an essay published in the official theoretical journal of the PCI, in April 1928, just as his brother Romolo was being arrested, he wrote:

> We don't risk being accused of lying when we affirm that the PNF [National Fascist Party] has received the support of solid groups of all Italian political parties except the Communist Party. There have been a very limited number of low-ranking members of the Communist Party who have gone over to fascism, notwithstanding the opposite fairy tale diffused by the [Socialist] reformists. But those elements, among which there was no party leader, went over to the Fascists as one goes over to the police. Their betrayal had no political importance.

Was Silone implying that contact with the police (i.e., Bellone) was not as morally corrupting as collaboration with the Fascists? Whatever the case, he was simply wrong on this point, as any history of the period can demonstrate that several political leaders of all parties, including the PCI, threw in their lot with fascism (an exception was Justice and Liberty). An interesting piece of philological detective work by Mimmo Franzinelli demonstrates that when Silone republished this essay in 1962, he omitted this passage, even though claiming in an editorial note to having reproduced a version faithful to the original, "with only the omission of some anachronistic and polemical digression."

Biocca published his research in an academic journal in 1998. It did nothing to quell the controversy; in fact, the tone of the debate descended from academic to contentious to acrimonious. Even the timing of the publication and the nature of the journal became grist for the controversy: The essay appeared when many people were preparing for official ceremonies to commemorate the twentieth anniversary of Silone's death, and some noted that the essay appeared in a journal that was founded by Renzo De Felice, the dean of historians of fascism, often accused of a "rehabilitation" of Mussolini and his regime.

The central document—the urtext of the controversy even if it was written last—is a letter of April 13, 1930 (two years to the day after Romolo's arrest), signed "Silvestri." The letter was removed from Silone's file in the Archivio Centrale dello Stato in Rome and leaked to the national newspaper *La Repubblica*, which published it in 1996. It is a classic example of the way a single document can be interpreted in different ways. For the colpevolisti it is the smoking gun of Silone's guilt; for the innocentisti it is proof of Silone's moral crisis in attempting to mitigate the fate of his younger brother in Fascist hands.

13.4.1930

Forgive me if I haven't written you any more. What you were interested to learn is no longer a mystery (the press already talks about it). I don't know what my friends and I will do. My health is terrible but the cause is moral (you will understand if you remember what I wrote to you last summer). I find myself at a very painful moment in my existence. The moral sense that has always been very strong in me now dominates me completely; it doesn't let

me sleep, it doesn't let me eat, it doesn't allow me the briefest
respite. I find myself at the resolution of my existential crisis, which
allows only one way out: the complete abandonment of militant
politics (I will seek some intellectual occupation). Aside from this
solution, nothing was left but death. Continuing to live an equivocal
life was impossible to me, is impossible for me. I was born to be an
honest landowner in my village. Life has thrown me down a slope

from which I now want to save myself. My conscience tells me I
have done a great harm to neither my friends nor to my country.
Within the limits of the possible I have always avoided wrongdoing.
I must tell you that, given your position, you have always behaved
like a gentleman. For that reason, I am writing this last letter so
that you *won't prevent* my plan, which will take place in two phases:
first, eliminate from my life everything that is falsehood, duplicity,
equivocation, mystery; *second*, begin a new life, on a new basis, in
order to repair the wrongs that I have done, in order to redeem
myself, to help the workers, the peasants (to whom I am tied with
every fiber of my heart), and *my country*.

Between the first and the second phase I need a bit of physical,
intellectual, and moral rest. No considerations of a material nature
have influenced my decision. Discomforts don't frighten me. What
I want is to *live morally*. The influence and popularity that I've
acquired in many emigration centers induce me to conceive of my
future activity (as soon as I've reestablished my health) in the shape
of a completely independent literary and editorial activity. I should
add that these days great modifications are taking place in my
ideology and that I feel greatly attracted again to religion (if not
the church) and that the evolution of my thought is facilitated by
the cretinous and criminal orientation the Communist Party is
assuming. The only thing about my separation from it that causes
me *regret* is that it is a party under persecution in which, except for
the leaders, there are thousands of workers in good faith. In order
to exercise a little influence on the base, I continue to hesitate about
publicly announcing my break from the party and will wait for an
imminent, propitious moment. This letter of mine to you attests to
my esteem. I want to *close*, definitely, a long period of loyal relations
with an act of loyalty. If you are a believer, pray God to give me the
strength to overcome my remorse, to begin a new life, and to *spend
it all* for the good of the workers of Italy.

Yours,
Silvestri

Anyone familiar with Silone's writing can here detect his familiar voice, and the letter certainly appears to be in his handwriting. Furthermore, a typed copy of this letter has a cover document marked with the customary blue pencil of the chief of the Fascist political police, Arturo Bocchini, that the letter was from "Secondino Tranquilli," thereby firmly establishing that "Silvestri" was indeed Silone. Another document from the archives, as early as October 7, 1924, refers to a "Silvestri" in the third person, with many biographical details paralleling Silone's own: his rise in the Communist Party hierarchy, personal obligations to a younger brother, grandmother, sisters-in-law, etc. Yet another letter, dated July 5, 1929, also signed "Silvestri," is in a quite different hand, is addressed to "Egregia Signorina" (Emilia Bellone was Guido Bellone's sister), and refers to Silone ("Tr.") in the third person.

Tr. has arrived here, where he is in a private clinic; he never leaves given that his health is still delicate. It is difficult to visit him in the clinic, because there are people who know him [or me?] among the staff.

It seems that he will remain in the clinic another 2–3 weeks and then go to a pensione. Then it will be possible to approach him.

I will write to you again in a few days. You justly complain of the scarcity of my letters: our *rapporti* ["reports," or "relationship"?] could be more regular and frequent if they change their nature and character. At this point in my moral and intellectual formation, it is *physically* impossible for me to remain in the same relationship as 10 years ago. I suppose that you also might be interested in a different arrangement of our relationship. The first thing to eliminate, because it leaves me indifferent or humiliated, is money. But of this we will speak privately with greater ease.

Cordial greetings,
Silvestri

While the letter of April 1930 might appear to be the proverbial smoking gun, its status is undermined by the earlier one. At the very least, this letter indicates that someone else—perhaps Gabriella Seidenfeld—was also aware of Silone's correspondence with Bellone. It was possible that Seidenfeld, knowing of Silone's exchange of letters with Bellone, drafted this one (and perhaps others now lost). A single sentence in this letter exploded like a bombshell in the controversy: "At this point in my moral and intellectual formation, it is *physically* impossible for me to remain in the same relationship as 10 years ago." It was supposedly proof that Bellone and Silone had carried out an exchange for a decade. (The word "physically" and its implications are examined below.) Later in July 1929, "Silvestri" sent the following letter, translated in its entirety. Whether or not it was addressed to Bellone is unclear.

> Yesterday I received your three letters, leaving a sanatorium where I
> was for a month and a half, afflicted with serious nervous disorders

[*gravi squilibri nervosi*]. In 15 days I will go to the Mezzogiorno to rest and then I will be able to write to you with greater ease.

Seemingly, the case was closed: Silone was guilty of spying for the Fascist police. Yet the letters before 1928 (that is, before the arrest of Romolo) are not signed "Silvestri." Romolo had been arrested on April 13, 1928, suspected in the bombing in Milan. A week later, an arrest warrant was signed for Silone for having "revealed political and military secrets concerning the security of the State." On April 23, 1928, chief of police Bocchini sent Mussolini a report that "the Inspector General of Public Security Guido Bellone has received a telegram from Basel from Tranquilli Secondino—one of the Communist leaders—giving notice of his arrival in Italy. The conversation with him could be interesting." A week later (April 30), Bellone received word from Silone that, owing to the fact that his name had been circulating at the frontier and that the Fascist police had standing orders to arrest him, the trip was canceled.

Silone's epistolary exchange might be explained in several ways. Most convincing, since the correspondence before 1928 cannot definitively be attributed to Silone, is that the letters were an attempt to mitigate Romolo's fate. If one accepts the Biocca-Canali claim that the letters pre-1928 are indeed Silone's, an alternative scenario unfolds. In September 1919, Silone's name (as Secondino Tranquilli) was entered into the file of the Questura of Rome as a "subversive." At the time, Guido Bellone was the police prefect of Rome and would have come across his name and paid him a visit. There is some speculation but no evidence that Bellone and Silone had already met, either in Pescina or in Rome, in the aftermath of the 1915 earthquake. By late 1919, Silone had been named editor of *L'Avanguardia*, the organ of the Italian Socialist Youth organization. In that capacity, he would have been required by the laws of the Kingdom of Italy to present his weekly newspaper to the Questura of Rome in order to abide by the censorship laws then in effect. In either case, it seems that Bellone may have established a kind of stern, paternal relationship with the young orphaned country boy lost in the metropolis.

Yet if Silone was spying for the Fascist regime, why did his name often appear on the lists of those to be apprehended, with permission granted for the subject to be shot if resisting arrest? In the immediate aftermath of the attempted regicide in Milan in April 1928 and Romolo's arrest, the name Secondino Tranquilli appeared on such a list.

This most recent caso Silone cannot be understood outside the unfolding of Italian domestic politics in the 1990s as the entire political establishment crumbled under the revelations of the Tangentopoli bribery scandal and "Mani Pulite" (clean hands) corruption investigation. Add the hyperpoliticization of historical writing in Italy and the stage was set. Biocca and Canali's essays were originally published in the journal of the increasingly conservative revisionist historian Renzo De Felice at precisely the moment when the anti-Fascist legacy was under virulent attack.

Many commentators have remarked that while the critical commentary on Silone's oeuvre always made mention of how closely Silone resembled his main protagonists, especially Pietro Spina/Paolo Spada, these new revelations make it seem that Silone was closer to the police spy Luigi Murica in the novel *Bread and Wine* (1936) and the play *And He Hid Himself* (1944). Murica is a member of the Communist Resistance who turns informer. Although he is despised by his colleagues, Murica achieves redemption after being tortured to death by the Fascist police. In the play, the scene of his interrogation, torture, and death is a replication of Christ's Passion. Of course, these critics now say, how could we have been so blind? It was there all along: Silone was confessing to his spying through the tragic figure of Luigi Murica. But perhaps we might propose an (admittedly) improbable but perhaps possible alternative scenario linked with another work: In *The Secret of Luca* (1956), the main character refuses to defend himself against a charge of murder and is imprisoned for forty years. Andrea Cipriani, long assumed to be another one of Silone's alter egos, is a native son reluctantly returning as a politician in the new republic after years of persecution for his participation in the anti-Fascist underground, determined to uncover Luca's secret. To defend the honor of a married woman whom he loved, Luca refused to offer a defense to clear his name of the murder. Perhaps Silone here was portraying himself not in the guise of Andrea Cipriani but in Luca himself and defending someone else, such as Gabriella Seidenfeld? As his companion during the decade of the 1920s when the letters in dispute were being written and sent to Bellone in Rome, Seidenfeld was in a position to be in the same cities as Silone (where the letters were mailed from) and to have the same inside information on the politics and movement of party members.

Other lines of defense have not proved to be convincing. The political and cultural commentator and dean of Italian journalism, Indro Montanelli, indignantly thundered in the pages of Italy's most authoritative newspaper that "even if Silone himself rose from the tomb and confessed, I would not believe that he was a Fascist spy. The man who stood up to Stalin cannot be reduced to a confidant of a minor Fascist functionary." Montanelli attempted to use his considerable cultural authority to foreclose any discussion or debate on the subject, but his tactic backfired and made it seem that Silone's defenders could not argue the case on its merits. Montanelli did, though, make an intriguing argument in his essay: "I have no doubts concerning the authenticity of the documents, but permit me to put forward some doubt about the equation: Document equals Truth."

Another line of defense soon developed: Silone, in his epistolary relationship with Bellone, was attempting to influence the fate of Romolo, then suffering in Fascist prisons. But this defense too proved implausible because the exchange supposedly began long before Romolo's arrest. More damaging than the letter of July 5, 1929, speaking of a ten-year relationship is a cache of forty pages of documents written by Silone detailing the underground organization and activities of the PCI. These, although carrying no addressee or date, were supposedly written for Bellone by Silone in April 1923. They are partially reproduced photographically in Canali's book and certainly appear to be in Silone's hand. Sending the materials from Genoa, Bellone drafted a cover letter to his superior in Rome, Cesare Bertini, that the documents were written by "our friend" (*dal nostro amico*) over the course of two days, in Bellone's presence. But these could also have been internal party documents drafted by Silone and seized by the Fascist police in one of their many raids against safe houses and party headquarters.

If this most recent caso Silone can be compared to France's trauma over the Dreyfus affair, Silone's Émile Zola is Giuseppe Tamburrano, president of the Fondazione Pietro Nenni and former professor of history at the University of Catania. The indefatigable Tamburrano has been the most vocal defender of Silone, publishing dozens of indignant letters, essays, and two books in reply to Biocca and Canali's claims. Tamburrano and his research assistants present what they claim is a point-by-point refutation of the charges, with some convincing arguments.

Several inconsistencies, they point out, are obvious: If Silone had been an informer since 1919, his productivity was exceedingly small. Considering his personal role in many of the historical moments of Italian and international communism (the founding of the PCI in January 1921; his subsequent trips to Moscow, Berlin, Paris, etc.; the momentous Moscow meeting in May 1927 when Stalin sought to expel Trotsky; the tortuous internal divisions within the movement), there seems to be relatively little pay dirt for the Fascists. Furthermore, it seems almost impossible to believe that Silone would have been allowed an "emergency exit" from spying if he was as valuable as Biocca and Canali claim. A parallel with organized crime is perhaps not inconsistent. There are no known cases of an informer being permitted to return to "civilian" life. In some cases, their work for the Fascists was leaked and they were dispatched by Stalin and his henchmen. Also, it seems impossible that the Silone/Silvestri–Bellone relationship would have been unknown to other Fascist officials. Guido Leto, Arturo Bocchini, Michelangelo Di Stefano, and Carmine Senise were all high-ranking Fascist police officials. None made mention of Silone's alleged spying for the Fascists after the war. In 1957, when a right-wing Christian Democrat political rival sympathetic to fascism,

Ferdinando Tambroni, taking advantage of his position as minister of the interior with full access to all police documents, sought damaging material on Silone in the files, he came away empty-handed. Many of the older Fascist police officials, such as Leto, were still alive in 1957. (Bocchini had died in 1940.)

Another line of defense has been to challenge the mathematical equation that Silvestri = Silone. This has been most authoritatively put forth by Dr. Paola Carucci, former director of the Archivio Centrale dello Stato in Rome (before her politically motivated dismissal). Carucci, having access to the list of police and OVRA informants (more than 360), has written that neither "Silvestri" nor his supposed code number (73) appears in the list; missing also is any mention of the names Silone or Tranquilli. A document from the Ministry of the Interior dated October 12, 1937, proves that Silone did write to Fascist authorities: "indifferently sending generic information about the activities of the fuorusciti." But the document goes on to say that the information sent was to mitigate the fortunes of Romolo in prison; it makes no mention of letters written to Fascist authorities prior to Romolo's arrest.

Darina vacillated, at times calling the accusations "a shameful slander," at other times seeming to consider the letters genuine. In an interview, she admitted to me that some of the letters may indeed be his.

Umberto Terracini, a high-ranking member of the PCI for many years, told the writer and critic Luce d'Eramo on the occasion of the publication of her book *Deviazione* in 1979 that Silone was actually a triple agent. Having met Bellone as early as 1915 in the aftermath of the earthquake, Silone continued corresponding with Bellone even after the official became a Fascist police officer. Revealing this relationship to the Communist hierarchy, Silone was ordered to maintain it for purposes of counterintelligence. This may be why Palmiro Togliatti, secretary-general of the PCI and minister of justice after World War II with access to the files and Silone's sworn enemy, failed to unmask Silone as a Fascist spy. In 1945, Togliatti would surely have welcomed an occasion to destroy the man he referred to as "the renegade." Once

Silone had extracted himself from communism with his "emergency exit" and submission to expulsion, Togliatti played the role of the "Grand Inquisitor" until his death in 1964.

This brings us to a question of paramount importance, best formulated in Arthur Conan Doyle's short story "Silver Blaze." "Is there any point to which you would wish to draw my attention?" asks Watson. "To the curious incident of the dog in the night-time," responds Sherlock Holmes. "The dog did nothing in the night-time," answers Watson. "That was the curious incident," concludes Holmes.

Why did neither the Fascists nor the Communists "bark"? Once Silone had become internationally known and respected as a writer and anti-Fascist with the publication of *Fontamara*, why did the Fascist police not release the incriminating letters? Was Bellone such a gentleman that he could have resisted the certainly incessant pressure from OVRA, Leto, Bocchini, Foreign Minister Galeazzo Ciano, and Mussolini? The latter two were not above assassination to silence their political opponents, such as Piero Gobetti, Giacomo Matteotti, Giovanni Amendola, and the Rosselli brothers (not to mention the slow assassination in prison of Antonio Gramsci). More than once, the Fascist police contemplated assassinating Silone. Or they could simply have revealed Silone's duplicity and had Stalin and the Communists extract their own "justice."

Biocca and Canali are careful to present their work in neutral terms, as objective scholarship. But it has not passed unnoticed that their work has appeared in revisionist and conservative venues. Nor do they offer a motive for Silone's spying. Several times they suggest that significant sums of money changed hands, yet Silone was chronically short of funds in the 1920s, sometimes dangerously so. In a January 1930 letter to Romolo in prison, Silone confessed that "financially I am in very bad shape. For the first time in my life I have had to take on debts." Throughout his life, Silone led an economically precarious existence, later shielded from the vagaries of finance by Darina. He refused to own outright a modest apartment in Rome, turned down lucrative positions in postwar Italy (including director of the state-run television program), was often shortchanged by Italian and foreign publishers, and died almost penniless. It seems incongruous to assume, as many Italian journalists did, that Silone was a paid informer.

By crafting an "emergency exit" from the party, Silone not only liberated himself from the depravity of the Stalinist system, he also freed himself from bondage to Bellone. He no longer was a useful informer. He could therefore dedicate himself to seeking redemption in literature. "It was over. Thank God."

And yet it wasn't. Togliatti didn't give up hope that the "prodigal son" might find his way back into the fold. Nor was Silone's relationship with the Fascist police completely severed. Documents archived in Rome that have not been published or discussed over the last decade reveal that during the 1930s, Silone continued to meet with Fascist spies and that the spies continued to follow Silone, one even suggesting assassinating the now famous writer.

In November 1934, police informer #87 wrote from Zurich that "the Socialist writer Ignazio Silone (who is called Tranquilli), coming from Paris, has had a brief meeting with the spy Dante Lombardo at the cooperative restaurant." (There is no indication that Silone knew Lombardo was a spy.) At this meeting, Silone told Lombardo that the leadership of the Italian Socialist Party was riven by jealousy and distrust, adding that "nothing would be accomplished without a revolt in Italy itself." Another police informer (#582), the double agent Aldo Sampieri, was charged with following Silone and Seidenfeld and discerning the evolution of their relationship. By late 1934, the informer was able to report back to Rome that there had been a "cooling of relations" between the two. Sampieri managed to invite Silone to dinner through the intercession of Fernando Schiavetti, an important figure in the exiled anti-Fascist community. The agent noted that Silone had been expelled from the party in 1930 [sic] but that Gabriella, even though sharing his "so-called demagogic thesis," had not been expelled. Curiously, as late as 1934, Sampieri had not been able to decode

Silone's politics. "He is for others, and even more so for me, an enigma . . . his companion is even more of an enigma." Even Schiavetti had unwittingly "confessed" to the informer that he could not pin down Silone ideologically. But within a few months, Sampieri felt he now understood enough of Silone's thinking to make a daring suggestion to his superiors in Rome:

> It seems to me that for our situation—national and international—it's not good that these pathetic scraps of an opposition, which exist only in their own minds, continue to shoot their poisonous arrows on all continents; it therefore seems to me that a system should be put in place to eliminate the evil, just as a sick person goes to a SURGEON . . . In this case it seems to me that *Tranquilli is very close to the surgeon, and it might be time to complete the cure.* (emphasis added)

The regime never "completed the cure," perhaps having learned an important lesson from the assassination of Socialist deputy Giacomo Matteotti in June 1924, a lesson described by Pietro Spina: "Killing a man who says no is a risky business. Even a corpse can go on whispering no, no, no, no with a tenacity and obstinacy that is peculiar to certain corpses. How can you silence a corpse?" Matteotti was "a corpse that no one can silence."

Sampieri was soon joined in Switzerland by Giovanni Bazzi, a former Socialist who had become a Fascist informer. In 1936, Guido Bellone began a long decline in mental health, suffering from amnesia and other neurological problems. He was treated in the neuropsychiatric unit of the Umberto I clinic in Rome, retired from the police, and moved to via De Rossi, not far from where Silone and Darina would find an apartment on via Villa Ricotti. He died in 1948. It's not known if Silone and Bellone ever met or saw each other on the streets of Rome.

Further complicating the story is another document, not without mistakes, seemingly a summation of Silone's career and a commentary on his relations with the Fascist police. Dated October 12, 1937, the eight handwritten pages were then typewritten and carried a cover from the Ministry of the Interior, noting that three copies were made and that one was sent "this evening" to Mussolini.

In 1931 Tranquilli's brother Romolo was arrested and tried for Communist activities in Italy [sic: Romolo was arrested in 1928, tried in 1931]. Secondino Tranquilli, who had a profound affection for his brother, suffered greatly. He tried to help him in every way possible, sending him money and even sweets and delicacies. In that period it appears that, having repented of his anti-Fascist attitude, he attempted an approach with the Italian authorities, sending, disinterestedly, generic information on the activities of the fuorusciti. He did this with the intention of helping his brother, who, in any event, stricken by a very grave disease, died on October 20, 1932, in the infirmary of the prison of Procida.

This paragraph was later incorporated whole into a report filed by the Ministry of the Interior on October 23, 1957. The Christian Democratic government of the time, seeking to discredit Silone, had commissioned yet another search. The resulting document mentioned that rather than being a Fascist spy, Silone was an Anglo-American agent: "In some political circles, Silone is considered a trusted confidant [uomo di fiducia] of the American embassy and, through his Irish wife, in contact with the English 'Intelligence Service.'" As late as March 1956, Silone was still defending himself against charges that he was an agent of the American State Department, filing a libel suit against the Socialist Lucio Libertini, who had so accused him. Libertini, extrapolating from Ignazio and Darina Silone's reentry into Italy in October 1944 aboard an American military plane put at their disposal by Allen Dulles, concluded that Silone was indeed an agent for the CIA. When pressed, he withdrew his accusations and Silone dropped the lawsuit.

In late 1937, another police spy had been charged with following Silone. Agent #507 ("Platone") also had some trouble pinpointing him:

I still have not been able to master the true soul of Silone [*ad impossessarmi dell'animo vero del Silone*]. From our first encounter, I pegged him as a dreamer, and he is a dreamer. But up to what point and in what manner? . . . Today I add: what does he dream of, and where does his sincerity begin? He prefers to listen rather than speak. He begins a discussion and then does not develop it, preferring to hear the response of the other person. At times he seems to look deeply into space with an air of apparent distraction, and in those distracted eyes one cannot read whether there is a thought and active intelligence or if he is merely tired.

Platone apparently had a warm relationship with Silone. In January 1939, "visiting" Zurich, he sought out Silone, but failing to find him at home, left an odd letter with Silone's editor Emil Oprecht. "How is your health?" he asks solicitously. "Do you need anything? Have the boots been useful to you? . . . Did you receive a postcard from Lugano before Christmas?"

Silone responded from near Davos on January 13, thanking him for the boots and letters and postcards from Lugano, Bern, Luxembourg, and other places. Silone, using a new pseudonym, wrote that he would remain for a while in Davos,

not because the climate does me any good but because the mountains remind me of the Abruzzo . . . I have need of nothing. It may seem a proud answer, but since my conscience is at peace, the right response. This does not mean that I am content with what I do, and even less with what I don't do, but the only criterion to do or not do something for me today is my conscience and not self-interest or vanity. Forgive me if, because of modesty, these sentiments must be silenced in public; I express them in a letter that wishes to be only an exchange of greetings. It is proof of friendship.

Saluti cordiali, Sud.

P.S. Today is the 13th of January, that is, the anniversary of the earthquake of 1915, which was for me the beginning of many misfortunes.

But surely the most curious, if not bizarre, meeting took place in
May 1939 when Platone was visited by Silone and Gabriella Seidenfeld
at his hotel. The three had dinner together and Platone recorded the
following conversation, with all three using the formal "Lei" throughout. It sounds very much like a game of cat and mouse:

GABRIELLA: What do you think? When do you think fascism will end?

PLATONE: You think I can tell you when fascism will come to an end?

GABRIELLA: This is what I want to know: When will fascism end? Is it
   possible that it will never end?

PLATONE: It would be better if you think of something else, signora.
   Don't concern yourself anymore about the end of fascism.

GABRIELLA: You believe that it will never die? You believe that he
   [Mussolini] will never die? You believe that Mussolini will die a
   natural death?

PLATONE: But what are you thinking of? You wish for more attempts
   against the life of Mussolini?

GABRIELLA: Are you so pessimistic?

PLATONE: On the contrary, I am optimistic! I myself am spiritually
   closer to Mussolini than to any other political person. What harm
   has he done, what evil has Mussolini done that he should be
   assassinated?

GABRIELLA: And yet we here [in Zurich] have heard news of
   demonstrations in Italy.

PLATONE: They have told you lies.

GABRIELLA: It was an Italian from Rome, in fact, and he himself had
   seen the demonstrations in Rome.

PLATONE: I assure you, signora, that he told you lies: How can it be
   possible to think of demonstrations in an Italian city like Rome? In
   any event, we watch everyone who criticizes, everyone, and in every
   corner of Italy.

SILONE: And such a state of affairs is a good thing?

PLATONE: This is not a case of good or bad. I assure you that there
   are no demonstrations in Italy. Today, Mussolini commands the

country, and there is no one who criticizes Mussolini. Mussolini is master of the people because the people feel themselves to be protected by Mussolini. And in fact, all the social reforms are in favor of the masses and the individual workers.

GABRIELLA: So it appears that the masses are content, but if tomorrow something happens . . . then you would see the masses!

PLATONE: But what do the people still demand? Which state, which government has created and continues to create social reforms and all for the benefit of the workers?

SILONE: There is poverty [miseria] in Italy.

PLATONE: Poverty is not only an Italian privilege; poverty is everywhere, especially in the so-called rich countries. In France there is no poverty? In London there is no poverty? In the Americas are there not more than twelve million unemployed?

SILONE: I agree with you. In fact, in one of my essays I said that the dictatorship has always been the emanation of the people, and that democracy has always represented the privileged class of the rich, etc. Even I agree with you in recognizing the defects of the democracies. But I would like Italy, our beautiful Italy, our country, to have another form of government. To take an example, I would like each citizen to be able to voice his own opinion. That the army, which represents the nation, in all countries, that the army, that is, the chief of staff, would frankly voice his opinion before the nation, before the government. I would like the elected class to give its opinion of the problems that are to be confronted.

PLATONE: Well, don't you understand that the entire privileged class of the nation stands side by side with Mussolini? Mussolini can be credited with burying all the old things and now the entire nation has been rearranged according to his orders. Mussolini knows how to educate an entirely new social class and to have himself enthusiastically obeyed and loved. Mussolini is master of the situation.

SILONE: Yes, I understand. It must be as you say. But I, for example, just to give an example, would like our Italy to govern itself under a federal system, so that Calabria, for example, could thrive through a reciprocal exchange with Lombardia.

PLATONE: But what are you saying? Are you losing your mind? Italy live in a federal form with itself? Italy, which has finally achieved national unity, should, according to your conception, subdivide itself into a confederation? What are you saying?

SILONE: Yes, you're right. I have confused ideas. It must be the wine that is confusing my ideas.

Platone slyly concludes to his superiors: "I will see Silone again next week, but I will see to it that the wine clouds his head as little as possible."

It is an extraordinary document, heavily laden with Gabriella's outraged innocence and Silone's familiar irony and sarcasm. More important, the conversation throws a very different light on the earlier correspondence, giving some credence to the position that Silone was consciously cultivating relationships with persons he knew to be Fascist spies. Twelve days later, the same Fascist spy sent another curious document on to the Ministry of the Interior in Rome. It seems that Silone, Gabriella, and "Platone" had another meeting, verbally circling each other, seeking weak points.

Lunching at the Ristorante San Gottardo in Zurich on May 18, 1939, Silone tries to convince Platone that he has definitively abandoned politics and is not a member of any political party. Consequently, Silone affirms that, his apolitical stance being well known, "I don't believe that I could be followed or under surveillance," surely an instance of Silone's sly irony, as he was undoubtedly aware of his guest's true character and task. Condemning the democratic parties as being (according to Platone) "demagogic," Silone insists that "every form of demagoguery is a dictatorship" and that "today democracy no longer exists." Gabriella instead baits Platone with a rumor floating around Zurich that Mussolini had made a secret trip to the Swiss city for an operation to remove cataracts. Platone reacts indignantly to this suggestion, claiming that Mussolini is "in enviably good health." And, even if true, Platone continues, why go to Switzerland when Italy has doctors who are "second to none. Italy has always been the cradle of knowledge: Dante, Leonardo da Vinci, Marconi, Mussolini, yes Mussolini is also great, truly great. Yes, in Germany there is Hitler, who is great, but not as great as Mussolini." Reading this protestation, one must ask: For whom is Platone writing? Is he acting merely as an objective chronicler of a conversation, or is he transforming his written report into a sycophantic performance for his superiors in Rome?

Platone's report ends by transcribing a telephone conversation with Silone (both using the familiar "*tu*"):

> SILONE: I thank you for the telephone call. I have been sick for three days with a fever of thirty-nine. Today I am somewhat better.
>
> PLATONE: Here the weather is terrible; I'm feeling very irritable. Say, would you like to visit me in a week?
>
> SILONE: Where?
>
> PLATONE: In Luxembourg.
>
> SILONE: Thank you, but it's impossible. I don't have a passport, Luxembourg is difficult. If I could, I would prefer Sicily.
>
> PLATONE: What?
>
> SILONE: I would prefer to go to Sicily! To Taormina, where there is so much sun!
>
> PLATONE: Your wish is sacred if it depended on me. I will telephone you tomorrow at noon; we'll see if we can meet one of the following afternoons.

The reference to Taormina is curious. Why offer to traverse the entire Italian peninsula when an order for your arrest is hanging over your head? Could it have been a coded reference to homosexuality? In the late nineteenth and early twentieth centuries, Taormina had developed a reputation as a hedonistic city with a vibrant homosexual subculture, fostered by the German aristocratic photographer Wilhelm von Gloeden. Both Biocca and Leake imply that Silone's ambiguous sexuality may have been a reason for the relationship with Bellone. Biocca writes that "it is nevertheless plausible to theorize that the relationship was of a more intimate nature . . . The context, the tone, and the language of the correspondence, along with the numerous encounters that took place in Italy, France, and Switzerland, and the protection accorded until the end, sometimes reciprocally, leave us to suppose that the relationship implied emotionally significant and perhaps, for both, unspeakable elements." In Zurich, Silone had met Dr. Magnus Hirshfeld, founder of the Institut für Sexualwissenchaft in Berlin and a pioneer in the study of homosexuality. (Garbriella Seidenfeld had worked for some months in his office.) Leake writes that "it has also been murmured that the intimate friendship between Silone and Bellone was strengthened by a mutual erotic interest." The letter of July 5, 1929, perhaps by Silone or perhaps by Gabriella, also contained an ambiguous line: "At this point in my moral and intellectual formation, it is *physically* impossible for me to remain in the same relationship as 10 years ago." Could Silone's yearlong experience of psychoanalysis in Switzerland have been undertaken with the purpose of "curing" him of the "disease" of homosexuality? Could this be why Darina Silone insisted in several of our interviews and in subsequent correspondence that Silone had never undergone psychoanalysis?

We do know that as late as December 1942, Sampieri was still spying on Silone, complaining that Zurich was a center of intrigue against Mussolini's regime ("boiled, roasted, or stewed, as long as it is Fascist flesh"). He notes a rumor that the recent arrest of Silone was precipitated by a transmission from Radio Moscow that an Italian writer, granted refuge by the Swiss government, had signed a manifesto urging an insurrection of the Italian people against the Fascist regime. This apparently was the fruit of Stalin's vendetta against Silone.

"Everything conspires to confuse," wrote Sampieri from Zurich in early 1943. "No angel watches over him," he continued, adding cryptically, "If that dear woman [Gabriella?] were to talk . . . it would be the ruin of many others." In an ominous report, an agent implied that a "vendetta" might yet take care of the problem.

As late as the spring of 1943, two years after Silone had met Darina Laracy, Gabriella Seidenfeld was still involved somehow in his life. It was Seidenfeld who taunted Sampieri with the information that Silone had entered a refugee camp in San Moritz, forbidden by the Swiss authorities to enter the city proper. Silone was preparing a new work (*And He Hid Himself*) while Seidenfeld "split her sides laughing at Mussolini's expense, unable to touch her Secondino." With the Fascist regime only weeks away from internal collapse, Sampieri wrote bitterly back to Rome that, notwithstanding his earlier arrest by the Swiss authorities, Silone was able to move about freely between Davos and Marcel Fleischmann's villa in Zurich.

In an exchange of letters, Darina Silone was frank with me about the possibility of her husband being a spy: "I tend to think that Silone was forced by his Communist Party superiors to exploit his friendship with this police official to pretend to inform; information that the party could afford to give away, in exchange for finding out about OVRA attitudes to Communists." "I think the real truth will never be known because all concerned are now dead. (There was undoubtedly *something*, but what? Everything must be taken in its context.) I don't agree with any of them." "I am not *innocentista oltranza* [believing Silone to be innocent to the bitter end], although neither am I *colpevolista*. I believe the documents to be authentic but I question the way they have been interpreted. There are 'official' documents 'proving' that I was a Nazi spy. I am still alive to explain the weird circumstances of this— Silone is not." The scandal was taking its toll: "As you can imagine, I have many sleepless nights."

At the centenary celebrations of Silone's birth, held in Pescina on May 1, 2000, Darina Silone referred to Biocca and Canali's book as a "black cloud" hanging over the festivities. The authors, Darina noted, were professional historians, and calls to have the book suppressed or sequestered were wrong. Instead, other, "possibly better," facts and documents were necessary to confront the accusations. Darina mentioned that Diocleziano Giardini of Pescina discovered in Bellone's files that Bellone had been in Pescina after the January 1915 earthquake and that Silone and Romolo had met him at the time (seven years before the advent of fascism).

Referring to the letters sent to Bellone, she recognized "Silone's tendency to exaggerate, to self-dramatize, as, for example, when he wrote that he had undergone psychoanalysis." In interviews, Darina was far more adamant that Silone had not undergone psychoanalysis than she was in defending him against the charges of spying. On Silone = Murica, as charged by Biocca and Canali: "I find it very much in malafede to quote, as they do, passages from Silone's novels . . . to prove he was a spy or informer since he wrote about a character who was. Not to dream of comparing Silone to the great Russians, but mutatis mutandis, Dostoevsky did not have to be an assassin to write *Crime and Punishment,* and Tolstoy did not have to give birth to be able to describe Kitty's birth pangs in *Anna Karenina.*" Silone was well aware of the tragedy of police informers within the party; he often spoke to Darina of Guglielmo Jonna, a Communist official turned Fascist informer.

Darina had a number of long conversations with the historian Paolo Spriano before he died. Spriano, author of a massive, multivolume history of the PCI, had access to the documents pertaining to Silone's expulsion from the party. In more than two thousand pages of text, Spriano's definitive history makes no mention of Silone informing for the Fascist police (nor does it mention that Silone may have been spying for the PCI). Unfortunately, Spriano died in 1988, before the allegations first surfaced. He did mention to Darina that Togliatti "hated Silone to death" and would have destroyed him if he could. Why then didn't Togliatti do so when he was minister of justice after the war? Perhaps because Togliatti was fully aware that Silone was acting on behalf of the party? An alternative explanation is that Silone was a spy and that Togliatti, discovering this in 1945, failed to publicize it, terrified that Stalin would extract his revenge in the form of Togliatti's assassination for his failure to prevent a Fascist spy from infiltrating the PCI. This possible scenario doesn't explain why Togliatti didn't reveal Silone's spying after Stalin's death in 1953.

The historian Mimmo Franzinelli, author of an exhaustive study of Mussolini's secret police, has pointed out that it would be absurd for a spy of Silone's caliber to report only to Bellone and not to OVRA. Franzinelli published the complete list of OVRA informants: Silone's name is not on it; neither is "Silvestri."

Equally curious is the reaction of the world press to Biocca and Canali's allegations. Many are marred by biographical and factual in-accuracies, some minor, such as the oft-repeated "fact" that Silone's entire family was wiped out in the 1915 earthquake, and some rather strange. One website (with a claim to "tracking the entire world") cites Silone's occupation as "Novelist, Spy," while its "executive summary" of the man reads, in its entirety: "Anti-Fascist novelist, Pro-Fascist informant." Rory Carroll, writing from Rome for *The Guardian*, man-aged to get the year of Silone's death wrong, claimed that the April 1930 letter was addressed to Emilia Bellone (there is no named recipi-ent), and wrote that "Silone allegedly infiltrated the Italian Communist Party." In America, a typical reaction was expressed by Alexander Cockburn and Christopher Hitchens, both writing in *The Nation*. Cock-burn's essay, "Even Worse Than Orwell," relied entirely on press re-ports in Britain and inscribed Silone onto a "dishonor roll" and guilty of a "considerably greater level of infamy" than Orwell. But Cockburn is simply mistaken and echoing Biocca and Canali when he claims that the April 1930 letter was addressed to Emilia Bellone. Other minor inaccuracies aside, it appears that Cockburn simply accepted the Biocca-Canali thesis without any reservations and even some embell-ishments. A more nuanced essay a week later by Christopher Hitchens spent more time excoriating Cockburn and trying to defend Orwell than examining the evidence. But Hitchens too accepted the charge that Silone acted as a "spy" as early as 1919. Hitchens is more sympa-thetic and willing to concede Silone's sincerity in the April 1930 letter, something that Cockburn merely sneered at as a typical example of "self-serving proclamations of the writer's character" and Silone as a victim of "habitual high respect for his own moral fiber."

To his credit, Hitchens returned to the debate four months later with an admirable mea culpa or, more precisely, a warning to his readers that the charges against Silone were built on shaky evidence. Referring to his earlier piece, Hitchens confessed that he had assumed, "for the sake of argument, that the published reports of Silone's collaboration were true." But in the intervening months, the scandal had evolved in ways unforeseen to both Cockburn and Hitchens. Specifically, Mimmo Franzinelli had published a withering critique of Biocca and Canali's book. "It now appears," Hitchens wrote, "that we may both have been party, with differing degrees of relish and reluctance, to a widely and prematurely disseminated falsehood." And, in an exceedingly rare moment of humility, he concluded, "I cannot myself be confident, and I lack the necessary linguistic and historical expertise, but I now feel fairly sure that the first draft in this argument was allowed too much authority."

Likewise, John Foot, writing in the *New Left Review*, simply accepted the Biocca-Canali thesis and repeated some inaccuracies (such as the letter of April 1930 being addressed to Emilia Bellone and that "certainly he was paid for his betrayals over a decade"). For Foot, the evidence compiled leads to the "chilling truth" that Silone was indeed an informer for the Italian secret police from 1919 to 1930, and "the desperate effort to reinvent Silone's activities as a heroic triple game holds no water." But Foot acknowledges that "the enigma that remains unsolved is the question of motive" and questions why the regime did not expose Silone in the 1930s. "Beyond the factual mystery of the reasons for Silone's service as a spy for the regime, the psychological mystery of his emergence from it as literary-ethical phoenix is yet greater."

Even Alexander Stille, the most astute and informed observer of Italy writing in America, takes a minor misstep in his otherwise thoughtful examination of the scandal. Quoting from the July 1929 letter, he fails to note that the letter is obviously written by someone other than Silone. Stille calls for a rereading of Silone in light of these revelations, noting, as have others, the figure of Luigi Murica in *Bread and Wine* and Silone's play *And He Hid Himself*. Stille gives what can be regarded as the most sympathetic reading of those who are convinced of the documents' authenticity. The recent scandals, concludes Stille, "don't diminish the power of Silone's writings."

> If anything, his heroic image may have obscured the darkness and complexity of his books. Readers who approached the novels as straightforward denunciations of social injustice may have missed the undercurrents of deceit and betrayal that now come into relief. And if Silone no longer seems a man of moral purity, one marvels at his ability to remake himself. He went on to do exactly what he vowed in his last letter to Bellone, "to start a new life . . . in order to do good," killing off Secondo Tranquilli and becoming Ignazio Silone.

Such is the central conceit of Elizabeth Leake's intriguing study, *The Reinvention of Ignazio Silone*. Through the inferno of his collaboration with Bellone and his expulsion from the PCI, "Silone succeeded in orchestrating the complete reinvention of his public image around the shift from professional revolutionary to novelist." But, continues Leake, "when the contradictions of his life and his fiction are taken into account, there is no way to determine where he lies on the moral spectrum. The paradoxical nature of his identity is thus insurmountable." Leake's book is a study of how Silone constructed those paradoxes in public over the course of his career. Her contention is that, after undergoing psychoanalysis with Carl Jung, Silone reworked Marxism, Christianity, and his own childhood experiences into a narrative where "he no longer distinguished between his fictional accounts of his experiences and his actual experiences." Silone's Italian readers colluded in this sleight of hand because "they have always had a particular need for this figure. He fulfills a crucial function in the collective Italian psyche by representing a political stance that transcends party politics and by challenging authority in good faith and without consideration of the personal consequences."

A curious effect of this recent scandal is the portrayal of the secret police official Guido Bellone. While Tamburanno makes Bellone out to be a minor version of Big Brother, the press has portrayed him as a caring, understanding, paternal, and sympathetic figure: the "good" Fascist. Several accounts mention his apocryphal death in an insane asylum. Maybe once the PCI had discovered that Silone had broken his relationship with Bellone, it decided the writer was no longer useful and had him expelled a year later.

This most recent caso Silone also echoes some comparable cases: Alberto Moravia's fawning letters to Mussolini, Cesare Pavese's thoughts regarding fascism in his diary, Günter Grass's revelations that he served with the Waffen SS in World War II, a Polish archbishop and many members of the Polish clergy spying for the Communists, and literally millions of East Germans spying on one another. In Italy, readers were treated to the rare spectacle of two ideologically diverse newspapers, the right-wing *Il Tempo* and the left-wing *L'Unità*, which had a long history of denigrating Silone, rising to his defense.

Robert Gordon, in reviewing Biocca and Canali's *L'informatore*, writes that the book "quashes once and for all any attempt to deny that Silone sent these reports to Bellone," but he warns that much remains unclear. Direct evidence "is still very thin." Most of the purported letters "give relatively little away . . . low-key nuggets of information that the regime would also receive from several lesser informants. Even when he appears to go in for outright betrayal, he does so in a way that some have construed as practically useless to Bellone." Gordon argues, somewhat contradictorily, that "Silone's information no doubt helped the regime immensely in its damaging assault on the clandestine Communists in the early 1930s" and concludes that "abandoning the myth has been a wrench, but the truth of Silone's double life makes him more, not less emblematic of his century."

The most ardent defense of Silone and the most effective critique of the Biocca-Canali accusations in English comes from the writer Michael McDonald. In an elegant and tightly argued essay, McDonald entered the arena after the publication of *L'informatore* and Tamburrano's *Processo a Silone*. McDonald wryly points out that with their book, Biocca and Canali have accomplished what "the fascists and the communists combined had been unable to achieve: level a near deathblow to Silone's reputation." In addition to a convincing rebuttal of the Biocca-Canali thesis, McDonald offers a critique of the manner in which the controversy unfolded in Italy and the United States, with a rabid press eager to join in a feeding frenzy. "In the scoop-driven age of journalism, the facts are never allowed to stand in the way of a good news story . . . The press, first in Italy, later in the United States, credulously retailed Biocca and Canali's story to the public as fact, doing its best to see to it that Silone's reputation as a man of uncommon integrity and moral courage would be broken once and for all . . . Most of the Italian press accepted at face value the attribution of the espionage reports to Silone, never thinking to question the authenticity of the documents." But there is another, just as troubling, operation under way in the caso Silone: the discrediting of the anti-Fascist tradition.

McDonald notes that Biocca and Canali "are careful never to express the slightest moral opprobrium at Silone's alleged betrayals." Instead, their neutral tone is meant to convince us of their disinterested scholarship, intent on cutting through the fog of "hagiographical" research that has surrounded Silone.

> The unspoken yet inescapable results of the authors' method of proceeding and their findings of "fact" are two: first, Silone is made out to be a badly compromised figure whose heretofore penetrating criticisms of fascism must inevitably be devalued; second, the moral stigma of fascist collaboration (either during the heyday of Mussolini or now) is diminished.

Another defense of Silone in a conservative venue was David Pryce-Jones's essay in *The New Criterion*. Although Pryce-Jones makes a few minor mistakes in his essay (confusing the drained Fucino lake with the town of Pescina and repeating—again—that Silone lost his entire family in the earthquake), he is perceptive in sensing that the moral of the so-called Abruzzo Trilogy (*Fontamara, Bread and Wine*, and *The Seed Beneath the Snow*) is voiced by Pietro Spina: "Honor poverty and friendship, and be proud." Pryce-Jones sees the latest Silone scandal as part of the larger denigration of anti-Communists: After Albert Camus, Arthur Koestler, and George Orwell, "now it is the turn of Ignazio Silone." Like McDonald but unlike Cockburn or Hitchens, Pryce-Jones could read the original Italian accusations and Tamburrano's original reply and does well to lay out the inconsistencies of the charges. Furthermore, Pryce-Jones notes that "here was a game in which we cannot be sure who was the cat, who the mouse." The Fascists failed to retaliate against their valuable spy when he broke with them, the letters between 1923 and 1928 are anonymous, and "common sense" suggests that the evidence exonerates Silone. Pryce-Jones scores a telling point when he notes that "Biocca and Canali make no allowance for the totalitarian context, but strikingly and invariably place the ugliest possible interpretation on everything to do with Silone." He concludes that "some wounds to the human soul go deep, too deep to be understood, let alone healable . . . The personal example stands. The writing speaks for itself."

The questions persist: Why did Silone report to a police official rather than to OVRA, the state apparatus specifically created by the Fascist regime to combat antifascism? Why, if Silone had been collaborating since 1919, could he not mitigate the circumstances of Romolo's trial and incarceration? Why didn't the regime reveal Silone's collaboration to discredit him and have Stalin eliminate a troublesome character?

As Diocleziano Giardini of Pescina pointed out to me, the documents attributed to Silone and reproduced in Biocca and Canali's book carry no signature. Only a precious few documents, all written after April 1928—that is, after Romolo's arrest—bear the signature "Silvestri." This was first noted by Tamburrano, and McDonald succinctly summarizes the case:

> The documents Biocca and Canali attribute to Silone invariably refer only to information that the police received from a "source." The name, pseudonym and code number of the "source" are never revealed. In other words, there is no way to identify who provided

the documents to the police. More precisely, the sequence of documents presented by Biocca and Canali runs from January 12, 1923 to March 3, 1930. The name "Silvestri," as the informer, appears only beginning in April 1928 (and as "Silvestro" not "Silvestri"). In short, the pseudonym "Silvestri" is only attributable to Silone after the arrest of his brother. None of the informational reports attributed by Biocca and Canali from January 12, 1923 to April 1928 contain any reference to "Silvestri" as their author. Biocca and Canali offer no explanation for this.

Diocleziano Giardini proposed another intriguing interpretation of the documents in Silone's file. Noting that the alleged letters from Silone to Bellone are far different in content and character from the "official" documents in the file, Giardini suggests that many of the incriminating documents were not letters to Bellone but rather PCI documents that Silone drafted for internal dissemination. As none of the documents in question carry a greeting to Bellone, this makes some sense. It is possible that these documents may be ones that the secret police confiscated in their many raids against the party; the handwritten documents were then typewritten and copies placed in files of various dissidents. Giardini even proposed rereading the "smoking gun" letter of April 13, 1930, as addressed not to Bellone but to Togliatti. This is plausible except for the fact that Silone always addressed Togliatti as "Ercoli" and signed almost all his correspondence with Togliatti as "Pasquini," his party name at the time.

In the end, with a resolution of the scandal just as ephemeral today as it was a decade ago, it may be necessary to fall back on Primo Levi's conception of "the gray zone." Levi, an Italian chemist, anti-Fascist, and Holocaust survivor, warned against wrapping Holocaust survivors in a halo of hagiography. A truly diabolical characteristic of the concentration camp universe was that it erased the "normal" boundaries between "good" and "evil" to such an extent that even its victims were stained. Levi focused on the notorious *Sonderkommandos*, prisoners who, for better living conditions and camp privileges, carried out the most horrific tasks of herding victims into gas chambers, transferring the bodies to the crematoria (after extracting any gold fillings), and disposing of the ashes. Levi called their formation "National Socialism's most demonic crime." After three months, these prisoners were themselves conducted into the gas chambers as others took their place.

> It is necessary to declare the imprudence of issuing hasty moral judgments on such human cases. Certainly the greatest responsibility lies with the system, the very structure of the totalitarian state; the concurrent guilt on the part of the individual big and small collaborators . . . is always difficult to evaluate.

Was Silone so wracked by guilt that he scripted the minor figure of Luigi Murica as a form of confession? The historian Mimmo Franzinelli, in his monumental study of the Fascist secret police, describes Silone as "a polyhedral personality and difficult to decipher" (*una personalitá poliedrica e di ardua decifrazione*) and the caso Silone as "incredibly complex, thick with psychological, familial, and political implications, ultimately entangled with the arrest of Romolo." Franzinelli argues that Silone was indeed the author of the letters to Bellone, but that those letters were drafted only after Romolo's arrest in 1928, and concludes that the episode must be seen in the context of the author's anti-Fascist novels, "an effective denunciation of the intrinsically tyrannical characteristics of the Mussolini regime." Silone's "posthumous misfortune has been the excessive hagiographers or detractors compared to the scholars interested in understanding his complex existential itinerary."

Writing to an aspiring writer and poet who had sent him some verses in 1938, Silone defended his coldness on their initial meeting. "Among the illnesses fascism has inflicted upon us, this is not the smallest: not being able to distinguish with certainty between friend and enemy." In his famous autobiographical essay "Emergency Exit," Silone, referring to the crisis that led to his expulsion from the Communist Party and his subsequent recounting of it, made a distinction between "disciplined, bureaucratic confessions which are imposed by orthodoxy" (surely thinking of the notorious Stalin show trials) and his own idealized "free" confession, made by one who has conquered his own fear. More ambiguously, he argued that "in determining the origins and development of questions of conscience the chronology of memory is more dependable than the chronology of archives."

The writer and critic Luce d'Eramo, who came to know Silone well at the end of his life and who had a murky Fascist past herself, wrote in her autobiography that one of our most tenacious and varied aspirations was "the eternal human dream of correcting the past." Silone's lifelong guilt over his relationship with Bellone was responsible for some of the most poignant and powerful fiction of the twentieth century.

Late in life, Silone intriguingly revealed in an interview that "there is a secret in my life; it is written between the lines of my novels." Was he referring to his relationship with Bellone or something else entirely? With most of the protagonists in this most recent controversy long dead, we may never really untangle the mystery of whether and why Silone may have spent as much as a decade (or as little as two years) writing to Bellone. The answer—if there is one—lies, like Silone, somewhere in the no-man's-land between hagiography and the archives.

THAT WHICH REMAINS

Tormented olive trees
on the tufa outcroppings of Matera
Oh the bitter poems
of dead seasons!
—*ROCCO SCOTELLARO*, "The Cavalcade
   of the Bruna"

In February 1970, the religious writer Sergio Quinzio, who had contributed to *Tempo Presente* for a decade and whose young wife, Stefania, had just died, was surprised by an unannounced condolence call from Silone. Old, tired, finding it physically difficult to navigate the increasingly chaotic streets of Rome, Silone still felt it necessary to pay his respects to a colleague. Although clearly moved by the writer's gesture, Quinzio was not susceptible to the hagiography that was to surround Silone after his death eight years later. In an essay recalling their collaboration on *Tempo Presente*, Quinzio asked some pointed questions concerning Silone's insistence that socialism could inspire hope, even after the moral catastrophes of the twentieth century. Silone's sentiments were, according to Quinzio, "noble, but weak." By the late twentieth century—faced with the "continuous defeat of hope suffocated within the coils of power"—was it still possible or ethical to insist on hope? Could the peasants and workers of the past and the present, having lost all ingenuity in waiting for the final, always imminent yet never-quite-arriving triumph, accept the idea of a hope that was destined always to fail? This was the tragic absurdity that Silone has asked us to accept and even embrace. Our only true dignity is our ability to fight against insurmountable odds, to move from hatred to indifference through tolerance to compassion and friendship to love. "*Amo ergo sum*," says Rocco De Donatis with an innocent smile to Stella. "It's the surest proof of all."

Silone has left us on a threshold, asking us to pursue an ideal of justice that may be illusory. Our only salvation is in a compassionate encounter with human beings who suffer and struggle against a common fate. "There can be nothing inevitable," Silone wrote in 1965, "about matters involving the human mind and heart." His socialism was tinged with irony and his fervent religiosity was tempered with skepticism. In March 1969, on receiving the Jerusalem Prize for literature, he concluded his acceptance speech with an impromptu quote from the founder of the mystical Hasidic movement, the Baal Shem Tov, which he had just read at Yad Vashem: "Forgetfulness leads to exile; remembrance is the secret to redemption." Simone Weil had taught him that those who seek justice cannot find it in the camp of the conquerors. But as Severina lies dying, her friend from the convent, Sister Gemma, desperately asks her if she still believes. Severina's last words are ambiguous: "I hope, Sister Gemma, I hope. What remains is hope."

To the director of the Soviet state publishing house, Silone once argued that "freedom is the possibility of doubting, the possibility of making a mistake, the possibility of trying, of experimenting, of saying no to any authority, literary, artistic, philosophical, religious, social, or political." She responded that there was no need for such freedoms when the state had sanatoriums instead. Reflecting on the absurd exchange, Silone could only conclude that "there is no worse slavery than the one of which you are unaware." While communism was a finite, historical experiment (four decades before the collapse of the Soviet Union, Silone had argued that "the experience of Communism itself would kill Communism"), socialism was an eternal longing embedded in the nature of human beings striving to be free, a "permanent aspiration of the human spirit, which thirsts after social justice." He called them "insane truths" (*verità pazze*):

> It is in essence an extension of the moral criteria of private life to all social life. It is an ideal for the further humanization of our earthly existence by bringing under man's domination the economic forces which tend to oppress him.

Added to these "insane truths" later in life was a reverence for "that which incessantly drives mankind to surpass itself and that which is at the root of his unallayable anxiety" (*inappagabile inquietudine*).

Decades of clandestine political life underground had been a long and sad adventure that had left him with "the ashen taste of a wasted youth." He recognized the essentially tragic nature of his fate: "a revolt inspired by the desire for freedom can be a trap," but even this was better than "supine acceptance of one's fate." Whenever he reflected on these "misfortunes," Silone felt rise within him "an unhappy bitterness which might have been impossible for me to escape." To those who accused him of writing the same book over and over again, Silone pleaded guilty but insisted that "if a writer puts all of himself in his writing (and what else can he put into it?), his work inevitably forms a single book." More ambiguously he claimed that "one who returns having made the journey is no longer the same." Carlo Levi recognized what Silone had discerned in the Mezzogiorno when, in his classic of empathetic ethnography, *Christ Stopped at Eboli*, he noted that "the greatest travelers have not gone beyond the limits of their own world; they have trodden the paths of their own souls, of good and evil, of morality and redemption."

Although Silone had left Pescina at fifteen, Pescina never left him. "Had I ever forgotten these people or this land? Had I ever imagined anything which did not have its beginning and its end in this place?" Once, when he was traveling on foot to a nearby town, he paused at the entrance to the village, stricken with an inexplicable fear. He wanted to turn and run away, "but in that village the bread must have been coming out of the ovens just at that moment," and perhaps he recalled an ancient memory of his grandmother plaintively asking him as he left Pescina about who would bake his daily bread. Rooted to the spot, "a gust of wind brought me the good smell of fresh bread, which moved and reassured me." Fifty years after the earthquake, he would still describe Pescina as a place "where the poor who had escaped from their ruined huts were living in the mud, in caves, and in barracks, and had to keep fires burning at night to frighten the wolves away."

Late in life and feeling the passing of time, Silone made a surreptitious visit back to Pescina for the purpose of choosing a site for his final resting place. He recounted the episode in the short story "At the Foot of an Almond Tree":

> What is the particular sadness felt by anyone who attempts, after years of absence from a region where he once lived for a long time, who stops to observe, without being seen or recognized, the ordinary unwinding of life? I am trying to understand it, while from the top of this hill I contemplate the heap of gray and black houses of my native town.
>
> I got off the train a little while ago and, not having any luggage, I was able to leave the station quickly. On arrival there were few people and nobody noticed me. So much the better. I hadn't told anyone of my return; even in town nobody was expecting me. Quickly I took the shortcut between the hedges of brambles and the vineyards, but on the slope I became short of breath. Eh, I'm not a kid anymore. In my memory this path was less steep and longer. Instead, as soon as I surmount the small hill, there it is already, in front of me, the town.
>
> It appears unexpectedly, in its ancient and dark abyss. At the sight of it, I don't know why, I lost my breath and I slowed my step. I

looked around, searching for a stone or some grass on which to rest. I am not in a hurry, since no one awaits me.

Now I find myself at the foot of an almond tree, a little distant from the path. A few steps below, at a bend in the main road, rises a cross that the Passionist fathers erected many years ago, at the end of a Lenten sermon.

From here I can observe the most ancient part of the inhabited area. It is the first hour of the evening; the Ave Maria must have just sounded. A light purplish fog, formed from the damp and from the smoke of the fireplaces, flutters on the ditch of the river and disguises, between the houses and the stalls, the voids left, around half a century ago, by the earthquake. I see a long line of wagons, returning from the countryside, rising up along the road close to the river and scattering between the houses. A few women and children leave the church: some novena must be in progress. I see a quiet man leaning at the door of an inn, with his shoulder resting against the doorjamb. However, no voice reaches me, not even the slightest sound, perhaps because the wind blows in the opposite direction. It's as if I were present at the projection of an old silent film, dark and slightly worn-out.

In other times I knew every alley of this confined place, every house, every fountain, and which young girl, at what times, drew water from the fountain; I knew every door, every window, and who leaned out facing you, at what time. For fifteen years this was the closed perimeter of my adolescence, the known world and its frontiers, the prefabricated scenery of my secret anguishes. But—now I realize—the feeling that just before stopped my steps is not the common anxiety of emigrants, nor the anguish or terror of certain elderly men before the inevitable flowing of time, but rather something else.

I try to understand. This reality that is now before me I have carried around with me for many years, it is an integral, indeed a central part of myself, and I felt myself in it; certainly not at its center, yet nonetheless an integral part of it. Instead, now that I have it before me, it reveals itself to me for what it is, an extraneous world that continues to live of its own account, even without me, in the manner that is proper to it, with naturalness and indifference. In other words, not unlike how an anthill would appear to me. This is the way, I think, that the final unwinding of a human life will be seen by a dead man, if, after a certain number of years, he is able to see.

Following this reflection, I feel the earlier, confused apprehension clarify into a humble and desolate state of mind: that of the irremediable loneliness and precariousness of individual existence. I wonder why I have returned and I think of leaving immediately. But the sound of footsteps drawing near holds me back. It is an old woman, dressed—as the poor do—in black, carrying a heavy bundle of dry branches on her back, a sight that is certainly not novel in our part of the world, halfway between the plain and the mountain. Careful about where to place her feet, she is not aware of my presence. It is I who recognize her. She is a neighbor of ours. One of her sons, in elementary school, was my friend and classmate. What misfortunes could have reduced her to such a state? Her husband, her children are no longer alive. I get up to join her. Perhaps she will accept some help carrying the firewood.

Today, the significance of the almond tree is regrettably lost; even Silone's contemporaries had forgotten it. Once, while driving with a friend through the Abruzzo in early March, the two came upon an almond tree that was in full bloom in the midst of a barren field. "It's a miracle," the driver exclaimed. "It is," Silone remarked. "Don't you know the explanation in Abruzzo for the early blooming of the almond tree?" The Holy Family, persecuted by the thugs of Herod, fled to Egypt with the Madonna and Child atop a donkey and St. Joseph leading them on foot. When Herod's assassins approached, Madonna and Child climbed into its branches while St. Joseph pretended to sleep at the foot of the almond tree. "Why an almond tree?" asked the friend. "Because it is the tree with the hardest wood in the Mediterranean," answered Silone "and has a configuration of branches that is easiest to climb." When the tree felt mother and child seek refuge in its branches, it immediately burst into a profusion of flowers to hide them both. "Unfortunately, it is a risky precociousness," Silone darkly warned his friend, "if, because of the season, there comes a frost." Life is precocious and precarious, as is love. "All real love," Silone wrote in 1965, "is inevitably tinged with a tragic sense of precariousness."

In life, Silone could not return to Pescina, as he could not return to the church, but in death he found his final resting place overlooking the place—the *paese dell'anima*—that he carried within him in exile and in Rome. "The olive oil" of the town, he once wrote, "had a slightly bitter flavor; incidentally just like the milk, the water, the wine, the fruit, the bread, and the whole rest of the region . . . To appreciate it you must not have a depraved heart."

On my last visit to Pescina, I made a pilgrimage of sorts to the cross mentioned by Silone in his short story. I tried climbing the mountainside but could not reach the summit. So I returned to Silone's tomb and from there spied a dirt path that led to a paved road and I reached the cross by a more roundabout route, passing an old shepherd tending his sheep who pointed out the way to me. There it stands, an iron cross, vigilant over the town, a symbol for Silone not of the promise of the Easter Resurrection but of an eternal Good Friday. The almond tree proved more elusive. After forty years could it have still been standing? I wondered whether I was searching for something that had been lost or something that had never really existed. Disappointed at not finding the tree, I turned to make my way back to the town with a melancholy heart. But there, by the side of the road, was a wizened old almond tree that I imagined as "Silone's" tree, still with some fruit despite the late season. I plucked a handful of almonds. Their milk had dried and they were bitter, reminding me of the line from García Márquez's *Love in the Time of Cholera*: "It was inevitable: the scent of bitter almonds always reminded him of the fate of unrequited love." It also called to mind a passage from Silone: "Giuditta . . . brought a basket of almonds to the table—the only fruit that is grown in the valley. They are very small, very hard almonds; one has to use force to crack them open, and they are often very bitter." As the hillside was strewn with garbage, there was no place to sit and rest. I remembered Don Benedetto's remark in *Bread and Wine*: "Perhaps," he cautioned his students, "the truth is sad."

Ignazio Silone struggled all his life—in politics and in literature—to bring dignity and humanity to those whose lives were often sacrificed to greed and power. His own internal struggle was no less titanic: an anguished entanglement with both the secular promise of socialism and the transcendent vision of Christianity. Unlike the biblical Jacob, Silone wrestled with *two* angels and *both* failed him. He was forced to realize that he had sought in politics that which politics could not grant him. And through Don Orione, Silone was left with the profound sadness that "Christianity's place in modern society was more tragic and contradictory" than the church would have us believe. Reading aloud Tolstoy's story "Polikushka" to a group of peasants in Pescina at age fifteen, Silone had come to the conclusion that divine compassion "does not relieve a creature of his pain, yet on the other hand does not abandon him but helps him to the end, without ever revealing itself."

In the darkest days of World War II, a German Communist Silone had known immediately after World War I came to see him. The man was now gray and had suffered greatly at the hands of the Nazis. In a voice filled with both hope and trepidation, he told Silone that he had come upon a great and new revelation: "We ought to treat other men the way we would like to be treated ourselves!" Silone could only smile with melancholy and did not dare to remind the man that this truth was already very old. But what did it matter? The man had come to the truth by his own path. "In the saddest trials of our lives," Silone concluded, "we save ourselves by having stubbornly preserved in our souls the seed of some incorruptible certainty."

As one scholar has noted, even when Silone's work seems "too romantic, absurd, or paradoxical," his masterful orchestration of realism, symbolism, and irony enabled him to "summon archetypal echoes that resonate with themes from universal history." In reading the entire corpus, one begins to see that his subject was always the same: an examination of "the dynamics of power and the struggle of the individual to thwart the dehumanizing forces of history." In one of his last published essays, "Quel che rimane" (That Which Remains), Silone insisted that "in spite of everything" he still considered himself a Christian and a socialist. R.W.B. Lewis memorably defined him as an "apprentice saint." What remains for the writer is a Christianity "without myths, reduced to its moral essence, and a great respect but very little nostalgia for that which has been lost along the way . . . In the sense of fraternity and an instinctive devotion to the poor, there also survives the loyalty to socialism."

Contrary to what might appear at first sight, the recent controversy and allegations of his collaboration with the Fascist police do not dispel this reality. In fact, although the documents may discredit Silone as unblemished hero of the left, they add shadow and depth to a figure who had been considered a secular saint, much to his displeasure. In his story, we might come to a better understanding not only of the man but also of the complicated moral choices demanded by his times.

Despite his desperate resolve to overcome the tragic essence of life, Silone never attained that state of grace so elusive to men and women of the twentieth (or any) century. "We are destined," he concluded, "to proceed under a dark ideological sky." George Orwell once described Silone as "a revolutionary and an honest man . . . one of those men who are denounced as Communists by Fascists and as Fascists by Communists." After coming to know him, Iris Origo sensed that "he carried within him wounds which he knew to be unhealable." Another writer saw in Silone someone who had "seen the truth before everyone else," but that given contemporary society and politics, this was "an unforgivable sin." His whole life was marked by paradoxical, even absurd ideas and events. Notwithstanding his earlier hope for the power of political change and his later faith in a "primitive" Christianity, Silone never managed to overcome a tragic vision. His trust in the power of politics to transform and redeem died with a "god that failed." The certainty of a divine Christian comedy likewise withered. The wolves—in their many manifestations—prevented any possibility of overcoming that revelation. Those multifarious and polysemous wolves were still haunting him more than sixty years later when Silone found himself confronting his own death. Speaking to Darina at the clinic in Geneva where he was to end his days, he solemnly told her, "My only fear is that when I'm dead the wolves will devour you."

"What wolves are you talking about? I've never seen any except in the zoo."

"Wolves in human form," he answered gravely.

"I don't know if I have been successful," he confessed in a speech in Jerusalem, "but from my first book, *Fontamara*, to my last, *The Story of a Humble Christian*, I have tried to represent the difficult experiences of man caught in the apparatus and web of tyranny . . . Our powers are limited, but our books will not be useless if they contribute to making human beings more humane."

Are we today any closer to understanding Silone? Do we recognize the reality he chose to carry within himself and in his writing, what he called the human predicament of our time stripped to its barest essentials? Can we truly fathom his decision to cast his lot with the cafoni, his participation in a revolutionary party, his acceptance of a life underground, his letters to Bellone, his embrace of exile, his expulsion from the PCI, his denunciation of totalitarianism in its many guises, his prophetic warnings against affluence, consumerism, conformity, and nihilism? Two decades after Silone's death, Gustaw Herling predicted that "one of the reasons that Silone's work is destined to remain is that it is profoundly honest in a world that tends to be dishonest."

After living with Silone for nearly forty years, Darina confessed, "It is always difficult to say that one knows a man . . . Many aspects of Silone remain a mystery even to me." He was, she insisted, "a man fundamentally alone and lived in a world that was sometimes impenetrable, beyond the usual geography, even until his last moments." He himself had once written that "everyone who has reflected seriously about himself and others knows that some decisions are secret and certain vocations mysterious and unaccountable."

Notwithstanding the shadow cast over his reputation by the spying scandal, the works remain what they always were: powerful testaments to a struggle for justice and liberty. Seventy-five years after its publication, *Fontamara* continues to be read by people around the world. Some see it as "a universal fable about poverty, suffering and freedom," while others read it as "a clarion call of protest against Italian fascism from an exiled son." Perhaps its power lies in the fact that readers the world over—from small villages in Peru to shantytowns in South Africa to huts in Vietnam—recognize it is both. "Only loss is universal," he wrote, "and true cosmopolitanism in this world must be based on suffering."

Silone requested that he be buried in Pescina under the old bell tower of the ruined church of San Berardo. The church, built into the mountainside, destroyed by the earthquake of 1915, overlooks the entire town and commands a panoramic vista of the Fucino valley. Arriving one late winter day, I made the laborious climb up to the site just before sunset. It was the time of day "favorable to humility," just before the stream would be "full of stars." The tomb, more grandiose than that stipulated by Silone, is a striking monument. Stones hewn from the mountainside have been brought together by local masons. On hearing footsteps, I looked up just as one of these rough and honest men was coming down from gathering herbs on the mountain with his niece. He recounted with pride his own labor in building the tomb. A simple cross is the only ornamentation and concession to tradition. "I would like to be buried like this," Silone once wrote on a photograph of the site, "at the foot of the old bell tower of San Berardo in Pescina, with an iron cross against the wall and the sight of the Fucino plain visible in the distance." Sitting by his tomb, as the late afternoon sun sinks behind the mountains, with the smoke of chimneys drifting lazily into a sky burning violet, orange, and bloodred, hearing mothers calling their children home, it is easy to imagine Silone's characters wearily making their way back to the town with their donkeys after a day of hard labor in the fields, only to drink from a bitter spring.

NOTES
BIBLIOGRAPHY
ACKNOWLEDGMENTS
INDEX

Notes

A NOTE TO THE READER WITH SOME THOUGHTS ON BIOGRAPHY

xv The destiny of names: Luigi Sturzo, "Has Fascism Ended with Mussolini?" *Review of Politics* 7, no. 3 (July 1945): 306.

xv Although he was born Secondino Tranquilli: Among the many names he took for the PCI were Sereno, Pasquini, Setra, Olivetti, Bibo, Gregorio, Ismera, Romano Simone, Marisco, Olivetti, Sormani, Fritz Nickel; for the OSS he often used Len, Frost, Mr. Behr, and, my favorite, Man of the Mountain. The name Silvestri is dealt with in chapter eight.

xv "compelled to use so many names": Silone, *The School for Dictators*, p. 39.

xv "We have acquired too many names": "The Situation of the 'Ex,'" in *Emergency Exit*, p. 101.

xvi "when suffering ceases": Silone, preface to *Fontamara*, 1933, now in *Ignazio Silone: Romanzi e saggi* (hereafter cited as *ISRS*), vol. 1, p. 10.

xvi "the insistence": James Atlas, "My Subject, Myself," *New York Times Book Review*, October 9, 2005, p. 24.

xvi "the biographer remains invisible": Jay Parini, "Goethe's Bright Circle," *Chronicle of Higher Education*, May 11, 2007, p. B10.

xvii "all historians are prisoners": Arthur M. Schlesinger Jr., "Folly's Antidote," *New York Times*, January 1, 2007, p. A19.

xvii "I can guarantee its sincerity": "Emergency Exit," in *Emergency Exit*, p. 63.

xviii Fish noted that: Stanley Fish, "Just Published: Minutiae Without Meaning," *New York Times*, September 17, 1999, p. A19.

xviii an address by the historian Joseph Ellis: Joseph Ellis, "Get a Life! Reflections on Biography and History," adapted from a paper presented at the annual meeting of the American Historical Association, January 10, 2004, published in *Historically Speaking* 5, no. 5 (May/June 2004): 18–19.

xix Jill Lepore's assertion: Jill Lepore, "Historians Who Love Too Much: Reflections on Microhistory and Biography," *Journal of American History* 88 (2001): 129–44.

xix "a tremendous fear": Quoted in Ines Scaramucci, "Silone e la letteratura," in *Ignazio Silone tra testimonianza e utopia*, p. 17.

PROLOGUE THE LANDSCAPE OF MY SOUL

3 he was reading Dostoevsky: "Primo incontro con Dostoievski," *La Fiera Letteraria*, March 4, 1956; reprinted in *ISRS*, vol. 2, pp. 1244–46.

3 "baptize the pagan surname": *Il pane di casa*, ed. Giuseppe Ardrizzo (Bergamo: Minerva Italia, 1971); quoted in Bruno Falcetto, "Cronologia," in *ISRS*, vol. 1, p. lxxv.

4 "a queer mixture": Silone at the time was teaching Wilson Italian in postwar Rome. Dabney, *Edmund Wilson*, pp. 321–22.

4 peasant priest: Nicola Chiaromonte, "Silone il rustico," *Il Mondo*, 1952.

5 "the absolute necessity": "Emergency Exit," p. 46.

5 Representativeness was imposed: Silone wrote the American critic that "in the future, your essay will constitute an indispensable source of consultation for whoever wishes to understand my work." Silone to Lewis, July 5, 1961, Archivio Silone, Florence, busta 3, fascicolo 23.

5 "He became a socialist": Lewis, "Ignazio Silone: The Politics of Charity," in *The Picaresque Saint*, pp. 113, 121.

5 "socialism was his": *Bread and Wine*, p. 438.

5 "Every man": Quoted in Bruno Falcetto, "Introduzione," in *ISRS*, vol. 1, pp. xxxiii, xxxiv.

5 "That situation was": Personal correspondence, letter of August 11, 2000.

6 "Look at Silone": Interview in the Parisian weekly *Demain*, November 15, 1957, p. 21.

6 "There is no single truth": Quoted in Peter Coleman, "Ignazio Silone," *Quadrant* 48, no. 1 (January 2004).

6 "I live in": See Silone's "Note on the Revision of *Fontamara*" in *Fontamara*, trans. Eric Mosbacher (London: J. M. Dent, 1985), p. xi.

7 as Irving Howe noted: Irving Howe, introduction to *Bread and Wine*, trans. Eric Mosbacher (New York: New American Library, 1988), pp. v–vi.

7 "a Socialist without": Interview in *L'Express*, Paris, January 23, 1961.

8 forbade its reprinting: Silone, *Der Fascismus*. In spite of Silone's clear instructions that the book was not to be translated into Italian, it appeared as *Il fascismo* in 1992 and again in 2002. Speaking of this last version, Darina Silone called it "a really splendid job." When asked about the possibility of an English translation, she noted that a British publisher was interested but she hoped they would not move forward as "it couldn't possibly be nearly as good as the Mondadori edition." Personal correspondence, Darina Silone to the author, July 7, 2002.

8 "a touch of irony": Author's Note (1962) to *Bread and Wine*, p. 180.

8 "our inhuman fate": Letter to Girolamo Valenti meant as a preface to a 1936

American edition of *Fontamara* that, for unknown reasons, was never published. The original letter is archived in the Taminent Institute of New York University and included in d'Eramo, *Ignazio Silone: Clandestino del Novecento*, pp. 146–48.

8   "But a great respect": Silone to Giovanna Berneri, February 11, 1959, Archivio Silone, Florence, busta 3, fascicolo 21.

8   "There's a kind of sadness": Don Severino speaking to Donna Maria Vincenza, *The Seed Beneath the Snow*, p. 590.

9   the subject of a biography in English: Two important studies should be mentioned here: Maria Nicolai Paynter's *Ignazio Silone: Beyond the Tragic Vision* and Elizabeth Leake's *The Reinvention of Ignazio Silone*. The first is not a biography but a fine work of literary criticism. As will become apparent, although indebted to Paynter's work, I question whether Silone ever transcended the tragic vision of life. Leake's work is not a full-fledged biography but a psychoanalytical reinterpretation of Silone in light of the charges that he spied for the Fascist regime. Perhaps the best critical work on Silone in English remains "Ignazio Silone: The Politics of Charity" in R.W.B. Lewis's *The Picaresque Saint*.

9   some discerning, insightful scholarship: Two outstanding works, to which I am much indebted, are Luce d'Eramo, *L'opera di Ignazio Silone*, and Bruno Falcetto's meticulous editing of Silone's collected works in two volumes as *Ignazio Silone. Romanzi e saggi*. Also of immense help were Vittoriano Esposito, *Vita e pensiero di Ignazio Silone*, and Diocleziano Giardini, *Ignazio Silone. Cronologia della vita e delle opere*.

10   "Ironically, the foreign writers": "Silone and His Critics," in *Fontamara* (London: J. M. Dent, 1994), p. 173.

10   "has now become": Origo, *A Need to Testify*, p. 312.

11   Documents from the National Archives: The documents have been reproduced by a Swiss scholar and are available at www.peterkamber.ch/ignazio.html.

12   "Perhaps the real cause": *Bread and Wine*, p. 260.

12   it was a classic case: See McDonald's essay on the most recent controversy, "Il caso Silone," pp. 77–89.

13   "But for the fact": *Bread and Wine*, p. 201.

13   "saints should always": "Reflections on Gandhi," *Partisan Review*, January 1949.

13   "Silone was the man": Darina Silone, *Colloqui*, pp. 87–88.

13   comparison with an earlier work: Pugliese, *Carlo Rosselli*.

13   As Elizabeth Leake demonstrates: Leake, *The Reinvention of Ignazio Silone*, p. 7.

14   "The difficulty Spina encounters": May 14, 1936, Zurich, Archivio Silone, Florence, busta 4, fascicolo 6.

15   "Unforeseen and unforeseeable": Silone to Mariapia Bonanate, January 1973, Archivio Silone, Florence, busta 10, fascicolo 1.

15 "Anyone who is deeply": Gustaw Herling, "Rome, December 2," in *Volcano and Miracle*, p. 28.

15 had no homeland: Interview with Ugo Alfassio Grimaldi in "Alcune domande a un francotiratore del socialismo," *Critica Sociale*, November 20, 1965; reprinted in *ISRS*, vol. 2, p. 1273.

16 "I saw once again": "Restare se stessi," *Il Resto di Carlino*, January 20, 1963; reprinted in *ISRS*, vol. 2, pp. 1264–65. Darina Silone recounts the episode in *Colloqui*, pp. 88–89.

17 "if the spring is not clear": Rocco De Donatis in *A Handful of Blackberries*, p. 168.

ONE **SAINTS AND STONECUTTERS**

20 "The wolves would come down": *A Handful of Blackberries*, p. 192.

20 "Eventually a voice": *Bread and Wine*, p. 461.

21 "It was a few days": "Incontro con uno strano prete," in *ISRS*, vol. 2, p. 772.

21 "You know": Darina Silone, "The Last Hours of Ignazio Silone," p. 81.

22 "I believe it was that night": A fictional version of the event is recalled by Don Benedetto in *Bread and Wine* (pp. 410–11) and with more detail in *The Seed Beneath the Snow* (pp. 822–24).

22 "Its glories": "Rethinking Progress," in *Emergency Exit*, p. 156.

22 "In the judgment": "Restare se stessi," pp. 1261–66.

23 "It is one of the most inhuman": "Some Facts of My Life," *Twice a Year*, Autumn–Winter 1938; translated and reprinted in *ISRS*, vol. 1, p. 1383.

23 "that other part": Levi, *Christ Stopped at Eboli*, p. 3.

23 What kinship did Silone: Interview with Grimaldi, "Alcune domande a un francotiratore del socialismo."

23 "quite ordinary, simple": "In Celestine's Footsteps," in *The Story of a Humble Christian*, p. 17.

23 "glimpsed the possibility": The encounter is described ibid., pp. 18–9. The South African veteran and author was Uys Krige and his book is *The Way Out* (Cape Town: Maskew Miller, 1955).

23 "everything that I may have written": "Emergency Exit," p. 64.

24 Twenty years later: Diocleziano Giardini recounted this story to me as we warmed ourselves by the annual St. Anthony's bonfire in Pescina, January 2007.

24 "When I came from Rome": *The Seed Beneath the Snow*, p. 726.

24 "made up of a hundred": "Simplicio," in *Mr. Aristotle* (English translation of *Viaggio a Parigi*), p. 93.

24 "the ruins of an ancient castle": "Visit to a Prisoner," in *Emergency Exit*, pp. 2–3.

25 "I drank that water": Silone to Gabriella Seidenfeld, July 29, no year, Archivio Franca Magnani Schiavetti; quoted in Biocca, *Silone. La doppia vita di un italiano*, p. 18.

25   "of a singular beauty": Ferdinand Gregorovius, preface to Bindi, *Monumenti storici e artistici degli Abruzzi*; quoted by Silone in "La terra e la gente," in *ISRS*, vol. 2, p. 1390.

25   Needless to say: "La terra e la gente," p. 1391.

26   "as sour as lemon juice": Foreword to *Fontamara*, p. 9.

26   "Just because you are from somewhere": Quoted in Judt, *The Burden of Responsibility*, p. 97.

26   "I had never seen it": "Visit to a Prisoner," p. 4.

27   "some good and some less good": Giardini, *Scorre la vita*, pp. 76–79.

27   In a 1937 letter: *ISRS*, vol. 1, pp. 1375–76.

28   "its only illustrious sons": "Emergency Exit," p. 64.

29   "I was born in 1900": Quoted in Castagnola Rossini, *Incontri di spiriti liberi*, p. 30.

30   (Yet as the town historian Diocleziano Giardini): See the parochial archive of the church of Santa Maria delle Grazie in Pescina, *Liber Baptizorum*, act no. 85, 2 May 1900, in Giardini, *Ignazio Silone: Cronologia*, pp. 7, 133n1.

30   "I remember the combination": *Partisan Review*, February 1938; translated and reprinted as "Un ricordo d'infanzia," in *ISRS*, vol. 1, pp. 1379–80.

30   In an interview: Origo, *A Need to Testify*, pp. 92–93.

31   One summer evening: Howe, *A Margin of Hope*, p. 1.

31   "there were three great events": Castagnola Rossini, *Incontri*, pp. 30–31.

31   "Look how funny he is!": "Visita al carcere," from *Uscita di sicurezza*; reprinted in *ISRS*, vol. 2, p. 751.

31   "the most restless": "Emergency Exit," p. 52.

32   As Silone himself admitted: "Some Facts of My Life," *Twice a Year*, Autumn–Winter 1938; reprinted in *ISRS*, vol. 1, p. 1383.

33   "In school": "Emergency Exit," p. 62.

33   "Many babies died": *Bread and Wine*, p. 256.

34   "My memories of childhood": "Dati di una vita," in Craxi, *Ignazio Silone. La via della verità*, p. 28. Not all was unrelieved misery. In a letter to Nicola Chiaromonte in 1956 from the seaside town of Pescara, Silone nostalgically recalled how his family had visited the Adriatic town in 1909, a vacation impossible to imagine for most of Pescina's peasants. Nicola Chiaromonte Papers, Gen. Mss. 113, box 3, folder 77.

34   The novelist Ferdinando Camon: *The Fifth Estate*, trans. John Shepley (Marlboro, VT: Marlboro Press, 1987); *Life Everlasting*, trans. John Shepley (Marlboro, VT: Marlboro Press, 1987); and *Memorial*, trans. David Calicchio (Marlboro, VT: Marlboro Press, 1983).

34   "it was not a very stimulating": "Parliamo di me," in *Il Resto di Carlino*, January 18, 1963; reprinted in *ISRS*, vol. 2, p. 1255.

35   "But the most interesting": Castagnola Rossini, *Incontri*, p. 31.

35   "its own laws": *Bread and Wine*, p. 253.

35   peasants all over the world: Foreword to *Fontamara*, pp. 5–6.

35 "At the head of everything": *Fontamara*, pp. 26, 36.

36 "peasants go caroling": Foreword to *Fontamara*, pp. 11, 12.

36 "intimate contact with": "Le idee che sostengo," in *ISRS*, pp. 1388–90.

37 "I am proud": "Emergency Exit," p. 85.

37 "those traits of generosity": "Emergency Exit," p. 85.

38 It left an indelible impression: "Parliamo di me," p. 1256.

38 "An imbalance": "La narrativa e il sottosuolo meridionale," *Quaderni di prospettive meridionali*, January 1956; reprinted in *ISRS*, vol. 2, pp. 1369–80.

38 "the work that today": Ibid.

39 "creative vision sprang": McDonald, "Il caso Silone," p. 77.

39 An incident from childhood: *Uscita di sicurezza*, in *ISRS*, vol. 2, pp. 806–808.

40 "When the earthquake": *The Seed Beneath the Snow*, p. 741.

41 "All of a sudden": "Quand Silone raconte sa vie," interview with Paul Guth in *Le Figaro Littéraire*, January 29, 1955.

42 A pathetic letter: Reprinted in its entirety in Giardini, *Ignazio Silone: Cronologia della vita e delle opere*, pp. 137–39.

43 "Any unlucky person": *Uscita di sicurezza*, p. 814.

43 "In an earthquake": Ibid., pp. 817–18.

45 a half century later: "Una piazza è una piazza," speech given at the conference "Incontro con l'architettura," March 26, 1962; reprinted in *ISRS*, vol. 2, p. 1383.

45 "must have been surprised": "Encounter with a Strange Priest," in *Emergency Exit*, p. 16.

46 Silone was astonished: "What Remains," in *The Story of a Humble Christian*, pp. 30–31.

46 "Try to encourage vice": "Ecco perché mi distaccai dalla Chiesa," in *La Discussione*; reprinted in *ISRS*, vol. 2, pp. 1266–71.

46 "How could one remain?": "What Remains," in *The Story of a Humble Christian*, pp. 30–31.

46 "was the object": *A Handful of Blackberries*, p. 84.

48 "how fond these": Hyde, *God's Bandit*, p. 81.

48 The train ride: "Encounter with a Strange Priest," pp. 15–30, and "Restare se stessi," pp. 1261–66.

49 the seminary's "donkey": Hyde, *God's Bandit*, p. 26.

49 "better an *asino di cartone*": Magnani, *Una famiglia italiana*, pp. 152–53. Magnani's mother brought the news of Silone's arrest to the family by saying "*hanno arrestato cavallo di cartone*," p. 177.

49 "the goodness and clear-sightedness": "Encounter with a Strange Priest," pp. 26, 29–30.

50 "Certain things that he told me": "Restare se stessi," p. 1266.

50 "I would prefer to remain": Quoted in Flavio Peloso, "Don Orione, lo 'strano

prete,' e i fratelli Secondino e Romolo Tranquilli," in Silone and Bagnoli, *Per Ignazio Silone*, p. 121.

50 "It's been so long": Ibid.

50 Silone's portrait: Ignazio Silone, "A costo di essere frainteso," *Vogue*, 1949; quoted ibid., p. 119.

51 "I have a great fear of myself": Ibid., p. 122.

51 "fountains of science": Quoted in *ISRS*, vol. 2, p. xlvi.

52 "Father, my health": Silone to Don Orione, July 29, 1918, in the Archivio Don Orione; quoted in Peloso, "Don Orione," pp. 125–26.

52 "the strategist of charity": Pronzato, *Il folle di Dio*.

53 "Lenin. I have met.": Hyde, *God's Bandit*, p. 121.

53 "The motive for the paradoxical paragon": Ignazio Silone to Don Paolo Bidone, September 15, 1957, in the Archivio Don Orione; quoted in Peloso, "Don Orione," p. 129.

53 "was a natural demagogue": Hyde, *God's Bandit*, p. 122.

53 The "strange priest": Ibid., 90–91. Silone, having read the book, sent Paolo Bidone a letter correcting four minor mistakes but not denying this episode. See Peloso, "Don Orione," p. 129n46.

53 Orione had a special desire: Hyde, *God's Bandit*, p. 77.

54 "if Christ had not": Ibid., p. 120.

54 "It is not among the palm trees": Ibid.

55 "It's not true! I bring the bread": Quoted in Peloso, "Don Orione," p. 132.

55 "Romolo was not a wicked boy": Ibid., p. 133.

55 On the sixth anniversary: Ibid., pp. 134–35.

56 "I'm sorry because": Ibid., p. 136.

57 Pomponio Tranquilli recalled: Ibid., p. 138.

57 "removing him from the malevolent influence": Silone's "malevolent influence" was from the perspective of Don Orione, not Romolo; quoted ibid., p. 139n76.

57 "I'm in trouble": Antonio Ruggeri, *Don Orione*, p. 61.

57 "It would be incorrect to conclude": "Emergency Exit," p. 55.

TWO THE CHOICE OF COMPANIONS

58 "A good Christian": "Emergency Exit," p. 59.

58 "In my rebellion": Ibid., pp. 63–64.

59 drowning out the voices of the speakers: *La Discussione*, October 31, 1965; reprinted in *ISRS*, vol. 2, p. 1268.

59 At the local school: Ibid., p. 1270.

61 "The women went to church": "Polikushka," in *Emergency Exit*, p. 31.

62 " 'What do we do now?' ": *Uscita di sicurezza*, pp. 816–17.

63 "The Great War": "The Choice of Companions," in *Emergency Exit*, p. 112.

63 "During my youth": Paul Guth, "Quand Silone raconte sa vie," *Le Figaro Littéraire*, January 29, 1955, pp. 1–4.

64 "The companions I preferred": "Emergency Exit," p. 48.

64 "That which defined": The Italian word *compagni* can be translated as "comrades" or "companions." "La scelta dei compagni," in *Uscita di sicurezza*, now in *ISRS*, pp. 883–84.

64 "a profound change": "The Choice of Companions," p. 119.

64 "Even in the best books": "Alcuni fatti della mia vita," in *ISRS*, vol. 1, p. 1384.

65 He once asserted: "Parliamo di me," p. 1259.

65 "I felt strangely attracted": "Polikushka," pp. 32, 34.

65 "I left at night": "The Painful Return," in *Emergency Exit*, p. 145.

65 On his leaving Pescina: The scene is recounted in Quinzio, *La speranza nell'apo-calisse*, p. 119. Quinzio contributed to *Tempo Presente*, the journal edited by Silone and Nicola Chiaromonte, for twelve years (1956–68) and Quinzio and Silone often spoke of Silone's life in Pescina.

65 "a sort of flight": "Emergency Exit," pp. 64–65.

66 "Those were times when": *Uscita di sicurezza*, p. 824.

67 the Church of Sant'Anna: The tale is told by Don Gaetano Piccinini in Ruggeri, *Don Orione*, and recounted in Gurgo and de Core, *Silone*, pp. 39–40. Darina confirms the episode in her *Colloqui*, pp. 91–92.

68 Silone was not alone: Gurgo and de Core, *Silone*, pp. 37–38.

69 Three points in particular: De Grand, *The Italian Left in the Twentieth Century*, p. 41.

70 Even an innocuous motion: Gurgo and de Core, *Silone*, p. 44.

70 Antonio Gramsci did not: Ibid., p. 45.

71 So began his clandestine career: Silone's intellectual contribution to the PCI can be traced through the nearly three dozen essays he wrote for the PCI, now collected in Gasbarrini and Gentile, *Ignazio Silone. Comunista*.

71 "living like a foreigner": "Emergency Exit," p. 66.

71 A half century after: "La valigia di Terracini," interview with Marco Cesarini, *Il Mondo*, January 24, 1971.

71 "there were no hotels": Interview on Antenne 2, quoted in Gurgo and de Core, *Silone*, pp. 50–51.

71 "The first time I saw him": Interview with Alfredo Todisco, *Corriere della Sera*, April 22, 1970, p. 3; quoted ibid., p. 48.

72 "bureaucratic involution": Ignazio Silone, "Lenin: le idee e la realtà," *Panorama*, April 23, 1970.

72 Silone refused to be cowed: Gasbarrini and Gentile, *Ignazio Silone. Comunista*, p. i. To his credit, Paolo Spriano, in his monumental *Storia del partito comunista italiano*, vol. 1, p. 267, recognized Silone's important role in the history of the party, even quoting from Silone's *Uscita di sicurezza*.

72 "even in truly exceptional": "Emergency Exit," p. 68.

73 "It's true that we": Quoted in Gasbarrini and Gentile, *Ignazio Silone. Comunista*, p. xl.

73 "Every little thing": Camilla Ravera interview with Daniella Ambrosino, reproduced in Gasbarrini and Gentile, *Ignazio Silone: Tra l'Abruzzo e il mondo*, pp. 275–76.

74 "I knew him well": Silone with Enzo Biagi, quoted in de Core and Gurgo, *Silone, un alfabeto*, pp. 71–72.

74 "fundamental ambiguity": Ignazio Silone, "Agenda," *Tempo Presente*, January 1958.

74 "stripping Gramsci": "Antonio Gramsci," *Tempo Presente*, February 1958; reprinted in *ISRS*, vol. 2, p. 1313.

75 "understood him very": Gasbarrini and Gentile, *Ignazio Silone: Tra l'Abruzzo e il mondo*, pp. 275–76.

75 Gabriella Seidenfeld, one of three sisters: For biographical material on Gabriella Seidenfeld, I rely here on her unpublished memoir, "Le tre sorelle" (The Three Sisters), and I thank Elizabeth Leake for making it available to me.

76 "He was a solitary": Ibid., p. 5.

76 "I wish I could": Quoted in Biocca, *Silone*, p. 88.

76 "It was a very agitated time": Seidenfeld, "Le tre sorelle," p. 6.

76 Vanni Buscemi: On Buscemi and his many guises, including Fascist spy, see Ottanelli, "Fascist Informant and Italian American Labor Leader," pp. 104–16.

77 Put on a train to Barcelona: Origo, *A Need to Testify*, p. 205.

78 Improbable as it may seem: "Primo incontro con Dostoievski," *La Fiera Letteraria*, March 4, 1956; reprinted in *ISRS*, vol. 2, pp. 1244–46.

79 "You'll see": Seidenfeld, "Le tre sorelle," p. 10.

79 To avoid detection: Ibid.

80 "What I want": Quoted in *Colloqui*, pp. 117–18.

80 Most damaging: See Spriano, *Storia del partito comunista italiano*, vol. 2, pp. 119–20.

81 "I've just realized": January 13, 1928, Collezione Franca Magnani Schiavetti, quoted in Biocca, "Ignazio Silone e la polizia politica," p. 78.

81 When Tresso was expelled: Seidenfeld, "Le tre sorelle," p. 22.

82 "In the party you": Ibid.

82 an evening twenty-three years earlier: "Emergency Exit," pp. 41–47.

83 He was only a child: Ibid., pp. 47–48.

83 "When you grow up": Ibid., p. 48. The Harvard University political scientist Edward Banfield, struck by this ancient piece of "peasant wisdom," crafted an entire theory of "amoral familism" from it. "Act only for the immediate short-term interest of the family, and assume all others will do likewise." Banfield argued that this accounted for the political and economic failure of the Italian south, confusing cause and effect. Banfield, *The Moral Basis of a*

Backward Society. See a critique in Silverman, "Agricultural Organization, Social Structure, and Values in Italy" and *Three Bells of Civilization*.

84 "sublime concepts": "Emergency Exit," pp. 48, 51.

85 breaking three ribs: Franzinelli, *I tentacoli dell'OVRA*, p. 83.

85 "If I get twenty years": *La Stampa*, March 14, 1928, p. 1.

85 "Dearest brother": Silone to Romolo, April 25, 1928, Archivio Silone, Pescina.

86 Someone who writes like this: Quoted in Peloso, "Don Orione," pp. 146–47.

86 The real perpetrators: See Franzinelli, *I tentacoli dell'OVRA*, pp. 77–90, and Canosa, *I servizi secreti del Duce*, pp. 69–78.

86 "From Basel, Guido": Quoted in Biocca and Canali, *L'informatore*, p. 123.

86 "I canceled my trip": ACS, Polizia Politica, Materia, b. 95; quoted ibid., pp. 258–59.

87 "Who will now help": Letter intercepted by the Fascist police, April 28, 1928; quoted in *Quaderni Siloniani*, January 1998, p. 7.

88 Don Flavio Peloso: Peloso, "Don Orione," p. 153n121.

89 redacted by prison officials: See letter, dated June 9, 1931, in Archivio Silone, Pescina. "Dearest Secondino, By now you will have heard that the Special Tribunal has sentenced me to twelve years in prison and three years of surveillance and the interdiction of holding public office; I didn't even want to write to you about the verdict to better tell you how it has left me indifferent and [redacted]. When my lawyer turned to console me, I spontaneously gave him an earful, loud and clear: [redacted]."

89 "Now, if I read": Quoted in Gurgo and de Core, *Silone*, p. 102.

89 "You said it well": No date, but from the prison in Perugia. Archivio Silone, Pescina.

89 A devoted exchange: The letters are archived in the Fondo Silone in Florence with copies at the Archivio Silone in Pescina.

90 "I must make": Romolo Tranquilli to Silone, April 7, May 5, May 23, 1931.

90 confess to Don Orione: Peloso, "Don Orione," p. 156. In a letter to Don Antonio Ruggeri of February 1, 1979, Don Antonio Cerasani recounted a conversation with Don Orione that the latter had heard Romolo's confession and "had a holy death . . . an enviable death." Darina Silone recounts the scene in *Colloqui*, p. 94.

90 Silone was notified: "Dear Secondino, With a sorrowful heart I must tell you that on October 11, I went to visit your brother Romolo at Procida and found him gravely ill; in fact on October 27, he peacefully passed away . . . Be strong, dear cousin (on this glorious All Souls' Day). I swear you have done your duty. I'll make arrangements for a tombstone in his memory." Pomponio Tranquilli to Ignazio Silone, November 2, 1932; Archivio Silone, Pescina. Pomponio Tranquilli paid 10 lire for the cross to mark Romolo's grave.

90 attempted to exhume the body: Ruggeri, *Don Orione*, pp. 78–79.

91 "I have tried": "Emergency Exit," p. 93; and "Alcune domande a un francoti-

ratore del socialismo," *Critica Sociale*, November 20, 1965; reprinted in *ISRS*, vol. 2, p. 1272. Quoted by Darina Silone in "Le ultime ore di Ignazio Silone," in *Severina*, p. 173. I have not, though, been able to find the letter, and some have speculated that Silone, by inventing such a letter, may have been adding more tragedy to an already tragic situation.

91 "A young Italian": Quoted in Sutro, "Note on Ignazio Silone," p. 208.

91 "The life of a revolutionary": "Le idee che sostengo," p. 1389.

92 "documents have nothing": The episode, recounted in "Emergency Exit," pp. 74–77, is corroborated by Togliatti, with some minor variations, in *L'Unità*, January 6, 1950: "It generally really went as Silone relates." Togliatti and Silone reported to leadership of the PCI a few weeks later (April 1927), documents preserved in the Archivio Antonio Gramsci in Rome and reproduced in Gasbarrini and Gentile, *Ignazio Silone. Comunista*, pp. 201–36.

92 "unanimously" condemned Trotsky: "Emergency Exit," pp. 82–83.

92 Silone's expulsion: For this episode, see the official party history in Spriano, *Storia del partito comunista italiano*, vol. 2, pp. 230–61. Interestingly, Silone fares well in Spriano's officially sanctioned study.

92 "to disappear": "Emergency Exit," p. 93.

92 The dispute revolved: E. H. Carr, *Twilight of the Comintern, 1930–1935*, pp. 239, 255.

93 Trapped by party intrigue: "Un caso di malavita politica," *Lo Stato Operaio*, May 1931, pp. 291, 294.

93 "the party must": Quoted in Gasbarrini and Gentile, *Ignazio Silone. Comunista*, pp. ix–x.

93 Silone's close confidant: On the relationship between Tasca and Silone, see Soave, *Senza tradirsi, senza tradire*.

94 parallel fates: Elisa Signori, "Ignazio Silone nell'esilio svizzero," *Nuova Antologia* 2132 (1979): 94.

94 "The young people": "Al colloquio con Silone," *Il Messagero*, August 22, 1966.

95 Between Tasca's expulsion: I am indebted to David Bidussa for making the Silone-Tasca letters available to me. See his careful reconstruction of the epistolary exchange and collection of letters in "Dialogato per un rinnovamento socialista," pp. 593–671; the quote here is from p. 625.

95 "Buying paper is": Silone to Tasca, December 2, 1930.

95 He dashed off: Originally published in 1934 as *Der Fascismus: seine Enstehung und seine Entwicklung*. The original Italian manuscript was lost in Silone's many moves across Europe. An unauthorized Italian edition appeared as *Il fascismo. Origini e sviluppo* in 1992; a more authoritative edition, translated from the German by Marina Buttarelli, appeared in 2002.

95 "Even at the risk": Silone to Tasca, December 2, 1930.

95 "Eating every day": Silone to Tasca, January 16, 1931.

95 On June 20, 1930: Ercoli (Togliatti) to Pasquino (Silone), June 20 and August 5, 1930; Archivio Silone, Florence, busta 1, fascicolo 1.

96   "Dream of not": Silone to Adami (Romano Cocchi), Zurich, May 30, 1931, Archivio Silone, Florence, busta 1, fascicolo 1.

96   "Certain comrades": Barbara Seidenfeld Tresso to Angelo Tasca, January 15, 1931, quoted in Bidussa, "Dialogato," p. 632.

97   "These were the charges": Silone to Tasca, June 24, 1931, ibid., p. 637.

97   only be expelled: "Communist parties do not tolerate resignations. They recognize only expulsions." "Emergency Exit," p. 95.

97   Summoned one last time: "L'espulsione di Pasquini dale file dell'I.C.," Lo Stato Operaio, July 1931, pp. 362–65. No official record of the meeting at which Silone was expelled has been published. For Togliatti's version of events, see Opere, vol. 3 (Rome: Riuniti, 1973), pp. 341–53.

97   "An outlawed revolutionary": The Seed Beneath the Snow, p. 585.

98   una piccola morte: "The Situation of the 'Ex,' " p. 101. It is unlikely that Silone—famously shy of sexuality in his writing—was consciously evoking the French la petite mort.

98   "for any motive": "Rethinking Progress," p. 158.

98   "In the struggle": "The Situation of the 'Ex,' " pp. 108–109.

98   When oppression: "Parliamo di me," p. 1257.

99   Silone would drink: Seidenfeld, "Le tre sorelle," p. 27.

99   Hungarian count Michael Károlyi: Mihály Károlyi, Memoirs of Michael Károlyi: Faith Without Illusion, trans. Catherine Károlyi (New York: Dutton, 1957).

99   It was Brupbacher: Seidenfeld, "Le tre sorelle," p. 27.

100 Gabriella continued to live: Ibid., p. 31.

101 "Two years ago": Quoted in Gurgo and de Core, Silone, p. 61.

101 "To a small number": Attachment n. 2 to will; photocopy of original in Gasbarrini and Gentile, Silone: Tra l'Abruzzo, p. 26.

101 "I propose to remain": Silone to Tasca, May 30, 1934; Tasca to Silone, September 14, 1934; in Bidussa, "Dialogato," p. 655.

102 "The truth is so sad": Balabanoff to Silone, November 19, 1936, Archivio Silone, Florence, busta 1, fascicolo 2, doc. 143.

102 "shoot the vipers!": Mosbacher to Silone, September 14, 1936, Archivio Silone, Florence, busta 1, fascicolo 2, doc. 113.

102 Just months after: Proving that instant celebrity-politico books are not new, Badoglio's La guerra d'Etiopia was published by Mondadori (Silone's future publisher after the war) with a preface by none other than Mussolini himself. It appeared in English as The War in Abyssinia (London: Methuen; New York: Putnam, 1937). Tellingly, there was no English translator listed.

102 "it is necessary": Rosselli to Silone, February 1937, Archivio Silone, Florence, busta 1, fascicolo 3, doc. 36.

102 "Give my regards": Silone to Balabanoff, Archivio Silone, Florence, busta 1, fascicolo 3, doc. 105.

102 "After the death": "Emergency Exit," pp. 73–74.

103 "side by side": "The Situation of the 'Ex,' " p. 104.

103 "a very sad day": "Emergency Exit," p. 97.

103 "the rashness": "Polikushka," p. 40.

103 no "superior moral virtue": "Emergency Exit," pp. 80, 83.

103 "There are many": "The Choice of Companions," p. 126.

THREE WRITING IN/AND EXILE

104 "Finally, the English": Silone to Eric Mosbacher, September 9, 1936, Archivio Silone, Florence, busta 2, fascicolo 1, doc. 110.

105 "private war against": The Situation of the 'Ex,' " pp. 105, 107.

105 "my second homeland": Quoted in Castagnola Rossini, *Incontri*, pp. 31–32.

105 "One is cured": "Emergency Exit," p. 90.

105 "So far, I have kept you": The letter, dated December 8, 1933, can be found in the Archivio Silone at the Fondazione di Studi Storici in Florence, busta 1, fascicolo 1. Curiously, Dr. Strasser's address, Mythenstrasse 23, Zurich, was the site of a Swiss society formed in February 1918 to combat venereal disease. See also the April 20, 1936, invitation to speak from Dr. Heinrich Meng, a Freudian psychoanalyst, in the Archivio Silone, Florence, busta 1, fascicolo 2.

105 "delays my convalescence": Quoted in Biocca, *Silone*, p. 135.

106 "I have been cured": Ibid., pp. 161–62.

106 "I continue to go": Ibid., p. 169.

107 "The beautiful young lady": The description is from the jacket copy of a novel by Eveline Hasler, *Aline und die Erfindung der Liebe* (Aline and the Invention of Love) (Zurich: Nagel & Kimche, 2000).

107 Silone spent much of his life: The correspondence between Silone and Aline Valangin Rosenbaum, along with Silone's poem, "le monde et la barque" and his version of "La Genese" (an alternate and irreverent version of Genesis) is in the Swiss Archives in Bern. I am indebted to Deborah Holmes and Elizabeth Leake for sharing them with me.

107 writing sporadic letters: The letters, in French, are at the Archivio Silone in Pescina, the Swiss State Archives in Bern, and the Archivio Aline Valangin in the Canton Library of Lugano.

108 "The spirit of the ark": Swiss State Archives, Bern, translated from the French into Italian by Vittoriano Esposito in *Quaderni Siloniani* 1–2 (2003–2004): 16–19.

108 "We wrote to each other": Aline Valangin, *Erinnerungen*, partially reprinted in Peter Kamber, *Geschichte zweier Leben: Wladimir Rosenbaum & Aline Valangin* (Zurich: Limmat Verlag Genossenschaft, 1990), p. 100; quoted in Falcetto, "Cronologia," pp. lxxxii–lxxxiii.

110 "The man was tall": Magnani, *Una famiglia italiana*, pp. 90, 98.

111 "Aber de Duce": Ibid., p. 68.

111 When Hitler appeared: Ibid., pp. 125, 132.

111   Established a complex network: Holmes, *Ignazio Silone in Exile*, pp. 137–39.

111   The process of "reinvention": *The Reinvention of Ignazio Silone.*

111   "The victory of my soul": Mercuri, *Memoir from a Swiss Prison*, p. 26.

112   "Driven by homesickness": "Rethinking Progress," p. 157.

112   "obeying at all times": "Letteratura e politica," *Critica Sociale*, April 20, 1957; reprinted in *ISRS*, vol. 2, pp. 1247–51.

112   "writing for me": "Parliamo di me," pp. 1255–60.

112   a fictional town: There is considerable dispute as to whether Fontamara was based on Pescina; Silone himself was sometimes ambiguous, perhaps purposely so. In the Angelo Tasca Archive at the Feltrinelli Foundation in Milan, there is a four-page typewritten résumé in French of *Fontamara: Roman de vie contemporaine.* Among the "advertissements": "*Fontamara existe réellement, mais son nom véritable est Pescina . . .*" See Judy Rawson, "Un riassunto di un Ur-Fontamara," in Silone and Bagnoli, *Per Ignazio Silone*, pp. 21–31. As the document is unsigned, it is not possible to determine whether this was Tasca's summary or Silone's. (The slight mistakes might lead a reader to suppose the latter, as Tasca's French was notably better than Silone's.)

112   "Ill and in exile": "The Painful Return," pp. 146–47.

113   "I believe they": July 29, 1930, Archivio Franca Magnani Schiavetti, quoted in Biocca, *Silone*, pp. 177–78.

113   "I am working": Silone to Tasca, January 22, 1931, in Bidussa, "Dialogato," p. 633.

113   so poor that: Remarks by Darina Silone at the centenary commemorations of Silone's birth, May 1, 2000, Pescina.

113   In his own personal copy: The book, inscribed on April 12, 1933, is on display at the Museo Silone, Pescina. The line is also inscribed on a painting of the Pietà where "Christ looked like a *cafone*," mentioned in *Bread and Wine*, p. 403.

115   "The art of storytelling": Foreword to *Fontamara*, p. 13.

116   "Fate has decreed": November 6, 1931, Collezione Franca Magnani Schiavetti, Rome; quoted in Biocca, "Ignazio Silone e la polizia politica," p. 90.

116   Silone turned to his circle: See Silone's September 30, 1955, letter (in French) to Arthur Koestler, who had created some controversy over his remarks about the genesis and original publication of *Fontamara*. Archivio Silone, Florence, busta 3, fascicolo 17.

116   Salvemini wrote back: Salvemini to Valangin, October 2, 1931, Archivio Silone, Florence, busta 1, fascicolo 1.

117   "My impression is": Tasca to Silone, October 18, 1931, in Bidussa, "Dialogato," p. 641.

117   "act of pure generosity": "Eric und Nettie," Zurich, October 14, 1967, quoted in d'Eramo, *L'opera di Ignazio Silone*, p. 18.

118   The book was typeset: Silone to Arthur Koestler, Rome, September 30, 1955, quoted in d'Eramo, *L'opera di Ignazio Silone*, pp. 18–1914.

118   "to be confiscated": Dietrich Strothmann, *Nationalsozialistische Literaturpoli-*

tik: Ein Beitrag zur Publizistik im Dritten Reich (Bonn: Bouvier, 1968), p. 230. In 1935, Silone's *Der Fascismus* was added to the list.

119 "I hastened in search": "Parliamo di me," p. 1259.

119 "to remain faithful": Silone to Borgese, May 12, 1937, Archivio Silone, Florence, busta 1, fascicolo 3, doc. 98.

120 Buonaiuti recalled: "Un artista maturato nella sofferenza e nella speranza," in Cristini, *Dal villaggio all'Europa*, p. 12.

120 an American professor at Florida State: Cunningham, "La pazienza come volontà," pp. 24–25.

120 Carlo Rosselli: Rosselli to Silone, November 17 and December 31, 1933, Archivio Silone, busta 1, fasciscolo 1.

121 "In *Fontamara* passion": d'Eramo, *L'opera di Ignazio Silone*, p. 60.

121 "From the first": Trotsky to Silone, July 17, 1933, printed in the Russian oppositionist journal in Paris, *Bollettino dell'Opposizione*, October 1933.

121 Silone, detecting: d'Eramo, *L'opera di Ignazio Silone*, p. 61.

121 "One hundred rich men": Ibid., p. 63.

121 "In *Fontamara* we": *Spectator*, November 2, 1934; quoted in Gordon, "Silone and His Critics," p. 174.

122 "the entire action": Interview with Grazia Coco, after a letter dated September 20, 1969, Archivio Silone, Florence, busta 10, fascicolo 1.

122 "life itself": "A Note on Ignazio Silone," afterword to *Mr. Aristotle*, pp. 203–11.

123 "My embarrassment": "Note on the Revision of *Fontamara*," in *The Abruzzo Trilogy*, p. 4.

123 Silone replied: Quoted in d'Eramo, *L'opera di Ignazio Silone*, p. 32.

123 "Who is he?": Ibid., pp. 65–66.

123 "the necessity of a deep consciousness": Petroni, "Testimonianza a Ignazio Silone."

124 Silone offered a three-part definition: Dave Renton, *Fascism: Theory and Practice* (London: Pluto Press, 1999), p. 67.

124 "revolutions, like trees": "The Choice of Companions," p. 117.

124 Croat and Polish: The Polish translation was published without the author's knowledge or consent. When Silone became aware of it, he wrote an angry letter to the publisher (who, unknown to Silone, had recently died). His widow replied by asking that Silone pay the Polish typesetter, as her husband had died in debt by publishing the book. D'Eramo, *L'opera di Ignazio Silone*, pp. 109–10.

124 blessings of Darina Silone: When I broached the subject of an English translation, Darina Silone was adamantly against it. She did approve of the 2002 Italian edition ("he's done a really splendid job"); letter of July 12, 2002.

125 "Was ist Fascismus?": Ignazio Silone, *information*, August–September 1932, p. 8.

125 "that the victory": *Il fascismo*, trans. Marina Buttarelli, p. 273.

125 "of the general moral": "The Choice of Companions," p. 113.

126   "development, movement, change": For the fourteen essays written by Silone for the review, translated from the original German into Italian by Lelio Cremonte, see *Gli articoli di "information" (Zurigo 1932–1934)*, ed. M. Antonietta Morettini Bura (Perugia: Guerra, 1994).

126   "the idea and": Silone to Tasca, July 8, 1937.

127   "Politics [for Machiavelli]": *School for Dictators*, p. 12.

127   "A deep knowledge": Ibid., p. 28.

127   "it mobilizes and marshals": Ibid., p. 93.

128   "work of art": Ibid., p. 35.

128   "The fascist leader's": Ibid., p. 72.

128   "Although a political movement": Ibid., p. 134.

128   "The only thing fascism": Ibid., p. 157.

128   "sacralization" of politics: Carlo Levi, *Fear of Freedom*, trans. Adolphe Gourevitch (New York: Columbia University Press, 2008); Gentile, *The Sacralization of Politics*.

128   "Nothing but an adequate liturgy": *School for Dictators*, pp. 212–13.

129   "modern melancholy": Kazin, "A Dialogue on Dictatorships."

130   "Silone knows too much": Tucci, "Bad News for the Thought Police."

130   "He is the only one": The thirty-four Silone-Oprecht letters, written between 1933 and 1958, are in the Zurich Central Library; see Castagnola Rossini, *Incontri*, pp. 21–34. On Musil, see Ignazio Silone, "Encounters With Musil," *Salmagundi* 61 (Fall 1983).

130   "today they ignore us": See J. M. Coetzee's introduction to Robert Musil, *The Confusions of Young Törless* (New York: Penguin, 2001), p. ix.

130   "Here I truly": Falcetto, "Introduzione," in *ISRS*, vol. 2, p. lviii.

130   "13 January 1941": My translation from the French of the handwritten letter, along with a typewritten page on St. Paul's thought on love from his letter to the Corinthians (1:13), in the Archivio Silone, Florence, busta 1, fascicolo 5. This is the famous passage that begins, "If I have all the eloquence of men or angels, but speak without love, I am simply a gong booming or a cymbal clashing," and ends, "There are three things that last: faith, hope and love; and the greatest of these is love." In a footnote, Silone makes clear his interpretation that Paul was not speaking only of love between a man and a woman, and argues for "*amitié.*"

132   thought him a tragic figure: d'Eramo, *L'opera di Ignazio Silone*, p. 154.

132   "I very much admired": Arthur Koestler, *The Invisible Writing* (New York: Macmillan, 1954), p. 279.

133   "he was a fanatical Stalinist": Silone to Rudolf Jakob Humm, March 22, 1957, Archivio Silone, Florence, busta 3, fascicolo 19.

132   "the sorrowful comedy": Lewis, *The Picaresque Saint*, pp. 160–61.

133   "a beautiful and painful book": *Quaderni di Giustizia e Libertà* 9 (November 1933): 100. I am grateful to Frank Rosengarten for making the entire run of the *Quaderni* available for consultation.

133 a correspondence began: On the relationship, see Pugliese, *Carlo Rosselli*, pp. 192–93. The correspondence between Silone and Rosselli is in the Istituto Storico della Resistenza in Toscana in Florence, Archivio di Giustiza e Libertà, sezione I, fascicolo I, sottofascicolo III, inserti 1–4.

134 "Besides, there is": Silone to Rosselli, June 12, 1934, sezione 1, fascicolo III, inserto 3.

134 "I understand perfectly": Rosselli to Silone, June 15, 1934, Archivio Silone, Florence, busta 1, fascicolo 1.

134 "today [1942] the": Silone to the Chief of Information Services of the Federal Swiss Attorney General, December 16, 1942; reproduced in Ignazio Silone, *Memoriale dal carcere svizzero*, p. 34.

135 promptly translated: *Die Reise nach Paris*, trans. Nettie Sutro (Zurich: Verlag Oprecht, 1934); *Mr. Aristotle*, trans. Samuel Putnam (New York: Robert McBride, 1935); also *A Journey to Paris*, trans. John Lehmann (London: Penguin, 1936). There were also Danish and Spanish translations. A Japanese translation appeared after the war, without the author's consent.

135 "What, don't you remember me?" Recounted in d'Eramo, *L'opera di Ignazio Silone*, p. 117.

135 "a book like yours": Humm to Silone, May 19, 1936, quoted in Holmes, *Ignazio Silone in Exile*, p. 99.

136 "to me entirely": Author's note (1962) to *Bread and Wine*, p. 179.

135 *Vino e pane*: Doctoral dissertations have been written on the variations of Silone's works, especially those between *Pane e vino* and the subsequent *Vino e pane*. For a summary, see d'Eramo, *L'opera di Ignazio Silone*, pp. 137–53. When Silone's English translator Eric Mosbacher suggested pursuing the idea of making *Bread and Wine* into a film, Silone demurred: "I'm a bit fearful; I would need to collaborate with too many people." Silone to Mosbacher, June 6, 1936, Archivio Silone, Florence, busta 2, fascicolo 1, doc. 44.

136 "The cause of my pain": *Bread and Wine*, p. 272.

137 "Perhaps the wolf": Ibid., p. 284.

137 "It's not your ideal": Ibid., p. 359.

137 "We live the whole": Ibid., pp. 214–15.

138 Murica has become ensnared: Ibid., pp. 428, 453.

138 "Dear comrade": Angela Balabanoff to Silone, August 15, 1936, Archivio Silone, Florence, busta 2, fascicolo 1, doc. 97.

139 "a compassionate parable": d'Eramo, *L'opera di Ignazio Silone*, pp. 155–56.

139 "Just another word": Archivio Silone, Florence, busta 1, fascicolo 3.

139 "I force myself": *Twice a Year*, Autumn–Winter 1938; quoted in *ISRS*, vol. 1, p. 1382.

140 "a novel cannot": "The Things I Stand For," appeared in English in *The New Republic* (November 2, 1942) as well as *La Parola* of New York and in Italian in *Il Mese* of London (October 1943). Reprinted in Italian as "Le idee che sostengo," pp. 1385–91.

140 "forgotten that in the best": Silone reconstructed the history of NEC in

"Le 'Nuove Edizioni di Capologo,'" in *Egidio Reale e il suo tempo* (Florence: La Nuova Italia, 1961), pp. 151–68. See also Castagnola Rossini, *Incontri*, pp. 61–121.

142   "At first I was afraid": *The Seed Beneath the Snow*, pp. 663–64.

144   "The Third Front": The document can be found in the Bern Bundesarchiv 8. 2070; it has been printed in its entirety in Silone, *Memoriale dal carcere svizzero*, pp. 64–67, and reprinted in *ISRS*, vol. 1, pp. 1392–1412.

146   Two weeks later: Riccardo Formica (pseudonym "Minotti"), born in Trapani, Sicily, joined the Socialist movement in 1921 but moved to the PCI that same year and fought in the Spanish Civil War in defense of the republic. By 1941, he had returned to the PSI. Olindo Gorni ("Giannini"), born near Mantova, was a professor of agronomy; he died of cancer in September 1943 in Geneva. Piero Pellegrini ("Pedroni"), from Turin, had been living in Lugano, where he was editor of the newspaper *Libera Stampa*. At the time, Silone was using "Sormani" as a code name.

149   "I was," he confessed: In an interview with Silone's widow, Darina, she stated that Silone had contemplated suicide several times in his life. During the course of their marriage, he more than once threatened to kill himself. Interview with author, March 16, 2000.

151   "The Spirit blows": "The wind, that is, the Spirit, blows where it chooses, and you hear the sound of it, but you do not know where it comes from or where it goes" (John 3:8). In his essay "Unpacking My Library," Walter Benjamin writes: "*Habent sua fata libelli*: these words may have been intended as a general statement about books. So books like *The Divine Comedy*, Spinoza's *Ethics*, and *The Origin of Species* have their fates. A collector, however, interprets this Latin saying differently. For him, not only books but also copies of books have their fates." *Illuminations*, trans. Harry Zohn (New York: Schocken, 1968), p. 61.

152   "What is the worth": *ISRS*, vol. 1, pp. 1269–72.

154   "vivid, living texts": Silone could not have known it at the time, but his former colleague in the Italian Communist Party, Antonio Gramsci, had surreptitiously written his *Prison Notebooks* while in Fascist prisons, a work that was to revitalize Italian Marxism after the war. He surely knew of Carlo Rosselli's *Socialisme libéral*, which had first been published in France in 1930 (and in an English edition as *Liberal Socialism*, trans. William McCuaig [Princeton: Princeton University Press, 1994]). Every educated person of Silone's generation was familiar with Silvio Pellico's memoir of time spent in Austrian prisons, *Le miei prigioni*, translated as *My Prisons* by I. G. Capaldi (New York: Oxford University Press, 1963). For more recent studies, see Charles Kloop, *Sentences: The Memoirs and Letters of Italian Political Prisoners from Benvenuto Cellini to Aldo Moro* (Toronto: University of Toronto Press, 2000), and Ellen V. Nerenberg, *Prison Terms: Representing Confinement During & After Italian Fascism* (Toronto: University of Toronto Press, 2001).

154   "archival madness.": The term in the original is "*cretinismo archivistico*" (not to be confused with Jacques Derrida's "archive fever"). The materials confiscated by the Swiss police are archived in the Institute for Social History in Amsterdam; I am indebted to the staff there for permission to consult the documents.

155 "I hope to be read": Here, I do not think Silone means Christian in a religious sense. In the lexicon of the southern Italian peasantry, *cristiano* meant a decent person, not necessarily a follower of the religion. Of course, this raises the question of why the word came to be used in such a way and what implications it has in how Italians thought of Jews and Muslims. Paradoxically, even Jews and Muslims could be *"bravi cristiani."*

156 "a grave threat": Silone, *Memoriale dal carcere svizzero*, pp. 89–90.

157 "the special representative": Darina Silone, letter to *Le Monde*, May 28, 2000, p. 13.

157 government in exile: *Colloqui*, p. 64.

157 communication to the Allies: Petersen, *From Hitler's Doorstep*, p. 255.

157 conductor Arturo Toscanini: Ibid., p. 8.

158 support the anti-Fascist Resistance: Ibid., p. 594.

158 also a Fascist spy: Ottanelli, "Fascist Informant," pp. 104–16.

158 "psychological value": Ibid., p. 11. See the telegram from Dulles to London, April 28, 1944, pp. 275–76.

158 When Silone requested: Petersen, *From Hitler's Doorstep*, p. 578.

159 "from the earliest days": Telegram 1593, March 12, 1943 (doc. 1–41), ibid., pp. 51–52.

159 In the spring of 1943: Telegram 60–66, April 14, 1943, ibid., pp. 57–58.

159 "states that the insurgents": Ibid., p. 81.

160 "take over Fascist corporations": July 20, 1943; ibid., p. 85.

160 "Badoglio's role is": July 27 and August 14, 1943; ibid., pp. 98, 91.

160 The newly created Italian: January 27, 1944; ibid., p. 205.

160 "it is impossible": Silone to Sforza, March 10, 1944; quoted ibid., p. 245.

161 "many things which": "Le idee che sostengo," p. 1385.

161 "My nostalgia for Switzerland": Silone to Luce d'Eramo, "Il mio amico Silone," in *Ignazio Silone: Clandestino del Novecento*, p. 18.

161 *"Their manner of acting":* Quoted in Falcetto, "Introduzione," in *ISRS*, vol. 1, pp. xxxiv–xxxv.

162 "a book once published": Author's Note to *Bread and Wine*, p. 179.

FOUR DARINA

163 One day Darina's father: *Colloqui*, p. 21.

164 During her first year: "Religious Experiences," unpublished essay, private correspondence with the author, March 2001.

165 "The curious thing is": "Esperienze politiche," unpublished essay of April 2001, presented to the author May 11, 2001.

165 "to become a heretic": "The Making of an Earth Citizen," unpublished remarks at a conference commemorating Indira Gandhi, New Delhi, January 1989.

165 "I understood that Mussolini": "Esperienze politiche," p. 1.

165 "During my school years": Ibid., p. 2.

166 In Zurich: A letter to her parents dated December 31, 1941, intercepted by the Fascist police, now in the Archivio Centrale dello Stato, Rome. Darina reads from this letter in *Colloqui*, pp. 100–01.

166 *"Gute Deutsche kaufen"*: *Colloqui*, p. 24.

166 One of these "good Germans": Ibid., p. 25.

167 "Anything, except killing": "Esperienze politiche," p. 4.

168 "wasn't like the movies": Interview with author, November 27, 2000, Rome.

168 Expelled by the Italian government: Darina Silone obituary by Desmond O'Grady, *Irish Independent*, August 10, 2003.

168 "Dear Signorina, I have heard": *Colloqui*, p. 45.

169 Darina immediately wrote: Ibid., pp. 46–47.

169 "Better to read a writer": Ibid., p. 48.

170 "In that single moment": Darina describes the revelation in 1974 during a visit to the temple of Chidambaram in "The Making of an Earth Citizen."

170 "I did quite a lot": *Colloqui*, p. 58.

170 Her attempt: Personal correspondence with the author, April 17, 2000.

171 found the whole episode: *Colloqui*, pp. 51–52.

171 "permanently scandalized.": Ibid., pp. 52–53.

172 "Good morning. May I": Darina recounts the episode in a letter to her parents, dated December 31, 1941, signed "*L'Enfant prodigue*" and intercepted by the Fascist police. She reads from the letter in *Colloqui*, p. 101.

172 "What a beautiful country!": Darina Silone, "Saluto conclusivo," closing remarks at an international conference, Pescina, May 1, 2001.

172 "The Allies are showing themselves": The memorandum to President Roosevelt dated October 23, 1944, prepared and signed by the director of the OSS, William J. Donovan, was copied to Secretary of State Cordell Hull and Assistant Secretary of War John McCloy. The document was declassified by the CIA and is now in the Records of the Office of Strategic Services, Record Group 226, entry 92, box 181, National Archives and Records Administration, Washington, D.C. I am grateful to Paul B. Brown of the Modern Military Records Textual Archives Services Division for making a photocopy available for use.

173 notorious Fosse Ardeatine massacre: On the so-called Ardeatine Caves massacre, see Robert Katz, *Death in Rome* (New York: Macmillan, 1967), and Alessandro Portelli, *The Order Has Been Carried Out* (New York: Palgrave, 2003); on the prison at via Tasso, see Stanislao G. Pugliese, *Desperate Inscriptions: Graffiti from the Nazi Prison in Rome* (Boca Raton, FL: Bordighera Press, 2002).

174 They lived on: *Colloqui*, p. 68.

174 "after years of using false papers": "The Situation of the 'Ex,'" p. 101.

174 "he was not capable": Interview with author in the Silone apartment on via Villa Ricotti, Rome, March 15, 2000.

175   He had a "repugnance": Author's Note to *Bread and Wine*, p. 180.

175   "Why do you live": Lewis, *The City of Florence*, p. 3.

176   One scholar has detected: d'Eramo, *Ignazio Silone*, p. 37.

177   so-called *guitti*: *Colloqui*, p. 61.

177   English "a fetish": Darina Silone to the author, August 11, 2000.

177   friend of Indira Gandhi: When Darina wrote to Indira Gandhi asking what she should bring from Italy, Gandhi replied, "A kilo of parmigiano cheese; it's very useful in the kitchen." *Colloqui*, p. 105.

177   "sixteen unexpectedly delightful": Darina Silone, postcard dated October 20, 1981, Vassar College, Mary McCarthy Papers, box 223, folder 223.6.

177   "Often he would seek refuge": Remarks at the centenary commemorations of Silone's birth, May 1, 2000, Pescina.

178   "poky, horrible little flat": Letter to the author, April 17, 2000.

178   Darina was fascinated: *Colloqui*, pp. 78–79.

179   "He had trouble understanding": Ibid., p. 14.

179   A surreptitious peek: Silone's study—complete with desk, typewriter, and the photos—has been transferred and re-created at the Centro Studi Silone in Pescina.

179   Gide, or Mann: O'Grady, *Irish Independent*, August 10, 2003.

179   Silone's 1942 call: Interview with the author, November 27, 2000, Rome.

180   did not undergo psychoanalysis: See her letter to *Le Monde* of May 28, 2000, p. 13: "I can say with confidence that the 'psychoanalysis with Jung in 1929' is a myth, nothing more: Silone did not meet Jung until around 1935. In 1929, as several letters show, Silone could not afford the luxury of psychoanalysis."

180   his journal *Monde*: "I can quickly write for you a two-column article on Jung . . . As you know, together with Freud and Adler, Jung represents one of the masters who are fighting for supremacy of modern psychology. Recently, Freud has begun to be translated in France; Adler and Jung are unknown. I would like to take advantage of the book that has just appeared to do a presentation on Jung: an informative, objective article." Ignazio Silone to Angelo Tasca, October 29, 1930; reproduced in Bidussa, "Dialogato," p. 626. Silone is probably referring to Jung's *Paracelsus*, published in Zurich in 1929.

180   "largely rewritten and fictionalized": The history of the "missing dedication" is recounted by Silone's niece, Maria Moscardelli. Seidenfeld's memoir, with Darina Silone's notation, is in the Archivio Silone in Pescina.

180   "I am becoming aware": *Colloqui*, p. 112.

181   In the summer of 2003: Don Flavio's testimony is in a letter to Michele Dorigatti and Maffino Maghenzani, editors of Darina Silone's *Colloqui*, and is cited on p. 127. The dream is recounted by Darina's sisters, Cecily, Moira, and Eithne, in a letter one year after Darina's death, to Dorigatti and Maghenzani, ibid., p. 128.

181   A small Christmas *presepio*: Don Flavio Peloso, "Ricordo di Darina Silone,"

unpublished eulogy, personal correspondence with the author, August 13, 2003. Father Peloso is the director of the Piccola Opera della Divina Provvidenza, the charitable organization founded by Don Luigi Orione, with headquarters in Rome.

181   "ethical adventure": *Colloqui*, p. 125.

FIVE **THE PROBLEMS OF POSTFASCISM**

182   "moral infection of nihilism": "The Choice of Companions," p. 113.

183   If Roselli argued: Gurgo and de Core, *Silone*, pp. 227–28.

183   "Trotskyist counter-revolutionary": Ibid., p. 228.

184   film based on *Fontamara*: A sketch of the screenplay was discovered in the summer of 1996 in the Usellini archive at the Università di Pavia. Gurgo and de Core, *Silone*, p. 229n7.

184   Serafino Romualdi: Romualdi left his papers to Cornell University, where they can be consulted in the Kheel Center for Labor-Management Documentation and Archives. His memoir, *Presidents and Peons* (New York: Funk and Wagnalls, 1967), was published the year of his death.

184   "gave us the impression": Quoted in Gurgo and de Core, *Silone*, p. 233.

185   In his diary, Nenni: Nenni, *Tempo di guerra fredda*, p. 121.

186   "it depends entirely": Gurgo and de Core, *Silone*, p. 235.

186   Writing in early 1945: Ibid., pp. 235, 237.

187   To the Honorable: No date but 1946, Archivio Silone, Florence, busta 2, fascicolo 8.

187   But before the end: A most beautiful and evocative portrait of Parri's fall from power, along with elegiac commentaries on time, memory, and history, is found in Carlo Levi's *The Watch* (South Royalton, VT: Steerforth Press, 1999).

188   In July 1944: Domenico, *Italian Fascists on Trial*, p. x.

188   "we should not pretend": *Avanti!* February 8, 1946.

189   "Many of us have remained": Quoted in Gurgo and de Core, *Silone*, p. 239.

189   "Let us leave the dead": Ibid., p. 250.

189   "gotten on my nerves": *La Fiera Letteraria*, July 4, 1948.

190   After the first course: *Colloqui*, pp. 75–76; the curious episode is confirmed by the Contessa Elena Carandini in her memoir, *Passata la stagione*.

190   An Orwell biographer: Agathocleous, *George Orwell*, p. 69.

190   "Silone doesn't have the qualities": Gurgo and de Core, *Silone*, p. 242.

191   "an act of life": *Avanti!* June 5, 1946, p. 1.

192   "sad epilogue": "Nel bagaglio degli esuli," in *Esperienze e studi socialisti* (Florence: La Nuova Italia, 1954).

192   On behalf of Zauri's illiterate mother: This episode is reconstructed from Silone, *The Secret of Luca*, and Darina Silone, *Colloqui*, pp. 72–74.

194 "I asked your mother": "Ritorno a Fontamara," *Comunità*, March–April 1949, p. 55.

194 His farewell editorial: "Autocritica," *Avanti!* July 14, 1946, quoted in Gurgo and de Core, *Silone*, p. 246.

195 Thirteen years later: Letter appeared in *Corriere della Sera*, quoted ibid., p. 248.

196 "If we do not make 'Europe'": "Missione europea del socialismo," in *Europa federata*, ed. Ernesto Rossi (Milan: Edizioni di Comunità, 1947); reprinted in *ISRS*, vol. 2, pp. 1002–13; the quote here is from p. 1013.

196 "Together with the social question": "L'internazionale socialista e l'unità europea," *Oggi*, November 1946.

197 "inexorable recognition of defeat": Pampaloni, "Tra letteratura e politica."

198 "Battle of the Births": Giovanna Berneri's plea for assistance and Silone's response in Archivio Silone, Florence, busta 2, fascicolo 11.

199 "the psychology of a renegade": Togliatti, "Contributo alla psicologia di un rinnegato."

199 "the six that failed": Roderigo di Castiglia, "I sei che sono falliti," *Rinascita*, May 1950.

200 "dear Comrade Silone": Natalia Sedova Trotsky to Ignazio Silone, July 6, 1951, Archivio Silone, Florence, busta 12, fascicolo 12.

201 "two eloquent Europeans": See the declassified CIA document "Origins of the Congress for Cultural Freedom, 1949–1950," www.cia.gov/library/center-for-the-study-of-intelligence/kentcsi/docs/v38i5a1op.htm.

201 "and I left communism": Arthur Koestler, *The Invisible Writing* (New York: Macmillan, 1954), p. 15.

201 "I have always wondered": Quoted in Coleman, *The Liberal Conspiracy*, p. 24. Coleman makes the common mistake that Silone lost both parents in the January 1915 earthquake; others have made a more egregious error, in killing off Silone's entire family in the quake. He is also mistaken in the claim that the name "Ignazio Silone" "meant nothing . . . he wanted an unattractive name to show his disgust with the literary world of the time" (p. 25).

202 "An unforgettable loss": Quoted ibid., p. 42.

202 State Department "operation": Darina Silone to Peter Coleman, August 29, 1984; cited ibid., p. 27.

202 "a democracy that": The speech, "Evitiamo di essere oltranzisti," was published by Enrico Franceschini in *La Repubblica*, July 7, 1990.

203 "spirit of its totalitarian crudeness": G. A. Borgese, "Errore di Belino," *Corriere della Sera*, October 8, 1950.

203 "If you still have ears": "Habeas animam!" in *ISRS*, vol. 2, pp. 1021–25.

204 "diabolical secret": Ibid., p. 1025.

205 In October 1950: Coleman, *Liberal Conspiracy*, p. 142.

205 Italian Association for Cultural Freedom: Ibid., p. 143.

205 "drug addicts of anti-Fascism": Quoted ibid.

206 "Don't you realize": "Testimonianza di Gustaw Herling," in *ISRS*, vol. 1, p. xviii.

207 "Vittorini compares himself": Roderigo di Castiglia, "Vittorini se n'è ghiuto, e soli ci ha lasciato!" *Rinascita*, August–September 1951.

207 "He might be an anti-Fascist": Carlo Salinari, *L'Unità*, July 14, 1952.

207 "The fundamental characteristic": Carlo Salinari, *L'Unità*, August 2, 1952.

208 "I considered him in good faith": Carlo Salinari, *L'Unità*, July 31, 1952.

208 "a failure, an ugly": Giuseppe Petronio, *Avanti!* July 14, 1952.

208 "Silone is one of the very few": Gurgo and de Core, *Silone*, p. 283.

208 "My dear, these humble": The book, with its inscription to Darina dated July 20, 1952, is on display at the Museo Silone in Pescina.

209 "everyone is a bit": Antonio Gramsci, "Nostro Marx," *Il Grido del Popolo*, May 4, 1918; reprinted in David Forgacs, ed., *An Antonio Gramsci Reader: Selected Writings, 1916–1935* (New York: Schocken, 1988), p. 36.

210 "I wouldn't have had him": Edmondo Paolini, *Altiero Spinelli. Dalla lotta antifascista alla battaglia per la Federazione Europea: 1920–1948* (Bologna: Il Mulino, 1996), p. 131.

210 As Herling points out: *ISRS*, vol. 1, p. xxii.

210 "This made me realize": The anecdote is found in *La Fiera Letteraria*, April 11, 1951.

210 "You believe you go": Quoted in *Colloqui*, pp. 70–71.

211 "There are many childish": "Restare se stessi," p. 1262.

211 "In my day": Interview with Bruno Falcetto, in *ISRS*, vol. 1, p. xvi.

211 "How happy I am": Herling, *Volcano and Miracle*, p. 78.

212 "I have never been tempted": "The Lesson of Budapest," in *Emergency Exit*, p. 135.

212 *America*: "A Trip to Paris," in *Mr. Aristotle*, p. 155. A different version is in *Bread and Wine*, p. 387:

>   Thirty days in the steamship
>   And we got to 'Merica
>   We found neither straw nor hay
>   We slept on the bare earth
>   Like beasts of the field.

213 "America is no land": Buttitta to Silone, n.d. (but 1937); Greenway to Silone, n.d.; Zito to Silone, October 23, 1937, Archivio Silone, Florence, busta 1, fascicolo 3, docs. 156, 179, 207. Silone responded to Zito: "Dear Carmelo Zito, Your letter gave me much pleasure; I spent a year and a half in Calabria during the war."

214 As Ferdinando Alfonsi: Alfonsi, *Ignazio Silone*, p. 80.

214 responsible for the patricide: Other antidotes to the streets-paved-with-gold mythos are Pietro Di Donato's powerful memoir of his father's death, *Christ in Concrete*, and Stanley Tucci's film *Big Night*.

215 "Note to the Present Edition": New York University, Tamiment Library, Giro-

lamo Valenti Papers, box 1, folder 13, Correspondence, 1930–1950. I am grateful to Gail Malmgreen of NYU for permission to view the papers. For unknown reasons, the 1936 edition was never published.

215 "a recent echo": See the original text "Inedito di Silone," in d'Eramo, *Ignazio Silone*, pp. 146–48.

216 "Beneath the rags of folklore": Ibid., p. 148.

217 "After *Fontamara*, no American": Diggins, *Mussolini and Fascism*, p. 251.

217 In 1940, Sumner Welles: Interview with Darina Silone, November 29, 2000.

217 "All things considered": Silone to Chiaromonte, June 6, 1963, Nicola Chiaromonte Papers, Gen. Mss, box 3, folder 77.

217 "rhetoric of boredom": "Silone negli Stati Uniti," *La Fiera Letteraria*, May 19, 1963.

218 "The General Assembly expresses": Silone's speech was reprinted in the AILC's (Italian Association for Cultural Freedom) *Bollettino per la libertà della cultura*, June 27, 1960.

218 At least one biography: Gurgo and de Core, *Silone*, p. 345.

219 "Though the origin": Letter to the Editor, "About a Louisiana Jail," *Transition* (Kampala, Uganda) 16 (1964): 35.

219 Nello Ajello recounts: Ajello, "Siamo ancora al Venerdì Santo."

220 "To discover what is being born": Ignazio Silone, "L'esperienza di Pasolini," *Tempo Presente*, December 1966.

220 Pablo Neruda who refused: Another Italian delegate, Antonio Barolini, described the scene in "Silone mortifica il servilismo di Neruda," *La Fiera Letteraria*, June 30, 1966.

221 "Change your seat immediately": Mirella Serri, "Dalla parte di Silone il maladetto," *La Stampa*, November 12, 1991.

SIX COLD WAR CULTURE

223 "a painful duty to perform": "The Situation of the 'Ex,'" pp. 102–103.

223 "Friends, remember that": Anita Galliussi recounted the episode at the conference "Processo al processo Silone" held at the Castello Cinquecentesco in L'Aquila on July 1, 1998; quoted in Gurgo and de Core, *Silone*, p. 288.

223 "the only compassionate": Henry Kissinger to Ignazio Silone, April 30, 1953. A copy of the letter is at the Silone Archive in Pescina.

224 "What do you want": Herling recounts the scene in his interview with Bruno Falcetto in *ISRS*, vol. 1, pp. xxv–xxvi; see also Gurgo and de Core, *Silone*, p. 303, where Herling tells how Silone approached him soon after to say, with a mischievous grin, that he had unwittingly returned to being a Communist. Herling was stupefied and asked how. Silone replied that Pajetta had "reclaimed" him in the press conference.

225 His most pointed question: Coleman, *Liberal Conspiracy*, p. 130. The stenographic record of the meetings was published in French in *Comprendre*, the journal of the Société Européenne de Culture, in September 1956.

225 exchange with Ivan Anissimov: The epistolary exchange is collected in Silone

and Anissimov, *Un dialogo difficile. Sono liberi gli scrittori russi?* A wry editorial note facing the title page states that Anissimov was, at one time, a fanatical Stalinist (*uno sfegatato stalinista*) and that the exchange of letters had not been published in Russia.

227 "the writer belongs": "Lo scrittore contro lo Stato," quoted in Gurgo and de Core, *Silone*, p. 305.

227 "Just as no well-raised child": Quoted ibid., pp. 310–11.

227 But neither the condemnation: Silone in *Nuovi Argomenti*, May–June 1956.

228 Sartre was emblematic: "The Lesson of Budapest," pp. 131, 136–38.

229 "The Russians we have": Ibid., pp. 141–42.

230 even his publisher: See Mondadori's letters to Silone in Alberto Mondadori, *Lettere di una vita: 1922–1975* (Milan: Mondadori, 1996).

231 "when I look at a fascist": *Encounter*, March 1962. Irving Kristol, along with Stephen Spender, was a founding editor in 1953.

231 nicknamed "Agnus Dei": See Silone's interview with Grazia Coco in 1969, Archivio Silone, Florence, busta 10, fascicolo 1.

231 Silone could not remain silent: "Agenda," *Tempo Presente*, September–October 1963.

232 "unjustified illusions": "Illusioni ingiustificate," *Tempo Presente*, December 1965.

232 "degrading the toga": Anonymous, "È cominciato al Viareggio il valzer degli scandali," *La Fiera Letteraria*, July 11, 1965. For a discussion of the scandal of the Premio Viareggio, see Gurgo and de Core, *Silone*, pp. 362–72, and d'Eramo, *L'opera di Ignazio Silone*, pp. 378–81.

232 The regret of many Italian: From the unsigned introduction "Siloniani in ritardo," in d'Eramo, *Ignazio Silone*, p. 7.

232 Carlo Bo attempted: Bo, "C'è qualche eccezione alla triste regole delle riviste."

233 "A Dominican [severe] with himself": Indro Montanelli, "Ignazio Silone," *Corriere della Sera*, June 5, 1965.

233 Giancarlo Vigorelli wrote: Giancarlo Vigorelli, "Il libro del giorno: Uscita di sicurezza," *Il Tempo*, June 30, 1965.

233 penned a mea culpa: Bo, "C'è qualche eccezione."

233 In a bitter essay: Carlo Bo, "Hanno avuto paura," *L'Europeo*, August 1, 1965.

234 In his acceptance speech: The speech of September 11, 1965, was reprinted in *La Fiera Letteraria*, September 19, 1965.

234 "Among living writers": Quoted in Gurgo and de Core, *Silone*, p. 372.

234 "His every word": Irving Howe's review of *Emergency Exit*, *New York Times Book Review*, December 29, 1968, p. BR5.

235 three broad periods of Silonian criticism: d'Eramo, *Ignazio Silone*, pp. 80–83.

235 "it is almost impossible": Kazin, *The Inmost Leaf*, pp. 176–79.

235 "Robert Frost of the Abruzzi": Michael Harrington, "The Political Novel Today," *Commonweal*, October 28, 1955.

236   "Sulla dignitá dell'intelligenza": in *ISRS*, vol. 2, pp. 1117–25.

236   "All those who contribute": *L'Express*, January 23, 1961.

236   a modern Don Quixote: See Gurgo and de Core, *Silone*, p. 352.

237   Fifty-two anti-Communist: The Fraschette d'Alatri concentration camp housed many refugees from the war: "There were some 50 nationalities imprisoned in this walled, machine-gun guarded camp. Some 200 Germans (mostly ex-SS), about one hundred American, British and French army deserters, hundreds of Yugoslavs and about twenty Czechs. There was a lonely refugee from Tibet who preferred to sleep on top of the soccer goal." Frantisek Bejcek (Frank Baychek) and Eric Ronge, "European Odyssey of Two Refugees," http://users.bigpond.net.au/magnetic-island/European _Odyssey.htm.

237   Silone recognized: d'Eramo, *Ignazio Silone*, p. 95.

239   "In every spiritual vocation": January 8, 1958, Archivio Silone, Florence, busta 3, fascicolo 20.

239   "To describe our method": Silone to Chiaromonte, October 11, 1955, Archivio Silone, Florence, busta 3, fascicolo 17.

239   vastly different personalities: On their sometimes acerbic relationship, see the letters archived in Nicola Chiaromonte Papers. I am indebted to Diane Ducharme of the Beinecke Library for access to the letters.

239   "They were different": Gustaw Herling, "L'importanza di una rivista," in Fofi et al., *Nicola Chiaromonte, Ignazio Silone*, p. 14.

240   a 1932 Chiaromonte essay: "Lettera di un giovane dall'Italia," *Quaderni di Giustizia e Libertà*, December 1932. Chiaromonte had written to Silone in 1935, asking the Abruzzesi writer to read the essay; Chairomonte to Silone, October 20, 1935, Chiaromonte Papers, box 4, folder 131.

240   Russian-born Andrea Caffi: In December 1942, when Caffi was fighting the Nazis in France, Chiaromonte sent a telegram to Silone: "Please send some money to Andrea Caffi." Chiaromonte Papers, box 4, folder 132.

240   Writing as "Sincero": "La morte si chiama fascismo," *Quaderni di Giustizia e Libertà*, January 1935, pp. 20–60.

241   a 1929 memorandum: Reproduced in Gasbarrini and Gentile, *Ignazio Silone. Comunista*, p. 124.

241   "for us Italians": Chiaromonte to Silone, October 27, 1935, Chiaromonte Papers, Gen. Mss. 113, box 4, folder 131.

241   "the antiquated flying coffins": Quoted in Coleman, *Liberal Conspiracy*, p. 89.

241   In his essays: Chiaromonte, *The Paradox of History*.

242   Malraux, in his role: The episode is recounted by Herling in "L'importanza di una rivista," p. 15. The book was eventually published as *Stalin: Aperçu historique du bolchévisme* by Plon in Paris in 1935. An excerpt from the foreword demonstrates why Silone found the work so congenial. There are echoes of Souvarine in Silone's own works, such as *The School for Dictators*.

> But this is nothing compared with the remarkable demonstration of December 21, 1929, Stalin's fiftieth birthday. The whole Soviet press displayed vast headlines, large portraits, and articles of enormous

length. The eulogies of the Dictator were not less portentous. According to the incense-burners of his entourage, all human and some
superhuman virtues were incarnate in Stalin.

His modesty, courage and devotion were paralleled by his knowledge and wisdom. He was the organiser of the Bolshevik Party, the
leader of the October Revolution, the head of the Red Army, and victor
in the Civil War as well as in foreign war. He was, moreover, the
leader of the world proletariat. The man of action proved himself as
great as the theorist, and both are infallible; there is no instance of a
mistake made by Stalin. One *leitmotiv* recurs constantly in the dithy-
rambs: man of iron, steeled soldier, allusions to the name he had
adopted, with variations on the invariable theme of steel and iron:
"iron Leninist," "granite Bolshevik." The same formula, the same
exaggeration, the same extravagant expressions of admiration and
submissiveness, in strict conformity with models sent down from
Moscow, recur in thousands of addresses, messages and telegrams
from all parts of Russia, which fill whole pages of the newspapers,
and then several columns daily for weeks. The State publishing-
houses issued thousands of copies of collections of these tributes in
which panegyrics filled over 250 pages, in addition to innumerable
messages simply indicated by the names of the senders. An official
portrait bust was manufactured by mass production and distributed
officially. The name of Stalin, already given to several towns, was
again given to factories, electricity stations, rural undertakings, barracks and schools.

From an online version of *Stalin: A Critical Survey of the Russian Revolution,* trans. C.L.R. James (New York: Longman, 1939), www.marxists
.org/history/etol/writers/souvar/works/stalin/.

242   a moving tribute: Nicola Chiaromonte, "Albert Camus: In Memoriam," in
     Camus: A Collection of Critical Essays, ed. Germaine Brée (Englewood Cliffs,
     NJ: Prentice Hall, 1962), pp. 11–15.

242   Chiaromonte questioned the title: Chiaromonte to Silone, March 9, 1952,
     Chiaromonte Papers, box 4, folder 132. Elinor Lipper, *Eleven Years in Soviet
     Prison Camps,* trans. Richard and Clara Winston (Chicago: Regnery, 1951).

243   "He looked at me": Herling and Falcetto, in *ISRS,* vol. 1, p. xxiii.

243   "He was truly": Interview with Bruno Falcetto, in *ISRS,* vol. 1, p. xi.

244   "the man always remained"; "Intervista a Sergio Quinzio," pp. 160–63.

245   "But back then": Herling, *Volcano and Miracle,* p. 70.

245   "I was just an eccentric": Herling, "L'importanza di una rivista," p. 13.

245   "It is, unfortunately, difficult": Silone to Chiaromonte, August 16, 1956,
     Chiaromonte Papers, box 3, folder 77.

245   It was common: Herling, "L'importanza di una rivista," p. 16.

246   "It was," Herling reported: Titti Marrone, "Il mondo a parte degli spiriti
     liberi," *Il Mondo,* November 28, 1996.

246   "In the past": Pieracci Harwell, *Un cristiano senza chiesa,* p. 43.

247   So rooted was this fear: "Reagan, agente dell'FBI, spiava Ignazio Silone," *Il
     Giornale,* March 31, 1992.

247 in 1959 she was pressured: Both Flamini and Leggeri were interviewed by Goffredo Fofi for *Linea d'ombra*, December 1991; I have taken their testimony from Giorgio Fabre's article, "Mamma la CIA," *Panorama*, December 8, 1991. See also Enzo Forcella, "Silone e la CIA? Non fatene un caso," *La Repubblica*, December 5, 1991.

247 he was no spy: See the documents collected by Peter Kamber at www .peterkamber.ch/ignazio.html.

248 money coming in from the CCF: Peter Coleman has estimated that the Congress for Cultural Freedom gave $45,000 to *Tempo Presente* in 1966.

248 "Silone loved this journal": Giovanni Spadolini, "Parliamo di me: Per un'autobiografia di Ignazio Silone," *Nuova Antologia*, July–September 1978.

248 extraordinary galaxy of writers: Gurgo and de Core, *Silone*, pp. 342–43.

248 "incredulous despair": Darina Silone, letter to *Le Monde*, May 28, 2000, p. 13.

248 "cannot be said to have had": Darina Silone, correspondence with author, September 5, 2000.

249 Repeated requests: The CIA is required by law to give a reason for refusing to release documents. My request was denied pursuant to FOIA exemptions (b)(1): "material which is properly classified pursuant to an Executive order in the interest of national security or foreign policy"; and (b)(3): "information pertaining to the CIA Director's statutory obligations to protect from disclosure intelligence sources and methods, as well as the organization, functions, names, official titles, salaries or numbers of personnel employed by the Agency, in accordance with the National Security Act of 1947 and/or the CIA Act of 1949." Letter to the author from Scott Koch, Information and Privacy Coordinator, Central Intelligence Agency, January 26, 2006. The same day the biographical entry for Silone was cataloged (January 7, 1944), Emmy C. Rado, an OSS analyst and wife of the Hungarian psychiatrist Sandor Rado, sent a letter to Mario Einaudi in Chappaqua, New York, containing a list of Italians "of which I would like to have as much information as possible." Rado had been, curiously enough, Wilhelm Reich's dance partner in Vienna and was rumored to be having an affair with Allen Dulles, a notorious ladies' man.

249 "Your problem as a writer": Chiaromonte to Silone, March 9, 1952, Chiaromonte Papers, box 4, folder 132.

249 a volume in honor of Silone: "Silone, scrittore veridico," in Cristini, *Dal villaggio all'Europa*. The original typeset manuscript of Chiaromonte's essay is in Yale University's Beinecke Rare Book and Manuscript Library, Gen. Mss. 113, box 5, folder 198, where the original title, "Silone, scrittore di verità" is crossed out. The difference might be translated as from "Silone, Writer of Truth" to "Silone, Truthful Writer."

249 nineteenth-century Russian writers: For Chiaromonte's idea that history could best be understood—perhaps only understood—through great narrative fiction, see his collection of essays, *The Paradox of History*. In "Silone, scrittore veridico," Chiaromonte notes that Silone's conception of simplicity mirrored that of Pasternak, who invoked the quality in one of his poems as the ideal for a modern writer.

251 "Colonialism," he wrote: Silone to Humm, March 22, 1957; Diego Rivera to Silone, June 25, 1957; Archivio Silone, Florence, busta 3, fascicolo 19.

251 "We defend the right": The handwritten speech is in the Archivio Silone, Pescina.

253 What most offended Silone: "Una protesta dell'Associazione: 50 anni di storia italiana secondo la RAI," *Bollettino per la libertà della cultura*, January 15, 1959.

253 A society that forced: *Bolletino per la libertà della cultura*, August–September 1961.

253 "acquired her sense of irony": "Emergency Exit," p. 68.

254 One day they were walking together: Ibid., p. 70.

254 "The truth," he claimed: "Le idee che sostengo," p. 1391.

255 "One can be free": *Bread and Wine*, p. 215.

255 "40 Questions for . . .": "40 domande a Ignazio Silone," *La Fiera Letteraria*, April 11, 1954; reprinted in *ISRS*, vol. 2, pp. 1211–13.

256 contacts with Italian anti-Fascists: Franzinelli, *I tentacoli dell'OVRA*, p. 81.

256 "without any evasiveness": Camilleri to Silone, January 31, 1953, Archivio Silone, Florence, busta 12, fascicolo 15.

256 Silone responded with a stinging letter: Silone to Piccinini, Rome, January 14, 1965; reprinted in *Quaderni Siloniani*, January 1998, p. 5.

SEVEN THE PAINFUL RETURN

258 When the pasta is al dente: d'Eramo, "Il mio amico Silone," in *Ignazio Silone*, p. 13.

258 "talks too much": Silone to Mosbacher, September 9, 1936, Archivio Silone, Florence, busta 2, fascicolo 1, doc. 110.

258 "give up our quest": "The Choice of Companions," p. 119.

259 "Certainly not because": "Restare se stessi," p. 1262.

259 to both Weil and de Foucauld: Interview with Darina Silone, November 13, 2000, Rome.

259 Silone who deserved the award: Gurgo and de Core, *Silone*, p. 330.

259 "I move ahead": Quoted in Rosselli, *La famiglia Rosselli*, p. 150.

260 Silone's own peasants: Gurgo and de Core, *Silone*, p. 334. Silone's eulogy was published in *Corrispondenza socialista*, November 1957; his thoughts on Salvemini and the crucifix are from "Crocifisso," *Tempo Presente*, September–October 1957.

260 "they will be less political": Pieracci Harwell, *Un cristiano senza chiesa*, p. 91.

260 Silone's speech: "Apparati di partito e partitocrazia," Silone's speech at Rodi, was published in *Tempo Presente*, November 1958.

261 "The social conditions": Interview with Ferdinando Virdia, quoted in Giancarlo Borri, "La perfezione del potere e il disordine dello spirito," in d'Eramo, *Ignazio Silone*, pp. 26–27.

262 "Many respectable people": "The Choice of Companions," p. 121.

262 While postwar Europe: "Rethinking Progress," pp. 163, 176, 186.

262 On another occasion: "Ecco perché mi distaccai dalla Chiesa," *La Discussione*, October 31, 1965; reprinted in *ISRS*, vol. 2, pp. 1267–71.

263 did not imitate her gesture: *Colloqui*, p. 95.

263 "Dear Don Piccinini": Silone to Piccinini, January 21, 1970, Archivio Silone, Florence, busta 10, fascicolo 1.

263 "by instinct I am allergic to celebrations": Silone to Gentile, January 15, 1970, Archivio Silone, Florence, busta 10, fascicolo 1.

263 "a great privilege": Silone to Kollek, no date (but 1970), Archivio Silone, Florence, busta 10, fascicolo 1.

264 Rouault prints and reproductions: *Colloqui*, pp. 85–86; Pieracci Harwell, *Un cristiano senza chiesa*, p. 30–52.

265 "sharp nostalgia": "The Choice of Companions," pp. 125–26.

267 "For us Abruzzesi": "La Maiella è il Libano di noi abruzzesi," in "Sulle tracce di Celestino," a sort of preface to *L'avventura di un povero cristiano*, in *ISRS*, vol. 2, p. 546.

267 "They summon it in": Paolo Morelli, "Majestic Maiella," *Megazine*, August 2001.

268 "Celestine can help us": "In Celestine's Footsteps," in *The Story of a Humble Christian*, p. 18.

268 "I am fairly satisfied": Silone to Margherita Pieracci Harwell, August 27, 1967, in *Un cristiano senza chiesa*, p. 63.

268 "What an ending!": "Presenza di Silone," in Gasbarrini and Gentile, *Silone: Tra l'Abruzzo e il mondo*, p. 17.

268 "CELESTINO: Will you restore me": *The Story of a Humble Christian*, pp. 185–86.

269 at home recovering: Gurgo and de Core, *Silone*, p. 391.

269 tape a message: Grazia Livi, "Un premio al pudore," *Epoca*, September 1968.

270 "If the idea of utopia": "L'eredità cristiano," in *L'avventura di un povero cristiano*, in *ISRS*, vol. 2, p. 556.

270 "In the depths of my soul": Interview with Grazia Coco, September 1969, Archivio Silone, Florence, busta 10, fascicolo 1.

270 "that group of twentieth-century writers": Howe, *A Margin of Hope*, p. 194.

271 "I no longer speak": Claudio Casoli, ed., *Bacchelli, Betocchi, Cassola, Luzi, Quasimodo, Silone interpretano la società del Novecento* (Milan: Marietti, 2005), p. 136.

271 "I have always aspired": Herling, "L'importanza di una rivista," p. 16.

272 "enriched by the slow": Herling, "Rome, December 2, 1971," in *Volcano and Miracle*, p. 27.

272 "one of the many things": "40 domande a Ignazio Silone," *La Fiera Letteraria*, April 11, 1954; reprinted in *ISRS*, vol. 1, p. 1212.

272   "'You know,'" she said": "Joy the Weeper," in *Mr. Aristotle*, pp. 85–86.

273   Silone again apparently contemplated suicide: Interview with Darina Silone, November 29, 2000.

273   "The Choice of Companions": The essay was first presented at a conference in Turin in 1954 and published in June of that year in *Comunità*; it subsequently appeared in the *Quaderni* of the Associazione Cultural Italiana and in the *Testimonianze* rubric of the Associazione Italiana della Libertà della Cultura. It was included in *Emergency Exit*.

273   "What a mournful band": "The Choice of Companions," p. 111.

273   "How can one possibly know": "Rethinking Progress," p. 188.

273   "Nihilism," Silone wrote: "The Choice of Companions," pp. 112, 114, 116.

274   Once, while attempting to visit: "The Beginning of a Search," in *The Story of a Humble Christian*, pp. 15–16. As with some other autobiographical stories, it is difficult to corroborate this episode. Italians might say, "Se non è vero, è ben trovato" (Even if not true, it is an illuminating tale well told).

275   "it would find me": Interview with Gino De Sanctis, in *Il Messagero*, October 17, 1972; reprinted in *ISRS*, vol. 2, p. 1287.

276   "a timid, courteous": *A Handful of Blackberries*, p. 32.

277   "Forgive me," said the dying man: Ibid., pp. 191, 201–02.

278   "I'll appeal to the Bishop": Ibid., pp. 180–81.

279   "Stella was driven": Silone was asked by the editors of the *New Republic* to comment on the promulgation of anti-Semitic legislation in Fascist Italy; "Italian Anti-Semitism," *New Republic*, November 23, 1938, pp. 67–69.

279   As Adele admonishes: *A Handful of Blackberries*, pp. 182–83.

279   in his capacity as priest: Alfonsi, *Ignazio Silone*, p. 54.

280   "I have only these names": Silone to Anissimov, January 15, 1957; in *Un dialogo difficile*, p. 56. Dovid Bergelson, a Yiddish writer and former member of the Jewish Anti-Fascist Committee during World War II, arrested during Stalin's anti-Semitic campaign of 1952, was executed on his sixty-eighth birthday. A similar fate was meted out to Peretz Markish, another Yiddish writer. Itzik Feffer was a more complicated case: A colonel in the military press corps and vice chairman of the Jewish Anti-Fascist Committee, he was also an informer for the secret police. This could not spare him in the 1952 purge and he too was shot. Moshe Kulbak from Vilna was taken from Minsk in 1937 and sent to a Soviet labor camp, where he perished, perhaps in 1940.

280   "I could not have found": Archivio Silone, Pescina. "It is no accident that the word *nebbish* originated in Yiddish," writes Franklin Foer, "a language without a nation that is spoken by a people repeatedly beaten down by pogroms and thus in a good position to empathize with nebbishes . . . According to the great Yiddish linguist Max Weinreich, Jews appropriated the word *nebbich* from their Slavic neighbors in the 11th century. Indeed, other European nations with similar histories of subjugation maintain similar words. In Ukrainian, for instance, the word *bidni* refers to an unfortunate, pitiable soul. Italian has *poverino*. The fact that *nebbish* made it into English owes

much to Jewish Borscht Belt comedians becoming '50s TV stars." Franklin Foer, "Nerd vs. Nebbish," *Slate*, July 12, 1998, www.slate.com/id/1873.

281 "a second life companion": Gurgo and de Core, *Silone*, p. 292.

281 "It was not easy": Interview with Darina Silone, November 29, 2000, Rome.

281 his old friend from Switzerland: *Colloqui*, p. 83.

281 "anguished and unconsummated love": Sontag, "Simone Weil."

282 "she was intensely Jewish": T. S. Eliot, preface to Simone Weil, *The Need for Roots* (New York: Putnam, 1952), pp. vii–viii.

282 "Jewish self-hatred": See, for example, Paul Giniewski, *Simone Weil ou la haine de soi* (Paris: Berg International, 1978), and Thomas R. Nevin, *Simone Weil: Portrait of a Self-Exiled Jew* (Chapel Hill: University of North Carolina Press, 1991).

282 very heart of prophetic monotheism: J. Edgar Bauer, "Simone Weil: Kenotic Thought and 'Sainteté Nouvelle,'" www.cesnur.org/2002/slc/bauer.htm#_edn10.

282 Carlo Levi's meditation: Carlo Levi, *Of Fear and Freedom*, trans. Adolphe Gourevitch (New York: Farrar, Straus and Giroux, 1950; Columbia University Press, 2008).

282 "One must always be ready": *Uscita di sicurezza*, p. 891.

282 simply noted the humiliation: "Semplicemente," *Tempo Presente*, April–May 1961; "Fine d'anno e fine di secolo," *Tempo Presente*, December 1966; reprinted in *ISRS*, vol. 2, pp. 1089, 1103.

282 equal to Camus, Orwell, and Sartre: See Silone's January 15, 1957, letter from Rome to Ivan Anissimov, published in *Tempo Presente*, reprinted in *Un dialogo difficile*, p. 68; also in *ISRS*, vol. 2, p. 1153.

282 "a spiritual itinerary": *Colloqui*, p. 83.

282 "If Silone had not encountered": Ibid., p. 85.

283 better imagine Severina: Darina Silone, "Premessa" and "Storia di un manoscritto," both in *Severina*, pp. 19–22, 131–44.

283 profoundly affected by *Bread and Wine*: Pieracci Harwell, "Silone e Simone Weil."

283 to visit Selma: The correspondence between Silone and Selma Weil can be found in the Silone Archive, Florence.

283 "the two volumes": Pieracci Harwell, *Un cristiano senza chiesa*, p. 48.

283 when the Russian writer was composing: Silone recounted this story to Annibale Gentile in "Quando Silone mi rivelò il 'Segreto di Luca,'" *Il Tempo*, August 22, 1979.

284 "The loss of my mother": Darina Silone, "Le ultime ore di Ignazio Silone," pp. 174–75.

284 "Through the glass": "The Painful Return," pp. 144, 147.

284 "When, as occasionally happened": McDonald, "Il caso Silone," p. 78.

284 "for me it is a good experience": Silone to Luce d'Eramo, quoted in *Ignazio Silone*, p. 18.

285 "I was already thirty": The letter requesting an interview, the questions, and Silone's responses can be found in the Archivio Silone, Florence, busta 10, fascicolo 1.

286 "I think that all ideological systems": "Un scrittore socialista," p. 1235.

286 "power to change": Note on the Revision of *Fontamara*, in *The Abruzzo Trilogy*, p. 4.

286 "When we came out": Origo, *A Need to Testify*, pp. 196–97.

286 In one of Silone's last public interviews: "Credere senza obbedire," *Il Messagero*, October 17, 1972; reprinted in *ISRS*, vol. 2, pp. 1285, 1290.

287 "I have no fear of dying": Appendix to *Severina*, p. 169.

288 "miraculous ways": Darina Silone to McCarthy, August 12, 1978, Vassar College, McCarthy Papers, box 223, folder 223.6.

288 "I have to consider his dignity": Ibid.

288 "indeed desperate": Darina Silone to McCarthy, August 8, 1978, ibid.

288 "How many years lost": *Colloqui*, p. 82.

289 "I greatly admire Solzhenitsyn": Herling, "Dragonea, August 28," in *Volcano and Miracle*, p. 79. Solzhenitsyn's Class Day speech was given at Harvard on June 8, 1978. Silone may have been referring to the following phrase: "But should someone ask me whether I would indicate the West such as it is today as a model to my country, frankly I would have to answer negatively. No, I could not recommend your society in its present state as an ideal for the transformation of ours. Through intense suffering our country has now achieved a spiritual development of such intensity that the Western system in its present state of spiritual exhaustion does not look attractive . . . A fact which cannot be disputed is the weakening of human beings in the West while in the East they are becoming firmer and stronger. Six decades for our people and three decades for the people of Eastern Europe; during that time we have been through a spiritual training far in advance of Western experience." www.columbia.edu/cu/augustine/arch/solzhenitsyn/harvard1978.html.

289 "My Abruzzo can be anywhere": Herling, "Dragonea, August 28," p. 77.

289 "his joy when he realized": Darina Silone to McCarthy, November 4, 1978, McCarthy Papers, box 223, folder 223.6.

289 In another version: "Le ultime ore di Ignazio Silone," appendix to *Severina*, pp. 167–82.

290 Darina was still outraged: Ibid. In the margin of her letter to McCarthy here, Darina wrote, "The pity of it, Horatio, the pity of it!"

291 "people stealing even more": Darina Silone to McCarthy, November 4, 1978.

291 "I simply had to *clear out*": Darina Silone to McCarthy, February 28, 1979, McCarthy Papers, box 223, folder 223.6.

291 Silone had stipulated: See Darina's appeal to collect Silone's vast correspondence after his death in the *New York Review of Books*, July 19, 1979.

292 revert to the city of Pescina: The handwritten document is reproduced in Gasbarrini and Gentile, *Ignazio Silone. Comunista*, pp. ix–x.

292 At the hour of our death: The document is translated here for the first time.

Darina Silone published a photocopy of the original and a transcription in the appendix to *Severina*, pp. 160–64. She judges it to have been written between 1963 and 1966.

293   "In his will": Remarks at the centenary commemorations of Silone's birth, May 1, 2000, Pescina.

293   She sent flowers: *Colloqui*, pp. 39, 123.

293   "the only serious way": Carlo Rosselli, "Il neo-socialismo francese" (1933); reprinted in Costanzo Casucci, ed., *Scritti dell'esilio* (Turin: Einaudi, 1988), vol. 1, p. 227.

294   "Everything Silone wrote": Howe, introduction to *Bread and Wine*, p. vi.

EIGHT   *"SILVESTRI"*

295   archival documents: The documents were first presented at a conference organized by Stanford University in Florence. See Biocca, "Ignazio Silone e la polizia politica," pp. 67–93, and Biocca, " 'Tranquilli' (nell'ombra)," pp. 53–76; Canali, "Il fiduciario Silvestri," pp. 61–86. Biocca and Canali used these essays as the basis for an expanded examination in *L'informatore*, as well as Canali's *Il caso Silone*. A forum that included Romolo Tranquilli Jr. appeared as "Silone: per favore non chiamatelo spia," *Reset* 54 (May–June 1999): 63–78. The charges are also scattered throughout Biocca's *Silone*. In English, see Canali, "Ignazio Silone and the Fascist Political Police," pp. 36–60.

295   Biocca's bombshell was primed: Giovanni Belardelli, "Silone. Con l'OVRA per amore del fratello," *Corriere della Sera*, March 7, 1996. Biocca's address two days later was titled "The Taste of Ashes."

295   a rival newspaper in Rome: "Silone: All'OVRA non collaboro più," *La Repubblica*, April 30, 1996.

295   specialist on the Fascist secret police: Canali, *Le Spie del regime*.

295   "There were already continuous slanders": Giorgio Bocca, "Ignazio Silone: 'abnormale politico,' " *La Repubblica*, August 23, 1978.

295   "that he risked being": Robert Gordon, "Emergency Exit," *Times Literary Supplement*, October 20, 2000, p. 12.

295   "Press Collect Via ITALRADIO": Archivio Silone, Florence, busta 2, fascicolo 8, doc. 106.

297   "He's lucky": Cutler, "Final Examination," in *Seeing the Darkness*, pp. 13–14. I have not been able to ascertain whether this story was apocryphal or based on a true event, as Cutler has died.

298   the archive is the locus: Jacques Derrida, *Archive Fever: A Freudian Impression* (Chicago: University of Chicago Press, 1996).

298   cannot be consulted by scholars: In contrast, Professors Maurizio Degl'Innocenti and Stefano Caretti and Dottoressa Paola Pirovani were collegial and helpful during the time I consulted the Silone Archive in Florence, as was the staff at the Centro Studi Ignazio Silone in Pescina.

298   several fine scholarly works: Alessandro Portelli, *The Order Has Been Carried*

Out: History, Memory, and the Meaning of a Nazi Massacre in Rome (New York: Palgrave Macmillan, 2003). See also Luisa Passerini, *Fascism in Popular Memory: The Cultural Experience of the Turin Working Class*, trans. Robert Lumley and Jude Bloomfield (New York: Cambridge University Press, 1987). For a survey of recent trends and debates in the methodology of oral history, see John M. Foot, "Words, Songs and Books: Oral History in Italy," *Journal of Modern History* 3, no. 2 (Summer 1998): 164–74.

299 "all different from Silone's": Anna Petrecchia, "Silone spia?" *Corriere della Sera*, April 28, 2001.

299 As one scholar has aptly: Tamburrano, Granati, and Isinelli, *Processo a Silone*, p. 6.

299 "We don't risk being accused": Secondino Tranquilli, "Borghesia, piccola borghesia e fascismo," *Lo Stato Operaio*, April 1928, quoted in Franzinelli, *I tentacoli dell'OVRA*, p. 311.

300 "with only the omission": Ibid., p. 311n1.

300 Biocca published his research: Biocca, "Ignazio Silone e la polizia politica," pp. 67–90.

300 The central document: "Silone, all'OVRA non collaborò più," *La Repubblica*, April 30, 1996. Curiously, *La Repubblica*, considered by many to be one of the finest newspapers in Italy and partial to a left-of-center politics, has been most vocal in publicizing the charges against Silone, while the former Communist daily *L'Unità*, which frequently vehemently criticized the writer, often rose to his defense in the scandal. The letter is in the Archivio Centrale dello Stato in Rome; ACS, Ministreo dell'Interno, Direzione Generale della Pubblica Sicurezza, Divisione Polizia Politica, busta 1370, fascicolo 51.

13.4.1930

Mi scusi se non le ho più scritto. Ciò che le interessava sapere non è più un mistero (la stampa già ne parla). Non so cosa io e i miei amici faremo.

La mia salute è pessima ma la causa è morale (Lei comprenderà se ricorderà ciò che le scrissi l'estate scorsa). Io mi trovo in un punto molto penoso della mia esistenza. Il senso morale che è stato sempre forte in me, ora mi domina completamente; non mi fa dormire, non mi fa mangiare, non mi lascia un minimo di riposo. Mi trovo nel punto risolutivo della mia crisi di esistenza, la quale non ammette che una sola via d'uscita: l'abbandono della politica militante (mi cercherò un'occupazione intellettuale qualsiasi). Oltre questa soluzione non restava che la morte. Vivere ancora nell'equivoco mi era impossibile, mi è impossibile. Io ero nato per essere un onesto proprietario di terre nel mio paese. La vita mi ha scaraventato lungo una china alla quale ora voglio sottrarmi. Ho la coscienza di non aver fatto un gran male né ai miei amici né al mio paese. Nei limiti in cui era possibile mi sono sempre guardato dal compiere del male. Devo dirle che lei, data la sua funzione, si è sempre comportato da galantuomo. Perciò le scrivo quest'ultima lettera perché lei <u>non ostacoli</u> il mio piano che si realizzerà in due tempi: <u>primo</u>, eliminare dalla mia vita tutto ciò che è falsità, doppiezza, equivoco, mistero;

secondo, cominciare una nuova vita, su una nuova base, per riparare il male che ho fatto, per redimermi, per fare del bene agli operai, ai contadini (ai quali sono legato con ogni fibra del mio cuore) e alla mia patria. Tra il primo e il secondo tempo ho bisogno di un po' di riposo fisico, intellettuale e morale. Nessuna considerazione di carattere materiale ha influenzato la mia decisione. I disagi non mi spaventano. Quello che voglio è vivere moralmente. L'influenza e la popolarità che in molti centri di emigrazione ho acquisito mi inducono a concepire la mia attività futura (appena sarò del tutto ristabilito in salute) nella forma di un'attività letteraria ed editoriale del tutto indipendente. Devo aggiungere che in questo tempo, delle grandi modificazioni si vanno compiendo nella mia ideologia e mi sento riattratto, molto, verso la religione (se non verso la chiesa) e che l'evoluzione del mio pensiero è facilitata dall'orientamento cretino e criminale che sta assumendo il Partito comunista. La sola cosa che mi fa allontanare da esso con rammarico è il fatto che è un Partito perseguitato nel quale, al di fuori dei dirigenti, vi sono migliaia di operai in buona fede. Per poter esercitare un'influenza sugli elementi della base, io esito ancora ad annunciare pubblicamente la mia rottura col Partito ed attendo, prossimamente, il momento propizio. Questa mia lettera a lei è un'attestazione di stima. Ho voluto chiudere, definitivamente, un lungo periodo di rapporti leali, con un atto di lealtà. Se lei è un credente, preghi Iddio che mi dia la forza di superare i miei rimorsi, di iniziare una nuova vita, di consumarla tutta per il bene dei lavoratori e dell'Italia.

Suo,
Silvestri

303 Another document from the archives: ACS, PS 1925, busta 130; quoted in Biocca and Canali, *L'informatore*, pp. 233–34.

303 Yet another letter: This letter too was leaked to the press and published as "Silone. Confesso che ho spiato," in *L'Espresso*, May 30, 1996. Both letters are reproduced in Biocca, "Ignazio Silone e la polizia politica," pp. 68–69, 82.

Egregia Signorina,
Tr. è arrivato qui, dove si trova in una clinica privata; non esce mai dato che il suo stato di salute è ancora delicato. Nella clinica è difficile visitarlo, perché fra il personale vi sono dei conoscenti.
Sembra che resterà nella clinica ancora 2–3 settimane e poi andrà in un pensione. Allora sarà possibile avvicinarlo.
Le scriveró nuovamente fra giorni. Lei giustamente si lagna della rarità delle mei lettere: i nostri rapporti potranno essere più regolari e frequenti se cambieranno natura e carrattere. Al punto in cui sono nella formazione morale e intellettuale, mi è fisicamente impossibile rimanere con lei negli stessi rapporti di 10 anni fa. Suppongo che in una sistemazione diversa dei nostri rapporti potrebbe anche lei avere interesse. La prima cosa da eliminare, perché mi lascia indifferente o umiliato, è il denaro. Ma di ciò parleremo a voce con maggiore comodità.

Saluti cordiali
Silvestri

304 "Yesterday I received": Quoted in Biocca, *Silone*, p. 147.

305 "an arrest warrant": ACS, CPC, busta 5195, Tranquilli, Secondino.

305 censorship laws then in effect: On the censorship laws, see Yannik Beaulieu, "La presse italienne, le pouvoir politique et l'autorité judiciaire durant le fascisme," in *Amnis: Revue de Civilisation Contemporaine* (1994), www.univ-brest .fr/amnis/pages_francais/archive_article_annee.php?annee=2004.

306 appeared on such a list: Franzinelli, *I tentacoli dell'OVRA*, p. 85.

307 "even if Silone himself": Indro Montanelli, *Corriere della Sera*, February 2, 1999.

307 Bellone drafted a cover letter: Canali, *Il caso Silone*, p. 31.

308 The indefatigable Tamburrano: Tamburrano, Granati, and Isinelli, *Processo a Silone*; Tamburanno, *Il "caso" Silone*.

309 A document from the Ministry: Both Carucci's letter and the document are reproduced in Tamburrano, Granati, and Isinelli, *Processo a Silone*, pp. 148, 144–47.

310 "financially I am in": The original letter is in the Silone Archive in Florence.

311 "It was over. Thank God": *Uscita di sicurezza*, p. 858.

311 "nothing would be accomplished": Zurich, November 25, 1934, ACS, Polizia Politica, busta 1370, fascicoli personali.

311 "cooling of relations" between the two: Zurich, December 7, 1934, ibid.

312 Even Schiavetti had unwittingly: Zurich, December 28, 1934, ibid.

312 "It seems to me that for our situation": Zurich, February 14, 1935, ibid.

312 "Killing a man who says no": *Bread and Wine*, p. 398.

313 "In 1931 Tranquilli's brother": Rome, October 12, 1937, ACS, PP, busta 1370, fascicoli personali; reproduced in Tamburrano, Granati, and Isinelli, *Processo a Silone*, pp. 144–47.

313 "In some political circles": Quoted in d'Eramo, *Ignazio Silone*, p. 118.

313 As late as March 1956: The episode can be reconstructed from Hal Draper, ed., *The Politics of Ignazio Silone* (Berkeley: Independent Socialist Press, 1974).

314 "I still have not": Zurich, April 12, 1938, ACS, PP, busta 1370, fascicoli personali.

314 "How is your health": Paris, January 12, 1939, ibid.

314 "not because the climate": Paris, January 16, 1939, ibid.

315 Platone recorded the following conversation: Zurich, May 14, 1939, ibid.

317 Silone tries to convince Platone: Zurich, May 26, 1939, ibid.

318 photographer Wilhelm von Gloeden: Wilhelm von Gloeden, *Taormina* (Pasadena: Twelve Trees Press, 1986).

319 "it is nevertheless plausible": Biocca, *Silone*, p. 206.

319 "it has also been murmured": Leake, *Reinvention of Silone*, p. 163n24. In another passage (p. 173n48), Leake, noting the lack of descriptions of or allusions to sex, writes that this may have contributed to the rumor that Silone was impotent. She notes, however, evidence of an active erotic life through

his correspondence, especially with Aline Valangin. Bellone was a lifelong bachelor who lived with his younger sister in Rome. As I note in chapter four, Darina Silone told me in an interview that their marriage was unconsummated.

319 Sampieri was still spying on Silone: Zurich, December 21, 1942, ACS, PP, busta 1370, fascicoli personali.

319 "Everything conspires to confuse": Zurich, January 9, 1943, ibid.

319 a "vendetta" might yet take care of the problem: Zurich, January 15, 1943, ibid.

320 "split her sides laughing": Zurich, March 5, 1943, ibid.

320 Silone was able to move: Zurich, June 3, 1943, ibid.

320 "I tend to think that Silone": Letter to the author, April 17, 2000.

320 "I think the real truth": Letter of July 18, 2002.

320 "I am not *innocentista oltranza*": Letter of May 11, 2001.

320 "As you can imagine": Letter of April 17, 2000.

321 "I find it very much in": Ibid.

322 complete list of OVRA informants: "Elenco dei 622 confidenti dell'OVRA," appendix to Franzinelli, *I tentacoli dell'OVRA*, p. 679.

322 One website: www.nndb.com/people/431/000117080/.

322 Rory Carroll: "Darling of Italy's Left 'Spied for Mussolini,'" *Guardian*, April 5, 2000.

322 Cockburn's essay: Alexander Cockburn, "Even Worse Than Orwell," *Nation*, June 5, 2000, p. 10.

322 A more nuanced essay: Christopher Hitchens, "Ignoble Ig-nazi-o?" *Nation*, June 12, 2000, p. 9.

323 an admirable mea culpa: Postscript to Christopher Hitchens, "The Former Yugoslavia," *Nation*, October 23, 2000, p. 9.

323 critique of Biocca and Canali's book: Mimmo Franzinelli, "Silone, l'infame," *L'Indice dei Libri* (June 200): 10–11.

323 Likewise, John Foot: John Foot, "The Secret Life of Ignazio Silone," *New Left Review* 3 (May–June 2000): 146–52.

323 examination of the scandal: Stille, "The Spy Who Failed," pp. 44–48, and his foreword to *The Abruzzo Trilogy*, pp. xvii–xxiv.

324 "If anything, his heroic image": Stille, "The Spy Who Failed," p. 48.

324 "Silone succeeded in orchestrating": Leake, *The Reinvention of Ignazio Silone*, pp. 3, 7, 8–9.

325 "quashes once and for all": "Emergency Exit," *Times Literary Supplement*, October 20, 2000, p. 12.

325 an elegant and tightly argued essay: McDonald, "Il caso Silone," pp. 77–89.

326 "The unspoken yet inescapable": Ibid., p. 82.

326 Another defense of Silone: Pryce-Jones, "The Exemplar: Ignazio Silone," pp. 28–32.

327 "the documents Biocca and Canali attribute": McDonald, "Il caso Silone," p. 86.

328 Primo Levi's conception: Primo Levi, "The Gray Zone," in *The Drowned and the Saved*, trans. Raymond Rosenthal (New York; Summit Books, 1988), p. 44.

329 "a polyhedral personality": Franzinelli, *I tentacoli dell'OVRA*, pp. 335–42.

329 "Among the illnesses": Letter addressed to Orlando, June 16, 1938, Archivio Silone, Florence, busta 1, fascicolo 4.

330 "disciplined, bureaucratic confessions": "Emergency Exit," p. 84.

330 "the eternal human dream": Luce d'Eramo, *Deviazione* (Milan: Mondadori, 1979), p. 343.

330 "there is a secret": Silone interview for *La Storia Siamo Noi*.

EPILOGUE **THAT WHICH REMAINS**

331 Silone's sentiments: Quinzio, "Ricordo di Silone," in *La speranza nell'apocalisse*, p. 123.

332 "*Amo ergo sum*": *A Handful of Blackberries*, p. 246.

332 "There can be nothing inevitable": "Rethinking Progress," p. 204.

332 his acceptance speech: The original handwritten text is archived at the Centro Studi Ignazio Silone, Pescina.

332 "I hope, Sister": *Severina*, p. 127.

332 "freedom is the possibility": "Emergency Exit," p. 69.

333 "the experience of Communism": Ibid., p. 97.

333 "permanent aspiration": "The Situation of the 'Ex,'" p. 109.

333 "It is in essence": "Emergency Exit," p. 98.

333 "that which incessantly drives mankind": Ibid.

333 "the ashen taste": Ibid.

333 "if a writer puts all": "The Beginning of a Search," in *The Story of a Humble Christian*, p. 12.

333 "one who returns": Quoted in Paynter, *Ignazio Silone*, p. 9.

333 "the greatest travelers": Levi, *Christ Stopped at Eboli*, p. 4.

334 "Had I ever forgotten": "The Painful Return," pp. 149, 151.

334 "where the poor who had escaped": "Encounter with a Strange Priest," p. 29.

334 "What is the particular sadness": "Ai piedi di un mandorlo," *Ausonia* (January–February 1960); reprinted in *ISRS*, vol. 2, pp. 1252–54.

336 "It's a miracle": "La terra e la gente," in *ISRS*, vol. 2, pp. 1397–98.

337 "All real love": "Rethinking Progress," p. 166.

337 "The olive oil": *The Seed Beneath the Snow*, p. 726.

338 "Christianity's place": "Encounter with a Strange Priest," p. 27.

338 "does not relieve a creature": "Polikushka," pp. 37–38.

338 great and new revelation: "The Situation of the 'Ex,'" p. 110.

338 "too romantic, absurd": Paynter, *Ignazio Silone*, pp. ix, x.

339 "apprentice saint": Lewis, "Ignazio Silone: The Politics of Charity," p. 129.

339 "without myths, reduced": "What Remains," in *The Story of a Humble Christian*, p. 33.

339 "We are destined": "The Choice of Companions," p. 127.

339 "a revolutionary and an honest man": Orwell's review of Silone's *The School for Dictators, New English Weekly,* June 8, 1939; quoted in McDonald, "Il caso Silone," p. 89.

339 "seen the truth": Ugoberto Alfassio Grimaldi, "Alcune domande a un francotiratore del socialismo," *Critica Sociale,* November 20, 1965; reprinted in *ISRS*, vol. 2, p. 1274.

340 "My only fear": Darina Silone, "The Last Hours of Ignazio Silone," *Partisan Review* 51, no. 1 (1984): 81; also in "Le ultime ore di Ignazio Silone," in *Severina*, pp. 169–70.

340 "I don't know if I": Speech on accepting the Jerusalem Prize for literature, March 1969, Archivio Silone, Pescina.

340 the human predicament: "Rethinking Progress," p. 155.

340 "one of the reasons": "L'avventura di un povero cristiano e un povero socialista," in *ISRS*, vol. 1, p. xxv.

340 "It is always difficult": *Colloqui*, p. 87.

340 "everyone who has reflected": "Emergency Exit," p. 63.

341 "a universal fable about poverty": Gordon, "Silone and His Critics," p. 175.

341 "Only loss is universal": "Le idee che sostengo," p. 1387.

341 "favorable to humility": "It was a time favorable to humility. Man returned to the animal, the animal to the plant, the plant to the earth. The stream at the bottom of the valley was full of stars." *Bread and Wine,* p. 429.

Bibliography

ARCHIVES

Archivio Centrale dello Stato, Rome
Archivio Silone, Centro Studi Ignazio Silone, Pescina
Archivio Silone, Fondazione di Studi Storici "Filippo Turati," Florence
Fondo Manoscritti di Autori Moderni e Contemporanei, University of Pavia, Italy
Girolamo Valenti Papers, Tamiment Library, New York University
International Institute for Social History, Amsterdam
Mary McCarthy Papers, Vassar College
National Archives and Records Administration, Washington, D.C.
Nicola Chiaromonte Papers, Beinecke Rare Book and Manuscript Library, Yale University
Swiss State Archives, Bern
www.amici-silone.net
www.peterkamber.ch/ignazio.html

SELECTED WORKS BY IGNAZIO SILONE

For outstanding reconstructions of Silone's body of work, the reader is referred to the extensive bibliography that runs more than fifty pages in Bruno Falcetto's meticulous *Ignazio Silone, Romanzi e saggi*, 2 vols. (Milan: Mondadori, 1998–99), vol. 2, pp. 1607–64, and Luce d'Eramo's *L'opera di Ignazio Silone: saggio critico e guida bibliografica* (Milan: Mondadori, 1971). Also instrumental in tracing Silone's work is the "Cronologia delle Opere" compiled by Diocleziano Giardini in *Ignazio Silone: Cronologia della vita e delle opere* (Cerchi: Adelmo Polla, 1999) and the selected bibliography in Deborah Holmes's *Ignazio Silone in Exile: Writing and Antifascism in Switzerland, 1929–1944* (Burlington, VT: Ashgate, 2005).

WORKS IN EXILE

Fontamara   Translated into German by Nettie Sutro-Katzenstein (Zurich: Oprecht & Helbing, 1933). First Italian edition (Paris: Nuove Edizione Italiane, 1933). Translated into English by Michael Wharf (New York: Harrison Smith & Robert Harris, 1934); Gwenda David and Eric Mosbacher (Harmondsworth, England: Penguin Books, 1938). Translated into twenty-seven languages.

Viaggio a Parigi   Translated into German by Nettie Sutro-Katzenstein as *Die Reise nach Paris* (Zurich: Oprecht & Helbing, 1934). First Italian edition translated from the German by Silvia Carusi and Karin Wiedemeyer Francesconi, edited by Vittoriano Esposito (Pescina: Centro Studi Siloniani, 1999). Translated into English by Samuel Putnam as *Mr. Aristotle* (New York: Robert M. McBride, 1935).

Der Fascismus: seine Entstehung und seine Entwicklung   Translated into German by Gritta Baerlocher (Zurich: Europa Verlag, 1934). First Italian edition translated by Maria Gabriella Canonico as *Il fascismo. Origini e sviluppo* (Carnago: SugarCo, 1992). Second, authorized, Italian edition translated by Marina Buttarelli, edited by Mimmo Franzinelli (Milan: Mondadori, 2002).

Pane e vino   Translated into German by Adolf Saager as *Brot und Wein* (Zurich: Oprecht, 1936). First Italian edition (Lugano: Nuove Edizioni di Capolago, 1937). Translated into English by Gwenda David and Eric Mosbacher as *Bread and Wine* (New York: Harper, 1937). Translated into nineteen languages.

La scuola dei dittatori   Translated into German by Rudolf Jakob Humm as *Die Schule der Diktatoren* (Zurich: Europa, 1938). First English edition translated by Gwenda David and Eric Mosbacher as *The School for Dictators* (New York: Harper, 1938). First Italian edition (Milan: Mondadori, 1962).

Il seme sotto la neve   Translated into German by Werner Johannes Guggenheim as *Der Samen unter dem Schnee* (Zurich: Oprecht, 1941). First Italian edition (Lugano: Nuove Edizioni di Capolago, 1942). Translated into English by Francis Frenaye as *The Seed Beneath the Snow* (New York: Harper, 1942).

Ed egli si nascose   (Zurich-Lugano: Büchergild Gutenberg-Ghilda del Libro, 1944). Translated into English by Darina Laracy Silone as *And He Hid Himself* (New York: Harper, 1945).

WORKS IN ITALY

Una manciata di more   (Milan: Mondadori, 1952). Translated into English by Darina Silone as *A Handful of Blackberries* (New York: Harper, 1953).

Il segreto di Luca   (Milan: Mondadori, 1956). Translated into English by Darina Silone as *The Secret of Luca* (New York: Harper, 1958).

La volpe e le camelie   (Milan: Mondadori, 1960). Translated into English by Eric Mosbacher as *The Fox and the Camelias* (New York: Harper, 1961).

Uscita di sicurezza   (Florence: Vallecchi, 1965). Translated into English by Harvey Fergusson II as *Emergency Exit* (New York: Harper, 1968).

L'avventura di un povero cristiano   (Milan: Mondadori, 1968). Translated into English by William Weaver as *The Story of a Humble Christian* (New York: Harper, 1970).

Paese dell'anima   Edited by Maria Letizia Cassata (Milan: Mursia, 1978).

POSTHUMOUS

Memoriale dal carcere svizzero   Edited by Lamberto Mercuri (Cosenza: Lerici, 1979). Translated into English by Stanislao G. Pugliese as *Memoir from a Swiss Prison* (Merrick, NY: Cross-Cultural Communications, 2006).

Severina   Edited by Darina Silone (Milan: Mondadori, 1981).

Ignazio Silone: Romanzi e saggi [*ISRS*]   Edited by Bruno Falcetto, 2 vols. (Milan: Mondadori, 1998–99).

The Abruzzo Trilogy: Fontamara, Bread and Wine, The Seed Beneath the Snow   Translated by Eric Mosbacher, revised by Darina Silone (South Royalton, VT: Steerforth Italia, 2000).

Esami di coscienza   Edited by Francesco de Core (Rome: Edizioni E/O, 2000).

Le cose per cui mi batto   Edited by Alessandro Bresolin (Santa Maria Capua Vetere: Edizioni Spartaco, 2004).

La coperta abruzzese   Edited by Maria Moscardelli (Rome: Aracne, 2004).

JOURNALISM

Editor of *L'Avanguardia* (Rome, 1920–23)

Editor of *Il Lavoratore* (Trieste, 1921–22)

Editor of *information* (1932–34)

Editor of *L'Avvenire dei Lavoratori* (1944)

Editor of *Avanti!* (1945–46)

Editor of *Europa Socialista* (1947–49)

Editor of *Tempo Presente* (1956–68)

L'Avvenire dei Lavoratori (1944–1945)   Edited by Stefano Merli and Giulio Polotti (Milan: Istituto Europeo di Studi Sociali, 1992).

Gli articoli di "information" (1932–34)   Edited by M. Antonietta Morettini Bura, translated into Italian by Lelio Cremonte (Perugia: Guerra, 1994).

Tempo Presente: Antologia 1956–1968   Edited by Tommaso E. Frosini (Florence: Liberal Libri, 1998).

CORRESPONDENCE

Un dialogo difficile. Sono liberi gli scrittori russi?   Edited by Ignazio Silone and Ivan Anissimov (Rome: Opere Nuove, 1958).

The Politics of Ignazio Silone   Edited by Hal Draper, with a prelude by Irving Howe (Berkeley: Independent Socialist Press, 1974).

"Ignazio Silone e Carlo Rosselli"   Edited by Paolo Bagnoli, *Nuova Antologia*, April–June 1984.

L'incontro di due uomini liberi. Don Orione e Silone   Edited by Giovanni Casoli (Milan: Jaca, 2000).

WEBSITES

www.amici-silone.net
Italian-English site developed and maintained by Silone's grandniece, Maria Moscardelli, with biography, bibliography, photos, and essays.

www.fondazionesilone.it
Silone Foundation in Rome.

www.italialibri.net/appendice/0600-2.html
Articles and essays related to the scandal of Silone's spying for the Fascist secret police.

www.ossimoro.it/silone.htm
Biography, bibliography, and essays relating to the spying scandal.

www.peterkamber.ch/ignazio.html
Documents relating to Silone's work with the OSS.

www.silone.it
Website of the Centro Studi Ignazio Silone in Pescina, with digitized archives.

www.siloneparma.com
Essays, photos, and history.

www.webalice.it/ninocapone/silone/casosilone.htm
Essays relating to the spying scandal.

SELECTED SECONDARY WORKS

Agathocleous, Tanya. *George Orwell: Battling Big Brother*. New York: Oxford University Press, 2000.

Ajello, Nello. "Siamo ancora al Venerdì Santo." *La Fiera Letteraria*, April 11, 1954.

Aliberti, Carmelo. *Ignazio Silone*. Foggia: Bastogi, 1990.

Alfonsi, Ferdinando. *Ignazio Silone, o della ricerca della permanente*. Catanzaro: Carello, 1991.

———. "Il vangelo secondo Silone: *Il secreto di Luca*." *Le Ragioni Critiche* 19–20 (1976).

Alsop, Kenneth. "Ignazio Silone." *Encounter* 18, no. 3 (1962).

Annoni, Carlo. *Invito alla letteratura di Silone*. Milan: Mursia, 1974.

Aragno, Piero. *Il romanzo di Ignazio Silone*. Milan: Mursia, 1974.

Banfield, Edward. *The Moral Basis of a Backward Society*. Glencoe, IL: Free Press, 1958.

Barbagallo, Angela. *Omaggio a Silone*. Catania: Editrice Milo, 1981.

Bergin, Thomas. "An Italian Novel Against Fascism." *New York Times Book Review*, September 23, 1934.

Bidussa, David. "Dialogato per un rinnovamento socialista. Un carteggio degli anni Trenta tra Ignazio Silone e Angelo Tasca." *Annali del Centro di ricerca Guido Dorso*. Avellino: Edizioni del Centro Dorso, 1986.

Bindi, Vincenzo. *Monumenti storici e artistici degli Abruzzi*. Naples: Giannini, 1889.

Biocca, Dario. *Silone. La doppia vita di un italiano*. Milan: Rizzoli, 2005.

———. "'Tranquili' nell'ombra. Ignazio Silone in Francia." *Nuova Storia Contemporanea* 3, no. 3 (May–June 1999).

———. Ignazio Silone e la polizia politica." *Nuova Storia Contemporanea* 2, no. 3 (May–June 1998).

Biocca, Dario, and Mauro Canali. *L'informatore: Silone, i comunisti e la polizia.* Milan: Luni, 2000.

Biondi, Marino. *Scrittori e miti totalitari: Malaparte, Pratolini, Silone.* Florence: Edizioni Polistampa, 2002.

Bloy, Myron B., Jr. "Ignazio Silone: Prophet of Liberation." *Commonweal,* October 23, 1973.

Bo, Carlo. "C'è qualche eccezione alla triste regole delle riviste." *L'Europeo,* April 4, 1965.

Bocelli, Arnaldo. "Itinerario di Silone." *Nuova Antologia,* May 1966.

Bolognese, Giuseppe. "Silone's Modern Quest and Primordial Discovery." *Perspectives on Contemporary Literature,* 1982.

Bondy, François. "'L'engrenage de l'existence' entretien avec Ignazio Silone." *Preuves* 186–87 (1966).

Brambilla, Rosa, ed. *Ignazio Silone tra testimonianza e utopia. Atti del seminario di studio.* Assisi: Biblioteca della Pro Civitate Cristiana di Assisi, 1977.

Bria, Camillo. *Ignazio Silone.* Milan: Cetim, 1977.

Brown, Robert McAfee. "Ignazio Silone and the Pseudonyms of God." In *The Shapeless God,* edited by Harry J. Mooney Jr. and Thomas F. Staley. Pittsburgh: University of Pittsburgh Press, 1968.

Camus, Albert. "*Le pain et le vin* d'Ignazio Silone." In *Essais.* Paris: Gallimard, 1965.

Canali, Mauro. *Le Spie del regime.* Bologna: Il Mulino, 2004.

———. *Il caso Silone. Le prove del doppio gioco.* Rome: Liberal, 2000.

———. "Ignazio Silone and the Fascist Political Police." *Journal of Modern Italian Studies* 5, no. 1 (Spring 2000).

———. "Il fiduciario Silvestri. Ignazio Silone, i comunisti e la polizia politica." *Nuova Storia Contemporanea* 3, no. 1 (January–February 1999).

Canosa, Romano. *I servizi secreti del Duce.* Milan: Mondadori, 2000.

Carandini, Elena. *Passata la stagione: Diari 1944–1947.* Florence: Passigli, 1989.

Carr, E. H. *Twilight of the Comintern, 1930–1935.* New York: Palgrave Macmillan, 1986.

Caserta, Ernesto. "The Meaning of Christianity in the Novels of Silone." *Italian Quarterly* 16, nos. 62–63 (1973).

Casoli, Giovanni. *L'incontro di due uomini liberi: Don Orione e Silone.* Milan: Jaca, 2000.

Cassata, Maria Letizia. *Ignazio Silone: Paese dell'anima.* Milan: Murisa, 1968.

———. *Gli uomini di Silone.* Gubbio: Oderici, 1967.

Castagnola Rossini, Raffaella. *Incontri di spiriti liberi. Amicizie, relazioni professionali e iniziative editoriale di Silone in Svizzera.* Rome: Piero Lacaita, 2004.

Cecchi, Emilio. "Il caso Silone." *Di giorno in giorno*. Milan: Garzanti, 1971.

Chiaromonte, Nicola. *The Paradox of History: Stendhal, Tolstoy, Pasternak and Others*. Philadelphia: University of Pennsylvania Press, 1985.

———. "Silone, scrittore veridico." Original manuscript in the Nicola Chiaromonte Papers, Beinecke Rare Book and Manuscripts Library, Yale University, Gen. Mss. 113, box 5, folder 198; printed in *Dal villaggio all'Europa*.

———. "Silone et l'espérance du 'cafone.'" *Preuves* 23 (January 1953).

Coleman, Peter. *The Liberal Conspiracy: The Congress for Cultural Freedom and the Struggle for the Mind of Postwar Europe*. New York: Free Press, 1989.

Craxi, Bettino, ed. *Ignazio Silone. La via della verità*. Rome: Edizioni del Garofano, 1982.

Cristini, Giovanni, ed. *Dal villaggio all'Europa: Omaggio a Silone*. Rome: De Luca Editore, 1971.

Crossman, Richard, ed. *The God That Failed: Six Studies on Communism*. New York: Harper, 1950.

Cunningham, Lawrence. "La pazienza come volontà." *La Fiera Letteraria*, October 14, 1973.

———. "Ignazio Silone Seen by the Novelist Luce d'Eramo." *Forum Italicum* 4, no. 4 (December 1972); 570–74.

Cutler, Bruce. *Seeing the Darkness*. Kansas City: BkMk Press, 1998.

Dabney, Lewis M. *Edmund Wilson: A Life in Literature*. New York: Farrar, Straus and Giroux, 2005.

de Core, Francesco, and Ottorino Gurgo. *Silone, un alfabeto*. Naples: L'ancora del Mediterraneo, 2003.

De Grand, Alexander. *The Italian Left in the Twentieth Century*. Bloomington: Indiana University Press, 1989.

———. *L'opera di Ignazio Silone: Saggio critico e guida bibliografica*. Milan: Mondadori, 1971.

d'Eramo, Luce. *Ignazio Silone*. Rimini: Editori Riminesi, 1994.

———. ed. *Ignazio Silone: Clandestino del Novecento*. Rimini: Editori Riminesi, 1996.

Diggins, John Patrick. *Mussolini and Fascism: The View from America*. Princeton: Princeton University Press, 1972.

Di Lorenzo, Angela. *Il pensiero politico di Ignazio Silone*. Pescina: Centro Studi Ignazio Silone, 1997.

Di Scipio, Giuseppe. "Christological Symbolism and Silone's *Il segreto di Luca*." *NEMLA Italian Studies* 6 (1982).

Domenico, Roy Palmer. *Italian Fascists on Trial, 1943–1954*. Chapel Hill: University of North Carolina Press, 1991.

Esposito, Vittoriano. *Ignazio Silone ovvero un "caso" infinito*. Pescina: Centro Studi Siloniani, 2000.

———. *Silone vent'anni dopo*. L'Aquila: Amministrazione Provinciale, 1998.

———. *Vita e pensiero di Ignazio Silone*. Cerchio: Adelmo Polla, 1993.

————. *Silone novelliere tra ironia e angoscia*. Avezzano: Centro Studi Marsicani, 1994.

Fadiman, Clifton. "Fontamara." *New Yorker*, September 22, 1934.

Falqui, Enrico. "Un po' di giustizia." *La Fiera Letteraria* 9, no. 15 (April 11, 1954).

Farrell, James T. "Ignazio Silone." *Southern Review* 4, no. 4 (Spring 1939): 771–83.

Fofi, Goffredo, Vittorio Giacopini, and Monica Nonno, eds. *Nicola Chiaromonte, Ignazio Silone: L'eredità di "Tempo Presente."* Rome: Farenheit 451, 2000.

Franzinelli, Mimmo. *I tentacoli dell'OVRA*. Turin: Bollati Boringhieri, 1999.

Frassanito, Giovanni. *Celestino V: Cristiano senza Chiesa*. L'Aquila: Ferri, 1983.

Frosini, Tommaso E., ed. *Tempo Presente: Antologia 1956–1968*. Florence: Liberal, 1998.

Galli, Sara. *Le tre sorelle Seidenfeld: Donne nell'emigrazione politica antifascista*. Florence: Giunti, 2005.

Garosci, Aldo. *Storia dei fuorusciti*. Bari: Laterza, 1953.

Gasbarrini, Antonio, and Annibale Gentile, eds. *Ignazio Silone. Comunista, 1921/1931*. L'Aquila: Angelus Novus Edizioni, 1989.

————. *Ignazio Silone: Tra l'Abruzzo e il mondo*. L'Aquila: Marcello Ferri, 1979.

Gentile, Emilio. *The Sacralization of Politics in Fascist Italy*. Translated by Keith Botsford. Cambridge, MA: Harvard University Press, 1996.

Georges, Robert A. "Silone's Use of Folk Beliefs." *Midwestern Folklore* 12, no. 4 (Winter 1962).

Giannantonio, Valeria. *La scrittura oltre la vita: studi su Ignazio Silone*. Naples: Loffredo, 2004.

Giardini, Diocleziano. *Scorre la vita*. Trieste: Trieste Grafica, 2005.

————. *Ignazio Silone: Cronologia della vita e delle opere*. Cerchio: Adelmo Polla, 1999.

Gordon, Robert. "Silone and His Critics." In Ignazio Silone, *Fontamara*. London: J. M. Dent, 1994.

Greene, Graham. "Fontamara." *Spectator*, November 2, 1934.

Guerriero, Elio. *Silone l'inquieto: L'avventura umana e letteraria di Ignazio Silone*. Cinisello Balsamo: Edizioni Paoline, 1990.

Gurgo, Ottorino, and Francesco de Core. *Silone: L'avventura di un uomo libero*. Venice: Marsilia, 1998.

Haller, Herman. "Cronostilistica dei romanzi d'esilio di Ignazio Silone." *Modern Language Studies*, Winter 1982.

Hanne, Michael. "Silone's Fontamara: Polyvalence and Power." *MLN* 70, no. 1 (January 1992).

Heiney, Donald. "Silone: Emigration as the Opiate of the People." *America in Modern Italian Literature*. New Brunswick: Rutgers University Press, 1965.

Herling, Gustaw. *Volcano and Miracle: A Selection from the Journal Written at Night*. Translated by Ronald Strom. New York: Penguin, 1996.

Holmes, Deborah. *Ignazio Silone in Exile: Writing and Antifascism in Switzerland, 1929–1944*. Burlington, VT: Ashgate, 2005.

Howe, Irving. "Socialism and Sensibility." *New Republic*, October 26, 1987.

———. *A Margin of Hope: An Intellectual Autobiography.* New York: Harcourt, 1984.

———. "Ignazio Silone's *Fontamara.*" *New Republic*, August 15, 1981.

———. "Malraux, Silone, Koestler: The Twentieth Century." *Politics and the Novel.* New York: Horizon, 1957.

Hyde, Douglas. *God's Bandit: The Story of Don Orione, "Father of the Poor."* Westminster, MD: Newman Press, 1957.

Judt, Tony. *The Burden of Responsibility: Blum, Camus, Aron, and the French Twentieth Century.* Chicago: University of Chicago Press, 1998.

Kazin, Alfred. "From an Italian Journal." *The Inmost Leaf.* New York: Harcourt, 1956.

———. "A Dialogue on Dictatorships." *New York Herald Tribune*, December 12, 1938.

———. "Ignazio Silone's Compassionate Parable." *New York Herald Tribune Books*, April 11, 1937.

Koestler, Arthur. *Arrow in the Blue.* New York: Macmillan, 1952.

Krieger, Murray. "Ignazio Silone: The Failure of the Secular Christ." *The Tragic Vision: Variations on a Theme in Literary Interpretation.* Chicago: University of Chicago Press, 1966.

Krige, Uys. *The Way Out.* Cape Town: Unie-Volkspers, Beperk, 1946.

Landuyt, Ariane. "Un tentativo di rinnovamento del socialismo italiano: Silone e il Centro Estero di Zurigo." In *L'emigrazione socialista nella lotta contro il fascismo (1926–1939)*, edited by Gaetano Arfè, pp. 71–104. Florence: Sansoni, 1982.

Leake, Elizabeth. *The Reinvention of Ignazio Silone.* Toronto: University of Toronto Press, 2003.

Leone, Giuseppe. *Ignazio Silone: scrittore dell'intelligenza.* Florence: Firenze Atheneum, 1996.

Levi, Carlo. *Christ Stopped at Eboli.* Translated by Frances Frenaye. New York: Farrar, Straus and Giroux, 2006.

Lewis, R.W.B. *The City of Florence.* New York: Henry Holt, 1995.

———. *Ignazio Silone: Introduzione all'opera.* Rome: Ragionamenti, 1978.

———. "Ignazio Silone: The Politics of Charity." *The Picaresque Saint.* Philadelphia: Lippincott, 1956.

Lombardi, Olga, ed. *Ignazio Silone.* Camposampiero: Edizioni del Noce, 1982.

Lorusso, Caterina. *Ignazio Silone: Cristianesimo e Socialismo.* Bari: Adriatica, 1988.

Lucente, Gregory. "Signs and History in *Bread and Wine*: Silone's Dilemma of Social Change." *NOVEL: A Forum on Fiction* 16, no. 3 (Spring 1983).

Magnani, Franca. *Una famiglia italiana.* Milan: Feltrinelli, 1991.

Magnani, Valdo, and Aldo Cucchi. *Crisi di una generazione.* Rome: Edizioni E/O, 1952.

Marelli, Sante. *Silone. Intellettuale della libertà.* Rimini: Panozzo, 1989.

Martelli, Sebastiano, and Salvatore Di Pasqua. *Guida alla letteratura di Ignazio Silone.* Milan: Mondadori, 1988.

Martin, Kingsley. "The New Machiavelli." *New Statesman and Nation*, February 4, 1939.

McDonald, Michael P. "Il caso Silone." *National Interest*, Fall 2001.

Milano, Paolo. "Annalisi di una fedeltà." *La Fiera Letteraria*, April 11, 1954.

Montanelli, Indro. "Ignazio Silone." *Corriere della Sera*, June 5, 1965.

Muraca, Giuseppe. "Rivolta e utopia in *Fontamara* di Ignazio Silone." *Utopisti ed eretici nella letteratura italiana contemporanea*. Soveria Mannelli: Rubbettino, 2000.

Napolitano, Daniela. *Il socialismo federalista di Ignazio Silone*. Pescina: Centro Studi Ignazio Silone, 1996.

Nenni, Pietro. *Tempo di guerra fredda. Diari, 1943–1956*. Milan: SugarCo, 1981.

Nicoli, Giovanni, and Thomas Stein, eds. *Zurigo per Silone: Atti delle giornate Siloniane in Svizzera*. Zurich: Tragelaphos, 2004.

Origo, Iris. *A Need to Testify*. San Diego: Harcourt, 1984.

Ottanelli, Fraser. "Fascist Informant and Italian American Labor Leader: The Paradox of Vanni Buscemi." *Italian American Review* 7, no. 1 (Winter/Spring 2000).

Padovani, Gisella. *Letteratura e socialismo: Saggi su Ignazio Silone*. Catania: Aldo Marino, 1982.

Pampaloni, Geno. "Tra letteratura e politica." *Prospetive nel mondo*, February 1979.

———. "L'opera narrativa di Ignazio Silone." *Il Ponte*, January 1949.

Paynter, Maria Nicolai. *Ignazio Silone: Beyond the Tragic Vision*. Toronto: University of Toronto Press, 2000.

Petersen, Neil. *From Hitler's Doorstep: The Wartime Intelligence Reports of Allen Dulles*. University Park: Pennsylvania State University Press, 1996.

Petrocchi, Giorgio. "L'antidoto di Ignazio Silone." *La Fiera Letteraria*, April 11, 1954.

Petroni, Guglielmo. "Testimonianza a Ignazio Silone." *La Fiera Letteraria*, December 11, 1949.

Petronio, Giuseppe. "Le acerbe more di Ignazio Silone." *Avanti!* August 14, 1952.

Pieracci Harwell, Maria. "Silone e Simone Weil." *Quaderni Satyagraha* 1 (April 2002).

———. *Un cristiano senza chiesa e altri saggi*. Rome: Studium, 1991.

Ploetz, Dagmar. *Ignazio Silone: Rebell und Romancier*. Cologne: Kiepenheur & Witsch, 2000.

Potts, Paul. "Not Since Dante." *New Road* 6 (1946).

Pronzato, Alessandro. *Il folle di Dio: San Luigi Orione*. Milan: Paoline, 2004.

Pryce-Jones, David. "The Exemplar: Ignazio Silone." *New Criterion* (September 2001): 28–32.

Pugliese, Stanislao G. *Carlo Rosselli: Socialist Heretic and Antifascist Exile*. Cambridge, MA: Harvard University Press, 1999.

Quinzio, Sergio. "Intervista a Sergio Quinzio." *Tempo Presente*, July–December 1990.

———. *La speranza nell'apocalisse*. Milan: Paoline, 1984.

Radcliff-Umstead, Douglas. "Animal Symbolism in *Vino e pane*." *Italica* 1 (Spring 1972).

Rahv, Philip. "The Revolutionary Conscience." *Nation*, April 10, 1937.

Riddei, Volfgango. *Ignazio Silone e Fontamara*. Rome: Ciranna, 1973.

Riepiloghi per Ignazio Silone. Consiglio Regionale dell'Abruzzo/Rivista di Cultura Oggi e Domani. Pescara: EDIARS, 1998.

Rigobello, Giuliana, ed. *Ignazio Silone*. Florence: Le Monnier, 1981.

Rosselli, Aldo. *La famiglia Rosselli. Una tragedia italiana*. Milan: Bompiani, 1983.

Rousseaux, André. "Les Vérités terriennes d'Ignazio Silone." *Le Figaro Littéraire*, May 17, 1953.

Ruggeri, Antonio. *Don Orione, Ignazio Silone e Romoletto*. Tortona: Edizione Don Orione, 1981.

Salinari, Carlo. "L'ultimo Silone." *L'Unità*, August 2, 1952.

Salvatorelli, Luigi. "Ignazio Silone ha scritto un *Principe* per il XX secolo." *La Stampa*, September 12, 1962.

Scalabrella, Silvano. *Il paradosso Silone: L'utopia e la speranza*. Rome: Studium, 1998.

Schneider, Franz. "Scriptural Symbolism in Silone's *Bread and Wine*." *Italica* 44 (1967).

Scott, Nathan A. "Ignazio Silone: Novelist of the Revolutionary Sensibility." *Rehearsals of Discomposure*. New York: King's Crown Press, 1952.

Scurani, Alessandro. "La religiosità di Silone." *Letture*, July 1966.

Silone, Darina Laracy. *Colloqui*. Edited by Michele Dorigatti and Maffino Maghenzani. Zevio: Perosini, 2005.

———. "The Last Hours of Ignazio Silone." *Partisan Review* 61, no. 1 (1984).

Silone, Ignazio, and Paolo Bagnoli, eds. *Per Ignazio Silone*. Florence: Polistampa, 2002.

Silverman, Sydel. *Three Bells of Civilization: The Life of an Italian Hill Town*. New York: Columbia University Press, 1975.

———. "Agricultural Organization, Social Structure, and Values in Italy: Amoral Familism Reconsidered." *American Anthropologist* 70 (February 1968).

Slochower, Harry. "Absolute Doubt." *Literature and Philosophy Between Two World Wars*. New York: Citadel Press, 1964.

Soave, Sergio. *Senza tradirsi, senza tradire. Silone e Tasca dal comunismo al socialismo cristiano (1900–1940)*. Turin: Nino Aragno, 2005.

Sontag, Susan. "Simone Weil." *New York Review of Books*, February 1, 1963.

Spaldolini, Giovanni, ed. *Ignazio Silone in Svizzera*. Lugano: Associazione "Carlo Cattaneo," 1994.

Spezzani, Pietro. *Fontamara di Silone: Grammatica e retorica del discorso popolare*. Padua: Liviana, 1979.

Spriano, Paolo. *Storia del partito comunista italiano*. 7 vols. Turin: Einaudi, 1967–98.

Stille, Alexander. "The Spy Who Failed." *New Yorker*, May 15, 2000.

Sutro, Nettie. "A Note on Ignazio Silone." In Ignazio Silone, *Mr. Aristotle.*

Taddei, Francesca, ed. *L'emigrazione socialista nella lotta contro il fascismo (1926–1939).* Florence: Sansoni, 1982.

Tamburrano, Giuseppe. *Il "caso" Silone.* Turin: UTET, 2006.

Tamburrano, Giuseppe, Gianna Granati, and Alfonso Isinelli. *Processo a Silone: La disavventura di un povero cristiano.* Rome: Piero Lacaita, 2001.

Togliatti, Palmiro. "Contributo alla psicologia di un rinnegato. Come Ignazio Silone venne espulso dal Partito comunista." *L'Unità,* January 6, 1950.

Tucci, Niccolò. "Bad News for the Thought Police." *New Yorker,* October 20, 1963.

Tuscano, Pasquale. *Introduzione a Ignazio Silone.* Modena: Mucchi, 1991.

Vandano, Brunello. "La storia di Silone." *Epoca,* September 19, 1965.

Vigorelli, Giancarlo, ed. "Per i settant'anni di Silone." *Il Dramma* 5 (May 1970).

Virdia, Ferdinando. *Ignazio Silone.* Florence: La Nuova Italia, 1985.

Voigt, Klaus. "Ignazio Silone e la stampa tedesca dell'esilio." In *L'emigrazione socialista nella lotta contro il fascismo (1926–1939),* edited by Gaetano Arfè, pp. 105–36. Florence: Sansoni, 1982.

Walzer, Michael. "Ignazio Silone: 'The Natural.'" *The Company of Critics: Social Criticism and Political Commitment in the Twentieth Century.* New York: Basic Books, 1988.

Zavoli, Sergio, and Aldo Forbice. *Silone.* Empoli: Ibiskos, 2006.

Zirardini, Alessandro. "Le Rôle de l'intellectuel: Silone s'explique." *L'Express,* February 9, 1961.

Acknowledgments

Over the course of a decade, I have incurred numerous debts to scholars, friends, and archivists on two continents, several countries, and half a dozen archives. They are listed here in no particular order with a preemptive apology for anyone inadvertently left out. Needless to say, they are not responsible for the errors that have crept into the text or the interpretations I have adopted.

Jeff Kehoe at Harvard University Press and Deirdre Mullane were the first to lend encouragement to this project. It is my extraordinary good fortune to have had Jonathan Galassi as wise and patient editor, shepherding the manuscript through to publication with graceful erudition. Thanks to Jesse Coleman (editor), Chris Peterson (production editor), and, especially, Cynthia Merman (copy editor) at FSG.

Archivists have been especially kind in permitting me to consult and reproduce documents. Dr. Paola Pirovano and Professors Maurizio Degl'Innocenti and Stefano Caretti of the Fondazione di Studi Storici "Filippo Turati" in Florence were friendly and professional in their assistance, as was the president of the Archivio Silone in Pescina, Professor Franca Mazzali. A special thanks to archivists Sebastiana Ferrari and Martorano Di Cesare and the entire staff of the Centro Studi Ignazio Silone in Pescina.

Thanks as well to the staff of the International Institute for Social History, Amsterdam, and the Beinecke Rare Book and Manuscripts Library at Yale University. I must acknowledge the work of Peter Kamber of Switzerland for maintaining a website containing hundreds of documents relating to Silone's work with the OSS and Ruth Stalder of the Schweizerisches Bundesarchiv in Bern, who kindly provided me with important documents concerning Silone's Swiss exile. I am indebted to Nadia Zonis of Columbia University, Elisabetta Zini of New York University, and Dr. Paul Arpaia for spending hours in the archives photocopying documents.

Professor Giuseppe Tamburrano kindly sent me books, essays, and articles from Italy, as did Professor Lamberto Mercuri of Rome.

The late Darina Silone was gracious in granting me several interviews and maintained a spirited correspondence with me until her death in 2003. Don Flavio Peloso, current director of St. Luigi Orione's Order of Divine Providence, shared with me documents and his memories of Darina Silone's last days. The Romolo Tranquilli Jr. I thank here and cite in the notes is not, obviously, Silone's brother who died in 1932 but the son of Pomponio Tranquilli, Silone's cousin, today living in Rome. I thank him for permission to consult documents and reproduce photos from his personal archive.

At Hofstra University I am fortunate to have the support of faculty and administrators, especially Dr. Herman A. Berliner, Provost; Dr. Bernard J. Firestone, Dean of the Hofstra College of Liberal Arts and Sciences; and the staff of the Joan and Donald E. Axinn Library. A special thanks to the Friday afternoon reading group organized by Dr. Massoud Fazeli for allowing me to present my work in progress. The research for this book was made possible by Hofstra research grants and a Presidential Award. I thank my colleagues in the History Department for creating a stimulating environment to work in and my mentor, Dr. Pellegrino D'Acierno, for intellectual guidance. Harris Manchester College at the University of Oxford awarded me a fellowship in the summer of 2004 that facilitated research and writing.

A special thanks to the members of the Society for Italian Historical Studies, especially Roy Domenico, Charles Killinger, and Walter Adamson, whose encouragement and criticism at the January 2007 meeting of the American Historical Association are greatly appreciated.

Professor Liliana Biondi of the Università d'Aquila, Professor Vittoriano Esposito, Professor Santa Casciani of John Carroll University, and Davide Bidussa, Director of the Fondazione Feltrinelli, Milan, all lent support to the project. For their encouragement and generous gifts of time, advice, and sharing of documents, thanks to Dr. Maria Nicolai Paynter of Hunter College, Michael P. McDonald, formerly of the National Endowment for the Humanities, translator William Weaver at Bard College, Dr. Deborah Holmes of the Ludwig Boltzmann Institut für Geschischte und Theorie der Biografie in Vienna, and Dr. Elizabeth Leake of Rutgers University.

Diocleziano Giardini, custodian of the town's history and the memory of Silone, was my guide in Pescina. *Mille grazie* to the people of Pescina who shared with me their generosity of spirit with warm welcomes on my winter visits. With the sharing of St. Anthony's bread on January 17, we became, as Silone would have said, *(cum pane)* companions.

A different version of chapter eight appeared as "The Double Bind of Ignazio Silone: Between Archive and Hagiography," in *Culture, Censorship and the State in Twentieth-Century Italy*, edited by Guido Bonsaver and Robert S. C. Gordon (Oxford: Legenda, 2005), pp. 142–48. A segment of chapter three appeared as "Ignazio Silone's Dark Night of the Soul," in Ignazio Silone, *Memoir from a Swiss Prison* (Merrick, NY: Cross-Cultural Communications, 2006), pp. 1–14, as well as in the summer 2006 issue of *Dissent* magazine. Passages of chapter five appeared in "Ignazio Silone and America," in the inaugural issue of the *Harvard College Journal of Italian American History and Culture* 1, no. 1 (Winter 2007): 8–11, edited by P. Justin Rossi and Sabino Ciorciari. My translation of Silone's short story "At the Foot of an Almond Tree" first appeared in *Words Without Borders* (July 2005) at www.wordswithoutborders.org.

Thanks also to Dr. Martin Schaden of Rutgers University for assistance in translating German documents. I am indebted to Antony Shugaar for help with some tricky Italian–English translations, always mindful of the old Italian proverb *"Il traduttore è un traditore"* (The translator is a traitor). Although hoping that I have not betrayed Silone, I will not go so far as Jorge Luis Borges, who wrote that *"El original es infiel a la traducción"* (The original is unfaithful to the translation).

Finally, an insufficient word of profound gratitude to my parents and extended family but especially to Jennifer, Alessandro, and Giulia for their patience as I wandered among archives and small towns far from home.

Index